D1716695

The Modern Jewish Experience

Paula Hyman and Deborah Dash Moore, editors

FRENCH JEWS,
TURKISH JEWS

FRENCH JEWS, TURKISH JEWS

The Alliance Israélite Universelle and
the Politics of Jewish Schooling
in Turkey, 1860–1925

ARON RODRIGUE

INDIANA UNIVERSITY PRESS
Bloomington and Indianapolis

The paper used in this publication meets the minimum requirements of American National Standard for Information Sciences—Permanence of Paper for Printed Library Materials, ANSI Z39.48-1984.
⊗™
Manufactured in the United States of America

Library of Congress Cataloging-in-Publication Data
Rodrigue, Aron.
French Jews, Turkish Jews : the Alliance israélite universelle and the politics of Jewish schooling in Turkey, 1860–1925 / Aron Rodrigue.
p.   cm.—(The Modern Jewish experience)
Includes bibliographical references.
ISBN 0-253-35021-2
1. Jews—Education—Turkey. 2. Jews—Turkey—History.
3. Alliance israélite universelle. 4. Turkey—Ethnic relations.
I. Title.   II. Series: Modern Jewish experience (Bloomington, Ind.)
LC747.T9R63   1990
370'.89924'0561—dc20   89-46327
                                                        CIP

1 2   3   4   5   94   93   92   91   90

To my parents
and
to the memory of the Jewish communities of Thrace

CONTENTS

ACKNOWLEDGMENTS

I am deeply grateful to Simon Schama and Yosef Hayim Yerushalmi for their support and encouragement. Their intellectual stimulus has had a major influence on my historical thinking in the fields of European and Jewish history. I thank Patrice Higonnet who played a crucial role in deepening my appreciation of the fundamentals of modern French history. My thanks also go to Omeljan Pritsak, who explored with me many aspects of Turkic and Ottoman history and who was instrumental in heightening my awareness of the need for the comparative perspective in all historical inquiry.

I am grateful to Esther Benbassa with whom I have been working closely in the field of Turkish-Jewish history for having read and commented on various drafts of this work. I have gained tremendously from our many discussions over the years. Jean-Christophe Attias has shared with me the insights of the medievalist and has often provided much-needed correctives to this unreconstructed modernist. I have discussed many aspects of the activities of the Alliance Israélite Universelle with Annie Benveniste, who opened up for me the sociological perspective on this subject.

Lois Dubin, David Fishman, and Peter Mandler read and commented extensively on earlier drafts, gave me the benefit of their learning in different areas, and thus illuminated my own field of research. Benjamin Braude gave me important advice during the revision process. Peter Baldwin, Riva Kastoryano, Daniel Sherman, and Christopher Waters all provided invaluable friendship and intellectual companionship. I thank Georges Weill, Chief Archivist of the Alliance Israélite Universelle, for giving me permission to consult the Alliance archives. I owe a special debt of gratitude to Yvonne Lévyne, the head librarian of the Alliance, for her tireless efforts to facilitate my research. I would also like to thank the Archives of the Ministère des Affaires Etrangères, and the Bibliothèque Nationale in Paris, the Public Records Office in London, the Ben Zvi Institute Library, the Central Archives for the History of the Jewish People, the Central Zionist Archives, and the National and University Library in Jerusalem, the Widener Library at Harvard, and the Indiana University Libraries at Bloomington, Indiana for allowing me to use their holdings. At various stages of research and writing, Michel Abitbol, Phyllis Albert, Jacob Barnai, Israel Bartal, Jay Berkovitz, Richard Cohen, Paul Dumont, Michael Graetz, Joseph Hacker, Otto Dov Kulka, Simon Schwarzfuchs, Michael Silber, Jacques Thobie, and Yaron Tsur gave advice, comments, suggestions, and help, for all of which I am deeply thankful.

The final draft of the manuscript was finished at the Institute for Advanced Study of the Hebrew University of Jerusalem, and I thank the Institute for its hospitality. Last, but not least, I am grateful to Indiana University, its Jewish Studies Program, and its History Department for providing me with a challenging, stimulating, and always supportive environment.

ix

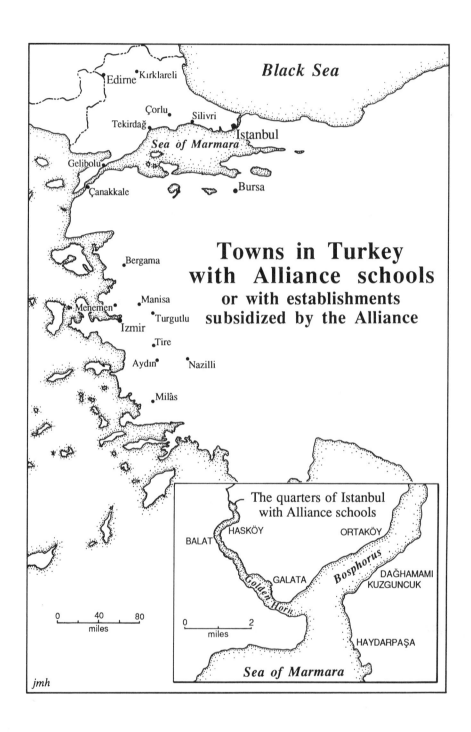

Black Sea

Edirne •Kırklareli

Çorlu•
Tekirdağ• •Silivri
Sea of Marmara •Istanbul
Gelibolu•
Çanakkale •Bursa

Towns in Turkey
with Alliance schools
or with establishments
subsidized by the Alliance

•Bergama

•Manisa
Menemen• •Turgutlu
Izmir
•Tire
Aydın• •Nazilli

•Milâs

The quarters of Istanbul
with Alliance schools

BALAT   HASKÖY   ORTAKÖY

          GALATA   DAĞHAMAMI
                        KUZGUNCUK
Golden Horn   Bosphorus

                              HAYDARPAŞA

Sea of Marmara

0   40   80
miles

0   2
miles

jmh

INTRODUCTION

If you believe that a great number of your coreligionists, overcome by twenty centuries of misery, of insults and prohibitions, can find again their dignity as men, win the dignity of citizens;

If you believe that one should moralize those who have been corrupted, and not condemn them, enlighten those who have been blinded, and not abandon them, raise those who have been exhausted, and not rest with pitying them . . .

If you believe in all these things, Jews of all the world, come hear our appeal. . . .[1]

With such fiery words the newly created Alliance Israélite Universelle emphasized in its appeal of 1860 the need to embark upon the process of educating and transforming the Jewish communities far removed from European civilization. The aim of the organization was to fight persecution and to bring about the emancipation of the Jews in those countries where it had not yet been achieved. But, apart from the legal component, emancipation also had a social dimension, and the Alliance saw the two as an indivisible whole. Social emancipation was especially important in "certain regions of the Orient where there [was] a whole work of regeneration to undertake."[2] The agent of "regeneration" was to be the modern school.

This kind of concern shown by elements within the Franco-Jewish elite for the fortunes of the Jews of the East is firmly rooted in the history of European Jewry in the modern period. The era of emancipation ushered in by the Enlightenment and the French Revolution, dissolving corporate communities and gradually integrating the Jews into the "national" life of their respective countries in the nineteenth century, brought about a hitherto unseen fragmentation in the Jewish world. Until the eighteenth century, all Jews had shared a common universe based upon the principles of rabbinical Judaism, of *halakhah* (Jewish law), and of communal autonomy. There were, of course, local variations in liturgy, language, dress, and custom. However, the bedrock of Jewish life, whether for the Ashkenazi or the Sephardi, was a well-defined and regulated religious tradition. This universe was transformed irrevocably by the rise of the modern state, by the European Enlightenment and its Jewish version, the *haskalah*, by the development of industrial capitalism, and by legal and political emancipation. The contours of modern Jewish history have been shaped by the challenges posed by these developments.

The transformation of Jewish life proceeded unevenly, affecting Western and Central Europe first, and then slowly spreading further East. By the middle of the nineteenth century, leading sections of Western Jewry were, from all points of view, quite different from their fellow Jews elsewhere. The *embourgeoisement* of this elite, the result of its growing acculturation and integration into European bourgeois culture and civilization, inevitably posed new questions with respect to its relationship to the mass of poor traditional Jews living either in close proximity, or in distant lands. Internalizing the Enlightenment critique of traditional Jewish society as well as the currently accepted notions about the need to moralize and redeem the poor, the elite, especially in France and in Germany, evolved an agenda of "regeneration" to "civilize" the "backward" traditional Jew, whether in Alsace, in Bavaria, or in Posen. As for the millions of Jews under the rule of the Tsars, it was widely expected that soon, under a more enlightened regime, the same processes that had brought change in Western and Central Europe would also spread further to the East to transform them into "civilized" citizens.

However, the Muslim world, under inefficient and neglectful rulers, did not look as promising. Growing European trade and commerce with the Middle East and North Africa, which brought increasing contacts with the Jews of these areas, the information brought by the press about the conditions of Sephardic and Eastern Jewries, and the appeals of local notables for help, all converged in the middle of the nineteenth century to create a "Jewish Eastern Question"[3] for the leadership of Western Jewry. For the latter, the Jews of the East were a poor, benighted lot, "backward" and "obscurantist," and in dire need of help from their brethren in the West to rejoin "civilization." The agenda of "regeneration" was hence expanded to cover these unfortunate co-religionists in Muslim lands. The aim was nothing less than the remaking of the Eastern Jew in the idealized image of the emancipated Western Jew.

It was French Jewry which developed the institutional and organizational framework to put this program of "regeneration" into practice in the shape of the Alliance Israélite Universelle, founded in 1860. The first Jewish community to be legally emancipated, administered by a highly centralized consistorial system, French Jewry was in a position of leadership vis-à-vis other European Jews, especially across the Rhine, who were still struggling to gain equal rights from their respective governments. With its own emancipation question resolved, French Jews could look beyond their own borders to help other communities gain the same rights and to embark upon the process of their "regeneration." The institution to implement this program, the Alliance Israélite Universelle, emerged as the very distillation of all the ideological and political forces that had created the emancipated, acculturated social and intellectual elite of modern French Jewry.

As its appeal of 1860 already indicated, change was to come through the modern school, and the organization soon became involved with the task of educating the young generations in the Sephardic world. By the first decade of the twentieth century, it had established a network of educational institutions among the Jewish communities of an area ranging from Morocco in the West to Iran in the East. On the eve of World War I, 43,700 students were attending 183 Alliance schools.[4] These were mostly elementary establishments offering more advanced classes than their counterparts in the West. The Central Committee of the Alliance devised its curriculum which was taught in French, the language of "civilization" par excellence, and based it upon the one used in schools in metropolitan France, with the addition of instruction in local languages and in Jewish subjects such as Hebrew and Jewish history. The schools were under the directorship of teachers who were themselves graduates of Alliance institutions and had received further education at the teacher training college created by the organization in Paris, the *Ecole Normale Israélite Orientale*.

By World War I, the Alliance had managed to establish a near monopoly over the field of education in most Sephardic communities, considerably weakening or displacing altogether the traditional educational system. It was responsible for the schooling of generations of Jews and had left its mark on wide sections of Jewish society. The organization acted as the central and most significant conduit which channelled European ideas and practices to the Jews of the Middle East and North Africa.

This study analyzes the ideology, politics, and consequences of the work of "regeneration" undertaken by the Alliance, focusing upon its activities in a specific region, the one that falls within the borders of the present-day Turkish Republic. It concentrates on the largest and most important Jewish communities of the area, namely those of Istanbul, Izmir, and Edirne (Adrianople), also referring to other smaller centers in Thrace and Asia Minor to illustrate the general aspects of the organization's work. It also mentions developments in Salonica and Bulgaria where these throw light upon issues that were of import to the three major communities.

The Alliance's efforts to transform Middle Eastern and North African Jewry, is, of course, situated within the larger context of the process of Westernization that affected the area in modern times. The aim here is to illuminate some of the implications of this trend as they applied to Turkish Jewry by examining the very site from which emanated many of the new ideas and customs that affected it profoundly, the Alliance school.

This is not a history of Turkish Jewry in the nineteenth and early twentieth centuries. It is also not a history of modern education among the Jews of Turkey, though it examines some of the most important developments in this domain. (It has proven impossible to gain access to relevant Ottoman archives without which an educational history would remain incomplete.) Nor does it cover the Alliance's activities in world diplomacy, a subject that merits a separate, full-length treatment. Rather, the central focus is the local and international politics of the Alliance's attempt to transform the Jews in the lands of Islam as illustrated by its activities in one area, Turkey. The encounter between European and non-European Jews in modern times is a theme that continues to have ramifications in our own day. This is a case study of the beginnings and evolution of the encounter in the nineteenth and early twentieth centuries.

NOTE

Simplified Hebrew transliteration, based on the general rules of the *Encyclopedia Judaica* transliteration system, has been used throughout the book. The only exception is that the *ayin* is designated by an apostrophe (').

FRENCH JEWS,
TURKISH JEWS

I

THE EMERGENCE OF THE "JEWISH EASTERN QUESTION"

The Damascus Affair and the Ideology of Emancipation

A new type of international action carried out by Jews emerged in the nineteenth century, first evident in the Damascus affair of 1840. This incident was of great importance in bringing the Jews of the Middle East to the attention of their coreligionists in the West.

The facts of the blood libel are well known.[1] A Capucin friar, Père Thomas, disappeared in early 1840 in Damascus. Sections of the Christian Arab population of the town accused the Jews of having murdered him to use his blood for ritual purposes. This was an old libel that had been especially common in premodern Europe,[2] but in this instance the French consul of Damascus, Ratti Menton, took the accusations seriously. The governor of the town was particularly concerned to be on his best behavior, as France was the only supporter of Mehmet Ali, the ruler of Egypt who had occupied Syria since 1832. The governor therefore immediately arrested the accused Jews, some of whom also happened to be the leaders of the community, and tortured them to extract a confession to the alleged crime. The terrorized Damascus Jews asked for help from the Jewish community of Istanbul, which immediately appealed for the intervention of the Jewish communities of Europe.

The news provoked widespread consternation among the Jews of Europe. The latter were, of course, concerned about the fate of their fellow Jews and did all that was possible to save them. But more was at stake. Sections of the French press, especially the clerical papers such as *La Quotidienne, La France,* and *L'Univers Religieux,* took the allegations seriously and reported them as if the Jews were indeed guilty of the crime. At the same time, another blood libel was reported from the island of Rhodes. If all was to be believed by the population at large, the hard-won emancipation of the Jews would be put into jeopardy. As Adolphe Crémieux, vice-president of the Central Consistory wrote to *L'Univers,* one of the newspapers which had appeared to support the veracity of the charges: "at the same time that the Jews of the Orient were accused in Damascus and Rhodes, the Jews of the Occident were [also] accused. . . ."[3] In another letter he appealed to public opinion, to the

1

"French Christians" who had shown the world "the example of the most gentle and the most pure toleration" not to abandon the Jews now.[4] Writing many years later, Albert Cohn, a close associate of the Rothschilds, who was to play a very important role in the fortunes of Middle Eastern Jewry, reminisced that "by mistreating the Jews of Damascus they [had] wanted to dishonor the Jews of Europe. . . ."[5] These statements reveal just how fragile the Jews perceived their newly gained emancipation to be. Any development that could, in any way, show them in an unfavorable light was taken as potentially dangerous. In 1853, after another blood accusation in the East, the editor of the *Jewish Chronicle* of London was moved to write that "some little latitude might be granted to him who, as a Jew, felt that the infamous charges brought against his brethren in faith, would, if true, have rendered him, as well as them, unfit to be received in civilised society."[6]

Furthermore, the affair put French Jewry in a delicate position vis-à-vis the government, which refused to condemn the actions of its consul in Damascus, who had encouraged the governor in his search for the culprit of the alleged crime among the Jewish community. Appeals by the Central Consistory of French Jews to Adolphe Thiers, the foreign minister, and to the king, Louis Philippe, went unanswered. French indifference was in marked contrast to the attitude and behavior of other European governments and their consuls in the Levant.

Motivated both by a sense of urgency to save their fellow Jews in Damascus and by a need to demonstrate to the Christian world the unfounded nature of the accusations, the Central Consistory of French Jews and the Board of Deputies of British Jews joined their efforts to bring about the release of the imprisoned and their full exoneration by the authorities. A joint mission, composed of Sir Moses Montefiore, the great British philanthropist, Dr. L. Loewe, his secretary, Adolphe Crémieux, the well-known French lawyer and vice-president of the Central Consistory, and Salomon Munk, the famous Orientalist, set out for the Middle East, and, to the jubilation of European Jewry, succeeded in having the prisoners freed and obtained proclamations asserting their innocence. Montefiore went on to Istanbul where, to convince European public opinion, he obtained from the Sultan a *ferman* (imperial edict) on the falsehood of the blood libel.[7]

What is striking about the episode of the Damascus Affair is the mixture of the old and the new it presents in the relationship between far-flung Jewish communities. The channels of communication had functioned in the traditional way. The distressed community of Damascus had written for help to the Istanbul community, with which it had been in contact for many centuries, to intervene with the authorities in the capital. (It had come under Egyptian rule only recently.) Jews from the nearby community of Beirut had written to Lehren, head of the *Va'ad ha-Pekidim* (committee of officials) based in Amsterdam which was in charge of the directing of funds from Europe to the Jews of Palestine.[8] Two Jews from Palestine, on a visit to Istanbul, had written to

James de Rothschild of Paris.[9] And the Istanbul community had sent an appeal to the Jews in London.[10]

Western Jews had acted in the age-old tradition of powerful Jews using their influence in high places to help their brethren in distress. Crémieux and the Consistory had appealed to the French government, though to no avail Montefiore and the Board of Deputies had succeeded in obtaining the support of Sir Robert Peel and Lord Palmerston. However, the British had, at that moment, no direct influence on Egypt and Syria. Hence a joint mission was embarked upon to try to influence the authority most directly concerned, Mehmet Ali of Egypt.

None of this was new. Many a Court Jew had behaved in similar fashion in the past. Jewish society had well-established patterns of dealing with adversity and distress. If a problem could not be solved locally, then another community's help was asked. Rich Jews with links to the authorities often used their influence to settle a problem concerning the Jews. Communities also had institutionalized help by putting aside funds specifically for the purpose of aiding Jews in trouble. One such fund was for the ransoming of captives.[11] Money, either from communal funds or philanthropists, was regularly sent when disasters like fire, earthquake, and destruction struck other communities. The help offered by Western Jewry to the Damascus Jews in 1840 certainly had a long and hallowed tradition behind it.

Most historians have focused on the impetus provided by the Damascus affair for the emergence of a Jewish press and public opinion in Europe and on its role in the making of a secular Jewish solidarity.[12] Indeed, a totally new aspect of the Jewish intervention at the time of the Damascus affair was its public nature. The leadership of Western Jewry took a public stand as full fledged members of European society. They orchestrated a steady flow of letters to the editors of newspapers. They lobbied their respective governments, used parliamentary tactics by having questions raised in the British House of Commons and in the French Chamber of Deputies. They organized an open protest meeting in London in 1840.

All this bore testimony to the fact that in spite of worries over the fragility of their newly gained civil rights, the Jewish leaders took themselves to be equal and full participants in the newly developed liberal public sphere in their respective countries. The appeal to public opinion was to be a common feature of most Jewish lobbying activities after the Damascus affair.

However, another facet of the intercession has been relatively ignored, the effort undertaken both by Crémieux and Montefiore to bring about internal changes in the Jewish communities of the Middle East while they were in the area. Upon arrival in Alexandria, Crémieux lost no time in preaching at a local synagogue on the advantages of European-style education.[13] He then moved to Cairo, where, with the help of resident foreign Jews, mostly Italian in origin, he founded one school for girls and one for boys. A committee was created to oversee the activities of the schools, and the first teacher was engaged.[14] These were the first modern Jewish schools in the Middle East that taught European languages and employed a European curriculum. It was here that was launched the first attack on the traditional Jewish educational system in the lands of Islam.

Sir Moses Montefiore also showed great interest in the education of Jewish youth when in Istanbul. He visited a traditional school where boys studied Hebrew, read the Talmud, and translated it into their mother tongue, Judeo-Spanish.[15] This was the immediate aftermath of the Imperial Rescript of 1839 which had inaugurated the period of reforms known as the *Tanzimat,* guaranteeing the life, property, and honor of all the subjects of the Sultan, irrespective of religion, the first step in the moves that were to transform the Ottoman Empire during the course of the nineteenth century.[16] Expecting these reforms to improve the condition of the Jews, Montefiore, in a meeting with notables, "rebuked them for their unwisdom in concentrating all their energies on the study of Hebrew, without giving due attention to the vernacular."[17] His secretary, Dr. Loewe, preached for three hours (!) in the Galata synagogue in Hebrew, Turkish, and Spanish on the benefits of modern education and of a knowledge of European languages and Turkish.[18] Under Montefiore's direction, Loewe drew up an appeal to the Jews of the Ottoman Empire, pointing out the importance of studying Turkish.[19] Montefiore pressed it upon the Chief Rabbi, Mosheh Fresco, who then used it as the base of a proclamation issued on 28 October 1840, asking every Jewish institution of education to hire a qualified teacher to teach the Turkish language.[20]

The attempts by Crémieux and Montefiore to introduce reforms in the Jewish communities of the Levant during the course of their visit in 1840 points to a new departure in the relationship between Western Jewry and their fellow Jews elsewhere. The elite of Western Jewry increasingly brought a specific ideological program to its dealings with Jewish communities outside Western Europe. Under the impact of the twin forces of Enlightenment and emancipation (the latter achieved either fully or in part), a particular *Weltanschauung,* firmly grounded in the ideology of emancipation, had come to dominate the thoughts and actions of the elite. Its central concern was to transform the community of which it was a part in the light of this ideology. However, the ideology also influenced the elite's perception of other Jewish communities which had not yet gone through the same process of change. Intercession on behalf of fellow Jews in distress and philanthropy had now become politicized. The aim was not only to give help when called upon but also to transform, to "regenerate."

Even before the Damascus affair, French Jewry had had to face the problem of what to do with the "backward" Jews of Algeria who had come under French rule since the occupation of the country in 1830. On 24 December 1837, the Central Consistory of French Jews in Paris wrote to the Consistory of Marseilles inquiring about the means that could be employed to "hasten the regeneration" of Algerian Jewry. The reply from Marseilles stressed the need to open schools with French teachers, to create consistories like those of France, and to send French rabbis to Algeria.[21]

The events of the past fifty years had made the concept of "regeneration" mentioned in the above letter such a permanent fixture in the ideology of the French-Jewish notable that he would export it whenever given the chance. In this he was helped by elements from other Jewish communities of Europe as deeply influenced by the ideology of emancipation.[22] The changes that Crémieux and Montefiore attempted to institute in the Jewish communities of the Levant that they visited during the course of the Damascus affair were some of the first manifestations of a new politics in the Jewish world, one deeply marked by the ideological and social differences between different Jewries.

What exactly was meant by the term "regeneration"? It is important to realize that the term is intimately associated with the Enlightenment and revolutionary discourse on the Jews, and with its logical conclusion—emancipation. For the rational functioning of society on the path of "progress," all corporate bodies with special rights and privileges had to be dissolved and replaced by a citizenry with equal rights. The individual, shorn of superstition and medieval habits, had the duty to become a useful and productive citizen. The question of utility preoccupied the Enlightenment discourse on the Jews. In 1781, Christian Wilhelm Dohm, a Prussian ministerial councillor, argued in his book, *Über die bürgerliche Verbesserung der Juden,* that the Jews could be rendered useful to the state by the amelioration of their status and the removal of the restrictions on their economic activities so that they could enter agriculture and engage in manual trades. The book was translated into French in 1782 and became well known in intellectual circles in France.[23]

The potential usefulness of the Jews was again in question in the competition organized by the *Société royale des sciences et des arts de Metz* in 1785 for the best essays on the subject of the means to be used to render the Jews "happier and more useful in France." The most important of the three essays awarded prizes was that of Abbé Grégoire, who was later to play an important role in the revolutionary assemblies emancipating the Jews and the Blacks. His work had the title *Essai sur la régénération physique, morale et politique des Juifs.* This was one of the first public occurrences of the term "regeneration" as applied to the Jews.

The argument of the book, stated very briefly, was that the improvement of the situation of the Jews would remove them from being outcasts in society, a position that encouraged all their "bad habits" such as superstitions, exclusiveness, and excessive predilection for commerce and usury. Grégoire recognized that the Jews were in a degraded state and of little use to the society they lived in. Together with all the other prizewinners, he argued that it was partially the fault of Christians that they had developed "bad habits," as persecution had shut off all avenues for amelioration, although he also implied that much of their "degeneration" was the result of their own religion and customs. Nevertheless, he did not believe that this was an irreversible state of affairs. Their "regeneration" would reverse the situation and integrate the Jews into society at large.[24]

The concept of "regeneration" as used by Jew and Gentile alike also presupposed the "degeneracy" of the current condition of the Jews. Hence, "regeneration" was not just a rhetorical device standing for "improvement." It also implied, by definition, a radical critique of traditional Judaism and of traditional Jewish society.

Therefore, for the ideology of emancipation, the granting of equal rights from without and the reform of Jewish society from within came as a package. Legal emancipation had to go hand in hand with the "moral betterment" of the Jews, whether such "betterment" was to be achieved by themselves or by the state, so that they could at last be integrated in society and transcend those peculiar characteristics that set them apart. Corporate communal autonomy and Jewish distinctiveness were deemed equally undesirable. "Regeneration" was that process of comprehensive reform by means of which Jews could become fully equal and "useful" citizens, virtually indistinguishable from others. As such, it constituted the foundation stone of the ideology of emancipation.

The consistory system instituted by Napoleon in 1808 had the very purpose of "regeneration" in mind. The consistories were to administer and police the Jewish communities and bring about their transformation by encouraging Jews to find useful professions such as artisanal trades and agriculture.[25]

Jewish leaders in France soon came to see their society with the same eyes and adopted the term "regeneration" to denote the desired process that would transform the Jews into "useful" citizens. A Jewish agenda emerged to accelerate this transformation as spelled out in books such as Berr Isaac Berr's *Réflexions sur la régénération complète des Juifs de France* (Paris, 1806), P. Wittersheim's *Mémoire sur les moyens de hâter la régénération des Israélites d'Alsace* (Metz, 1825), and even in a newspaper, *La Régénération,* published in Strasbourg in 1836–1837. The adoption and internalization of the Enlightenment and revolutionary discourse on the Jews by the Jewish leadership meant that the community as a whole had to transform itself radically.[26]

The *locus classicus* of the transformation was to be the school. Its aim was to correct "bad habits" and socialize future generations of French Jews.[27] The Jewish reformers looked with great disfavor upon traditional education with its stress on Hebrew and the Talmud. The new Jewish schools were all designed to educate the poor, as it was assumed that the more well-to-do Jews would send their children to public or private French institutions. Hence the French state left the Jewish schools in the hands of philanthropists and the charity agencies of the consistories.

The first modern Jewish school opened in 1818 in Metz to be followed in 1819 by another one in Paris. By 1821, there had been established a total of twelve schools in seven *départements,* all supported by Jewish philanthropy.[28]

Educational reforms went hand in hand with moves to diversify the Jewish social structure by promoting manual professions and agriculture. From 1810, the Central Consistory assigned the task of teaching the manual professions in Paris to the *Comité de bienfaisance* which supervised the distribution of Jewish charity. An apprenticeship system was developed in 1819. An *Ecole de travail* was founded in Strasbourg in 1825. After 1830, a *Comité des dames* supervised the apprenticeship of girls. Many societies for the encouragement of manual trades sprang up. The most important and long lasting of these was the *Société de patronage des apprentis et ouvriers Israélites de Paris,* founded in 1853 with the involvement of the Rothschilds and many of the future founders of the Alliance.[29]

The reshaping of Jewish society also had to involve changes in the training of rabbis. This necessity led to a debate that raged throughout the first half of the nineteenth century. The Central Consistory founded an *école rabbinique* in Metz in 1827, which replaced the traditional *yeshivot* and offered secular as well as rabbinical learning. The school drew heavy criticism for not having well integrated secular studies in the curriculum. Nevertheless, with piece-meal reforms, especially after its transfer to Paris in 1859, the *séminaire rabbinique,* as it came to be known, totally transformed the character of the French rabbinate.

The concern by the Jewish leadership with education and with the reform and moralizing of the Jewish masses paralleled the stance taken by bourgeois philanthropy in the face of *la question sociale* in nineteenth-century France, testifying to the assimilation of this elite into the larger French bourgeois culture. The *sociétés de patronage* and the apprenticeship system designed by Jewish leaders were not unique to the Jews. They were, in fact, measures adopted by French philanthropy in general.[30] The attack on traditional Jewish popular culture certainly sprung from a specifically Jewish program of "regeneration" to integrate the Jewish masses into wider French society. But the program was also a Jewish reflection of the larger bourgeois agenda to remould popular culture, an agenda that had originated in the early modern period[31] and reached its crescendo with the activities of the public school teacher in the Third Republic.[32] The Jewish elite, composed of bankers, intellectuals, notables, and important segments of the consistorial rabbinical class, was united around a philanthropy designed not only to give old-style *zedakah* (charity) but to reform and transform the recipient of the charity into the model moral citizen. Composed of new members of a triumphant metropolitan bourgeoisie, the elite adopted with the zeal of the neophyte all the latter's cherished values and attitudes about the poor and the masses and adapted them to the Jewish context. Ultimately, the obsession with "regeneration" was a powerful reflection of the growing *embourgeoisement* of French Jewry.

Three issues, educational reform to socialize the Jews, vocational instruction to turn them to "useful" trades, and the transforming of rabbinical training to produce new spiritual leaders of the community constituted the central themes of "regeneration." Implicitly and explicitly, the ideology posited the remaking of French Jewry. Nevertheless, the program was not unique to France but was common to the *haskalah* (the Jewish Enlightenment) as a whole which affected most of Western and Central European Jewry in the age of Enlightenment and emancipation. *Régénération* was a local, French variant of a much wider phenomenon, written about and debated throughout the century. This explains the resonance of these ideas also outside France when the reform of other Jewries was to be the question of the day.

The transformation of the Jewish community by reforms instituted by Jewish leaders themselves to suit the requirements of the modern nation-state in particular and of bourgeois "civilization" in general constitutes the central dynamic of the evolution of the inner life of French Jewry in the nineteenth century. There was, of course, opposition from traditionalist quarters, and the need for and validity of reforms was accepted by varying degrees by different groups of French Jews. Nevertheless, there did emerge a consensus on the desirability of change in the Jewish community to bring it closer to the rest of French society.[33] The ideology of emancipation, with "regeneration" as its cornerstone, thus became the dominant world view of French Jewish public life. It was inevitable that the image of the Jew outside the borders of France was refracted through the prism of this world view and that, when called upon to act, French Jewry produced the same agenda for these other Jewish communities that it had set for itself.

The Image of the Eastern Jew in the 1840s and 1850s

French Jewry, upon France's conquest of Algeria in 1830, was the first modern Jewish community which came into direct contact with a non-European one. As early as 1833, the Central Consistory decided to act to convince the authorities of the need to extend the consistory system to Algeria. There were similar attempts throughout the 1830s, all to no avail, as the government did not seem to be overly concerned with the "regeneration" of Algerian Jewry. Only at the end of the decade did the authorities begin to show interest in regularizing the situation of the Algerian Jews. In 1842, the government approved a proposal from some Marseilles politicians to send Jacques Isaac Altaras, president of the Marseilles consistory, and Joseph Cohen, a lawyer from Aix-en-Provence, to Algeria on a mission of information.

The report written by Altaras and Cohen on Algerian Jewry is a fascinating case study of how French Jewish officialdom saw non-European Jews and the means by which it sought to reform them. It is the earliest, full-blown, detailed *exposé* produced by Jews in Western Europe in the emancipation era about their coreligionists in a predominantly Islamic country. It reveals all the concerns that preoccupied the French Jewish leadership about its own society and prefigures the issues that were to be of great import to the Alliance in its dealings with the Jews of North Africa and the Levant.[34] Its whole thrust was to demonstrate the utility of the Jews of Algeria to France as intermediaries between the metropolis and the indigenous Arab population.

The report drawn up by Altaras and Cohen was highly critical of Algerian

Jews. It depicted them as fundamentally backward and superstitious. The community was in disarray. It was run by old-style rabbis and was in deep financial trouble. The authorities neglected the education of the youth. Traditional education was badly organized and run according to outdated principles in dirty, unhealthy rooms.[35] To improve this state of affairs, Altaras and Cohen were convinced of the necessity of action from the outside to activate the "forces of civilization." The reform of the educational system was of primary importance to bring about the fusion of Algerian Jewry with French society.[36] Local Jews had to be banned from wearing the local costume, encouraged to settle on the land and become farmers, and serve on the local *milice*. Civil law and civil courts had to replace religious law and tribunals. A consistorial system, based on the one in France, had to be instituted. But since the future belonged to the children of today, their education was the single most important issue that needed attention. For Altaras and Cohen, the solution was clear:

> Primary education, here is the real need of the masses; it is through it that one moralizes society, but it has to be *religious,* as what is morality without the salutary sanction of religion? *Vocational,* as geared to the people, it has to prepare them for work. *Agricultural,* as designed for men who ordinarily labor in the fields, it must make them get used early to this work which comes before all others. . . . [37]

As a result of their findings, an Algerian central consistory based in Algiers was created, with two provincial consistories in Oran and Constantine. These were to oversee the administration of the synagogues, the education of children, the finances of the community, and the spread of manual and agricultural occupations among the Jews.[38] In short, their function was to be the same as the consistories of France proper, to administer and to "regenerate." What was good for French Jewry also had to be good for the Jews of Algeria.

The same diagnosis and the same remedies are to be found in the columns of the nascent Jewish press when the Jews of the Levant came under scrutiny in the 1840s and 1850s. The Damascus affair had given an important impetus to the development of this press in Europe. The new sense of Jewish unity reflected itself in the newspapers that came to create a transnational Jewish public opinion in Europe, exchanging news and addressing issues of common concern. Before 1840, only Germany had a well-developed Jewish press, the most important newspaper being the *Allgemeine Zeitung des Judenthums*, edited by Dr. Ludwig Philippson of Magdeburg.[39] The *Archives Israélites* was founded in France in the very year of the Damascus affair and was followed four years later by its more traditionalist counterpart, *L'Univers Israélite*. These two newspapers, very influential in shaping Jewish public opinion in France, survived until World War II. The *Jewish Chronicle* of London saw the light of day in 1841 together with a rival, *The Voice of Jacob,* with which it merged in 1844. Austria, Italy, Gibraltar, the United States, all saw the emergence of a Jewish press in the 1840s. The Judeo-Spanish press also had its origins in these years with the publication for a brief period in Izmir in 1845–1846 of the *Puertas del Oriente*.[40]

The press took great care to report events concerning Jews throughout the world. From 1840 on, there were continuous reports about the conditions of the Jews of the Middle East and North Africa. These were very important in fashioning the perception of the Jew of Muslim lands in the West and influenced Western Jewry in the reforms it tried to institute to "improve" them.[41]

The first report on the Jews of Turkey was published in the *Allgemeine Zeitung des Judenthums* early in 1840, before the Damascus affair. The unsigned article had first appeared in the *Magazin für Literatur des Auslands,* was repeated verbatim in the *Allgemeine Zeitung,* and was translated and published in the *Archives Israélites* in the same year.

The picture depicted was a somber one. The Jews lived isolated from the rest of society in Turkey, attached to their rabbinical traditions, resigned to injury and outrage, consoling themselves with the hope of a glorious future. They were "ignorant, superstitious, and intolerant." They did not educate their children, did not know any European languages, and they spoke a corrupted Spanish. They thought of the Talmud as divinely inspired and believed in angels and demons. The rabbis exercised great influence and used excommunication frequently. From the point of view of morality, they seemed beyond reproach. But early marriages were the rule and, together with the lack of artisanal professions, were, for the reporter, the principal cause of the misery that reigned in the community.[42]

All these criticisms were repeated in a series of letters by an anonymous correspondent of the *Allgemeine Zeitung des Judenthums* on the Jewish community of Istanbul in 1841.[43] They were summarized in the *Archives Israélites* of the same year.[44] The letters took on an importance beyond that of their initial appearance, for parts of them were republished in 1854 by the Jewish press of Germany, France, and England to make the case for a reform of "Oriental Jewry" designed to follow their being granted equal rights with the Muslims of the Ottoman Empire.

For the author of the letters, the most important task for Western Jewry was to break the all-encompassing apathy of the Eastern Jew. Help for these Jews could come only from their European brethren whose primary task was the instilling of a new conscience, a new pride:

> What is the first thing that has to be given to them? *The feeling of being men* [emphasis mine]. Without this, no change is possible. The Oriental Jew must first of all understand . . . that he too is a man, that he has a right . . . to live as a man. . . .[45]

The similarity with Enlightenment discourse on the Jews is striking in this passage. It was indeed the *credo* of the Enlightenment that the Jews were "men" like others, and it was on that foundation that the whole edifice of the "regeneration" was erected. The internalization of this discourse by European Jewry is nowhere more apparent than in these reports on Eastern Jews and in the program for their betterment.

The letters then went on to outline the means to remedy the situation. The answer, predictably, lay in education. Because of the impracticality of setting up schools in the area, the best option was to bring young Turkish Jews to the West, who, after their education in the capitals of Europe, would return to spread the message of civilization to their brethren. The letters concluded with an appeal to European Jews to set up a committee which would oversee the creation and running of a school for young Turkish Jews who would be educated in Western Europe.[46]

Both the *Archives Israélites* and the *Allgemeine Zeitung des Judenthums* were newspapers which supported some degree of reform in religion, though stopped far short of the views of the more extreme reformists. The hostility shown to traditional Jewish society, as seen in the reports that they published on the Jews of the East, was also for domestic consumption. Nevertheless, the more traditionalist papers such as the *Jewish Chronicle* and *L'Univers Israélite* agreed with the stance taken by their more reform minded colleagues. All were firm believers in the benefits of emancipation, and all agreed that it was through education and social reforms that Jews could participate in European civilization. This was the public consensus that informed the united critical stance taken toward non-European Jewry and the proposals for its transformation.

Nothing came from the suggestions for action in the letters published in the *Allgemeine Zeitung des Judenthums* in 1841. Nevertheless, what is striking about them is the similarity in tone and conclusion with the Altaras-Cohen report, which they predated by one year. The answer to all the perceived ills facing these Jewish societies lay in educating the youth in the ways of Europe. The future would be a far better one if the slumbering forces of civilization could be awakened by instruction. The image of the school as the ultimate panacea for all the problems of society and as the most important agent for change and reform was, of course, not unique to the Jews, but was a constant of nineteenth-century middle class civilization. The fervor with which the Jews of nineteenth-century Europe embraced education as the principal means for improving their situation is too well known to need repetition. Faced with coreligionists steeped in a value system that no longer accorded with their own, it was all too natural that they would offer "modern" education as the entry ticket to the civilization that had only recently allowed them in.

This cult of education was later taken up by the Alliance, which, twenty years after the publication of these letters, produced a similar critique of non-European Jewish society and, remarkably, fulfilled all their programmatic aims. The only difference was to be in the Alliance's opting for schools in the localities, rather than educating Jewish youth in the West, though its teacher training institution in Paris did also fulfill the latter task.

The characterization in the 1840s of Eastern Jewry as "backward" and "degenerate" represented a remarkable turnaround in the perception of the

Sephardim among the "enlightened" elements of Western Jewry. In the literature of the *haskalah* of the late eighteenth and early nineteenth centuries, the heritage of the Golden Age of Spanish Jewry had constituted the yardstick with which current Jewish communities in Central and Eastern Europe were judged and found wanting. The assumed state of grace of the Sephardim of the Golden Age, full-fledged participants in the high cultural life of the learned elite of Spain as well as devoted followers of a Judaism fully open to the outside world, had to be attained once again. Hence, for example, Hartwig Wessely, a leading *maskil* and champion of the *haskalah* in the late eighteenth century, looked to Italian Jewry to find supporters for his call to Jews to study secular subjects as well as religious ones. He thought that the Sephardic component of Italian Jewish culture rendered it open, tolerant, and accessible to his project.[47]

But the idealized image of the Sephardim among the *maskilim* had suffered a rude shock by the middle of the nineteenth century. Familiarity did indeed breed contempt. Increased trade and commerce with the Middle East and improvements in transportation led to greater contact with actual Eastern Sephardim. The press became the conduit through which a new image, that of the "fanatical," "obscurantist," and "backward" Eastern Jew, was disseminated throughout the Jewish world. The new image was particularly galling to the new emancipationist liberal Jewish bourgeoisie of Western Europe. The latter feared to be tarred with the same brush as its Eastern brethren by Europeans who were increasingly present in the Middle East and North Africa for purposes of trade and commerce.

It is undoubtedly true that the new perception of the Eastern Jew was also influenced by the current ideas of European superiority vis-à-vis all non-European societies. The middle of the nineteenth century was also the period when the Middle East had come to assume a place in the psyche of the liberal European bourgeois as the repository of all the values taken to be the opposite of those that characterized the "advanced" European civilization. Whereas Europe was dynamic, the "Orient" was apathetic. Whereas Europe was forward-looking, well-launched upon the path of endless "progress," the "Orient" was indolent and backward. Europe represented order and rationality while the "Orient" was irrational and chaotic. Europe was the cradle of liberalism and democracy while the "Orient" was steeped in barbaric despotism.[48]

For the liberal Jewish bourgeoisie of Western Europe, the Middle Eastern Jew had been heavily contaminated by all the negative features of his surrounding society. The level of civilization of the Jew was very low, like that of the Turks and the Greeks who surrounded him.[49] He had to be transformed, through education, to regain his place in world civilization which was, of course, coterminous with that of Europe.

But while this essentially imperialist vision did influence the Western Jewish perception of Eastern Jewry, it would be a mistake to assign to it a determinant role. For the same negative image, with an identical vocabulary, was also very much in evidence in the perception of Central and Eastern European traditional Ashkenazi society by the "enlightened" and emancipated of Western Jewry.[50] The problem of the *Ostjude* was to haunt the German and Hapsburg Jewish elite well into the twentieth century.

The fundamental fissure in the nineteenth-century Jewish universe was not that between the European and the Middle Eastern Jew, or between the Ashkenazi and the Sephardi. The rupture that prevailed was between the "enlightened," the emancipated or emancipationist Jewries that were rapidly integrating into the bourgeois culture of their surrounding societies, and the rest of world Jewry still steeped in Jewish tradition and popular culture, whether in the East or in the West. The uneven development of the processes of *haskalah* and emancipation with all their accompanying social, political, cultural, and economic changes had brought about a polarization in Jewish society. The central motifs of the attack in the Jewish press on Middle Eastern Jewry, the inordinate power of the rabbis, the lack of productive trades and skills among the Jews, and the lamentable state of the educational system were all themes that developed from the *haskalah* movement onward. They were applied by the social and intellectual elite of Western and Central European Jewry to its own large reservoir of Jews steeped in tradition, whether they be in Alsace, in Bavaria, in Posen, or in Galicia. The editor of the *Archives Israélites* added a very revealing note at the end of the French version of the first article on Turkish Jewry published in the *Allgemeine Zeitung des Judenthums* in 1840.

> This judgment of our coreligionists in Turkey applies also . . . to those of other countries where many of the superstitions reported here have or have had equally numerous partisans. . . . The last fifty years have made a large number of [these superstitions] disappear, especially in France and in Germany.[51]

In non-European Jewry there could be seen the past that the elite of European Jewry had transcended or was still striving to transcend. Hence the biting quality of much of the reporting on the Jews of the Middle East and North Africa and the dark picture that emerged as a result.

Newspapers continued to publish articles on Turkish Jewry in the 1840s and early 1850s, reporting on local events such as blood libels[52] and echoing sentiments similar to the ones discussed above about the need to educate Turkish Jews,[53] stressing their present fallen condition.[54] However, no concrete action was taken until the outbreak of the Crimean War when the Eastern question became once again of paramount interest in European public affairs. The increasing Western presence in the Middle East, Turkey's alliance with European powers against Russia, and the projected changes in the status of the non-Muslim subjects of the Sultan, focused the attention of European Jewry on the fate of their fellow Jews and sparked the second stage in the attempt to "regenerate" the Jews of the Levant. In this respect, the Crimean war was as important as the Damascus affair in bringing about the active involvement of European Jews in the affairs of Middle Eastern Jewry.

An important consequence of the alliance between the European powers and Turkey was the increasing pressure put on the Porte, especially by the British ambassador, Stratford de Redcliffe, to improve the status of the Christians in the Empire and to open its administration to them. As a result, the Sultan issued a Reform Edict in 1856, promising the equal treatment of all the subjects of the Empire, irrespective of religion.[55]

From early 1854, European Jewish public opinion became greatly concerned with the fact that no mention was being made of Jews in the debates about the granting of equal rights to the Christians of the Ottoman Empire. The Central Consistory appealed to Napoleon III,[56] and the Board of Deputies to the British Foreign Minister, Lord Clarendon, to make sure that the provisions of any edict issued by the Porte on the matter would also apply to the Jews. These appeals were received positively by the British, who were the principal movers for the reform.[57] The French and English Rothschilds also acted, raising the subject directly with the Turks during the course of negotiations over a loan.[58] There is no indication that the Turks ever intended to exclude the Jews from the provisions of the forthcoming reforms. Nevertheless, the final Reform Edict, granting equal rights to "Christians and other non-Muslim subjects"[59] was received with much jubilation by the Jewish press,[60] strengthening the already Turcophile sentiments of European Jews who compared favorably the Turkish treatment of their brethren with that of Christendom, especially Russia.

This episode is important not only because of the mobilization of Jewish public opinion in favor of their fellow Jews in the Ottoman Empire but also for what it reveals about the dominant emancipation ideology. The European Jews perceived themselves as directly involved, since the exclusion of their brethren from the granting of equal rights would also have reflected negatively on their status in the West. Dr. Ludwig Philippson, the editor of the *Allgemeine Zeitung des Judenthums* put it thus:

> Besides the most intense sympathy elicited by this condition of our Oriental fellows in descent and religion . . . it cannot escape us that this event cannot remain without its influence on us European Jews. If the Turkish Jews are passed over and excluded from so great and world historical an opportunity, then OUR doom is also sealed, and we almost hear the proclamation resounding through the whole earth: "The descendents of Judah remain a rejected and oppressed race!" Should the Sultan, on the contrary, pronounce the equalization of the Jews with the Christian population, it must sooner or later affect also those Christian states which hitherto yet deny us that equality. We ourselves are therefore immediately concerned thereby.[61]

Once the emancipation of Turkish Jewry was placed on the agenda, the other side of the coin of the ideology, their "regeneration," became topical again. "It is now up to the Jews of Turkey to show themselves worthy . . ." wrote the traditionalist *Univers Israélite* when speaking about the benefits of emancipation.[62] Indeed much of the debate in 1854–1855 was built on the premise that Turkish Jews now would have to show that they merited the granting of equal rights.

The principal contributors to the debate were the Central Consistory in Paris, the *Archives Israélites,* and the *Allgemeine Zeitung des Judenthums.* The latter's editor, Ludwig Philippson took an especially active part, devoting most of the space in his weekly paper from March to October 1854 to the "Jewish Eastern Question," as he called it.[63] He reprinted substantial sections of the 1841 letters discussed above to summarize and indict the state of Turkish Jewry. He published a lengthy memorandum on the subject in the May 8, 1854 issue of the *Allgemeine Zeitung des Judenthums,* translated it into several languages, and sent it to important Jewish figures and communal bodies such as the Board of Deputies in London and the Central Consistory in Paris. The arguments of the memorandum were summarized in the *Archives Israélites,*[64] while the *Jewish Chronicle* printed a full translation.[65]

The ideas propounded in the memorandum were familiar ones. Turkish Jews were in a state of decline due to their ignorance. It was imperative that European Jews come to their aid, and the only remedy was education. Young Turkish Jews had to be educated in Europe. These students would, upon their return, form the nucleus of reform and civilization. He appealed to Jewish institutions in Europe to make special provisions for the education of Turkish Jews, to private charities to provide funding, and proposed the setting up of a "general management" to supervise these efforts. The arguments made in the 1841 letters had gained added urgency, as the Jews of Turkey were now on the verge of emancipation.

For Philippson, the natural center [*Mittelpunkt*] with sufficient authority to run this work was the Central Consistory in Paris.[66] After all, the Central Consistory was already involved with a similar set of circumstances in Algeria. To convince the Consistory, Philippson traveled to Paris in May 1854 and had meetings over the question with prominent Jewish leaders. The Consistory accepted his proposals and wrote to him in June 1854, announcing that it had consented to undertake " . . . the direction of the work of civilizing the Jews of the Orient . . ." and that it was sending Albert Cohn, president of the *Comité de bienfaisance* and secretary to the Rothschilds to the Middle East to report on the local conditions.[67]

Albert Cohn traveled to the Middle East with Rothschild money, founded two schools in Alexandria, a hospital, a school for girls, and a vocational school for boys in Jerusalem, a school in Izmir, and finally a school in Istanbul.[68] He saw the Sultan and the Ottoman foreign minister in Istanbul and conferred with them about the inclusion of the Jews in the provisions of any future reform edict on the status of the non-Muslims in the Empire.[69] The schools founded by Crémieux in Cairo in 1840 had closed soon after his departure. Albert Cohn's schools were, therefore, the renewal of the effort to implant Western institutions in the Jewish communities of the Middle East.

The foundation of schools in the Middle East was not in Philippson's plan. He was highly critical of the speed with which Cohn set up these establishments and predicted that they would not last for very long. He still wished to pursue his plan to educate Turkish Jews in Europe.[70] But by then, the rift between him and the Central Consistory had grown wider, and his project died for lack of funding.

It was natural that Philippson should have looked to the Central Consistory of French Jews to lead the work of "civilizing" the Jews of the Ottoman Empire. No other Jewry in the West had such a centralized umbrella body that administered the Jewish community of one country. The weight of the name Rothschild was also associated with the Consistory, as many members of the family served in its leadership positions. As Michael Graetz has argued persuasively, the Rothschilds, the Central Consistory, and the *Comité de bienfaisance,* which oversaw philanthropy and "regeneration" in France, formed a kind of leadership, a center, for French and European Jewry.[71] But the international action of the Consistory was limited by the fact that it was first and foremost a French administrative body, created by the French state, and it was hesitant to involve itself directly in a course that transcended its defined functions. And, indeed, the Albert Cohn mission in 1854 and his work in the Middle East was really a Rothschild enterprise, financed by Rothschild money.

Much of the interest shown in the Jews of the Levant in this period was also the result of growing concern over the condition of the Jews in the Holy Land. The war between Turkey and Russia had cut off the flow of *ḥalukah* (funds for the support of the Jews in Palestine) contributions from Russia, the source of most of the support for the Ashkenazim in the Holy Land. News of the widespread distress caused by the situation soon reached Europe. Meetings were held in all the major Jewish centers and funds were collected. The Albert Cohn trip was also part of this relief effort. Cohn carried 50,000 francs given to him by the Rothschilds, and he drew upon a further 300,000 francs of the Touro estate from New Orleans entrusted to the Rothschilds for this purpose.[72]

Philanthropy from rich individuals in Europe and *ḥalukah* contributions from the Jewish communities throughout the world had been the traditional means of support for the Jewish communities of Palestine. These contributions were given to emissaries who went from community to community to collect money. Funds were also sent to special bodies created to centralize collections, such as the *Va'ad ha-Pekidim* (committee of officials) of Istanbul in the eighteenth century[73] and its counterpart in Amsterdam in the nineteenth century. From the 1830s on, there was increasing immigration of Ashkenazim from Eastern Europe to Palestine. Most of the *Yishuv* (the Jewish settlements in Palestine) concerned itself with prayer and study and was dependent on the *ḥalukah* for survival.[74] By the mid-nineteenth century, this system was coming under attack from those sections of West European Jewry at the forefront of the transformation of their own communities. As early as 1842, Philippson had suggested the foundation of a *Missiongesellschaft des Judenthums* to oversee the introduction of modern schooling and of artisanal and agricultural trades to the *Yishuv.*[75] Philanthropists had also started to echo these views. Sir Moses Montefiore attempted to start a weaving school in Jerusalem, an effort which failed because of opposition from religious quarters.[76]

The philanthropic leadership of Western Jewry continued to maintain what can be termed a "Palestinophile" attitude throughout the nineteenth century, believing in the importance of the Holy Places for Judaism. As the Central Consistory put it in 1854, it could not, as a religious administrative body, " . . . refuse our sympathy to the holy places, objects of veneration and sacred equally by memories and by hopes."[77] This "Palestinophilia" was not motivated by any belief in the "national redemption" of the Jews in their ancestral homeland. It was aimed at the eventual transformation of the Jewish community of the Holy Land into a modern, productive Jewry that would honor the memory of the past. Montefiore's plans to introduce artisanal trades to the Jews of Jerusalem, the Alliance's creation in 1870 of an agricultural school, *Mikveh Yisrael,* outside Jaffa, and the Rothschilds' support of agricultural settlements toward the end of the nineteenth century, were all part of the "Palestinophile" philanthropy that had no Zionist aims. It was motivated by the wish to bring a modicum of modernity to the pious, traditional Jewish community of the Holy Land.

In short, for European Jewish public opinion of the mid-1850s, a clear agenda had emerged. The task at hand was the "regeneration" of the Jews of the Ottoman Empire in general and those in Palestine in particular by the introduction of modern schooling, modern trades, and agriculture. Palestine and Turkey were part of one large picture. The Central Consistory could not act with complete freedom; wealthy philanthropists could open schools here and there (as they continued to do in Jerusalem), but they could not sustain a long-term project of education on a mass scale. What was needed was an organization to effectively create and supervise a whole *oeuvre* of schooling and vocational training and channel European ways and ideas through an institutional framework to transform and to "regenerate." This organization was to be the Alliance Israélite Universelle, founded six years after the debates of 1854 and Albert Cohn's trip to the Middle East.

The Foundation of the Alliance Israélite Universelle

Recent scholarship has modified the hitherto accepted picture of nineteenth-century French Jewry characterized by an inexorable process of "assimilation" into the larger French society. There is no doubt that the process of socio-economic change and the impact of the program of "regeneration" did lead to the considerable acculturation and Gallicization of the French Jewish community. However, integration into the surrounding society was by no means complete by the second half of the nineteenth century. The position of Jews in France, though far better than most other communities in Europe, was fraught with problems. The struggle for acceptance was a protracted one.

Unlike other corporate bodies which were dissolved during the course of the revolution of 1789, Alsatian Jews had been made responsible for the debts of the old community. Rabbis started to receive state salaries only in 1831, while other clergy had been doing so since the days of Napoleon I. A special oath, the *more judaico,* which Jews had to take while giving evidence in court was not abolished until 1846. The revolution of 1848 saw extensive anti-Jewish rioting in Alsace. The swing toward the Church in the field of education, epitomized by the *Loi Falloux* of 1850, ushered in a campaign against Jewish teachers in public education which led to the dismissal of a number of Jews such as Isidore Cahen, the son of the editor of the *Archives Israélites* and one of the future founders of the Alliance.[78]

As if fulfilling the worst fears of Western Jewry, the reporting of blood libels in the East frequently provided occasions for attacks against the Jews in the right-wing clerical press. The period saw also the rise of antisemitic diatribes from the Left, from people like Proudhon and Fourier. The latter's disciple, Alphonse Toussenel, published the first secular antisemitic work, *Les Juifs, Rois de l'époque,* in 1844. The Jewish press was meticulous in recording each attack and responding vehemently to each accusation. It showed confidence in the age of progress, in what the future was to bring, and thought that antisemitism was destined to disappear. Nevertheless, it had to be combated in all its manifestations.

At the same time, attacks on Jews in France strengthened the resolve to fight for Jewish rights throughout the world. The zeal with which French Jews approached the task of "regenerating" the Jews of Algeria, and eventually the Jews of North Africa and the Levant, was certainly motivated in part by the perception that no Jewish community could isolate itself from other communities whose fate could, in time, have an impact at home. An attack on any Jew, anywhere, was also an attack on the hard-won position of the French Jew and could be used as such by his enemies.

Apart from the defensive concern with fellow Jews outside France, a specific sense of Jewish solidarity also marked the era of emancipation. Growing integration and acculturation into the surrounding societies and cultures did not lead to the disappearance of the emotional and intellectual bonds that united far-flung Jewish communities. Phyllis Albert has shown how this solidarity and identity was expressed in the language employed by French Jews who frequently used the terms *nation, peuple, nos frères, famille,* when speaking of Jews in general.[79] The ideology of emancipation transforming the *Juif* into the *Israélite,* could not, of course, allow for a specific Jewish nationality. Nevertheless, the tie forged by a common past of suffering was too strong to discard. As the *Archives Israélites* put it: " . . . even if we have become the sons of different homelands, we have not repudiated the religious fraternity that has been bequeathed to us by thirty centuries of glory and of suffering."[80] The term *coreligionnaire* or *nos frères en religion* expressed the link between the Jews united by a common memory of suffering. This tie meant that other Jews in distress had to be helped. For Samuel Cahen, the editor of the *Ar-*

chives Israélites, the duty was clear: " . . . if all men are brothers, those who have the same religion cannot observe in cold blood the distress of their brothers in religion."[81]

Paradoxically, the consistorial system created by Napoleon I to fuse the Jews of France with the rest of the population was perhaps the single most important factor in the creation of a sense of unity and purpose among French Jews. Its overarching organizational structure, its active intervention in the administration of the communities, and the institutions of charity that it created or took under its wing developed a certain cohesion in French Jewish life which was lacking elsewhere. Jews outside France saw it as a leading institution, a place to appeal to in time of crisis. Since French Jewry achieved emancipation first, the Central Consistory, which represented it as an institution, was perceived as a vanguard, possessing a sort of " . . . moral hegemony over a great part of the Judaism of contemporary times."[82]

Within the constraints imposed on it as a French administrative body, the Central Consistory did act many times during the course of the century to help Jews outside France. It was very concerned that French Jews should not be subject to legal discrimination when traveling in countries like Switzerland and Russia not yet affected by emancipation. Its appeals to the French government on the issue did not meet with success. These episodes can be seen as attempts to defend the position of French Jews. Nevertheless, there were occasions when the Consistory intervened when no French Jew was directly involved, such as in the Damascus Affair and over the question of equal rights for the Jews of the Ottoman Empire at the time of the Crimean War. It also interceded on behalf of the Jews of Rome during the French intervention in 1849 and it repeated its appeals ten years later when Napoleon III was again embroiled in Italian affairs.[83]

Still, the Central Consistory, composed of notables highly conscious of the ambiguities inherent in acting in favor of Jews outside France, could not go beyond a self-imposed circumspection. With a few exceptions, the Consistory limited its interventions to cases where French Jews were directly involved or where French and Jewish interests could be shown to coincide. But by its very existence as an organization representing the Jews, it set a precedent and offered a concrete example to others, who, freed from the constraints of ties to the French state, could imitate the consistorial structure and start where it left off, picking up the mantle which the Central Consistory could not wear, that of representing not only French but world Jewry. This was to be the task of the Alliance.

The story of the events that led to the foundation of the Alliance has been told many times.[84] A recent study has also supplied a thorough analysis of the ideological currents that motivated the founders of the Alliance.[85] We will give here only a brief summary of the efforts which prefigured the creation of the Alliance, followed by an examination of its world view in the first years of its existence.

From the 1830s onward, there were several moves to form an organization that would coordinate efforts for Jewish emancipation and bring relief to Jews in distress. A proposal was made in the *Archives Israélites* in 1841 for the creation of a society to propagate and encourage instruction among the Jews of Algeria.[86] In 1844, the same newspaper published an article by Ben Levi arguing for the foundation of committees to help Jews abroad, echoed later in the proposal of Samuel Cahen for the creation of a *Comité européenne de colonisation israélite* to relieve Russian Jewry.[87]

Then came the publication of two appeals in the *Univers Israélite* in 1851 and 1853 for the creation of an international Jewish Congress by Jules Carvallo, one of the future founders and presidents of the AIU. Carvallo was a Sephardic Jew from Bordeaux, a *polytéchnicien* and an engineer with close links to the St. Simonians. His appeals constitute important documents, not only because of the author's future involvement with the Alliance but also because of their particular configuration of the concepts of emancipation, "regeneration" and solidarity which was later to become the hallmark of the Alliance. They illustrate perfectly the intellectual trends that Michael Graetz has identified as most influential on the outlook of the founders,[88] trends that Carvallo masterfully interwove with Jewish concerns.

Carvallo's main interest was to foster Jewish unity, to transcend "the state of isolation" in which the Jews found themselves. Some enjoyed full liberties in certain countries, while others languished as pariahs. The situation could not last long, Jews could not be left out of the achievements of the spirit of the age which saw as inevitable the victory of emancipation.[89]

Carvallo proposed a congress that would work for the emancipation of oppressed Jews, to provide moral and material support to those persecuted and help in their "regeneration." He repeated his appeal in 1853, with a distinctively messianic tone. Jews had been persecuted in Rome, in Germany, even in France. The most terrible persecutions were in the offing, and the last battle between the good and the bad was about to be waged. Unity among Jews was imperative for survival. " . . . Providence itself appears to invite you: Create a central committee. . . . Convene a meeting, and in a few days, you will see converge upon this spiritual Jerusalem all the worthiest representatives of this dispersed Zion."[90]

The ideology of emancipation shared with the Franco-Jewish elite was transformed in Carvallo's appeal into a quasi-messianic vision whereby all Jewry, emancipated and "regenerated," could bring into fruition its divine mission. The idea of the mission of the Jews, the mission to spread monotheism and divine justice, popular among Reform Jews in Germany, never stood at the forefront of the ideology of the Franco-Jewish establishment but did have a certain impact in intellectual circles, especially those associated with the Alliance.[91] However, it is interesting to note not only the rhetoric, but the fact that it was now French Jewry itself which was charged with a mission of its own, that of spreading emancipation and "regeneration" to other Jews. In Germany, the concept of "mission" became part of the theology of Reform Judaism. Across the Rhine, closely paralleling the dominant notion of

France's *mission civilisatrice* to disseminate the principles of the revolution of 1789, the *mission civilisatrice* of French Jews went beyond the realm of theory and was put into practice by the Alliance.

The growing awareness of the international dimensions of the problem of emancipation, the growth of a vocal Jewish press, the precedent of the Central Consistory and important Jews intervening with governments in favor of their less fortunate brethren, the survival of antisemitism in France itself, and the debate at the time of the Crimean War about the means to be used to "regenerate" the Jews of the Levant form the background for the emergence of the Alliance. The specific event that marked its foundation, however, was the Mortara affair of 1858. Edgar Mortara, a Jewish boy in Bologna, had been secretly baptized by a Christian servant of his family while a baby. When the servant revealed the fact to the Church authorities, the seven-year-old boy was taken away to be brought up as a Christian. The case soon became a *cause célèbre* for the Jews of Europe who appealed to all Western governments for justice, to no avail. Edgar Mortara remained with the Church and eventually became a priest. The whole episode was a rude shock to the self-confidence of European Jewry. Traditional means of intervention had again been shown to be ineffectual.

The only organization which was sympathetic to the Jews was the Universal Evangelical Alliance, founded by Sir Culling Eardley in London in 1855, a Protestant group believing in the necessity of the restoration of the Jews for Christian messianic reasons. Pastor Petavel of Neuchâtel, Switzerland, who was prominent in the organization, had links with several future leaders of the Alliance.[92] What impressed the Jews, however, was neither the millenarianism of the Evangelical Alliance nor its suspect philosemitism, but its organizational structure made up of three committees, one for charity, one for schools, and one for propaganda. As early as 1855, Isidore Cahen, the son of the editor of the *Archives Israélites,* who himself had directly suffered from antisemitism when he was removed from his post of teacher of philosophy at the *Lycée Napoléon* at the Vendée, wrote of the need for the Jews to emulate the organization and also "create an Alliance."[93]

After the Mortara affair, both the *Archives Israélites* and the *Univers Israélite* propagandized actively for such an organization. For the *Archives* it was imperative to create a *Comité de défense israélite* " . . . to centralize in Paris the efforts of the emancipated Jews . . . as it is in Paris that is . . . formulated the ideas of the Occident. . . . Jewish civilization founds its . . . council and holds its assizes in Paris."[94] Isidore Cahen practically outlined the future work of the Alliance in an article in the *Archives* entitled *L'Alliance Israélite Universelle,* thus giving the projected organization a name.[95] In 1860, Simon Bloch, the editor of the *Univers Israélite* which had published the appeal of Carvallo nine years before, took up the issue again and pushed for immediate action with the fiery words: "Let us consider all of Europe as a vast Palestine and Jewish verity as an imperishable Jerusalem."[96]

On May 17, 1860, seventeen Jews met in the house of a wealthy Jewish merchant of Alsatian origin, Charles Netter, and nominated six of their group to direct the creation of the Alliance. The six were Charles Netter, Isidore Cahen, Elie-Aristide Astruc, Eugène Manuel, Narcisse Leven, and Jules Carvallo. Younger than the leadership of the Central Consistory, mostly engaged in the free professions, this group had the support of Adolphe Crémieux, the veteran in the struggle for Jewish rights in France and abroad. Crémieux had retired from Jewish communal affairs in 1845, after his wife had converted his children to Christianity, but he had continued to be active in support of Jewish causes. He had been minister of justice in the revolutionary government of 1848, and was again to occupy the same post after the fall of Napoleon III in 1870. He joined the Alliance in 1860 and was persuaded to become its president in 1863, a post he held until his death. His support for and participation in the activities of the fledgling organization were a great *coup* for the Alliance, as his fame had spread far in the Jewish world after his intervention during the course of the Damascus Affair. His presence was a principal factor in the world-wide legitimation of the Alliance as a responsible institution.

In July 1860, the six founders published a manifesto and an appeal to the Jewish world which were translated into English, German, Italian, and Hebrew. The manifesto was disseminated far and wide in the Jewish world. It traced previous attempts to coordinate efforts for the emancipation of the Jews and for defense in the face of attack and argued for the necessity of a concentration of forces to redeem the word Jew from all that was negative associated with it. Only the Jews did not have a state to protect them. The Alliance was to fill the vacuum. It was to become a "center of moral progress, of religious solidarity and of protection for all those who suffer for being Jewish."[97]

These three points were elaborated by the fiery *Appel* which reads like a roll call of all the themes debated in the Jewish press and elsewhere in the previous twenty years. First, *solidarity*—"If, dispersed in all the corners of the earth . . . you remain attached in heart to the old religion of your fathers. . . . If you believe that union is a good . . . and that you can unite . . . your sentiments, desires and hopes. . . ." The next topic was *emancipation*—"If you believe . . . that the influence of the principles of '89 is all-powerful in the world . . . that it is to be desired that its spirit penetrates everywhere. . . ." On *regeneration,* the *Appel* stated: "If you believe that a great number of your coreligionists, overcome by twenty centuries of misery, of insults and of prohibitions, can recover their dignity as men, win the dignity of citizens, if you believe that one should moralize those who have been corrupted and not condemn them, enlighten those who have been blinded, and not abandon them, raise those who have been exhausted and not rest by pitying them. . . . If you believe in all these things, Jews of the world, come hear our appeal, give your membership, your help, the work is a great one. . . ."[98]

The initial coldness shown to the Alliance by the Central Consistory did not last long. Almost immediately there came to be considerable interpenetration between the leadership of the two bodies.[99] There was some opposition from abroad. Philippson, still piqued by the Central Consistory's dropping of his plan for the education of Turkish Jews in Europe, received the news of the creation of the AIU negatively. He feared that it could inflame the old preju- dice against the Jews as a sort of Freemasonry, even though in 1854, in an article entitled "The Solidarity of the Jews," he had himself appealed to the very sentiments that motivated the Alliance.[100]

French, Italian, Dutch, and Belgian Jewry were the ones most favorably inclined toward the Alliance in its initial years, and English and German Jewries also got involved after a period of hesitation. Any person could be- come a member of the organization by paying a subscription of six French francs per year. The Alliance saw a phenomenal rise in membership in its first twenty-five years, increasing from 850 members in 1861 to 3900 in 1865, to 13,370 in 1870, and to over 30,000 in 1885. By 1880, it had 349 local commit- tees in direct communication with the Central Committee in Paris. Of these, 56 were in France (including Alsace-Lorraine, incorporated into Germany after 1870), 113 in Germany, and 20 in Italy. The French membership declined from constituting 80 percent of the total in 1861 to approximately 50 percent in 1864, and to less than 40 percent in 1885.[101]

The Alliance tapped a reservoir of solidarity in the name of a Jewish collec- tivity that transcended national borders. The Central Committee remained French in composition, but it remained sensitive, especially in its first de- cades, to the international "universal" character of the society, and did not want to consider itself a specifically French body.[102] Nevertheless, the French leadership put its stamp on the whole organization which expressed the poli- tics, ideology, and culture of French Jewry.

The question of the "regeneration" of the Jews outside Europe came up soon after the foundation of the Alliance, Charles Netter negotiating with the Board of Deputies in London for the opening of a school in Tetuan in 1862. The moral progress mentioned in the Manifesto of July 1860 could only be brought about by education. "[E]mancipate, instruct, raise our brothers in Israel"[103] was the aim, fulfilling the agenda debated at the time of the Crimean War. It was thus that " . . . the children of Israel will pursue, in the distant corners of Africa and Asia, the civilizing mission that divine Providence has entrusted them."[104] Local committees of the Alliance were forming in North Africa and the Levant, and Jews there started to appeal for schools.

The Alliance soon recognized the enormity of the task, and asked for further, mainly financial, support from the Jewish world by launching another appeal in 1865, entitled *L'oeuvre des écoles*. Again, the discourse is identical to that of the Jewish press in the years 1840–1860. There were hundreds of thousands of Jews in North Africa and the Middle East who were vegetating in complete ignorance and apathy. Civilization had not yet reached these areas. They were becoming aware of their own backwardness. Many appeals to create schools had come from these regions. "Thus our brothers in Asia and Africa are ready to be regenerated."[105]

While the image of the traditional East European Jew was as negative as that of the Sephardic and Oriental Jew in the eyes of the elite of Western Jewry and the Alliance, the latter could not do much in this domain. The Russian authorities brooked no interference from the outside. Furthermore, the organization, like most of West European Jewry, expected in the 1860s that as the Russian regime became more enlightened, it would grant the Jews legal equality and increase its efforts to "regenerate" them.

The same was not true for the Muslim rulers of the Middle East and North Africa. The latter were not overly concerned with the inner life of the Jewish communities under their rule. Furthermore, growing European influence in these regions had weakened their power of resistance to the intervention of Western Jews. Hence, it was the Middle East and North Africa which was the area easiest for the Alliance to penetrate. And it was this region which was the classic site of the "Jewish Eastern Question," the outlines of which had been well-defined in the two decades preceding the foundation of the organization. Hence, the Alliance focused right from the beginning upon Sephardic and Eastern Jewry.

By the middle of the nineteenth century, philanthropists, the consistories, intellectuals, and the press had set a well-established agenda. The obtaining by the Jews of legal equality and their "regeneration," integrating them into Western civilization, had emerged as its cornerstones. This was motivated by defensive reasons over the embarassment caused by "backward" Jews to the acculturated elite, as well as by a strong sense of solidarity with fellow Jews in political and social distress. The Alliance incarnated all the impulses that had gone into the creation of the Jewish emancipationist world view. Already in 1851, one of its founders, Jules Carvallo, had argued for the inevitable victory of the process of emancipation:

> Everyone can appreciate the benefits resulting from the emancipation of the Jews of France. Once they formed a foreign population . . . now they are devoted citizens, loving and serving their country. . . .
>
> . . . *this state of the Jews, exceptional and proper to [those of] France only, will become their normal state amongst all the peoples.*[106] (Emphasis added.)

This was indeed the crux of the matter, the basic principle running through the work of the Central Consistory in Algeria and the future work of the Alliance in the Mediterranean basin. There was one normative path which other Jewries had to follow and that was the French one. Jewish solidarity called for consistent action in this direction.

As Narcisse Leven put it, it was through the creation of schools that " . . . the emancipated Occident will have paid its debt to the regenerated Orient."[107] The symmetry between emancipation and "regeneration" in this statement summarizes the essence of the ideology that guided the work of the Alliance. It was this ideology that Turkish Jewry was to encounter in the network of schools created by the organization in the next half century.

II

TURKISH JEWRY IN THE AGE OF THE *TANZIMAT*

Most Turkish Jews were the descendents of the exiles who had arrived in the Ottoman Empire in the two centuries that followed the expulsion from Spain in 1492. Soon becoming the dominant group by the sheer weight of numbers, they had imposed by the seventeenth century their Judeo-Spanish language and culture on the local, Greek-speaking Romaniote Jews who formed the remnant of Byzantine Jewry. In addition, there continued to live in the cities of Istanbul, Izmir, and Salonica a few small foreign Jewish communities composed of Italian Jews or Ashkenazim. In the middle of the nineteenth century, it is estimated that there were 150,000 Jews in the Empire,[1] with the Judeo-Spanish communities of the Balkans and Western Asia Minor constituting about half of this population. Their numbers had increased considerably by the eve of the Balkan wars of 1912–1913, when Salonica was annexed by Greece. In 1911, there were close to 140,000 Jews in an area within the borders of present-day Turkey.[2]

The consensus among scholars is that by the nineteenth century, Turkish Jewry was a community in economic and social decline. In the mosaic of religious and ethnic groups that made up the Ottoman Empire, the Jews had lost the distinction that they had enjoyed in the sixteenth century in the sphere of international trade and commerce. Iberian exiles, familiar with European ways, had been ideal intermediaries in the financial and commercial links between the Ottoman Empire and the West. The end of the Jewish influx from the peninsula in the course of the seventeenth century led to a relative decrease of contacts with Europe. The Greeks and the Armenians, increasingly dynamic entrepreneurs, began to replace the Jews as middlemen in the lucrative trade with the West.[3]

The isolation of Turkish Jews from Europe was, however, by no means absolute. There was an important channel of contact with Western Jewish communities which did remain open. Small groups of Jews from Italy, settled in major centers such as Istanbul, Salonica, and Izmir, had a significant place in trade with Europe. These Jews were to be in the vanguard of moves toward the Westernization of Turkish Jewry, and will be discussed below. Furthermore, there is some evidence to suggest that the decline in Jewish participation in commerce with the West was a relative one. For example, there are seven Jewish names in the list of 107 merchants in 1815 in Istanbul put in the category of *Avrupa tüccarları*, "merchants trading with Europe."[4] This was a group of non-Muslim merchants given special privileges by the Porte to counteract the growing tendency of local non-Muslim traders to use the protection provided by foreign consulates to escape Ottoman restrictions and taxation. Though their small number confirms that the Jews did not play an important role in this trade, especially when compared with the Greeks who make up the overwhelming majority of the list, it also demonstrates that they had not been eliminated altogether. When one takes into account the fact that Jews are abundantly represented in the lists of merchants "protected" by the consulates of Western powers—for example, fifty-three out of the 100 merchants protected by the French consulate in Izmir in 1812, singled out by the Porte as local non-Muslims, were Jews[5]—it becomes apparent that Jews continued to remain a factor in the commerce between Europe and the Levant.

The place of the Jews in this trade has also to be put in the context of the relative smallness of the community compared to the Greeks and Armenians. Of the three tolerated main non-Muslim groups in the Ottoman Empire, the Jews were by far the smallest. While they numbered 150,000 in the middle of the nineteenth century, the Empire contained 2,000,000 Greeks and 2,400,000 Armenians within its borders.[6]

Turkish Jews might have had a low profile in the domain of international trade in the eighteenth and early nineteenth centuries. But they were well integrated in the local economy. The ethnic division of labor in the Empire, attested by observers in the late nineteenth and early twentieth centuries, was also true for earlier periods. Jewish guilds and artisans concentrated in certain fields like textiles, silks, and clothes dyeing were an important presence in the economic life of the major cities.[7] In Asia Minor, Thrace, and Macedonia, Jewish traders were involved with regional commerce, often acting as intermediaries between markets in towns and the peasant economy of the surrounding area.

Furthermore the Jews were active as *sarrafs* (bankers, or moneylenders), tax farmers, and provisioners and were especially involved with the Janissary corps,[8] that uncontrollable military group that had become a thorn in the side of all reform-minded Sultans. Although Jews like everybody else suffered from the behavior of these troops who rioted all too frequently, many a Jewish merchant and banker's economic well-being was tied to the economy revolving around them. At the turn of the century, the Gabay, Aciman, and Carmona families, the leaders of the Jewish community, were all *sarrafs* engaged with the finances of the janissaries.[9]

The importance of this for the history of Turkish Jewry can hardly be overstated. The Jews were associated with the *ancien régime* and were to suffer initially from its dismantlement by the Turkish reformers and Westernizers. The reign of Mahmut II (1808-1839) was, in this respect, a fateful one. Its most notable achievement, the abolition of the Janissary corps in 1826, known as the *Vakayi Hayriye* (the Auspicious Event), proved to have a diametrically opposite connotation for the Jews with the literal decapitation of the communal leadership by the strangulation of Behor Isaac Carmona, the *nasi* (head) of the community and one of the principal tax farmers of the Empire.

Behor Isaac Carmona came from a family which rose to financial prominence in the second half of the eighteenth century. His grandfather, Moshe Carmona, established a banking enterprise in Istanbul during the reign of Selim III (1789–1807) and had close relations with the Sultan. He was given the monopoly of the trade of alum, and from then on the family was also known by the Turkish name of *şabçı* (dealer in alum). His grandson, Behor Isaac, further enlarged the family fortune and became the banker and money lender of many high Janissary officials as well as of Esma, the sister of Mahmut II. He played a leading role in Jewish communal affairs and was, for many years, the leader of the Istanbul community, presiding over the council of notables. His munificence went to support many institutions, and he was instrumental in securing the necessary permission from the authorities to build new synagogues, a very difficult task under Muslim rule. He distributed money for the Jewish poor and founded *yeshivot* in Jerusalem, Izmir, Bursa, and Edirne. He was also the head of the *Va'ad ha-Pekidim Kushta* (the Committee of Constantinople Officials), the organization responsible for sending money to the Jewish communities of Palestine.[10] In short, Behor Isaac Carmona was the most influential lay notable of the Jewish community.

At the time of the abolition of the Janissary corps, he was murdered upon the orders of the Sultan, his fortune confiscated, and the debts owed to him by several *vezirs* were used to build new quarters for the military.[11] His death and the abolition of the Janissary corps, with which the Jews had many economic links, plunged the community into deep financial chaos.

The marked decline in the activity of the *Va'ad ha-Pekidim Kushta* and the decline in the economic situation of the Sephardic community in Jerusalem, which began in this period, were accelerated by the incident and were related to the turmoil that followed in the affairs of the Istanbul community. The situation was commented upon by many of the letters of the newly created *Va'ad ha-Pekidim* (Committee of Officials) of Amsterdam, which now definitively replaced the Istanbul organization in centralizing the sending to Jerusalem of financial help from diaspora Jewry.[12]

Many observers noted later that it was the Armenian *sarrafs* who benefited most from the fall of the Jewish bankers, replacing them in important financial positions at the Porte.[13] For Turkish Jewry, this episode marked the onset of a dramatic decline, the *coup de grâce* delivered to a community which had already been supplanted by the Greeks in international trade and which was now displaced in the banking and moneylending fields by the Armenians. *The Jewish Intelligence,* the newspaper of English missionaries, was to put it thus twenty-five years after the event:

... the Jews have lost all offices of trust and emolument which they frequently
held, with them much of their influence is gone. They are no longer the collec-
tors of revenue, the farmers of the customs, the bankers of Turkish grandees. In
all these offices they have been supplanted by their dextrous rivals, the Armenians. The loss has been deeply felt by them, not merely in regard to the
degradation it involves, but through the more perceptible inroads of poverty. . . . [14]

The number of wealthy merchants or bankers is not so much significant in
itself as in what it reveals about the financial situation of the community. The
presence of wealthy personalities was often of decisive importance since it was
with the higher taxes that they paid and with their philanthropic activity that
many of the communal institutions, especially the schools and the *yeshivot*
(Jewish academies of higher learning) flourished or died. The poverty commented upon by observers in the middle of the century and the disarray in
which the communal institutions found themselves were no doubt the result of
processes which went back deep into the past of Turkish and Ottoman Jewry.
But from the mid-nineteenth-century perspective, the long term decline had
been compounded by the disastrous episode of 1826.

The Ottoman State and the Jewish Community

Until the nineteenth century, Turkish Jewish communities, like all traditional
Jewries, were run according to Jewish law, enjoying considerable internal
autonomy. Indeed, the religious foundations of Jewish communal existence,
of Jewish identity, was the determinant factor in the constitution of a Jewish
ethnicity, to a degree that far surpassed other groups in the Middle East.
While there were Gregorian, Catholic, and eventually even Protestant Armenians, or Arabs and Bulgarians who were Greek Orthodox Christians together with the Greeks, the principles of Jewish ethnicity and Judaism were
predicated upon one another.
    The tie between ethnicity and religion[15] was legitimized both by Jewish
tradition in the form of Jewish law, the *halakhah,* and by the ruling Ottoman
state which recognized the Jews, as dictated by the *dhimma* (pact) stipulations
of Muslim religious law, as a protected people. Under the *dhimma,* Jews and
Christians were tolerated, but were socially and juridically inferior to the
Muslims. They were free to practice their religion and run the internal affairs
of the community in return for the payment of special taxes.[16]
    Much has been written about the autonomy enjoyed by the traditional
Jewish community, the *kahal.*[17] This autonomy covered large areas of societal
life and was underscored by the application of the *halakhah* by rabbinical
courts in civil, commercial, and even criminal cases, by the right to collect
internal taxes, and by the existence of extensive welfare and administrative
bodies within the community. Nevertheless, though much of this picture was

undoubtedly true for different periods and places, it should really be taken as an ideal type. There continued to be considerable interference from outside, especially in the judicial domain. For example, recent research demonstrates quite clearly that the decision of rabbinical courts in the Ottoman Empire very often remained inoperative if not approved by the Muslim courts, and that in many cases, the ensuing ambiguity led many Jews to go directly to Muslim courts to make sure that they received definite redress for their grievances.[18] However, in spite of such limitations, autonomy on the symbolic as well as practical levels was an important reality for most areas of Jewish life in Turkey until the nineteenth century.

New revisions in our understanding of the so-called *millet* system have brought further clarification to the status of the Jews under Ottoman rule. Until recently, the dominant view in scholarship was that from the beginning, the Greeks, Armenians, and the Jews of the Ottoman Empire each consti- tuted distinct groups, called *millets,* with Patriarchs appointed by the Sultan in the case of the Christian communities and a Chief Rabbi in the case of the Jews. It has now become quite clear that such a formally recognized unified, hierarchical "system" did not in fact exist. As far as the Jews were concerned, a series of local arrangements prevailed whereby the local communities en- joyed a relative autonomy and had appointed representatives who acted as interlocutors with the authorities. For a group like the Jews who had no religiously sanctioned hierarchy, there was in fact no internal organizational precedent to have a Chief Rabbi to oversee the affairs of the community for the Empire as a whole.[19]

By the end of the seventeenth century, the fragmentation in communal affairs that followed the arrival of the Sephardim had given way to more organized and united forms of organization. Each Jewish center came to constitute an independent unit, had its own *Rav ha-Kolel* (rabbi of the commu- nity), the spiritual leader who, together with a *Bet-Din,* religious court, ruled over the legal and religious affairs of the community, while an assembly of notables, the *ma'amad,* concerned itself with the general administration. Sometimes the *Rav ha-Kolel* acted as the representative of the community vis- à-vis the state, in which case, but not always, he might be known as the *Hahambaşı* (Chief Rabbi) by the authorities, without however necessarily receiving official patents *(berat)* to this effect. Often, it was a lay notable who would carry out the function. There was no hierarchy among the large Jewish communities. The Istanbul rabbinate and administration was *primus inter pares* with that of other cities. Nevertheless, the proximity to the Porte put the leaders of the Istanbul community in the position of the *de facto* leaders of the other Jewish centers of the Empire.[20]

From the point of view of the internal organization, there were distinct similarities between this arrangement and the one that obtained for most European Jewish communities up to the eighteenth century. Its legitimation, in terms of the formulation in the *dhimma,* came from different sources under Islam than that of the regulations governing the status of the Jews that had evolved from the early Middle Ages in Europe. But in practice, both systems rested upon the fundamental premise of the distinctiveness, separateness, and relative internal autonomy of the Jewish community.

In Europe, the fundamental transformation of the position of the Jews came as a result of modern state-building practices. Jewish corporate autonomy was slowly eroded as the absolutist state evolved in Western and Central Europe. The French revolution, bringing about the elimination of all corporate groups, abolished the juridically accepted Jewish "nation" when it emancipated the Jews in 1790 and 1791. The concepts of citizenship and equality also entailed the divesting by hitherto distinctive groups of all that had made them legally and culturally separate. The emergence of the modern nation-state brought with it a concerted effort to "nationalize" all groups under its rule, to forge and often create from scratch a nation, one and indivisible.

This process was to be also relevant to the history of Turkish Jewry. However, its evolution was to be marked by some of the particular features of its Ottoman setting and the nature of the Ottoman state.

The Ottoman Empire did not develop feudalism. Instead, it was ruled by a strong patrimonial state that received its legitimation both from Islam and from the pre-Muslim Middle Eastern and Asian empire traditions. There was no division of religion and state, with the Sultan-Caliph being responsible for the implementation of the *sharia,* the Muslim religious law, in the pursuit of justice. He was also technically the owner of all the land and of his subjects. The strong centralized bureaucracy, the military with a slave army, the janissaries, at its core, and the religious clergy constituted the three pillars of the ruling elite. These were the groups exempted from paying taxes. The rest of the population, the taxpaying subjects, known as the *reaya* (flock), were strictly separate from the ruling class. However, access to the latter was not through hereditary succession but through education and military achievement.[21]

Ottoman society was marked by the lack of a large scale landowning class. The social base was constituted by a free peasantry tilling the soil on relatively small plots over which it had the usufruct. The ruling elite whose economic existence was dependent upon the reproduction of the system, and upon the extraction of surplus in the form of essentially tributary taxes from the *reaya,* systematically eliminated all concentrations of power, whether economic or social, that could challenge its authority. Hence, no horizontal ties could be developed that could eventually evolve autonomous forms of authority and legitimation. All power and status was dependent upon a vertical linkage to the center. The result was a weak civil society in the face of a strongly bureaucratized ruling apparatus.[22]

Non-Muslims who were by definition outside the ruling elite open only to Muslims were an important part of the *reaya* class. Nevertheless, the fact that they were outside the dominant systemic paradigm of society and were allowed a degree of autonomy in their internal affairs meant that they were in some respects better off than their Muslim counterparts. They were the only groups that could function with their alternative power and legitimation systems and develop their own institutions. In many ways, they were the only legitimate corporate groups within the Empire. This would prove to be pregnant with consequences for the development of nationalism among the Christian populations under the conditions that evolved in the nineteenth century.

Economic, political, and military factors all converged from the end of the sixteenth century onward to bring about the decline of the Empire. Growing inroads made by international commerce proved to be corrosive for the Ottoman economy, aligning certain areas of the Empire toward export-oriented agriculture and away from the control of the bureaucracy. Inept leadership and defeat in war precipitated a crisis in the body politic that was to last centuries. The control by the center began to slip considerably in the period of decline. Tax farming, a favorite means of raising revenue in the Empire, proved to have disastrous consequences in a period of weakening supervision and leadership, with a large amount of wealth siphoned off from the coffers of the state into private hands. Peripheral landed elites, the *ayan,* began to emerge, challenging the authority of the bureaucracy and demonstrating hitherto unseen independence from the center.[23]

By the end of the eighteenth century, segments of the bureaucratic section of the ruling elite began increasingly to look upon the West for blueprints to put the tottering Ottoman house in order. The Westernizing reforms that were to be adopted as the panacea for all the ills facing Ottoman society were, hence, not merely acts of mimesis, of blind emulation of a victorious West, but measures designed to reassert control by the center over the periphery, of destroying the emergent alternative loci of power. The rationalizing and streamlining of the ruling apparatus by the borrowing of the centralizing measures of European states, especially of the strong French state,[24] were all designed with this aim in sight.

The new policies of centralization were to have consequences for the non-Muslims also. The measures were designed to reassert control by the center, but the growing familiarity with contemporary European political systems made the maintenance of the status quo with respect to the non-Muslim communities undesirable.

The age of reforms, referred to collectively as the *Tanzimat,* inaugurated the period of change in the legal status of the non-Muslims. The *Hatt-ı Şerif* of Gülhane (the Noble Rescript of the Rose Chamber) of 1839 introduced the new principles with the announcement by the Sultan of a series of reforms guaranteeing the life, honor, and property of all the subjects, those who belonged to "the people of Islam and other nations."[25] The latter clause, implying a certain equality between "believer" and "unbeliever," clearly designed to please European powers concerned with the welfare of the Christians of the Empire, represented a potentially radical departure from the *dhimma.* The innovation, implicit in the rescript of 1839, became explicit with the Reform Decree of 1856 which granted equality to all non-Muslims. This constituted a dramatic change in their status, and was perceived in the West as heralding the emancipation of the Christians and the Jews. In the following

decades, Christians and Jews began to participate in local municipal and regional councils.[26] In 1869, a new citizenship law formulated explicitly the new
conception of Ottoman citizenship which included all the subjects of the
Sultan, irrespective of their religion, with rights and obligations now theoretically flowing mutually between the state and the individual without any medi-
ating bodies in between.[27]

The Ottoman reformers were concerned, at least in theory, to create a
unified patriotic citizenry and to downplay the importance of ethnic and religious divisions. In this respect, the 1856 decree and the citizenship law of 1869
can be interpreted as having legally emancipated the non-Muslims, and
among them, the Jews of the Ottoman Empire.

However, legislation that set the non-Muslims apart still remained. The poll
tax (the *cizye)* was abolished in 1856 but was reinstituted in 1857 as a military
exemption tax *(bedel-i askeriye)* to be paid by the non-Muslims. The tax was
raised by the heads of the *millets* until 1887 when local bureaucrats were made
responsible for its collection.[28] The military exemption tax was finally abolished in 1909, after the Young Turk revolution, with all males now being made
subject to conscription.

The moves toward equality were slowly accompanied by legislation that
seriously eroded the communal autonomy of the *millets.* New conceptions of
citizenship were incompatible with old privileges. According to the provisions
of the Reform Decree, criminal, civil, and commercial cases were to be tried
by mixed tribunals of Muslims and non-Muslims established in the 1840s.[29] In
1850 the French commercial code and in 1858 the French penal code were
adopted and were made to apply to all subjects of the Empire.[30] Indeed, for
all intents and purposes, the autonomy of the *millets* in matters concerning
civil, criminal, and commercial cases had come formally to an end in 1856.
The decree gave the non-Muslims the option of continuing to use their own
courts in cases involving family, inheritance, and divorce litigation (clause 12).
Matters concerning personal status were all that remained of the juridical
autonomy of the *millets.*[31]

The decree of 1856 also called upon the non-Muslims to institute "reforms
required by the progress of civilization and the age."[32] New regulations reorga-
nizing communal bodies prepared by the Greeks, Armenians, and the Jews
came into effect in the decade following the decree. The *millet* administrations
were now explicitly hierarchical organizations with the laity having a major
say in the running of communal affairs.[33] The religious leaders of the *millets,*
in the case of the Jews, the Chief Rabbi, were now formally the juridically
recognized leaders of the communities and acted as their representatives. The
new organs appear to have been mainly confessional bodies, with most matters outside the religious realm falling outside their purview.

In spite of the introduction of new law codes, the Ottoman legal system was
not rationalized. The reformers, introducing the changes from above, did not
replace already existing legal systems, but simply added to them. Hence, until
the end of the Empire, there continued to exist at least four different and

often competing legal systems: the new secular courts, the Islamic courts, the *millet* courts, and the consular courts with jurisdiction over non-Ottoman citizens.

The dualism between Western and Eastern that was to mark the last century of the Empire reflected to some extent the balance of forces. The Westerniz-ing Ottoman Empire, while acquiring the trappings of the European state, remained at the same time firmly anchored to its more traditional moorings; the Islamic character of its legitimation system could not be challenged under the Sultan-Caliph. The tradition of bureaucratic action from above precluded any real understanding of societal developments. The role of the economy in the reforms was neglected by a bureaucracy long accustomed to an essentially tributary financial relationship with the subjects. Military and bureaucratic reforms in the age of capitalist industrialization in the West was not enough to "save the state," the major concern of the reformers. By the 1870s, the Empire was bankrupt, and large sections of its economy had entered under the control of foreigners.

In fact, the multiple competencies in the legal arena point to the essentially hybrid nature of the reforming state in the nineteenth century. The weight of conservative Muslim forces and the protection by Western powers of the Christian groups of the Empire seriously hampered the implementation of the Ottomanist agenda of the reformers. Old and new coexisted uneasily side by side, diluting the impact of the reforms on the practical level.

This is further in evidence in the failure of the state to forge a common Otto-man identity for all its citizens. Indeed, the state was relatively late in attempt-ing to reform the system of education, the primary element in the making of nations in the West. The cultural realm proved particularly intractable to cen-tralization because of the multi-cultural composition of the empire, the growing nationalism among several ethnic bodies, and the resistance from the devout Muslim population to the notion of a common educational system that would have had to divorce itself from Islam to have any appeal to non-Muslims.

The *Tanzimat* announcements of 1839 did not even mention education. The reforms introduced slowly in this field in the following decades concerned only the Muslim schools, and concerned themselves exclusively with secon-dary education, neglecting elementary education which until the 1870s re-mained in the monopoly of Muslim clergy. The autonomy of Christian schools was jealously guarded by Western powers which reduced considerably the freedom of action of the Ottoman reformers. The schools established by the state to create a modern army, such as the naval school founded in 1773, the artillery school founded in 1796, and the medical school created in 1827 were all theoretically open to non-Muslims, and indeed a few did attend these schools in the course of the nineteenth century.

Following the Reform Decree, the *rüşdiyes* (lower secondary schools), which the state had begun to establish, became open to all non-Muslims in 1861, while the principle of separate elementary education for each religious group remained intact.[34] This was changed in the 1870s when secular primary

schools, the *iptidais,* were created following a reorganization of the educational system by the Public Education Law of 1869. Non-Muslims could now
attend the newly founded institutions (clauses 33 and 42).[35]

Although the number of educational establishments at all levels increased
substantially in the following decades, the overwhelming majority of non-
Muslims did not attend Ottoman state schools.[36] The separate educational
systems of the non-Muslims, although under attack by the early twentieth
century,[37] remained intact until World War I. The Ottoman state schools were
too few and weak to have any appreciable impact on the non-Muslim masses.
In 1895, two decades after state elementary education had become open to
non-Muslims, only eighty non-Muslims were attending these schools in all of
the Empire.[38] Both the order of priorities of the reformist bureaucracy, unused to the mass mobilization policies of activist social engineering, and the
constant pressure from European powers to safeguard the privileges of foreign and non-Muslim schools prevented the implementation of an "Ottomanist" educational policy.

The belatedness in the creation of an education system that would also
accommodate and integrate the non-Muslims into a united citizenry was part
of the general problems faced by the Ottoman state in the course of its
Westernization attempts. Non-Muslims were given equality in 1856, and yet
the poll tax remained, hidden as the exemption tax, separating the Muslim
from the non-Muslim. The juridical system was reformed, but no unitary
system emerged. Overlapping competencies in all areas of life together with
the impossibility of finding a unifying ideology that would cement the various
groups together and provide a centripetal force meant that in spite of its
centralizing impulse, the impact of the reforming Ottoman state on civil society remained highly uneven.

This had important consequences for the Jews. In Europe, one of the major
factors in the "modernization" of the Jewish communities was the crucial and
decisive impetus given by the state which, from the period of the Enlightenment onward, steadily dismantled corporate bodies and intervened in the life
of the Jewish community by sponsoring a policy of "nationalization" with
education as its mainstay. Even in states such as Russia or the Hapsburg
Empire where, unlike in France, the erosion or dissolution of Jewish corporate body was not accompanied by the granting of civic equality, the governments had embarked upon a policy of creating schools for the Jews with the
ultimate aim of hastening their assimilation.[39] This European model applies
only partially in the case of the history of Turkish Jewry in the last century of
the Ottoman Empire. A mobilized civic culture did not emerge, and the Jews,
together with other non-Muslims, continued to remain dissociated from and
nonintegrated into a poorly developed public sphere.

Hence the crucial importance of the role played by Western Jews in the life
of the Jewish communities under Ottoman rule in the modern era. It was they
who took upon themselves the task of "regenerating" their fellow Jews of the
East. The relative absence of the state in the sphere of education of the non-

Muslims until the twentieth century gave the freedom of action to the European Jewish reformers to proceed to the transformation of the educational system of the Jewish community. Montefiore's action in 1840 pressuring the Chief Rabbi in Istanbul to issue a declaration asking all Jewish schools to introduce the teaching of Turkish was the opening salvo of a campaign that would continue until the last days of the Empire. It represented the initial reaction to the *Tanzimat* not of Turkish Jewry, but of Western Jewry. The Jews of the West interpreted, characteristically, the *Tanzimat* and later the Reform Decree of 1856 in the light of their own experience in Europe in the preceding half century,[40] and immediately focused their attention on their preferred field of action, that of education.

Traditional Mass Education among Turkish Jewry

Traditional Jewish education of the masses in Turkey, like elsewhere, consisted first and foremost of religious instruction. Second only to the family, the school played a crucial role in socializing the child into the habits and customs of a society where religion constituted the central matrix. The task of the Jewish elementary school was to impart a knowledge of the Hebrew of the sacred texts, the study of which was an all-important religious duty. It also taught the daily prayers which were decisive both for religious reasons and for enforcing communal solidarity by preparing the eventual participation in the synagogue around which so much of Jewish life revolved. The meaning of the school in Jewish life is summed up well by the Judeo-Spanish song that was sung during the first days of the child's entry to the *meldar* (also called *ḥevrah,* especially in Salonica), the equivalent of the Ashkenazi *ḥeder*:

la Tora, la Tora	[the Torah, the Torah
el ijiko la dira	the son will say (read) it
kon el pan y el kezo	with bread and cheese
el livriko en el peço	(with) the book on the chest
onde vas ijo del Dio	where do you go, son of God
a meldar la ley del Dio	to read the law of God
vida larga ke te de el Dio	may God give you long life
a ti y a tu madre y a tu	to you and to your mother and
padre y a todos los cudios[41]	father and to all Jews]

The name of the institution of elementary education, *meldar,* meaning "to read" in Judeo-Spanish, underlined its purpose: the teaching of the reading of the *Torah*. The song highlights the function of traditional education, that of preserving and transmitting religious truth, and through this transmission, the perpetuation of the existence of the Jewish people.

Girls did not receive instruction in any formal sense. They could acquire some learning in the domestic sphere which was assigned to them, depending on the wealth of the family, but there is no evidence to suggest that it consisted of more than the reading and writing of Judeo-Spanish and the recitation of prayers in Hebrew. For the boys, the situation was quite different. Before attending the *meldar,* they were often sent to a *maestra,* a woman who took charge of them from the age of three to the age of six or seven.[42] The *maestras* who ran what now would be called kindergartens taught the children songs and perhaps a few prayers. But real education began in the *meldar* which the boys began to attend from the age of seven. This establishment often consisted of one large room near a synagogue, where 50–60 children would sit on the floor around the *melamed* (teacher) who was usually a rabbi. He would begin by teaching them the letters of the Hebrew alphabet.[43] After the alphabet, the next task was the mastering of the vowel signs. Then would follow the cantillation and finally the reading of a Biblical text and its translation into Judeo-Spanish.[44]

The institution of elementary instruction was often also called a *Talmud Torah.* Initially, this was an establishment where Jewish education would be pursued much further than in a *meldar* and would include advanced rabbinical study. The most famous of the *Talmudei Torah* in the Judeo-Spanish speaking communities was that of Salonica. It had become an important center of rabbinical learning and its fame had spread far and wide by the seventeenth century, attracting students and scholars from all over Europe by its rich endowment and library.[45] By the nineteenth century it had lost its great prestige, and learning had declined. Nevertheless, in the middle of the century, it still had close to 1000 students.[46]

By this time, the distinction between a *meldar* and a *Talmud Torah* had become increasingly blurred and many an institution, run by a needy rabbi who had no more than 50 or 60 students and which taught just the reading and writing of Judeo-Spanish and the reading of some prayers in Hebrew, called itself a *Talmud Torah.*[47] Nevertheless, most *Talmudei Torah* had more than one class, took studies a little further, and had some degree of communal support. In such an establishment, the translation of the Bible into Judeo-Spanish had pride of place, which, if the institution were sufficiently large, would be followed in the upper divisions by the translation of Rashi's commentaries and readings in Judeo-Spanish of the very popular commentary on the Bible, the *Me-am Lo'ez.*[48] The readings had a fixed calendar attached to them and would follow the timetable of the synagogue and of the Jewish religious year.[49] The Talmud was introduced in the last division,[50] and its further study with learned rabbis could eventually lead to the rabbinate. Then there were the *yeshivot* which were centers established by wealthy benefactors which provided a forum for study and discussion for all those interested in learning.[51]

It is important to realize that for the vast majority of the youth, the program of studies outlined above was interrupted by the necessity of work to support poor families. By the middle of the nineteenth century, the traditional educational system was in deep decline, poverty taking its toll even in the best institutions. Most *Talmudei Torah,* starved for funds by communities who could no longer pay for their upkeep, had become a collection of *meldarim* and did not offer much education beyond reading, writing, and the translation of the sacred texts into Judeo-Spanish. Western commentators were quick to condemn these schools. According to a typical report, the Jewish school in Turkey consisted of " . . . a small closet exhaling a putrid and infectious odour, where crawling pell-mell, sprawling on the ground, pupils and masters cry and vociferate one against each other."[52] The incomprehension and hostility with which the traditional education system was treated by the reformers, a hostility stemming from ideological preconceptions, was magnified by the fact that it was floundering in a deep economic crisis. Local partisans of reform also echoed increasingly this severe criticism in the columns of the newly established Judeo-Spanish press. Newspapers such as *El Nasional* and *El Tiempo* were both relentless in their attacks on the traditional *Talmudei Torah.*[53]

It is impossible to determine with any accuracy the number of schools in the Jewish communities of Turkey before the introduction of European-style institutions from the middle of the nineteenth century onward. As mentioned above, Salonica had one great *Talmud Torah,* with close to 1000 students, and many *meldarim* and *yeshivot.*[54] Izmir had a new *Talmud Torah,* built in 1847.[55] According to Ludwig August Frankl who visited the city in 1856, it had "twenty-five schools teaching the Hebrew language and the Talmud."[56] The principal Jewish quarters of Istanbul, Hasköy, and Balat each had a large *Talmud Torah.*[57] In 1858, the *Archives Israélites* reported that there were 44 Jewish schools in Istanbul with 2552 students and 3 Karaite schools with 100 students.[58]

One should also note the increasing number of Protestant missionary schools which began to operate in the Ottoman Empire from the first decades of the nineteenth century, schools specifically designed to evangelize among the Jews. "The London Society for Promoting Christianity amongst the Jews" began its work in Turkey by opening its first school in Izmir in 1829.[59] It founded two institutions in Istanbul in 1855, one in the quarter of Ortaköy and another in Balat,[60] and in 1864 established its most successful school, that of Hasköy.[61] The Church of Scotland also established schools in 1846 and in 1873 in Izmir and Istanbul.[62] In spite of the many *herems* (bans) launched by rabbis against parents who sent their children to these establishments, the free clothing and food distributed by the missions and the lack of resources of the Jewish community to properly subsidize and extend its own educational system, made some of them quite popular among the Jewish poor. For example, by 1881, 3219 Jewish children had attended the Hasköy school founded in 1864.[63] Though these institutions and later the Catholic missionary schools that were frequented by Jewish children never succeeded in making a significant number of converts, they did remain a constant source of worry both for the traditionalist rabbis and the Jewish reformers. The comparatively large number of Jewish children who flocked to them is effective proof of the breakdown of the traditional education system even before the arrival of the Alliance.

The tremendous changes undergone in the domain of education in the last two centuries and the emergence of categories such as "childhood" and "youth" as distinct periods before the reaching of adulthood obscure a clear understanding of the true nature of traditional education by the modern observer. The latter did not just entail a process of acquisition of knowledge or the learning of skills that would prove to be useful for "life." This took place outside the school, in the arena of the struggle for jobs and livelihood. Traditional Jewish education was, above all, a distinct *praxis*, that of reproducing Jewish existence through the study of the sacred texts. The term *meldar*, to read, illuminates the process at the heart of traditional Judaism, the establishment of a firm relationship to the holy texts that is supposed to last for a lifetime. Education in the institution of the *meldar* brought with it a skill that was not value-neutral but which acted to reaffirm the continuing validity of the eternal values of tradition.

The introduction of modern schooling in the second half of the nineteenth century considerably weakened, and in many places, altogether eliminated the transmission of tradition through education. But for this process to begin, serious conflicts had to be resolved, conflicts which broke out in the middle of the century and which involved both internal as well as external agents of change.

Educational Reform, Communal Crisis, and the Foundation of New Schools

The circular sent by the Chief Rabbi in 1840 at Montefiore's instigation urging the Jews to learn Turkish remained a dead letter. There were no qualified Turkish teachers to be found, the communities and the schools were too poor to support the extra charges, and there was no interest in the matter shown by the state. The next stage in the involvement of Western Jews came in 1854, at the time of the Crimean War, with the growing debate about the "Jewish Eastern Question," especially within the context of the pressure put on the Ottomans by the European powers to improve the status of the Christians of the Empire. It was in 1854 that Albert Cohn embarked upon his historic mission to the East and founded schools in Jerusalem, Izmir, and Istanbul.

The action taken by Western Jews to reform Jewish education in Turkey could never have come to a successful fruition without the presence among the Turkish Jewish communities of forces that were predisposed to change and were prepared to collaborate and indeed actively push for reforms. Usually it was the rich merchants and notables who were the most fervent supporters of the new schools.

The economic context in the middle of the nineteenth century had rendered these groups increasingly aware of the necessity of European education for Turkish Jewry. The period saw the domination of the Levant by Western capitalism. The Anglo-Ottoman trade convention of 1838 heralded the beginning of free trade with Europe, with the lowering of taxes on trade and the abolition of state monopolies.[64] Accompanied by the introduction of the steamboat to the Mediterranean, trade with the West increased substantially in the middle of the century. The Greek and Armenian commercial classes, by now the traditional intermediaries with Europe, benefited from this development, and were transformed into the commercial bourgeoisie of the Empire.

The acquisition of European languages was essential for success in the international and indeed local marketplaces now dominated by Western economic interests. The popularity of foreign schools in Turkey in the second half of the century was the result of this larger development. A Western orientation in general, and knowledge of Western ways and languages in particular, came to be considered crucial for Turkish Jewry by its commercial elite to compete effectively with the Greeks and Armenians, and to improve the lot of the desperately poor masses. As Moïse Allatini, the most important Jewish banker in Salonica put it in 1856, increased trade relations with Europe had begun to induce "the necessity of imparting a higher education to the young men."[65] In the context of the larger Westernization of the Empire and the domination of its economy by Europe, Western education constituted for the Jews a major tool for the reestablishment of economic links with the West that had grown weaker in the previous two centuries.

In the key communities of Istanbul and Salonica, the leading segment of the Jewish elite, foreign Jews mostly of Italian origin long settled in the Levant for the purposes of trade, played a particularly significant role in the introduction of European education among Turkish Jewry. They were known as *Francos,* a term probably originating from Crusader times when all Europeans in the Middle East were called *Francs.* The names of the leading *Francos,* such as Camondo, Allatini, Fernandez, Modiano, and Morpurgo are inseparable from the history of the new educational institutions in the two cities.[66]

The *Francos* were part of an international Italian Jewish commercial class concentrated in some of the major cities around the Mediterranean basin such as Tunis, Alexandria, Aleppo, Izmir, Istanbul, and Salonica. They continued to maintain close links with Italy. Most were under the protection of foreign consuls in the Ottoman Empire.[67] They thus benefited from preferential taxation in trade and enjoyed a relative independence from the local Jewish communities, often forming separate groupings outside their jurisdiction. Until the middle of the nineteenth century, the leaders among the *Francos* had remained aloof from the local Jews, maintaining traditional family ties with Italy, often sending their sons to be educated there.

The increased European economic presence in the Eastern Mediterranean as well as the growing involvement of Western Jews with the affairs of their Eastern coreligionists brought the *Francos* into close contact with the new political and economic developments affecting world Jewry. In outlook and ideology the natural allies of the West European Jewish elite, they soon came to accept the reforming impulse of the latter vis-à-vis their less fortunate brethren in the East. Dr. Moïse Allatini, for example, expressed in a memorandum to Ludwig August Frankl on his trip to the Middle East in 1856 the need for Western Jews such as Montefiore, Rothschild, and Philippson to continue to help the Jews of the East "to work their way out of their present miserable state of degradation. . . ."[68] He was to be the founder of the Alliance school in Salonica in 1873.

Another *Franco,* the rich banker Abraham Camondo of Istanbul, also known as the "Rothschild of the East,"[69] collaborated closely with Albert Cohn. With his bank rising to international prominence from the 1840s onward, Camondo, who had close contacts with the Rothschilds and the Bleichröders, was an ideal associate of the Western reformers.

Albert Cohn had ostensibly arrived in Istanbul to make sure that the Jews were included in the provisions of any decree granting equality to the non-Muslims of the Empire. Once this was obtained, he turned his attention to the creation of a Jewish school in Istanbul which would teach European languages. A committee headed by Camondo and some Ashkenazi Jews who were Austrian subjects raised the necessary funds to cover the costs of the new institution. Upon his return to Paris, Albert Cohn sent a French teacher to direct the school which opened on 23 November 1854 in the predominantly Jewish quarter of Hasköy with 76 students. This was the first Jewish establishment of education in Turkey which taught European languages and secular subjects, as well as Hebrew and Turkish.[70]

The Westernizing measures of the Ottoman state and the Reform Decree of 1856 with its stated directive to the non-Muslim communities to reform their institutions, all helped the cause of the reformers among the Jews such as Camondo. They were supported by the European Jewish elite which interpreted the Reform Decree as the act of emancipation of Ottoman Jewry. It is highly significant that Baron Alphonse de Rothschild, a leader of the Central Consistory in Paris, was present in Istanbul at the time of the promulgation of the decree. It was he who called for a meeting of the Jewish notables in Istanbul "to search the best means to use to raise the moral and social condition of our Turkish coreligionists and to render them more worthy of the good deeds of His Majesty the Sultan."[71] The result was a circular drawn up by the Chief Rabbi to be sent to all the communities of the Empire, outlining the reforms to be instituted. In this respect, Alphonse de Rothschild's action paralleled that of Montefiore who in 1840, as a response to the Rescript of 1839, had prodded the Chief Rabbi of the time to issue a declaration in favor of the teaching of Turkish in Jewish schools. The new international Jewish politics of Western Jewish reformers, in its infancy in 1840, had become well established by 1856.

The circular stressed the need to institute reforms as required by the Decree of 1856 and asked all the communities of the Empire to follow the measures to be undertaken by the Istanbul community. The latter would create two committees, one to oversee and reform the communal administration and another one to supervise the creation of a new educational system among the Jews which would teach secular subjects, as well as European languages and Turkish. Hebrew instruction would be rationalized, and schools for girls would also be instituted. The committees were to include representatives of foreign Jews *(Israélites francs)* resident in Istanbul.[72]

The stipulations of the circular reflected the reforming agenda of the Western Jewish leadership vis-à-vis Eastern Jews which had been discussed in full in the European Jewish press in the preceding years. The education of girls, the teaching of Hebrew in a systematic manner based upon the study of Hebrew grammar, the introduction of secular subjects and European languages into the schools system were all projects dear to the heart of European *maskilim* and reformers. Their allies, the *Francos,* given leadership positions in the committees, had now risen formally to important positions of power and influence. All seemed poised for an era of major change and reform.

However, opposition from the more traditionalist quarters was not long in coming. Once the dust had settled, and the initial reforming *élan* from the Ottoman state had died down, resistance to the reforms manifested itself, leading to major conflicts within the community.

Under the provisions of the circular, the school established at Hasköy in 1854 had become a communal institution and had moved to a large building on land donated by Abraham de Camondo.[73] A quarrel between a rabbi teaching at the school and its French director led to the dismissal of the former in 1858.[74] The rabbi promptly accused the director of religious laxity, a charge taken up by other rabbis who came to his aid. The school was excommunicated and 50 rabbis appealed to the Chief Rabbi for its closure, condemning the teaching of French as contrary to the Jewish religion.[75] The uproar led to the closing of the institution.

The lay notables reacted with the classic course of action of most reformers in the face of traditionalist attack in countless similar cases in Europe: They appealed to the state to come to their help. As a result, the minister in charge of education, Hayrullah Effendi, ordered the reopening of the school.[76] Under pressure from the government, a compromise was reached between the two sides. French was to continue to be taught. In return, Hebrew teaching and religious instruction would be strengthened. The offending French director would be replaced by a new teacher from France. Furthermore, subventions would be given to the *Talmudei Torah* by the communal administration.[77]

The latter point throws light on an important aspect of the conflict that can be lost sight of under the predominantly ideological nature of the stances taken by the two sides. Of course, on a fundamental level, the quarrel was over two diametrically opposed world views, one which recognized nothing outside the all-encompassing Jewish religious universe and another for which religious knowledge was one among many sources of wisdom, and which wanted to expose the Jews to outside influences. In this respect, it had all the bearings of the classic struggle between the traditionalist and the reformer in the Jewish centers of Central and Eastern Europe from the period of the *haskalah* onward.

But the conflict was also fuelled by more mundane considerations. The introduction of a new educational system announced by the circular of 1856 threatened many rabbis with the loss of livelihood. The systematization and formalization brought by the reforms and the inevitable diminution in the time devoted to the teaching of the sacred language and texts meant the erosion of the traditional educational system which had constituted the main source of employment to the hundreds of rabbis in the capital. Many eked out a bare existence teaching in the *meldars* and the *Talmudei Torah*. Their attack on the new school serving as a model for others and their demand for financial support for the traditional institutions of education were both defensive reactions of this group threatened by extinction.

The result of the 1858 struggle was a draw, to be followed by another conflict which rocked the Istanbul community in 1862. The action of the committee created according to the provisions of the circular of 1856 to reform the communal administration raised the ire of all those who stood to lose by the new reforms. The committee, headed by Abraham de Camondo, inspected accounts, encroached upon the action of the religious courts, and asserted increased control over the affairs of the community.[78] It also created the first long-lived Judeo-Spanish journal in Istanbul, the *Jurnal Israelit,* to propagandize for the reforms.[79]

An article defending Freemasonry in the newspaper precipitated the new confrontation.[80] Bans were issued against the paper, and Camondo himself, the principal force behind the reforms, was excommunicated in his house by a rabbi who had been invited there to discuss the crisis. Camondo in return had the offending rabbi imprisoned which led to new uproar within the community. Mass demonstrations in the capital and petitions to the Sultan managed to obtain a pardon for the imprisoned rabbi.[81]

The conflict within the Istanbul community led to the intervention of the state. The Chief Rabbi of the time, Jacob Avigdor, was dismissed and was replaced by the Chief Rabbi of Edirne, Yakir Astruc Geron, a friend of the reformers. He became the *kaymakam,* the acting Chief Rabbi of the Ottoman Empire in 1863.[82] Opposition to him in the form of mass demonstrations in the capital was crushed by the authorities. Administrative statutes for the community were prepared under his supervision and approved by the state in 1865. The new *nizamname* (regulations) gave increased power to the lay element and limited the say of the rabbinical corps.[83]

These statutes seemed to confirm the victory of the Westernizing lay element of the community over the traditionalists. In both of the conflicts of 1858 and 1862, opposition from the traditionalist side was defeated. However, it is important to note that in both cases, it was the intervention by the state that settled the matter. Without having recourse to the authorities, it is quite clear that the Westernizers would not have succeeded, as they did not have the critical mass within the community behind them to achieve their goals.

But, unlike similar cases in Europe, the state's intervention in the internal life of the Jewish community was intermittent at best. The reforming of the Jewish community, the smallest of the main non-Muslim groupings in the

Empire and the least problematic from the point of view of its nationalist aspirations, was very low in the order of priorities of the Ottoman state. The latter reacted as matters presented themselves, as in the conflicts of 1858 and 1862. But no sustained action in terms of supporting the Westernizing agenda of the Jewish reformers is in evidence in the next half century. Indeed, the vagaries of reform in the Ottoman Empire in general with the rise of Abdul Hamid's despotic regime after 1878 precluded any such effort.

This is corroborated if one follows the fate of the institution of the Chief Rabbinate of the Empire, through which one can assume the state could have carried out any plans of reform of the Jewish *millet*. The institution had, after a brief period of existence, ceased to exist in the sixteenth century.[84] Very little is known about its formal revival. It appears that in 1835 the Istanbul community appealed to the Porte for the appointment of a rabbi of its own choosing to the position of the *hahambaşı* with the appropriate *berat* (imperial patent), pointing out that the Greeks and the Armenians already enjoyed such a privilege.[85] This was duly accepted, and the communal candidate, Abraham Levi, was formally appointed as *hahambaşı*.[86]

The timing of the episode is significant, coming as it did a decade after the elimination of the Jewish *sarrafs* in 1826. It might reflect the need felt by the community to establish a direct, formal liaison with the Porte, now that its usual intermediaries had been removed. But more importantly, the revival of the institution of the Chief Rabbinate has to be seen as keeping with the general policy trends of the reign of Mahmut II, a reign marked by reforms, growing centralization, the dismantlement of local sources of power, and closer control of the affairs of all the communities.[87] The latter factor was no doubt important for the Ottoman state after the Greek revolt. Nevertheless, apart from the formal recognition of the Chief Rabbi, there is no evidence to suggest that the Porte was interested in the Jews in this period. The revival of the Chief Rabbinate in Istanbul did not change the internal life of the Jewish communities of the Empire. It also did not elevate the Chief Rabbi of Istanbul to a position of authority over the other rabbis of other Jewish centers. The one change after 1835 was that the other communities also started to receive *berats* for their Chief Rabbis.[88] Otherwise the status quo remained intact.

The *nizamname* of 1865, which was supposed to have rationalized the administration of the community and defined the role of the Chief Rabbi, did not, in fact, function well in practice. Continuing in the old tradition prior to 1835, no *hahambaşı* was formally appointed between 1865 and 1909. The position was held by acting Chief Rabbis. The communal councils all resigned in rapid succession. Long periods without these *meclises* meant that, in effect, the acting Chief Rabbi and a small coterie of his protégés ruled over the administrative affairs of the community. Furthermore, new *nizamnames* in the provinces that were supposed to have followed the one adopted by the community of the capital did not materialize until decades later, and they were as ineffectual.[89]

So, the appeal by the Reform Decree of 1856 for the reforming of the communal administrations of the non-Muslim *millets* did not meet with much concrete success in the case of the Jewish community. The stalemate and paralysis in communal affairs that followed the new regulations of 1865, as well as the nature of the conflicts that preceded them, all point to the fact that without the concrete backing of the state, the reforms of the Westernizers through the communal administrations were doomed to failure in the current balance of forces. The fact that the Ottoman state was not yet interested in a European style "regeneration" of its Jewish subjects meant that change could only come from the outside, independently from the institutional framework of the community. It is in this context that the work of the Alliance Israélite Universelle proved to be crucial in the next half century. Not surprisingly, all the major Westernizing *Franco* actors in the conflicts of 1858–1862 are to be found next in the Regional Committee of the Alliance Israélite Universelle in Istanbul, founded in 1863 with Abraham de Camondo as its president.

One important conclusion to be drawn from the crisis of 1856–1865 in Istanbul is that the major conflict between the traditionalists and reformers was played out *before* the Alliance came on the scene. Even though the result was a stalemate, the principle of education in European ways was tacitly accepted after the events surrounding the school established in Hasköy by Albert Cohn, as is shown by the accord that ended the conflict. It cannot be said that the reformers won, but they had prepared the ground for the Alliance. The same was true in the other major Judeo-Spanish communities of the Empire.

The developments in Istanbul had parallels in other Judeo-Spanish centers. From 1854 until the early 1860s, these communities saw attempts to establish new institutions of education.

Unfortunately, given the current state of research, it is impossible to clarify adequately the early history of the new establishments in Izmir. Albert Cohn opened a school there in 1854 on his way to Jerusalem,[90] but the institution appears to have closed soon thereafter. Izmir was the first Jewish community to respond to the circular of the Chief Rabbi in 1856. By the end of the year a new school opened where French was taught.[91] However, the institution appears to have had as ephemeral an existence as the one founded by Albert Cohn and collapsed soon thereafter.

Izmir also had its community of notables, some of them *Francos,* who pushed for the creation of new schools.[92] One of them, Alexandre (Alessandro) Sidi, played a leading role in this field in the 1860s. The school that he founded in the early years of the decade, called the *Aziziye* in honor of Sultan Abdul Aziz, had a tumultuous existence with many closures and reopenings due to financial problems and communal conflicts and finally closed its doors definitely in 1868.[93]

The Jewish community of Edirne saw the same movement for new schooling in the 1850s. The leading force behind it was the *maskil* Joseph Halevi. There has been controversy about the personal and intellectual background of this noted Hebraist who was to make a name for himself later as an Orientalist in Paris. He became famous in the Jewish world after he was sent in 1867 by the Alliance to Ethiopia to investigate the Falashas. It is now quite clear that he was an Ashkenazi Jew from Hungary.[94]

While Narcisse Leven claimed that Halevi founded a new school in Edirne in 1850,[95] an account by Halevi states that he started to be active in public life there in 1856. The later date seems more likely as it is also confirmed by another account of his arrival.[96] His considerable learning in Hebrew and the Talmud led to his initial acceptance by the rabbinical corps of the town. He was taken under the wing of Rabbi Bekhor Danon, the secretary to the Chief Rabbi of the town and the father of Abraham Danon, a noted *maskil* in his own right a generation later. Halevi became the director of the *Talmud Torah* of the Portuguese congregation of the town, one of the thirteen congregations that made up the Jewish community. He slowly began to introduce reforms at his school, teaching Hebrew grammar systematically and introducing the teaching of French. A group of reformers coalesced around him and managed to bring about the fusion of many *meldarim* into one big *Talmud Torah* with Halevi as its director.

Opposition soon made itself manifest, however, especially to the teaching of French and to Halevi's *haskalah* ideas. It proved to be too strong to overcome and he had to abandon Edirne. His experiment lasted five years, and it sowed the seeds of the *haskalah* and the revival of Hebrew in Edirne, which was later to produce two of the most important Sephardic *maskilim* of the second half of the nineteenth century, the religious nationalist Barukh Mitrani and the rationalist historian and Hebraist, Abraham Danon. Both were involved with the activities of the Alliance Israélite Universelle in Turkey.

In Salonica a school teaching European languages was founded in 1857. *Francos* such as Moïse Allatini and *maskilim* such as Yehudah Nehama collaborated in supporting the establishment. There too, however, opposition from the conservative camp soon emerged, and the school closed in 1861.[97]

A survey of developments in these Sephardic communities leads to one conclusion. The 1850s saw reforms in the field of education in all of them. New schools were established, and the principle of teaching European languages was introduced for the first time. The principal impetus for the increasingly Western orientation of the leadership of Turkish Jewry was the growing European economic and financial penetration of the Ottoman Empire. The lucrative consequences of the acquisition of the knowledge of European skills and languages were all too apparent to a community suffering from the social ills of economic backwardness. It was this necessity that created the base of support for modern schooling.

Of course, the same trend was also at work in the surrounding society and highlighted for Turkish Jews the importance of prompt action in this domain. The Greeks and Armenians established extensive education networks in the course of the nineteenth century, beginning this process much earlier than the Jews. The Armenians had 44 schools and one higher education academy in the capital in 1844.[98] In the same period, Armenian leaders started to give great

importance to the teaching of French.[99] The communal leadership established
a commission in 1853 to supervise the Armenian educational system. Under
its influence, reforms were instituted which put added emphasis on secular
subjects in the school curricula, and French began to be taught as a second
language in the upper levels of all elementary establishments and beyond.[100]
The expansion of the Armenian education system proceeded apace in the
second half of the century. By 1900, there were 80,000 students in the Armenian schools in the empire.[101]

The Greeks were even more active than the Armenians in the educational
field. Secular educational institutions such as the Izmir gymnasium, the
Ayvalık and Kuruçeşme academies were already functioning in the first decades of the nineteenth century.[102] The education and literary societies, the
syllogoi, founded from 1861 on in all the major Greek centers of the Empire,[103] embarked upon a major drive and founded or subsidized hundreds of
schools which dispensed a secular as well as a religious education, and also
taught foreign languages. There were 26 *syllogoi* in the capital in the early
1870s.[104] In the same period, Istanbul alone had 105 Greek schools with
15,000 students.[105] By the end of the century, many *lycées* teaching business
skills and modern languages also dotted the Greek educational landscape.

After the Reform Decree of 1856, the Ottoman state itself threw its full
weight behind the introduction of new Westernized secular education among
the Muslims. Between 1867 and 1895, the number of secular elementary
schools and students attending them doubled while the number of secondary
rüşdiye schools and their students quadrupled.[106] The *lycée* of Galatasaray was
founded in Istanbul in 1869 to train the future Westernized leadership of the
state.[107] The 1869 education law systematized the school system in the empire
by creating the administrative framework for the running of the new institutions. However, the Ottoman state remained outside the educational system
of the non-Muslims.

The conjunction of these circumstances presented a golden opportunity to
Western Jewish reformers to take their *mission civilisatrice* to the Jews of the
East, the outlines of which had taken shape in the debates about the "Jewish
Eastern Question" since the Damascus affair of 1840. The schools founded by
Albert Cohn in 1854 represented the first stage of the implementation of this
mission. Local forces to benefit most from Westernization, the lay notables,
the *Francos,* and some *maskilim,* provided the main support for these schools.

However, by the beginning of the 1860s, the first stage of the reforms had
come to an end. The opposition from the conservative camp had brought the
closure of the new schools in Izmir, Salonica, and Edirne and had put the
Istanbul school and the reformers on the defensive. The local forces working
for reforms were as yet too weak and the action of Western Jewish personalities
too intermittent to tip the scales definitely in their favor. This would only be
done by the sustained, *organized* work of the Alliance Israélite Universelle.

III

THE POLITICS OF SCHOOLING
THE ALLIANCE ISRAELITE AND THE
JEWISH COMMUNITIES OF TURKEY

The Establishment of the Schools

The local elements that had been involved in the movement for the reform of the educational institutions in the Judeo-Spanish heartland of Ottoman Jewry in the middle of the nineteenth century established contact with the Alliance soon after its foundation. Lay notables as well as local *maskilim* saw in the organization an outside force which could galvanize moribund institutions and open the path toward European education for the Jews. They considered this an absolute necessity for the improvement of the moral and material situation of the Jews of Turkey. Only then could the latter compete in the market place increasingly dominated by Western interests and cast off the weight of obscurantism and fanaticism.

The first person from the region to contact the Alliance formally was Yehudah Nehama, the leading *maskil* of Salonica, who had been instrumental in the foundation of a new elementary school there in the 1850s. He wrote to Paris to become a member on April 14, 1863.[1] By August of the same year, he had propagandized sufficiently to create a local Alliance committee in Salonica composed of leading notables.[2]

A visit by Adolphe Crémieux, the president of the Alliance, to Istanbul in 1863 precipitated a similar development there. The Regional Committee of the Alliance in Turkey was founded in his presence on November 31, 1863, with Abraham de Camondo as president, Jacques de Castro as vice-president, Emmanuel Veneziani as secretary, Daniel Fernandez as treasurer, and J. R. Servi, Hermann Klarfeld, and Adolph Barbier as members.[3] All of these were *Francos* and foreign Jews, and they had been involved with the Albert Cohn school founded in 1854. At the time of the creation of the Committee they were in the thick of the communal conflict that was dividing the Istanbul Jewish community. The new organization gave the local reformers another base from which they could pursue their objectives in the capital. The Regional Committee invited like-minded Jews in other communities to found similar organizations. These were created in Gelibolu (Gallipoli), Izmir, and Volos in 1864 and in Edirne in 1865.[4]

The Judeo-Spanish press also was to emerge as an important local ally of the organization. The editors of newspapers such as *El Jurnal Israelit, El Tiempo, El Nasional,* and *La Epoka* were tireless crusaders for reforms, especially for the creation of news schools teaching European languages. The press militated actively in favor of the Alliance. It also constituted a major vehicle for the transmission of the news of the work of the society, publishing lengthy reports on its activities, and translating the minutes of the meetings of the Central Committee in Paris.[5]

The question of schooling had been on the agenda of the Alliance from the beginning. The first appeal for it to take over the task of instruction in a non-European Jewish community had come from Tetuan, Morocco in 1861, a request which it accepted.[6] Similar requests came from Baghdad and Damascus.[7] The Alliance saw the spread of new schools in Eastern Jewish communities as central to its mission of "regeneration." Abraham de Camondo heartily seconded this view. According to him, "only instruction [could] open the path of progress" to the Jews of the Orient "so backward in civilization."[8] Both the Central Committee in Paris and the Regional Committee in Istanbul propagandized actively in favor of new schools.

Jacques Isaac Altaras, who had previously been involved with the "regeneration" of Algerian Jewry, used the occasion of a trip to the Middle East in 1864 to sound out local notables on the possibility of their help for such institutions.[9] This underscores the continuity between French Jewry's civilizing mission in North Africa after the conquest of Algeria in 1830 and the activities of the Alliance after 1860. The organization enlarged the scope of this work to cover the whole of the Mediterranean basin.

Nevertheless, the task of opening new institutions of education was far from easy and it would take many years before the hopes of the Alliance could be realized. There were many questions to be solved before a school could be established. First and foremost, the Central Committee had to secure the active support of a group of local notables. Unlike missionary organizations to which it has been frequently compared, on no occasion did the Alliance teacher arrive unsolicited in a locality and simply create a school, waiting for students to come. The Central Committee saw the collaboration of local elements as vital for the functioning of its establishments.

Once the demand from a locality was established and local support secured, the next question that had to be solved concerned the finances of the institutions. The Alliance did not see itself as a philanthropic organization and, though more than ready to contribute funds to a school, wanted the active financial involvement of local groups. It was only after local funding was secured that the Alliance agreed to send a director. The latter more often than not took over an already existing establishment, earmarked by the local notables and community, and transformed it into a full-fledged Alliance school.

The importance of financial support from the locality for the longevity of an

Alliance institution cannot be overestimated in the early years of the organization. Although there were to be some notable exceptions, local support emerged as a *sine qua non* in the first decade of the Alliance. This is best illustrated in the case of the school of Volos, in present-day Greece.

Volos was situated in one of those cotton-growing areas in European Turkey that had benefited from the collapse of American cotton during the Civil War. Jewish merchants there, most originating from Salonica, had prospered from the cotton trade in the early 1860s. Yehudah Nehama of Salonica was in touch with the leading family of Volos, the Faraggis, and he informed them of the activities of the Alliance.[10] In 1864, the Faraggis and other members of the Jewish community, which numbered approximately 1500 people, asked the Alliance for a teacher to found a school in Volos that would teach European languages. They made the necessary financial commitment to satisfy the Alliance, which then consented to subsidize the institution.[11] Volos, then, became the first town in the Judeo-Spanish areas of the Ottoman Empire where an Alliance establishment was founded.

Nevertheless, the school was to be short-lived. The end of the boom in the area, as cheap American cotton returned after 1865, severely undercut the financial position of the community. The school, after going from one financial crisis to another, closed in 1874 for lack of money.[12] At least in the early years, the Alliance was not prepared, and indeed was not sufficiently wealthy, to subsidize totally its educational institutions in the Levant.

These questions dogged the activity of the organization in its initial years in Istanbul and prevented it from establishing schools there until the mid-1870s, when new circumstances allowed it to sidestep the financial problem. The Regional Committee, composed of the most influential Jewish notables of the city, did try to coordinate efforts for new schools. By 1864, it had recruited many new members to the Alliance and had made a special effort to add not only *Francos* but also local Jews to its ranks. In March 1864, the Committee had been enlarged to include a notable from each Jewish quarter, and it was Camondo's hope that they would help the work of the Alliance.[13]

Nevertheless, only a month later, even though the membership in Istanbul had increased to 169 and the acting Chief Rabbi, Yakir Geron, a friend of the reformers, had himself become a member, Camondo was much more pessimistic. "The task [was] difficult and required a lot of work and perseverance."[14] Giving the example of what happened to the Albert Cohn school, which was now under his tutelage, he predicted that schools would not be able to function in Istanbul for a long time to come. The only hope was "to wait for the minds themselves to turn toward civilization, and seek in instruction the only means of leaving the profound ignorance in which they find themselves at the moment."[15] Even though Yakir Geron had remained the acting Chief Rabbi, it was impossible to rely on the communal bodies for any concrete help. The experience of the communal conflict of the past few years had rendered Camondo and other reformers wary of any new attempt that would disturb the fragile peace that they had gained only recently.

   The Istanbul community, in fact, existed only in name. Each Jewish quarter, divided into subquarters called *hashgaḥot,* maintained its own independence, ran its own affairs, and supported its own communal institutions. The *Francos,* the Karaites, and the Ashkenazim constituted semi-independent subgroups. The topography of the city, the existence of waterways such as the Bosphorus and the Golden Horn that physically separated its different areas, encouraged the independence of the quarters. The task of organizing new schools, especially in the aftermath of a long conflict between the traditionalists and the reformers proved a very difficult one.

   To this was added the initial reluctance of the Istanbul notables, even those in closest collaboration with the Alliance, to relinquish control of already existing institutions. The Hasköy school founded in 1854 by Albert Cohn would have been the most likely candidate for an Alliance takeover. Indeed, there were long deliberations between the organization and the concerned parties over the question. By 1868, a Committee for the Instruction of the Jews of Turkey had been founded, again composed of leading *Francos* such as Jacques de Castro and Abraham de Camondo. The Committee had decided to reorganize the Hasköy school and asked the Alliance for a director and teachers.[16] When in return the Alliance expressed the wish to have complete control of the institution to implement its program as it saw fit, the Committee of Instruction, Camondo included, retracted its offer.[17] This decision might have reflected its desire to maintain independence but might also have been motivated by the fear of repercussions from the rabbinate, as the school was still bound to the contract with it. As it was, nothing came of these negotiations. Though the institution was directed from 1873 by an ex-Alliance teacher, Félix Bloch, and copied the curriculum of the Alliance schools as much as possible, it remained an independent establishment. It was supported financially by the Camondo family until its closure in 1890.

The Edirne and Izmir Schools

As in Istanbul, the Alliance found an elite in Edirne which had already tried to modernize education in the 1850s. The chief protagonist of that attempt, Joseph Halevi, again played a significant role. Having abandoned his attempt to reform the *Talmud Torah* because of opposition from the traditionalist elements, Joseph Halevi had reopened his first school. In 1865, getting in touch with the Regional Committee in Istanbul, he began to recruit members for the Alliance and informed the Central Committee in a letter written in Hebrew of the creation of a provincial committee for Rumeli, the Ottoman province of which Edirne was the capital.[18] The president was the wealthy banker, Moïse de Toledo. The five other members consisted of another banker, three merchants, and one interpreter in the Austrian consulate.[19]

   The Edirne Jewish community, composed of eight to ten thousand Jews, was not particularly cosmopolitan, and the *Franco* element was totally missing. In this respect, it was quite different from the other large Jewish communities of Istanbul, Izmir, and Salonica. Nevertheless, it was situated in an important provincial capital which sat on the crossroads of trade routes from the Northern Balkans to the Aegean sea, and from the Adriatic and Salonica to Istanbul. Most Jews were shopkeepers and petty artisans. The richest families were involved with long and short distance trade, especially in textiles, animal skins, and colonial produce.[20] There were thirteen synagogues in town, over which two rabbinical dynasties, the Geron and the Behmoiras, had held sway for the last two centuries.[21]

The work of Joseph Halevi in the 1850s had borne some fruit. There was a small group in town which had come under his influence and was in touch with *haskalah* ideas through the reading of Hebrew newspapers such as *ha-Magid*.[22] It was from it that the invitation came to the Alliance in 1867 to take over Halevi's school. This invitation is almost a prototype of the letters the Alliance would receive in the next decades from local communities, inviting it either to send directors to already existing schools or to open new ones:

> We, the undersigned, directors of the Jewish school of Edirne called the *Talmud Torah 'im derekh ereẓ* [Torah study together with knowledge of the world], convinced of the necessity of giving a good French education to our students in order to introduce them to European civilization, we beg the very honorable Central Committee of the Alliance Israélite Universelle to give its valued assistance by providing us with a suitable teacher for the teaching of the French language and of the elements of modern sciences . . . [23]

The letter guaranteed a local subsidy of 2000 French francs per year for three years and agreed to all the stipulations that the Alliance might wish to make. Among the signatories were two traders in colonial produce (Salomon Bohor Eliakim, Samuel Pisa), one broker in cereals and wool (Yohai Nardea), one rabbi (Elia Navon), and one accountant in the banking house of Moïse de Toledo (Joseph Suhami). Only the latter knew French, having been educated in Marseilles. He had in fact been the French teacher of Joseph Halevi.[24]

The contents and tone of the letter matched neatly the Alliance's own world view, and the guarantee of financial support fulfilled one of its important requirements. The influence of Joseph Halevi is certainly in evidence in this request for a teacher. In fact, the letter was seconded by one from Halevi himself, who was then leaving Edirne on his way to the Falashas, charged by the Alliance to inquire into their state. Halevi waxed ecstatic over the changes that he saw in the Edirne Jewish community:

> The dissensions that reigned since the awakening of the people, between the secularist partisans of progress and the conservative casuists (the *ḥakhamim)* have ended with the total defeat of the latter and everybody wishes an enlightened education for their children. The fanaticism . . . which causes such devastation within the communities of North-Eastern Europe is thankfully unknown among the exiled from the Iberian peninsula. Once one manages to shake the laziness . . . which the climate of this country seems to engender, our

coreligionists embrace progress from which no refined casuistry can separate
them . . .[25]

The Alliance accepted the invitation and sent Félix Bloch, a recent Alsatian
graduate of the Paris Rabbinical Seminary, to head the school. But it was only
as a result of a *fait accompli* engineered by its partisans that the Chief Rabbi of
the town attended the inauguration in October 1867. A big ceremony was
organized, and for the first time in the annals of the Jewish community of
Edirne, all of the foreign consuls as well as the Turkish *vali* (governor) were
invited to attend. It would have been highly impolitic for the Chief Rabbi not
to attend a Jewish event graced by the presence of the highest Turkish official
of the region. He was obliged to come and give his blessing.[26] As the school
now appeared to have the support of the Turkish and the consular authorities,
it was safe from outright attack.

Indeed, the fanfare that accompanied the inauguration impressed the Jewish community as a whole. Mordechai Rodrigue, the president of the Alliance
local committee put it thus: "Never has the Jewish community received such
an honor; twenty years ago, the name of Jew was uttered with contempt while
today, thanks to your good works, gentlemen of the Central Committee, it is
uttered with respect."[27] The prestige of association with the Parisian institution always played a role in the success of the Alliance. It was an important
factor that motivated the local supporters of the schools. By the second half of
the nineteenth century, everything that came from Europe had come to assume an aura of superiority and of power for increasing numbers of people in
the Levant. An association with the triumphant West often yielded positive
results in the locality. Still, the Edirne school had to traverse a long and
tortuous path before it became *the* Jewish institution of the town. Nevertheless, it was now safely established and was followed by a school for girls two
years later.

Many of the elements seen in the foundation of the Edirne school were
present in the creation of Alliance institutions in other towns. The existence
of a group that appeared to have sufficient power and which supported the
institution wholeheartedly was the single most important factor. The Alliance
almost always came upon the invitation of a group that also promised to
contribute financially to the expenses of the institution. The Izmir establishments would follow the same pattern.

The 1860s were a period of turbulence for the Jewish community of Izmir.
As in the other centers of the Ottoman Empire, communal conflicts erupted
not only because of the friction between traditionalists and reformers but also
because of questions of internal taxation, the prestige of lay notables, and the
powers of the rabbinate. Galanté has described in detail the origins and
course of the conflict that broke out in 1865 and lasted until 1869, ending with
the election of Abraham Palacci to the Chief Rabbinate left vacant after his
father Haim Palacci's death.[28]

The Alliance had entered into serious negotiations with the local notables as early as 1864. Nissim Crispin, the head of the Alliance local committee, had shown Jacques Isaac Altaras, during his visit to the city in 1864, a school which had already been established. He had promised that the local Alliance committee would pay 3000 French francs a year to the director.[29] There were now 172 members of the Alliance in the town.[30] However a cholera epidemic at the end of that year closed the school. It could not be reopened due to the communal conflict of 1865, during which even the Alliance local committee, then headed by the wealthy merchant Alexander Sidi, disbanded itself.

This conflict which originated in a dispute over the *gabela* (meat tax) led to the complete paralysis of communal affairs until its resolution in 1869. The *Francos,* headed by Alexander Sidi, even tried to form themselves into a separate community under the protection of the French consul and they appealed to the Alliance for its help.[31] The documentation does not reveal whether they succeeded, but as there is no further mention of a separate *Franco* communal organization in any account of the history of the Jews of Izmir, it appears that the attempt failed. Or perhaps it was not pursued any further.

Alexander Sidi in the interim established a school in which French and Turkish were taught, but this institution which he supported financially lasted for a couple of years and had disappeared by 1868.[32] It was only in 1871 that another Alliance local committee was created.[33] By 1872, the situation appeared calm enough to renew negotiations over a new school. In the words of the president of the local committee, the rabbis had come to accept the necessity of the new education.[34] Answering the questions of the Central Committee about the projected school, he went on to add that the institution would have at least 200 students and that all the expenses, except for the salary of the director which the Alliance was expected to pay, would be met locally through tuition fees from the students or through contributions and donations.[35] The society founded previously to support the communal *Talmud Torah* also promised an annual subsidy to the school. The Alliance then agreed to send a director.

By 1873, Alexander Sidi was once again the president of the local Alliance committee, and it was he who oversaw the beginnings of the new establishment. The institution was inaugurated in August 1873 with the usual fanfare. The occasion was marked by a sermon given by the Chief Rabbi, Abraham Palacci, on the need for education and the acquisition of foreign languages for the improvement of the state of Izmir Jewry.[36] The rabbinical elite in the city had come to accept the need for educational reform. A school for girls was established five years later.

That something had to be done to alleviate the socioeconomic condition of the Jewish community of Izmir is one of the conclusions that can be drawn from the report addressed by David Cazès, the new school director, to the Central Committee in the same year. The economic situation of this community of "approximately 3500 families, numbering close to 20,000 souls" was stark indeed. One hundred families were more or less prosperous, all dealing in trade. 1500 to 2000 families made up a middling group, composed of petty brokers, merchants, artisans, porters, etc. There were "about 500 families whose heads had the title rabbi." 1000 families were without any means of subsistence and depended on public charity.[37] Both local philanthropists and the Alliance were convinced that the only way out of misery, all too common in the Turkish Jewish communities, lay in modern education which would impart new skills to the new generation.

The Istanbul Schools

The situation in Istanbul was no different. In the late 1860s and early 1870s, there began to appear in all the Jewish quarters a movement toward new schools with more modern curricula. The Judeo-Spanish press reported these activities extensively and encouraged the reformers in their efforts.[38] In 1867, the relatively wealthy Jewish quarter of Kuzguncuk announced plans to reform the already existent *Talmud Torah* and build a new institution where "French, Turkish, and Torah" would be taught.[39] A similar school was to be built in Balat, one of the poorest Jewish quarters of the city. These two establishments, the Camondo school, two new ones founded in Hasköy, and one new one founded in Ortaköy in 1871 received some financial support from the Committee of Instruction mentioned above, which was working with the Chief Rabbinate.[40] A school for Jewish girls was created in Hasköy by a Christian Frenchwoman in 1872.[41] The establishment in 1868 of a Protestant missionary establishment in Hasköy, which offered free education to the poor, raised great concern, and part of the new zeal for schools can be seen as a defensive reaction to this development.[42]

Nevertheless, these institutions did not last for long. The interest of the notables of the quarters proved transitory, and financial commitments were soon forgotten. Quarrels over who was to head the committees supporting the schools led to paralysis.[43] The subsidies from the Istanbul *kolel* (communal council), itself lacking real infrastructure and power, were erratic at best.[44] With the exception of the Camondo school in Hasköy, none of these establishments led a continuous existence. Foreigners living in Istanbul were hired as teachers,[45] but there was no coordinated, rationalized action either from the *kolel* or from the local *hashgahot* to support the new schools. Whatever money there was seems to have gone to the *Talmudei Torah*. And even these did not receive much from the *kolel*, eking out an existence by whatever contributions the *hashgahot* could spare and by the meagre tuition fees collected from an indigent population. As the Judeo-Spanish newspaper *El Tiempo* pointed out, what was needed was an organization that would coordinate all efforts.[46]

Such an organization already existed in the form of the Regional Committee of the Alliance. However, until 1873, its activities had been hampered by the lack of money and communal divisions. Seeing the chaotic situation in Istanbul, the Central Committee in Paris was more than prudent in its response to the inevitable appeal for subsidies that came from the new schools. This stance was supported by the Regional Committee in Istanbul. The latter at first aimed to have the communal council subsidize the schools. One of Abraham de Camondo's last actions before leaving definitely for Paris in 1869 was his attempt to secure such a subsidy and create committees in all the Jewish quarters of the city.[47] But, as pointed out above, he was not successful.

Even in his absence, Camondo continued to be the president of the Istanbul Regional Committee until his death. Real power, however, passed to the vice-president of the Committee, Emmanuel Veneziani, another *Franco* who was one of the directors of the Camondo bank in Istanbul.[48] Under his leadership, the number of Alliance members in Istanbul had increased to 390 by 1873,[49] and the Regional Committee took a more activist stance in general.

In the summer of 1873 the Central Committee in Paris sent Samuel Hirsch, who had been the director of the Alliance school in Tangier, to the Ottoman Empire to report on educational institutions. Hirsch saw the already established schools as the nuclei of future Alliance establishments. But he reported that the elements most favorable to the Alliance in Istanbul greeted the prospect of new schools with pessimism, unless the Central Committee was "prepared to cover all the costs."[50] The Chief Rabbi Yakir Geron himself was prepared to help. But he could not create the necessary financial resources without the communal council and as the latter had recently dissolved itself, there was not much to be expected from this quarter.

The Alliance Regional Committee tried to deal with the problem by attempting to reconcile the opposing elements to "organize the community into a *consistoire*."[51] This had been one of the aims of the new statutes of 1865, but conflicts over taxation and personalities that erupted periodically continued to undermine the regular functioning of the Istanbul *kolel*. The attempt of the Regional Committee failed after several meetings with communal leaders.[52] As the Chief Rabbi indicated to the Committee, the idea of seeking financial support through new taxation was a good one, but the moment was not right, as personal bickering divided and paralyzed the communal institutions.[53]

At this period a very important development occurred in Paris which allowed the Alliance considerable independence from local financial support. The wealthy railway magnate, Baron Maurice de Hirsch, the man who financed the first railways in Turkey, made a donation to the Alliance in December 1873 of 1 million francs, expressly for the education of Turkish Jewry. The letter announcing his decision shows a total identity of views with those of the Alliance:

> During my many and long stays in Turkey, I have been painfully struck by the ignorance and misery of the great majority of the Jews who inhabit this empire. There is progress everywhere in Turkey, but the Jews hardly profit from it because of their poverty and lack of enlightenment. To provide for the instruction and education of the youth is the most efficient remedy that one can bring to this evil. I know that the Alliance does not ignore this state of affairs, that it

deals with it specifically and that it has already founded a number of schools which are working well, but I also know that the limits of its financial resources do not permit it to do what is necessary, and that it has not even been able to turn its efforts toward the city of Constantinople . . . I have decided to create a foundation of one million francs in Constantinople designed specially to improve the situation of the Jews of the Ottoman Empire by instruction and education.[54]

The administration of the foundation was to be given to the Alliance.[55]

Baron de Hirsch was well informed about the activities of the organization. His uncle, Salomon Goldschmidt, a wealthy philanthropist in his own right, and his cousin Sacki Kann, were both members of the Central Committee. From 1873 on until their deaths in 1896 and in 1899 respectively, Hirsch and his wife Clara would continue to donate hundreds of thousands of francs to the Alliance and to its institutions.[56] It was with the beginning of their involvement in 1873 that the Alliance came into its own financially.

The members of the Regional Committee of Istanbul received with great jubilation the news of the donation of 1 million francs. Money brought with it a new confidence. Triumphalism replaced pessimism. As one member of the committee put it, the Alliance could now act without worrying too much about the views of the rabbis "who would remain behind."[57] It would not have to rely on the local community, though it was to be hoped that rich Turkish Jews would be emboldened by this move and would also contribute to the finances of the schools,[58] a hope that was not to materialize.

However, the subsequent decision by the Central Committee to spend the income on the 500,000 francs of the Hirsch money on its agricultural school in Palestine, *Mikveh Yisrael* [hope of Israel], came as a rude shock to the Istanbul Regional Committee. The latter protested, as it had been prepared to act throughout Turkey.[59] Now it would have to limit itself to Istanbul only. However, the Alliance did not change its mind. Agricultural education was seen as one of the keys for the "regeneration" of the Jews of the East, and *Mikveh Yisrael* would always occupy a special place in the considerations of the Central Committee. In direct continuation with European Jewry's concerns over Palestine in the 1850s, the "Palestinophile" orientation of the Alliance leadership also laid great stress on the transformation of the Jews of Palestine into a productive population. It tried to wean it away from dependence on the *halukah* contributions from abroad. The agricultural school was designed to further this end. Furthermore, Paris was certainly not prepared to involve the Istanbul committee in real decision making and always jealously guarded its prerogatives in this domain. Hence the protest fell on deaf ears.

Nevertheless, with funds now at its disposal, the Alliance soon responded to the new appeals from already existing schools in Istanbul and was more than happy to have the Regional Committee supervise its entry onto the educational scene of the capital. Many of these institutions began to receive subsidies from Paris, and, with the arrival of new directors sent by the Central

Committee, were ultimately transformed into Alliance schools. This was to be the case in the Jewish quarters of Ortaköy, Dağhamamı, and eventually Hasköy. Others were founded from scratch, such as the Balat and the Galata institutions. Between 1875 and 1882, a network of eleven schools was created in Istanbul.[60] Each major Jewish quarter now had its Alliance school. The city was to have a record number of Alliance institutions in its midst.

The Hirsch donation freed the organization from becoming a prisoner of local financial considerations. Although it still insisted on tuition fees from those students who could pay, as well as on donations from the locality, the Alliance could maintain its institutions irrespective of the ups and downs of local contributions.

An analysis of the finances of the Alliance schools in Istanbul, Edirne, and Izmir after the Hirsch donation of 1873 to World War I reveals a variegated situation. Some institutions, such as all the schools of Hasköy and Balat and the schools for girls in Dağhamamı and Kuzguncuk in Istanbul, never received communal subsidies. They relied entirely on subventions from Paris as well as on tuition fees. Others, such as the Goldschmidt school for the Ashkenazi community, the Kuzguncuk and Ortaköy school for boys in Istanbul, and the Edirne and Izmir boys' schools, received, with the exception of the odd year, regular subsidies from communal councils. Still others show a more complex financial trajectory. The Galata schools for boys and girls, the Dağhamamı school for boys in Istanbul, and the schools for girls in Edirne and Izmir received communal support, though with frequent interruptions before the twentieth century.[61]

Such support depended upon the political situation within the communities and on their financial condition. Both were exceedingly chaotic in Turkey. The Alliance schools were inevitably involved with communal finances, the Central Committee always insisting upon the maximization of local subsidies. Nevertheless, after the Hirsch donation, these institutions no longer had to depend on such funding.

Teachers, Committees, Communities

The relationship that evolved between Paris and the different localities where the Alliance schools were established varied considerably from place to place and depended to a large extent on the personality, caliber, and political dexterity of the teachers involved. Each school had a director sent by Paris who administered the institution and taught certain subjects. In larger establishments, they were seconded by other teachers sent from Paris as well as by some locally trained personnel who acted as monitors. The directors were the most important people for the organization, and they played a key role in the history of the Alliance. They were the ones who put its policy into practice, who reported on the locality to Paris, and who conveyed Paris's views to the locality.

Theoretically, the Central Committee believed in a division of labor between the Alliance affiliates in a community. The local Alliance committee was supposed to recruit members and propagandize in favor of the organization as a whole. The school committee was to oversee the finances of the institution and contribute to its smooth functioning. The school director was to concern himself with pedagogy only. The system, however, worked differently in practice. In many places, committees were established intermittently, or not at all, leaving the whole field to the director. In other places, school committees interfered with the curriculum, leading to friction with the school and with Paris. Competencies were ill-defined, and opportunities for conflict over personalities, pedagogy and finances remained manifest. In the end, it was the school directors who emerged as the principal actors, and it was upon them that the Alliance relied. The analysis of the activities of a few of these important personalities throws much light on the functioning of the organization in Turkey.

Félix Bloch and Edirne

The Alliance opened a teacher-training school in 1867, the *Ecole Normale Israélite Orientale,* to which the best graduates of its own schools in the Middle East and North Africa would be admitted for training as Alliance teachers.[62] Until then, the teachers had been French Jews, mostly of Alsatian origin. One of the most important members of this group who played an important role in Turkey was Félix Bloch.

Félix Bloch inaugurated the Edirne school in 1867. He was then twenty-seven years old and was an ordained rabbi, a recent graduate of the Rabbinical Seminary of Paris.[63] He was ideologically committed to the "regeneration" of Eastern Jewry. He was appalled at "the ignorance" he found in Edirne where, according to him, there were perhaps fifteen people who wanted to instruct themselves.[64] His task was to "improve the moral level of all these men who, alas, [were] nothing more than the degraded sons of the ancient Spanish school."[65]

Bloch proved to be a shrewd politician. He secured the help of the foreign consuls in Edirne and orchestrated the inauguration ceremony of the school, which, with all the dignitaries attending, attracted attention to the new institution.[66] He urged the Central Committee to write directly to Mordechai Rodrigue, the president of the Alliance local committee, to encourage him in his task and fuel his zeal.[67] He was gratified when a similar letter which he himself had solicited transformed the attitude of the president of the community, Simon Ben Nissim, turning him into one of the most ardent champions of the Alliance in town.[68]

A year after the foundation of the school, 102 students between the ages of five and fifteen were in attendance.[69] Three rabbis taught Hebrew. The sacred language and the Bible would always be taught by local rabbis in the Alliance institutions. This was an effective way of securing the cooperation of the local rabbinate, and it satisfied the more traditionalist elements in the school *clientèle*. Bloch himself was responsible for the teaching of French and, for the first time in the history of Edirne Jewry, arithmetic.[70]

There were problems from the start. The school building mysteriously went up in flames in 1868 and had to be rebuilt with donations from the fathers of the students.[71] Bloch complained regularly of the miserliness of the richer Jews in the community and was often in despair about finances.[72] It took much coaxing to raise money for the girls' school. In the end, the effort bore fruit, and the new institution was founded in 1869.[73] The education of girls was of cardinal importance for Bloch. His aim was to "destroy an old prejudice widespread among our coreligionists of this country who maintain that the education of women is dangerous and superfluous . . . to remove the children from an environment where no rules of order and propriety are known . . . [and] to destroy the laziness which is one of the most shameful vices of the Jewish woman of the Orient."[74]

Bloch was always wary of the local rabbinate and acted prudently so as not to alienate it. He was relieved that the school did not rely totally on subsidies from the community but subsisted chiefly out of tuition fees from students, donations from notables, and subsidies from Paris. Otherwise "backward rabbis" could stop his "progressive" movement.[75] In fact, the main concern of the community was not the Alliance school but the communal *Talmud Torah* with 800 students.[76] In addition, there was a private institution where only Hebrew was taught.[77] The Alliance establishments did not gain real popularity and become an integral part of Jewish communal existence until the 1880s, long after Bloch had left Edirne. As the wealthy banker Moïse de Toledo, the principal supporter of the Alliance school in Edirne, pointed out in 1875, the community as a whole was not really interested in the school with the exception of "a few of us."[78] Nevertheless, Bloch and the small elite around him succeeded in establishing the foundations of the Alliance institutions in Edirne on a secure basis.

Surprisingly, Bloch and his successor from 1874, Bendelac, had most trouble not with the traditionalists but with a local *maskil*, Barukh Mitrani. Mitrani merits a study on his own. This student of Halevi in Edirne, passionately concerned with the revival of the Hebrew language as a living medium, is a fascinating personality, combining religious messianism and moderate *haskalah* into an ideology which prefigured many of the elements of religious Zionism.[79]

His world view, strongly influenced by the writings of Yehuda Alkalai, was most clearly spelled out in his Judeo-Spanish book, *Diskorso de Perashat Shemot*, published in Salonica in 1868. Pointing out the achievements of the nations of Europe and their changing attitude to "the chosen people," Mitrani identified the lack of education as one of the principal causes of the backwardness of the Jews compared to the advances made by other nations.[80] Listing all the traditional reasons to account for their dispersion, he added that salvation was impossible if the Jews did not gather their forces. "The sacred language is not well known . . . [and we] lack science and the arts of government [*artifisios de reinado*]. . . . As long as we are lazy, Judaism is weak, the sacred language is unknown and there is no education, God is right to castigate us and to leave us in *Galut* [exile]."[81] His book was intended as an appeal to the Jewish nation, to "awaken it from the sleep of fanaticism and to make it understand what the Law, science and the civilized times of today requires from us."[82] Schools and more schools were needed where science and the "rules of civilization" would be taught, and the sacred language learnt well. Only with this learning would "the arts of government be acquired again and then "we will be redeemed and saved, and settled in the Holy Land, prosperous with the *melekh ha-mashiyaḥ* [King Messiah]."[83]

Mitrani had published violent critiques of traditional Jewish education in Judeo-Spanish newspapers such as the *Jurnal Israelit*[84] of Istanbul criticizing its lack of method, and was to publish a textbook of Hebrew with Judeo-Spanish explanations for the Jewish schools of the Levant.[85] In Mitrani's view, the critique of traditional education and society were all part of a world view which saw the reform of Jewish society as indispensable for the coming of messianic redemption.

He was well acquainted with *haskalah* ideas and published extensively in the Hebrew press. It was in this domain that he was perceived as a troublemaker by the Alliance. Mitrani's father was the teacher of Hebrew at the Alliance school in Edirne,[86] and he himself taught Hebrew at the newly opened Alliance institution in Şumla (present day Shumen in Bulgaria) in 1869–1870.[87] He came back to Edirne at the end of this period and wanted to become the director of the new girls' school opened by Bloch. Not receiving much encouragement, he opened a rival school for girls. Bloch, of course, did not receive this very well.[88]

Throughout the early 1870s, Mitrani remained in communication with the Alliance. He and Bloch quarreled and made up many times. The tug-of-war between them over the control of the girls' school continued until after Bloch's departure. In the end, Mitrani published several vitriolic diatribes against Alliance teachers in the Hebrew press of the time, in newspapers such as *Ḥavaẓelet* and *ha-Magid,* accusing the teachers of diverging from the original path of the organization, desecrating the Sabbath, giving more importance to French than to Hebrew, and looking down on the people.[89] He reiterated these accusations in long letters in flowing Hebrew to the Central Committee. For him, the origins of all the evil sprang from the faulty education received in the Alliance teacher training institution in Paris, the *Ecole Normale Israélite Orientale.*[90]

Mitrani founded a society with over 200 members, the *Mikveh Yisrael,* which supported the new school directed by him and his father and bombarded the Alliance from 1874 on with letters requesting financial help and a teacher of French. It is interesting to note that his ideal heroes were East

European *maskilim* with whose writings he had become acquainted through his reading of the Hebrew press. He wanted Jewishly observant teachers, enlightened *maskilim* such as Haim Selig Slonimsky and Abraham Beer Gottlober, who would teach foreign languages but who would not transform the school into a French institution.[91]

The Alliance at first tried to conciliate Mitrani. It then ignored him. Mitrani was too demanding for the Alliance to enter into any kind of long-lasting relationship with him. Furthermore, it did not like being attacked publicly and responded in the way that it would always respond to such attacks, with silence. It stood by its teachers. Mitrani did not have a real power base in the Edirne community, was hated by the Alliance local committee,[92] and soon had to close his school for financial reasons. He left the town sometime in the late 1870s, and he took up journalism in the Balkans and in Palestine in the following decade.[93] He returned to Edirne in the 1880s but did not become involved again in the public life of the community.

The conflict between Mitrani and Bloch and other Alliance teachers was unique in that the opposition to the organization came from the quarter in which it was used to having friends, that of the *maskilim*. The feud was sparked by the personal grievances of Mitrani, who was excluded by Bloch from a position in the schools in Edirne. But one should also note the great ideological differences between the position of Mitrani and that espoused by the Alliance. The latter wanted to "regenerate" Eastern Jewry in order to remake it in the image of the "enlightened" sections of French Jewry, into honorable citizens, proud of their religion but also fully conversant with "civilization"—that is, Western, especially French civilization. The admixture of traditional messianism and modern nationalism in Mitrani's thought, reminiscent of Yehudah Alkalai, with its stress on the revival of Hebrew, the centrality of the Holy Land, and religious tradition, was compatible with the ideals of the Alliance only up to a certain point. Both shared a critique of traditional Jewish society, but arrived at opposed conclusions. Bloch's views were colored by the ideology of emancipation espoused by the Alliance with its stress on "regeneration." Mitrani's proto-Zionist ideas, on the other hand, cast education and reform in a mold which, though messianic in tone, pointed in the direction of the future "national regeneration" of Jewish nationalism and Zionism.

The Mitrani episode in Edirne is significant in that it provides a perfect illustration of a wider trend that characterized the relationship between pre-Herzlian Zionists such as Alkalai, Hess, or Kalischer and the Alliance. This group greeted news of the latter's creation with great jubilation and interpreted the actions of the first modern Jewish political international organization, especially its call for Jewish solidarity, as heralding the dawn of "national redemption."[94] They were all to be disappointed when the Alliance remained steadfast in its commitment to the ideology of emancipation. The Mitrani episode epitomized locally this important break and prefigured the future Alliance-Zionist conflict in Turkey three decades later.

It also pointed to a larger development that would emerge in the coming years. The most serious conflicts that the Alliance would have to face would all concern differences of opinion between it and other local personalities already committed to change. The model of a clash between "traditionalists" and "modernizers" is inadequate to explain the history of the organization in Turkey. The struggle between the reformers and the traditionalists had been played out before its arrival and would form, at best, a muted backdrop to its activities. The most serious frictions, when they arose, were almost all to be within the camp of the reformers.

Bloch's relationship with the local Alliance committees was a relatively smooth one. There were few occasions when he and the school committee had a falling out, and almost all of these concerned the question of finances.[95] It was in the Alliance's interest to have as much money as possible collected for the school from the locality. Bloch frequently complained about the lack of financial help from the richer elements in the community.[96] By 1871, the institution was 3600 francs in debt. The Alliance subsidized half of the 120 children in the boys' school, who paid only a symbolic sum in fees.[97] Bloch wanted the community to contribute and had many negotiations with the Chief Rabbi over the subject, all to no avail. It was only in 1873 that the community began to provide small sums to the school. The bulk of its revenues continued to be the annual Alliance subsidy from Paris and the tuition fees paid by the students.

The director in the provinces always had a high visibility, and very often acted as the local *shtadlan* (intercessor), intervening with the Turkish authorities and the foreign consuls on matters concerning the community at large. Bloch's position in Edirne was no different. He was the principal defender of the Jews during a blood libel case in 1872 and managed to have the foreign consuls settle the matter.[98] He succeeded in persuading the Turkish governor to supply, free of charge, a teacher of Turkish at the boys' school,[99] another first for the Jewish community of Edirne.

The seven years spent by Félix Bloch in Edirne, until his departure in 1874 for Istanbul, were crucial ones for the Alliance in the town. These early years were later to be seen as the heroic age of the Alliance schools, when they established a foothold, began to attract students, and introduced a new system of education. In the coming decades they were to emerge from the relative isolation of the early years and become an integral part of Jewish communal life in Turkey. Much of this development was due to the work of the new generation of school directors trained by the Alliance in Paris.

Shemtob Pariente and the Schools of Asia Minor and Istanbul

David Cazès and Shemtob Pariente, the directors sent by the Alliance to head the newly established school in Izmir, were among the first graduates of its teacher-training institution in Paris. They both originated from Tetuan in Morocco, came from a background where Judeo-Spanish was spoken *(haketia,* its North African version), and were the products of the Alliance institution of their native city.[100]

David Cazès became the first Alliance director in Izmir in 1873 and stayed for five years, establishing cordial relations between the school and the local community. The institution benefited from the subsidy granted to it from the charity society which was in charge of the *Talmud Torah.*[101] Cazès worked closely with the leading Jewish notables, the Sidis and the Polacos, and laid the groundwork for the establishment of the girls' school, which in the end was opened immediately after his departure from Izmir.[102] As will be discussed below, he was the principal instigator of the Alliance vocational training system to be established throughout the Levant and North Africa.

The religious behavior of the directors was of cardinal importance in the first years of the Alliance in Turkey. No matter what their personal beliefs, they could not afford to alienate the more traditional elements. The latter had had to grudgingly accept the teaching of secular subjects and European languages but the institutions had to be beyond reproach as far as the religious conduct of the teachers and the students was concerned.

It is quite clear from the tenor of his letters that David Cazès was something of a free thinker. Responding to inquiries from the Central Committee, he was firm. He would "conform to *their* beliefs" (emphasis added), would frequent the synagogues, would insist on daily prayers by students in school, and would punish any infraction. But once the door of his room was closed, he was "free." He was, indeed, proud of the fact that he had a certain prestige among the rabbis, as he had a good knowledge of Hebrew and had many Hebrew books in his possession. "The rabbis [were] happy to see a *Franc* know their language."[103] Cazès's designation of himself as a *Franc,* the latter the name given to Europeans throughout the Levant, is ironic, given the fact that he was a native of Tetuan. This sort of total identification with the West was to become quite typical among a substantial element within the Alliance teaching corps.

Nevertheless, in the end, it was his behavior in the domain of religion that led to his departure. He was seen by his servant lighting a candle in his room during the night of *Yom Kipur* of 1875 and was promptly denounced.[104] Even though the affair did not lead to a major controversy, the Alliance, always prudent in these cases, chose to terminate his stay in Izmir. Cazès was to have subsequently an illustrious career, first in Tunis where he founded the Alliance schools and later as the Alliance representative in the new Jewish Colonization Association settlements in Argentina.[105]

It was another Jew from Tetuan who replaced him in 1878. Shemtob Pariente stayed in Izmir for sixteen years and played a decisive role in the establishment of the Alliance as a powerful force in the life of the Jewish communities of Asia Minor and the Aegean.

A few months after his arrival, the difficulties that had stood in the way of the opening of a school for girls were finally overcome. Increasing Protestant missionary activity in Izmir and the fact that there were sixty Jewish girls

attending various missionary establishments, fired the zeal of the more enterprising sections of the community. A society called "Progress" came into
being which, together with leading notables such as Alexander Sidi and Haim
Polaco, succeeded in raising funds to inaugurate the school.[106] The Chief
Rabbi, Abraham Palacci, always friendly to the Alliance, congratulated
Pariente for his efforts and supported fully the measures to make the institution well-known in the community.[107] With the granting of an annual subsidy
by the Central Committee in September 1878, the new institution became a
part of the growing Alliance network.[108]

Pariente was a consummate politician and managed to establish good relations with the different elements within the Izmir community. His pedagogic
skills, common sense, and good judgment endeared him to the Central Committee which began to consider him not only as a director but as a partner. In
1884-85, he was entrusted with the very important mission of inspection of the
Alliance schools in Bulgaria, Turkey in Europe, and Istanbul.

The mission presented a very delicate task. Pariente had to visit the schools
and the communities and report on local conditions without alienating his
fellow school directors. He did acquit himself very well in this regard, with a
minimum of conflict and controversy. The Central Committee in Paris wanted
to know everything about the state of its institutions, the physical aspects of
the school buildings, the cleanliness of the students, the effectiveness of the
teaching, and the importance given to the various languages taught.[109] But
even more important, it wanted to find out the exact degree of influence
enjoyed by the schools, their relations with the notables, local Alliance committees, the rabbinate, and the *Talmudei Torah*.[110]

It is important to note that in none of the reports addressed by Pariente to
Paris is there any mention of conflict with the rabbinate. In Edirne he found
that relations were good, and he managed to confirm the annual subvention
for the school from the communal council.[111]

In Istanbul the situation was much more complicated and chaotic. The
acting Chief Rabbi, Mosheh Halevi, did not actively oppose the Alliance
establishments. He maintained cordial relations with the director of the
school of the Kuzguncuk quarter in which he lived. Nevertheless, even though
he expressed sympathy for the Alliance to Pariente,[112] his general stance
toward the organization was, on the whole, negative. For example he refused
to sign an appeal for funds prepared by the Regional Committee in Istanbul in
favor of the Alliance until it made him a written declaration promising to have
all the religious prescriptions observed at the schools.[113] His attitude illustrates the rather tense relations between the Alliance and most of the Istanbul
rabbinate in this period. The traditionalists did not prevent the schools from
operating, but they remained suspicious and aloof.

There were, of course, exceptions. As was seen above, the Chief Rabbi
Abraham Palacci of Izmir showed himself a friend of the Alliance on numerous occasions and approved of the teaching of foreign languages. The same
was true of the attitude of the spiritual leader of the Hasköy community in

Istanbul, Jacob Ben Yaesh, who was an important supporter of the schools in this most populous of the Jewish quarters of Istanbul.[114] But, by and large, the organization and the mass of the local rabbinate remained mutually suspicious and antagonistic. This was hardly surprising as the traditional rabbinate in the Levant and the Alliance had totally opposing world views. But the friction between the two sides never broke out into outright conflict, and the uneasy *modus vivendi* that characterized their relationship from the beginning was maintained throughout the existence of the schools.

At the time of Pariente's tour of inspection, the main problem for the Alliance in Istanbul continued to be an organizational one. It is quite clear from the instructions sent from Paris to Pariente that the Central Committee was dissatisfied with the activities of the Regional Committee of Istanbul. The latter was now headed by Salomon Fernandez, a wealthy *Franco* notable who he had been active in the introduction of European-style schools in Salonica in the 1860s. Between them, Salomon and his son Isaac Fernandez headed the Regional Committee from 1874 until World War I. They were important personalities in the capital and were particularly useful to the Alliance as intercessors on its behalf with both communal and governmental authorities.

Where they were not particularly effective, however, was in organizing and supervising the schools and the local committees of Istanbul. Salomon and Isaac Fernandez were busy individuals who could not be expected to take an active part in the day-to-day affairs of the Alliance institutions. Even though the Regional Committee was theoretically composed of many members (the number was never fixed), the notables elected to it by the Alliance membership in Istanbul rarely took part in its deliberations. In actual fact, for much of its existence in the last quarter of the nineteenth and the first decade of the twentieth centuries, the Regional Committee was not much of an organization. The president was the committee. Félix Bloch became the secretary in 1874 when he moved to Istanbul to be the director of the Camondo school in Hasköy, an institution which remained independent of the Alliance until its closure in 1890, and he acted intermittently as the inspector of the Istanbul Alliance schools. But since he was employed as a full-time director, he could not devote himself thoroughly to the task. In the words of the Secretary General in Paris in 1885, "the Regional Committee does not exist, even though it has been renewed recently and has promised to work."[115]

The chaotic nature of the Jewish community in Istanbul reproduced itself in the Alliance institutions. Unlike the situation that prevailed in the provinces, the teachers did not enjoy much prestige and were eclipsed in the capital by richer Westernized notables. Many of the committees, especially the ones in Galata overseeing the running of the three Alliance institutions in the quarter, maintained a degree of independence that was displeasing to Paris, as they intervened too much in the work of the directors.[116] The latter were often divided among themselves, intriguing against each other and against the Regional Committee and its secretary.[117]

There was not much that Pariente could do but report what he saw. Félix

Bloch had been seriously offended by the sending of an outside inspector,[118] and he had to tread carefully, always appearing to act, in the Central Committee's designation, as the "auxiliary" of the Regional Committee,[119] since the Alliance did not want to alienate Salomon Fernandez because of his stature in the capital. Pariente wrote long reports on each school, pointing out the strengths and the shortcomings of each institution in matters of pedagogy, finances, and relations with the local committees. His major recommendation for Istanbul was the constitution of a "Committee of Schools" for the whole city to oversee and coordinate the Alliance establishments.[120]

The Alliance did not act upon the recommendation. It was not clear how the school committee would differ from the Regional Committee, and it was convinced that the latter would never permit a rival committee on its turf.[121] The tone struck by the Alliance on the matter was uncharacteristically pessimistic: "Our experience shows that there is (almost) no one in Constantinople who wants to occupy himself seriously with anything, or that there are obstacles in front of those who want to devote themselves to the public interest."[122]

The Central Committee's judgment on the last point proved to be correct. Istanbul remained a trouble spot for a long time. The problem that hampered its efforts was not so much opposition as organizational stalemate. The friction between school committees, the Regional Committee, and the directors led to a great waste of resources and dogged the activities of the Alliance institutions throughout their existence.

The divisions within Turkish Jewish communities and the crises that erupted with great regularity could have seriously affected the functioning of the Alliance establishments. This is illustrated well by the communal conflicts that occurred in Izmir during Pariente's stay there.

The Izmir community was an unusually turbulent one. Friction between the rich and the poor, the Jewish guilds, the communal institutions, and the communal council were all exacerbated by mass indigence.[123] According to the report drawn by Cazès in 1873, 1000 out of the approximately 3500 Jewish families of Izmir lived on public charity,[124] and begging was widespread.[125] The various charitable societies that had been set up to combat the problem inevitably ended up by quarrelling with each other. As the Alliance became a force in the Turkish Jewish communities, it was also drawn in to settle these conflicts. In Izmir, this happened first in 1879, when Emmanuel Veneziani, now the director of the Camondo bank in Istanbul and the vice-president of the Regional Committee, came into the city as a delegate of the Alliance and reconciled the feuding parties whose quarrel was threatening to endanger the finances of the school. Some leaders had precipitated the problem by attempting to reform taxation by abolishing the levy on kosher meat, the *gabela,* an initiative which created a furor in the community. This was the principal source of income of the communal council, direct taxation having become impossible to implement. If the income from the *gabela* dried up, all subsidies to schools and other institutions would have to be cut. Veneziani restored peace. The *gabela* was maintained and a new committee was created to oversee its collection and the distribution of funds to the various communal societies.[126]

A similar crisis occurred in 1887–88 that once again threatened the communal subsidy to the Alliance institutions. It began when Pariente dismissed a rabbi who was one of the Hebrew teachers at the school for boys. Powerful friends of the rabbi in the communal council protested, insisting on his reinstatement and on his teaching a special class on the ritual slaughter of animals in the Alliance school.[127] This was met by a categoric refusal by Pariente. The communal council appealed to the Central Committee in Paris which, predictably, sided with Pariente.[128] This alienated the council, which cut the subsidy to the school, and created a rival institution, the *Keter Torah* (crown of Torah) school where instruction would be in Hebrew and Turkish.[129] The Chief Rabbi Abraham Palacci attempted to reconcile the two parties but did not succeed.[130]

In the meantime, Pariente had begun to have problems with a prominent member of his school committee, Elia Ganon, who wanted it to have a more direct say in the running of the school. Ganon appeared to have scored a major coup when he obtained a promise from Baron de Hirsch during a visit by the philanthropist to Istanbul of a donation of 50,000 francs for schools to be founded in Asia Minor. Pariente was furious upon hearing the news.[131] Hirsch had donated important funds for the new Alliance school buildings in Izmir in 1881 and regularly contributed to charitable causes. But his donations had always been channeled through the Alliance. Pariente complained about the sort of indiscriminate use that Ganon could put the money to, and the Central Committee effectively quashed the promise by intervening with Hirsch when he returned to Paris.[132]

This episode illustrates well the tensions between school committees and the directors over their prerogatives. Even though the Alliance wanted to rely on the former for local support, more often than not the relationship proved to be a stormy one. Many of the notables who formed part of these organizations were directly involved in power struggles within the communities, and dragged the schools into the fray. In time the Alliance itself became convinced that the committees were more trouble than they were worth.[133]

In the meantime a new conflict erupted in the Izmir community, again on the question of the *gabela*. Many opponents of the reigning communal council tried to bring it down by undermining the revenues that came from the meat tax. An Ashkenazi butcher began to sell kosher meat without paying the proper dues,[134] and eventually some Sephardic ritual slaughterers were brought from outside Izmir for the same purpose. Recriminations flowed from both sides, the activities of all communal institutions ground to a halt, and the Turkish authorities were forced to intervene.

The Alliance was appalled at these developments, and even though the communal council had recently shown itself unfriendly, it did not approve of the suppression of the *gabela*,[135] as it realized that no Jewish community in the Levant could survive institutionally without this principal source of revenue.[136] Isidore Loeb, the Secretary-General of the organization, came to Izmir at the end of 1888, and like Veneziani a decade earlier, managed to reconcile the two parties.[137] The *gabela* was maintained, and the subsidy to the Alliance school was renewed.[138] Loeb thought that the *Keter Torah* school could render good services to a community where there were so many school-age children and so few schools,[139] but the *Keter Torah* did not survive for long. It closed its doors in 1892.[140]

In Izmir, as elsewhere, the Alliance schools always found themselves in the midst of such conflicts. The moment they received any subsidy from local sources, they became implicated in the quarrels over power in the communities, which invariably revolved around revenues and finances.

Pariente's stay in Izmir saw a phenomenal increase of involvement with the Alliance of the Jewish communities of Asia Minor and the Aegean. In the late 1870s, the organization began to expand its network to cover the smaller communities. Cazès had already indicated in 1875 that these wanted to emulate Izmir and found new schools.[141] Çanakkale (Dardanelles) became the first such community outside a major Jewish center to realize this goal by establishing an Alliance school in 1878. Pariente was particularly active in propagandizing in favor of the organization, and communities such as those of Turgutlu (Kassaba), Bergama (Pergamon), Aydın, Milas (Melasso), and Chios had created Alliance local committees by 1879.[142] He made frequent trips to these communities and reported extensively on their lives, customs, mores, and the state of their educational institutions.[143] His visit to Bursa during his tour of inspection of 1884–85 opened the way for the foundation of the local Alliance school, and he closely supervised the state of Jewish educational establishments in Chios and Rhodes, which would both eventually establish Alliance schools.[144]

The institutions founded in the major Jewish centers gradually opened up their hinterlands to the work of the organization, and the school directors in these cities played an important role in this development. Salonica influenced the Jewish communities of Macedonia; Edirne, those of Thrace and Eastern Rumelia; and Izmir, those of Asia Minor and the islands of the Aegean. By the early 1890s, much of the school network of the Alliance in the Judeo-Spanish heartland of the Ottoman Empire was already in place.

Pariente was one of those school directors who did not limit himself to the tasks of pedagogy, but became a public personality, an important member of the Jewish elite. He maintained close relations with the Europeans living in the city and with the Jewish notables of the community. By the time Pariente left in 1893, the Alliance was no longer perceived as a radical force intruding from the outside but as an integral part of Jewish communal existence.

In conclusion, one element emerges as striking in the saga of the Alliance in Turkey, the relative weakness of opposition from the traditional quarters. No doubt there was considerable mistrust and opposition, yet it was not strong enough to pose a serious threat. The very foundation of the schools was a symptom of the declining power of the more conservative groups in Turkish

Jewry. The struggle between the reformers and the traditionalists had occurred *before* the arrival of the Alliance, in the 1860s. There was going to be no repetition of the ban put on Camondo in 1862. The resolution of the crisis of 1862–64 with the new statutes for the internal religious administration of the Jewish *millet* had sent a clear signal that the Ottoman state would, when forced to act, come down on the side of the reformers. All the major communal conflicts over reforms had been settled before the establishment of the Alliance schools. The latter did not precipitate conflict. On the contrary, the neutralization of opposition beforehand made possible their foundation in the first place.

In the light of this trend, the traditional image of the early years of the schools, years full of fierce battles against "obscurantists" and "fanatics," has to be considerably modified in the Turkish case. The ground had been well prepared before the arrival of the Alliance. Friction between the schools and the traditionalists continued during the following decades. Nevertheless, opposition had been rendered powerless. In Turkey, the existence of the Alliance institutions was never seriously challenged from this direction.

There were sufficient numbers of local supporters to render these establishments viable. These, mainly *Francos* and other notables as well as *maskilim* favorably disposed toward European-style schools, had all been involved in the conflicts of the 1860s and were instrumental in inviting the Alliance to Turkey. The organization relied on the active support of these groups to establish its network.

The Alliance never founded a school without an invitation from the locality. But, moral support was not enough. Financial help had to be forthcoming also. In fact, it was the mundane problem of financing which remained the greatest headache of all for the Alliance, not the opposition from the traditionalists based on ideological grounds. The communal councils could not be relied upon for regular funding, as their activity was erratic at best, and they had little money at their disposal. As a result, all the Alliance schools functioned as private institutions, relying on the support of the wealthier elements in the localities, on tuition fees from the students, and on subventions from Paris especially after the Hirsch bequest of 1873. In principle, the Central Committee wanted the schools to be financially self-sufficient. This was a hope never to be realized. The tug-of-war between Paris and the localities over money, begun in the foundation years, continued unabated throughout the existence of the Alliance institutions in Turkey.

It was a testimony to the increasing prestige of Western Jewry in general and the Alliance in particular that the organization found itself increasingly in the role of arbiter in many local conflicts. As an alternative locus of power, it could act to settle disputes and influence the internal political evolution of the community. Well established, bureaucratized administrative structures such as the French consistorial system were alien to the local traditions of the Jews in the lands of Islam, including those of the Jews of Turkey. The 1865 statutes could have led to a "consistorial" system but could not do so without the active support of the Ottoman state. The latter continued to prefer to deal with individuals rather than institutions as intermediaries with the Jewish community. Hence Mosheh Halevi was appointed only Acting Chief Rabbi and dispensed with communal councils during his long tenure of office, a situation that did not displease the Abdülhamid regime, which preferred not to have too many representative institutions among its subjects.

In the absence of any real administrative system for the Jews of the Empire, and in the ensuing instability of communal affairs, the Alliance schools were the only local institutions that had some longevity due to their support from the outside. The elite that had invited the organization and supported its activities could also at times drag the schools into communal conflicts. However, they usually managed to extricate themselves as a result of their independence. If the question of subsidies from local communities led to periodic crises, the fact that, in the final analysis, they remained private institutions also saved them from going under.

The Alliance took over an aspect of communal life, that of education, which had come increasingly under the control of the state in nineteenth-century Europe. The relative absence of the Ottoman state in this domain created the favorable ground for the Alliance's activities in Turkey. Weakly developed communal institutions offered little, if any, resistance and were slowly won over by the organization. The schools created a parallel network of power and influence to that of the community. Slowly but surely, they moved from the margins of Turkish Jewish life to the very center.

IV

EDUCATING TURKISH JEWRY

The kind of instruction provided in the Alliance schools has been examined in detail elsewhere,[1] and I will provide only a brief summary here. All these schools began as institutions of elementary education. In the first years, the directors exercised considerable freedom of action, and while always fulfilling the wishes of the Central Committee in Paris, could supervise the teaching in the manner they saw fit. This was changed in 1883–84 when the Central Committee fixed the school program. According to the new instructions sent to the teachers, there were to be four classes corresponding to the four years that the students were supposed to spend in the school.[2] In addition, there could be two additional classes for the young children which would constitute a kind of kindergarten.[3] The subjects taught consisted of religious instruction, Biblical history, Hebrew (reading, writing, translating and grammar), written and spoken French, arithmetic, geography, history, the rudiments of physical and natural sciences, French calligraphy, and a "useful language." The girls' schools would also teach needlework.[4] The language of instruction in all the schools was French.

The program was expanded over the years, and often the four year school became a seven and eight year one, reaching the level of a junior high school, with subdivisions in each class. The age of the students to be admitted was fixed as between six and fifteen in the new instructions of 1903.[5] As in the system employed by most schools in France, the subjects were covered in a concentric fashion. All the materials were studied in one year and then studied in greater depth and detail in each following year.[6]

The Teachers and the Moralizing Impulse

The program of "regeneration" set the parameters of the educational activities of the Alliance. Moralizing and modernizing constituted the two poles on which rested its educational work. This is illustrated well by a circular of 1896:

> What was, what is the aim of the Alliance . . . ? In the first place, to cast a ray of the civilization of the Occident into the communities *(milieus)* degenerated by centuries of oppression and ignorance; next, to help them find jobs more

secure and less disparaged than peddling by providing the children with the rudiments of an elementary and rational instruction; finally, by opening the spirits to Western ideas, to destroy certain outdated prejudices and superstitions which were paralysing the activities and development of the communities. But in addition, the action of the Alliance principally aimed to give to the Jewish youth, and subsequently, to the Jewish population as a whole, a moral education rather than a technical instruction, to create rather than semi-scholars tolerant good men, attached to their duties as citizens and as Jews, devoted to the public good, and to their brothers, knowing how to reconcile the needs of the modern world with the respect of ancient traditions.[7]

This text is almost paradigmatic for the educational ideology of the Alliance. "Regeneration," progressing through Westernization, would reform "degenerate" populations that would not only acquire the skills needed to obtain secure occupations but would form a moral, upright citizenry who were also good Jews.

Moralizing was deemed the most important of the tasks entrusted to the schools. It constituted the essence of the Alliance's "civilizing mission." Neither the Central Committee nor the teachers hesitated to liken their work to that of missionaries. For Narcisse Leven, then the Secretary General of the Central Committee, the teachers were the "missionaries of progress."[8] The teachers also frequently referred to themselves as "secular missionaries."[9] The mission of the Alliance was further elaborated upon in the instructions of 1903:

The object of elementary schools, especially in the Orient, is not so much instruction as education. Education consists of both intellectual and moral education. Teaching as a whole should have a moral content, must aim by secret ways and continuous but invisible efforts to elevate the soul and the spirit of the child . . . one of the principal aims of the teacher will be to especially combat the bad habits more or less widespread among Oriental populations, egotism, arrogance, exaggerated expressions of feelings, insipidity, blind respect of force and fortune and the violence of petty passions. The virtues that one seeks to inspire in the child are love of country, love of all men, love and respect of parents, love of truth . . . dignity of character, nobility of sentiment, love of the public good, the spirit of solidarity . . . love of work.[10]

The perception of the local population by the Alliance had been shaped by the negative image of the Jews of the East that prevailed in Western Jewish public opinion in the middle of the nineteenth century. It was not to change. Hence, the moralizing aspect of education was given pride of place, beyond any other concern with instruction.

Most Alliance teachers railed constantly against the "vices" of the local population. For Nissim Behar, later to play an important role in the revival of Hebrew in Palestine, the Jews of Balat, one of the large Jewish quarters of Istanbul, were in 1875 "irascible, loud, self-seeking, none too scrupulous about the means of earning money, enemies of all work."[11] According to another teacher writing about the same community twenty-five years later, the Jews of Istanbul were not immoral, since to be immoral one had to be able to appreciate the difference between good and bad. Rather they were "amoral." This was not surprising, as four hundred years of "slavery" had destroyed all their better instincts, leaving only "guile and lying, all of them vices of slave peoples."[12] In Bursa they were keeping "with a jealous intransigence their prejudices and superstitions belonging to another age. Profound ignorance, dirt, vulgarity in language and manners, total absence of dignity, reluctance to do any hard work, here are what characterize the majority of our coreligionists of Bursa."[13] "Nonchalance and indolence [were] characteristics of this country of the Orient," according to a teacher writing from Aydın in 1902.[14]

What gives the negative perception an added twist in the case of the Alliance teachers is that they themselves were of "Oriental" origin. Initially, the organization had recruited its teachers from the students of the Rabbinical Seminary in Paris, and most were Alsatian in origin.[15] Difficulties of finding a suitable personnel led to the adoption of a new course of action. In 1867 the Alliance founded in Paris a teacher-training school, the *Ecole Normale Israélite Orientale* (ENIO). From this period on, the organization recruited teachers only from the graduates of its own schools in the Middle East and North Africa. The best students passed an examination at the end of their studies and were sent to Paris to the Alliance *Ecole Normale* to be trained as teachers. Upon the completion of their training they were sent to direct and teach in the Alliance schools around the Mediterranean basin.

Unfortunately, information about the kind of education provided in Paris to these students is extremely scant, as the archives are not available. Initially, the ENIO had a three year program, similar to the French normal schools. At the end of this period of study, the students had to pass the French national examination for the *brevet élémentaire,* which was the diploma that all French elementary school teachers had to obtain before they could teach. In addition, they had to study Hebrew, Jewish history, the Bible, and other Jewish subjects. A further year of study was added in 1876, and it became compulsory to take the *brevet supérieur* exam established as a requirement by the French educational system for all *instituteurs.* Girls followed the same program, though their study of Hebrew was optional, and they attended classes at two Parisian educational establishments for Jewish girls, the Institut Bischoffsheim and the boarding school of Madame Isaac.[16]

It is important to note in retrospect that a large section of the Alliance teaching body came from the Judeo-Spanish communities of the Ottoman Empire. Of the 403 ENIO male and female graduates who became teachers between 1869 and 1925 (on whom there is available biographical information), the area corresponding to the present-day borders of Turkey, Greece and Bulgaria alone provided close to 60 percent of the total. This percentage increases to close to 70 percent in the case of the female teachers. Indeed, the communities within the borders of present-day Turkey alone supplied 34.8

percent of the male and 48 percent of the female teachers of the organization. These figures offer a great contrast to the 10.1 percent represented by Morocco, the one country in which the Alliance was present the longest.[17]

As many teachers mentioned, those students whose mother tongue was Judeo-Spanish found it much easier to learn French, a kindred Romance language, than those who spoke Judeo-Arabic or Judeo-Persian at home. The mastery of French facilitated considerably the admission to the ENIO. Spanish Morocco, with the major communities of Tangier and Tetuan, is a case in point. Twenty-two of the thirty-one male teachers and all nine women teachers from Morocco came from this region whose Jewish communities also spoke Judeo-Spanish.[18] Furthermore, the Judeo-Spanish cultural area, part of an Empire which was increasingly opening up to the West in the nineteenth century, was more receptive to the process of Westernization. These two factors contributed to the predominance of the Judeo-Spanish speaking element among the Alliance teaching corps.

A career with the Alliance represented considerable upward social mobility to those who opted for it. Mostly coming from poor backgrounds, the teacher could aspire to the position of notable in the community to which he or she was sent. His or her association with an organization invested with all the prestige of the West transformed the teacher into an important personality, a figure that would henceforth, especially in the smaller communities, take his or her place among the ruling elite.

In the case of the women, the act of becoming a teacher of the Alliance was nothing short of revolutionary. Coming from profoundly patriarchal societies where their place was rigidly controlled by convention, a career with the Alliance was perhaps the only one available to young Jewish women from the Middle East and North Africa who wanted to lead an independent existence. What is surprising and hard to explain is the acquiescence of parents in the Levant of the nineteenth century to the departure of their female offspring at the age of fourteen to Paris for training and then their appointment to distant posts in alien lands. The existence of hundreds of such cases points to the need for further study of the changes in the position of Jewish women in the Middle East in the past century.

The graduates of the Alliance teacher-training institutions in Paris embarked upon their careers in the Middle East and North Africa fully imbued with the ideology of the Alliance. They all had the zeal of neophytes. For the teachers, the West represented the absolute good and Westernization the universal panacea for all the ills that plagued the Jewish communities of the East. Their sometimes violent critique of traditional Jewish societies in the East had all the bearings of a self-justificatory ardor to legitimate the path that they themselves had taken in rejecting the values of their own culture and society. As a group, they formed the first aggressively Westernized and Westernizing autochthonous elite within the Sephardic world.

Although there were differences between the teachers and the Alliance Central Committee over individual questions concerning curricular matters, mostly over details, the correspondence between them does not, with a few exceptions in the twentieth century, reveal any ideological divergence between the two. The teachers, like the Central Committee, believed firmly and fervently in their mission. As almost all of them repeated year after year, it was the school dispensing a Western education that was to constitute the principal agent of the "regeneration" of the Jews of the East.[19]

The cult of education dispensed by the Alliance was of course fuelled by the particular nature of the emancipation process of European Jewry in the nineteenth century. As discussed above, legal emancipation and the reforming of the Jews, their *education* into "modern civilization," were two sides of the same medallion for the elite of French and indeed of much of European Jewry. It is not surprising that this world view colored all aspects of the relationship between Western and Eastern Jewry and shaped the education in the Alliance schools.

It is also easy to place the Alliance in the fundamentally imperialist nexus between the West and the East. Indeed, the organization was very much the product of its time and place, and its negative vision of the Orient was one that was common in the Europe of the nineteenth century, which, in the flush of the material achievements accompanying the Industrial Revolution, was convinced of its moral superiority. The echoes of this Europe, and more specifically, of the French concern with a *mission civilisatrice* designed to spread French language and culture, are very much present in its variant espoused by the Alliance. The moralizing aims of the schools created by the French state in Algeria for the natives, designed to Westernize by instilling the virtues of "cleanliness, exactitude, obedience, politeness, sincerity, openness, probity, goodness" and to extirpate "Oriental vices" such as "hypocrisy,"[20] are identical to those adopted by the Alliance as seen by its circulars quoted above. The latter was quite open about its mission, "to integrate into Western civilization those groups of Jews which historical or political events had left outside."[21]

However, too much emphasis on the similarities between the imperialist discourse on the "natives" and that of the Alliance on Eastern Jews can also obscure larger general developments of which the organization was the expression in the Jewish world. For the moralizing and "civilizing" agenda adopted by both imperialism and the Alliance was nothing more than the extension of the fundamentally bourgeois attempt to transform and "civilize" lower classes and popular cultures in nineteenth-century Europe. The whole thrust of the educational system gradually put in place in France between 1815 and 1882 was the dissemination through the school of an officially sponsored culture aiming to replace traditional popular culture.[22] The *instituteur* of the Third Republic was, like the Alliance teacher in the East, the missionary of this "higher" bourgeois civilization.

Forming the "man" and the "citizen" had been the set goals for Republican education in France since the time of the French Revolution. The sensationalist view of human nature, popularized by Condillac and Rousseau, saw education as the panacea for all the ills of society, as education was taken to be the central formative agent in the making of the individual.[23] All educational reform in nineteenth-century France took this to be axiomatic, even under non-Republican regimes. Under the Orléanist monarchy, the Guizot education law of 1833 listed moral instruction for the making of the "man" as the first task of schools.[24] This was further emphasized by the Ferry education law of the early 1880s. In a letter sent to the primary teachers of France in 1883, Jules Ferry listed as all important the instruction of the students "in ethics and citizenship" and "in the first principles of morality."[25]

The leadership of the Alliance was deeply influenced by the liberal educational ethos. Leading pedagogues such as I. Carré and Ferdinand Buisson had taught at the ENIO in the early years of the establishment. The principle of concentric education adopted in the Alliance schools was identical to the system recommended in the règlement Gréard, which adopted it for all French primary schools in 1868.[26] Indeed the goal of making the "man" and the "citizen" was identical to that of the task of "regeneration."

The educational activities of the Alliance is best understood in a continuum that spans the attack upon all popular local cultures begun during the French Revolution by the Abbé Grégoire with his Rapport sur la necessité et les moyens d'anéantir les patois et d'universaliser l'usage de la langue française (1794),[27] and which reached its climax with the instituteur who punished his students for speaking patois under the Third Republic.[28] French Jews were one of the many groups in France such as Bretons and Provençals that encountered the process of "Gallicization" in the course of the nineteenth century. The Alliance, having deeply internalized the dominant metropolitan discourse on local cultures, spread the process beyond the borders of France.

Within this perspective, the moralizing impulse of the Alliance with its attack upon all the "vices" of local communities appears as a variant, in a Jewish context, of the larger work of moralization entrusted to the school in nineteenth-century France. The defects in local peasant populations earmarked for correction by the official program of lower primary schools in the France of the 1880s, such as "superstitions" and "prejudices," and the dissemination of positive virtues such as "personal dignity," "self-respect," and "modesty,"[29] are identical to those expressed in the Instructions générales of the Alliance. Ultimately, both imperialist pedagogy and that of the Alliance were variants of the larger mission civilisatrice undertaken by French schools first within the borders of metropolitan France.

The Alliance's mission was essentially a paternalist one. For the organization, the Oriental Jew was like a child and had to be educated away from his bad habits. Isidore Loeb, the secretary of the Central Committee from 1869 to 1892, and a distinguished Judaic scholar, considered that " . . . these Jews [were] children, thoughtless, light-minded, superficial."[30] For the school director in Hasköy, the local Jews were like children who sinned because of ignorance.[31] The personnel of the organization was itself subject to this paternalism. The teacher had to write to the Central Committee with the respect that was "due from him to his superiors."[32] He or she was under an obligation to continue his or her education by reading suitable books.[33] The teachers had to ask permission from the Central Committee to get married.[34] They could not become members of other organizations and were forbidden to write for periodicals and newspapers.[35] The secretary general in Paris marked the grammatical mistakes in the letters coming from the teachers and would often make observations on them by return post. The books ordered by the teachers for the school library were first screened by the Central Committee. In one such request, several books were deemed unsuitable by Isidore Loeb. Louis Blanc's interpretation of the French Revolution was wrong, George Sand's romanticism was "violent," and the Goncourt brothers' naturalism was "frenzied and unwholesome."[36] Centralization set severe limits on the freedom of action of the teachers.

The paternalism had its underpinnings in the fundamentally bourgeois outlook of the members of the Alliance Central Committee in Paris and echoed the accepted views of the time on the question of the poor. Many members of the Central Committee were involved with Jewish charity and educational organizations in Paris such as the *Société de patronage des apprentis et ouvriers israélites de Paris* and with the *Comité des écoles* of the Paris *Consistoire*.[37] The main task of these societies and committees was to organize the education of the Jewish poor and provide them with vocational training. The work involved both moral and practical instruction, with the goal of creating "honest workers, faithful Jews, and good Frenchmen."[38] This was, of course, the aim of the Alliance for Eastern Jewry, except that, instead of "good Frenchmen," the Eastern Jews theoretically had to become "good citizens" of their own countries. The Alliance's stance was influenced considerably by the experience of its leadership in the area of philanthropy and education in France, and it applied the same remedies to what it perceived were the same ills. Hence, as will become clear below, the vocational training system established by the organization throughout the Mediterranean basin was a copy of the one in existence for the Jewish poor in France.

As the perception of the indigenous poor and the Eastern Jew overlapped to a considerable extent, it was fitting that the students of the Alliance *Ecole Normale Israélite Orientale* were at first housed at the *Ecole de travail* in Paris, which had been founded in 1865 to provide vocational training for French Jews. Narcisse Leven organized evening courses there for Jewish workers.[39] In tandem with this, the girls being trained as Alliance teachers took courses at the Bischoffsheim trade school for girls.[40]

Since the primary aim of the Alliance was to transform the poor of the Eastern Jewish communities into productive, "useful" members of society, there was concern that the schools might be over-educating their students. This was a fear common to most pedagogues of the time, over-education being perceived as opening the way to social instability by the creation of *déclassé* individuals.[41] Hence, the Central Committee resisted for a long time the demands from the localities to institute additional classes in the schools in which accountancy and commerce would be taught. According to it, the school program was sufficient to impart the necessary skills to those who wanted to engage in commerce.[42] Many school directors were distressed that the Jewish poor did not like to engage in manual trades. For them, it was the rich who should be encouraged to continue with their education, but not the poor.[43] Isaac Fernandez, the head of the Regional Committee in Istanbul, shared the sentiment. According to him, the instruction given to "the poor class" in the schools was sufficient and he would have liked to see students and parents less interested in careers in commerce and more inclined toward manual trades.[44] Sylvain Bénédict, the inspector of the Alliance, was quite pleased to see that the level of studies in the Galata and Hasköy schools in Istanbul was higher than those of the communal and consistorial schools in Paris, but could not help but ask himself if all that much study was really necessary and relevant for these Jews.[45] As Isidore Loeb wrote to one director who was complaining that the students had not spent much time studying the great classics of French literature, the purpose of the Alliance was not to produce *"des petits cultivés."* These students did not need to know and were indeed incapable of appreciating the beauties of Lamartine and Victor Hugo.[46]

In its own self-perception, the core of the Alliance's work remained that of moral education. Many school directors took it upon themselves to extirpate "vices" such as smoking and drinking by making students sign certificates proclaiming that they would abstain from cigarettes and alcohol for the rest of their lives.[47] The virtues of solidarity and self-help were to be reinforced by the creation of mutual-aid and charity societies at school.[48]

In the moral economy of the Alliance, the education of girls and the "regeneration" of the Jewish woman of the East occupied a very important place. The woman, as wife and mother, was indispensable for the moral and material improvement of the situation of the Jews. According to Crémieux, if one wanted to have honorable and pure men, one had to raise the condition of women to "pay homage to their intelligence and to their domestic virtues."[49] Their "regeneration" was all the more important as it was the woman who as mother would transmit the most important values to the children. "The girls become women, the women become mothers; it is through the mother that the first principles are received, the first ideas which become imprinted in the heart of the child. . . . "[50]

For the teachers, the aim was clear: " . . . to form young women, enlightened, simple in taste, industrious housekeepers, intelligent, conscious of their role and [well-prepared] to bring up their children in a serious manner."[51] All the Oriental vices had to be extirpated and women emancipated from their ignorance. The woman of the Orient passed half the day in superficial work in the house and the other half in a demoralizing idleness, "drinking cup after cup of coffee and playing cards," and worse still, smoking cigarettes as much if not more than her husband.[52] Naturally she did not know how to educate her children.[53] Through the school, she would learn "good faith, simplicity, love of that which is truly good, beautiful and useful,"[54] which she would transmit to the next generation.

The ideal was that of the mother-educator of the European *bourgeoisie*. A circular of the Alliance put it succinctly: "The only aim one should pursue . . . is to form good mothers. . . . "[55] The Alliance's discourse on women again echoed the accepted notions by French pedagogues on the subject. Already Rousseau had given pride of place to the education of women as crucial for the education of men.[56] Victor Duruy stressed the importance of the education of the mothers because of their influence on their sons.[57] For the Third Republic, the stability of society rested upon the stability of the family which in returned rested upon the wife and the mother. As Jules Ferry put it in 1870 in language close to that of Crémieux mentioned above, "he who controls the woman controls everything, first because he controls the children, then because he controls the husband."[58]

In spite of the conservatism of the educational ideology of the Alliance when it came to women, in the local context its work of female education constituted a revolutionary development in the Middle East. Until the coming of the organization, there had been no place for girls in the traditional education system. Most received whatever instruction they had in the home. The Alliance introduced the very principle of female education, which then gradually became widely accepted as normative by the Sephardic communities. Even though the goal of the organization was a limited one of making of women good mothers and wives, it is incontrovertible that by opening the doors of its schools to girls, it liberated them from ignorance and opened new horizons to the female section of the population. It changed subtly the relationship between husbands and wives by approaching their cultural and intellectual perspectives. The Alliance was far from being "feminist." Nevertheless, what was conservative in Europe could become radical in the Middle East.

In conclusion, moralizing constituted the motor of the educational work of the Alliance. The aim of transforming the indigent and ignorant populations into a sober, industrious, and moral class of citizenry received perhaps its best expression in a missive sent by an Alliance director in Aydın to the Central Committee in 1906. Noting the progress in the "moral state" of the population, the director commented on the need for better housing for the Jews of the town, as European tastes and mores were spreading fast. Hence the need for better school buildings which would profoundly affect the Jewish population.

> The day [will come] when our schools will stand proudly in the middle of the fields, in the entrance of the town. That day will be seen, as if by magic, pretty little cottages emerging from the ground, clean and cheerful, surrounded by stylish little gardens. They will come to group themselves and nestle around our school buildings, like timid chicks around their mother.[59]

This rather lyrical rendition of the nineteenth-century bourgeois utopia for the lower classes captures exceptionally well the spirit of the Alliance's vision of transforming and "civilizing" the "backward" Jewish populations of the East.

Jewish Education

The Alliance meant to have Westernization go hand in hand with a real attachment to Judaism by the students. Indeed, it considered Judaism an eminently "moral" religion and an integral part of the education provided in the schools. Judaism was that

> . . . source of interior joy and energy which have enabled the Jews to live through centuries of persecution and an oppression without equal in history. The men who created the Alliance, as those who direct it now, wanted . . . to strengthen and purify the religious sentiment among the Jewish populations of the Orient and North Africa, to give to all students, and by them to their parents, the ideas of moral dignity, to make them attached to all that is good and noble, to Judaism, to its history and to its traditions.[60]

Religious instruction and the teaching of Hebrew occupied an important place in the curriculum of the schools. The classes in the boys' institutions had to study Hebrew from a minimum of five to a maximum of ten hours a week and receive one to two hours of religious instruction. The girls, on the other hand, did only two hours of Hebrew a week.[61] Hebrew was not taught as a living language (except by Nissim Behar in the Jerusalem school).[62] Its teaching was designed to make the student understand the Bible and the prayer book. In the ideal case of a student remaining in the school for seven years, he was to have studied all of the books of the Bible. Reflecting the views of European *maskilim,* the Alliance thought that the teaching of the Talmud did not belong to the elementary school. It saw all books other than the Bible as useless for the purposes of instruction in Hebrew.

Ideally, the program set out by the Alliance aimed to provide a good Jewish education. However, there were several factors that militated against the reaching of this goal. Perhaps the most important one identified by the Alliance was the fact that the teaching of Hebrew and religious instruction was left in the hands of local rabbis. This was both a political move, as it secured the cooperation of the local rabbinate, and a necessity. The Alliance teachers, though having a good command of Hebrew as a result of their studies in Paris, were not trained to teach the language and were too burdened by instruction of other subjects to devote much time to it.

There were some very good locally recruited teachers of Hebrew in some Alliance schools in Turkey.[63] Nevertheless, by and large, they had not been exposed to the modern methods of pedagogy which the teachers of French and other subjects had studied during their stay in Paris. The traditional method of teaching the language by rote was discontinued in the schools. The director was supposed to oversee the rational teaching of Hebrew grammar.[64] Still, the local teachers had not received modern training as to how to teach. The supervision of the director, reluctant to criticize because of the fear of alienating the local rabbinate, was not sufficient to coordinate Hebrew teaching on a serious basis.

The level of Hebrew instruction varied widely from place to place, from teacher to teacher. But, by and large, it does not appear to have been a favorite subject for the students.[65] It was compared negatively with French, which was taught according to the latest methods. The coexistence of two alternative systems of education in the same school with one receiving all the attention and the other relegated to the background did not prove beneficial to the teaching of Hebrew. The inspector of the Alliance as well as some teachers noted again and again that the language was badly taught in some Alliance schools, especially in places like the Galata quarter of Istanbul where European influence was paramount.[66] French eclipsed Hebrew.

Another important factor was the relative lack of interest in the subject shown by the Alliance teachers. The teaching corps was an aggressively Westernized and Westernizing elite and was bound to give more importance to those subjects in the school curriculum that validated its own *raison d'être*. The teachers did not attempt to intervene effectively in the rationalization of the teaching of Hebrew (Nissim Behar was again a notable exception in Jerusalem), and indeed the contempt they expressed for the local rabbinate and for their "superstition" contributed to the relative delegitimization of subjects such as Hebrew. It was all too common for the Alliance teachers to use the kind of language favored by Samuel Loupo, the director of the Edirne school, to describe the attitude of an opponent: "He belongs to an honorable family all of whose members have studied much Hebrew and Talmud and are hence led to like chicanery. . . ."[67]

To improve the level of Hebrew in the schools and to further its plans to "regenerate" Turkish Jewry, the Alliance tried to reform and Westernize the local Rabbinate. It thought that future Hebrew teachers for its schools could come from the new rabbinical elite. It began to subsidize in 1897 a rabbinical seminary in Edirne under the leadership of the noted *maskil,* Abraham Danon.[68] The seminary moved to Istanbul in 1899. Though the institution lasted until 1917, its influence proved to be minimal. Heavily dependent on the community's subventions, it became entangled in communal politics and was starved for funds. It failed to have any appreciable impact on the Turkish rabbinate.[69]

Occasionally, the Central Committee tried to brake some of the more extreme manifestations of secularization increasingly in evidence among the Turkish Jewish communities. It was well aware that the Westernizing zeal of some of its teachers surpassed the boundaries of what was acceptable. In an important circular dated June 1, 1896, it drew attention to the fact that many graduates of the Alliance schools "exhibited a scandalous disdain for the most respectable practices of religion."[70] This was mitigated by the fact that the youth which had not passed through its schools were also behaving the same way. However it was not enough that Alliance graduates were no worse than those of other schools. The Alliance wanted them to be better. It would be regrettable if the result of its work was the "extinguishing of faith in Jewish souls . . . , and those of our teachers who have not understood thus their duties have betrayed our thought or misinterpreted it badly."[71]

In a revealing note, the circular continued to point to some of the reasons why some teachers had not paid too much attention to Jewish matters. "Arriving in the midst of ignorant and superstitious populations," they had tried to obtain quick visible results, to combat ignorance with all their might and to instruct the children in languages such as French, to teach them useful subjects such as arithmetic. "But in many cases the teachers have lost sight of the fact that instruction is not enough, especially with children, that it is inefficacious—harmful even—when not combined with a strong moral discipline."[72] Religion was the most natural way of providing the latter.

There were several occasions when the rabbinate attempted to regularize and coordinate Jewish religious instruction in the Alliance schools,[73] but the lack of a real communal organization, especially in Istanbul, rendered impossible the implementation of any reform. The Central Committee itself tried in several instances to have Hebrew taught directly by its personnel,[74] but this proved to be impossible as the teachers were none too enthusiastic and the rabbinate objected. In the end, the system adopted at the beginning was continued, and the teaching of Hebrew and of religious instruction was left to the local rabbis.

In retrospect, it is clear that the Alliance erred seriously in not heeding the calls for the establishment of a teacher training school for Hebrew (this was done only in 1952 in Morocco),[75] calls such as the one made by Nissim Behar in 1909.[76] The essence of the Alliance's achievements in the domain of schooling in general was predicated upon the fact that it trained its own teachers and put into practice its own educational system which sidestepped the already existing one in the communities. Given the chaotic nature of the local communities, it is doubtful whether the Alliance institutions could have survived if they had not declared their independence from the beginning. Yet, paradoxically for an organization which criticized severely the traditional sectors of Jewish society, the sphere of Hebrew education and religious instruction was left in the hands of its traditional teachers, the rabbis. It could not, at that stage, compete with European style schooling.

Another contradiction lay in the fact that the organization did not treat Jewish education seriously in the schools for girls. These schools provided Hebrew and religious instruction for a maximum of two hours per week for each. The Alliance criticized traditional education for having ignored the girls, for not considering it important for them to learn anything more than the recitation of certain prayers. Yet when it opened its own schools, it reproduced the traditional stance by deemphasizing the Jewish instruction for girls. This is all the more striking in light of its view that it was the mother who as educator was directly responsible for the correct upbringing of the future generation and that the education of girls, the future mothers, was of decisive importance.

These paradoxes stemmed from the inherent contradictions in the ideology of the Alliance, from the unresolved tensions between its *Israélite* and *Universelle* components that it tried to straddle at the same time. Faced with traditional societies firmly rooted in the particularism of Jewish tradition, the teachers saw it as their first task to introduce to them those aspects of universalism which they interpreted as being coterminous with European civilization. This eclipsed the specifically Jewish dimension of education which was relegated to the background.

But the Alliance was increasingly disturbed by reports about the decline of Jewish religious practice in the societies in which its schools were operating and by the Zionist critique that not enough Hebrew was taught in its institutions. In 1908 it sent a delegation composed of Rabbi Israël Lévi of Paris and Dr. Nathan Porges of Berlin on a mission of inspection to the Middle East. The ensuing report defended vigorously the work of the Alliance. It deemed the education provided in its schools to be the one most suited to the needs of the locality.[77] It confirmed that the demand for French was as strong as ever and was in fact increasing. The report drew attention to the fact that the decline in the religious observance of Alliance graduates paralleled the wider development in the societies in which these graduates found themselves and that the responsibility could not be laid on the shoulders of the Alliance.[78] It found that Hebrew was taught adequately in most schools but confirmed that it could be substantially improved if good teachers of Hebrew could be found to replace old-style rabbis. It recommended that the latter be gradually phased out and that a larger place be given to the teaching of Hebrew at the Alliance teacher training school in Paris.[79]

The organization had already embarked upon a reform which it believed would strengthen the Jewish ties of its students with the introduction of Jewish history into the curriculum, a first in the history of Sephardic Jewry. In the school year 1892–93, it asked all the teachers to introduce post-Biblical Jewish history into their programs and to utilize as guides the works of Heinrich Graetz, Salomon Munk, and Theodore Reinach, the most important of the European Jewish historians.[80] Until then, only Biblical history had been taught as part of religious instruction, and general history was an integral part of the larger curriculum. By 1897, Jewish history was made "the pivot" of the teaching of all history. All topics had to be taught focusing on events which had affected the Jews directly.[81]

According to the Alliance circular, post-Biblical Jewish history was to be taught one to two hours every week in the upper two classes of the school. It had to be taught by an Alliance trained teacher, unlike religious instruction and the Bible, which was left in the hands of the rabbis. The program could be covered in two years and spanned the period from the destruction of the First Temple to the French Revolution. It ended, rather teleologically, but predictably, with the foundation of the Alliance Israélite Universelle.[82]

The teaching of Jewish history was to strengthen the Jewish ties of the student and to illustrate the ideology of emancipation that the Alliance wanted to transmit:

> We want the teachers to devote to Jewish history all their attention and zeal. Perhaps never before have Jews needed to know their past as much as now, the long and painful martyrdom of their ancestors and the frequent and bloody violence that marked their settlement in their different countries of adoption. How instructive is this history . . . it shows on the one hand that the same prejudices have always been nourished . . . and the same excesses committed against the Jews. On the other hand, one also sees in it how in the end human reason, the idea of tolerance and love always win out over hatred and superstition . . . Jews should force themselves, always remaining faithful to their glorious past and attached to their faith, to surpass their compatriots in loyalty, courage, honesty and patriotism. It is here that lies the moral of Jewish history.[83]

In the ideal world of the Alliance, the virtues enshrined in Judaism were the same that characterized the model modern citizen.

The organization left the field of religious instruction and Hebrew in the schools to the traditionalists. When it occupied itself with specifically Jewish topics, it was secular Jewish history to which it gave the overriding importance, a history which it saw as testifying to the ultimate victory of Jewish solidarity and emancipation. The main motivating force for the leaders of the Alliance was provided by a secular Jewish solidarity springing from a common "community of fate" shaped by history. In nineteenth-century France, this stance could be maintained together with a passionate belief in the benefits of emancipation and assimilation without any apparent contradiction. In areas where conditions were very different, the message of solidarity informed by the moral of Jewish history as taught in the schools could have different consequences. A polity such as the Ottoman Empire, where each religious and ethnic group remained distinct and separate and where Western-style emancipation remained in the realm of theory, was a radically different one than the society the Alliance was familiar with in the West. In this context, the ideas of solidarity and the "community of fate" transmitted by the organization had a deeper and different resonance for a rapidly secularizing Turkish Jewry than those aspects of its ideology which stressed legal emancipation and integration. The same A. H. Navon, the school director of Balat and future director of the *Ecole Normale Israélite Orientale,* who heaped abuse upon the local rabbinate and described the local Jews in language couched with deep contempt, could write in a very different vein in 1898 on the subject of the introduction of Jewish history. "Around our old race and forming as if a natural frame [to it] will come to be fixed [the study of] history and the hope

for better days. This is the origin of all these movements of national regeneration that we have been witness to in the last few years and . . . the reason of
the importance given to Jewish history in our schools."[84]

The step from the "regeneration" of the Jews to Jewish "national regeneration" was one that the Central Committee in Paris was not prepared to take.
But as will become clear, many a graduate of the Alliance schools in the very
different conditions that prevailed in the Levant took precisely this step as the
logical conclusion of the education they had received.

The Alliance School as the Emporium of Languages

The hostility shown by the Alliance toward the manifestations of Jewish popular culture was in full evidence in its perception of local Jewish languages. As
part of its "civilizing mission," it was determined to eradicate the usage of
Judeo-Spanish, the language which, by the nineteenth century, was the
mother-tongue of all the Jews of Turkey except for the small Ashkenazi community of Istanbul. The negative image of local languages and cultures in late
eighteenth century France, perhaps expressed best by the Abbé Grégoire's
*Rapport sur la necessité et les moyens d'anéantir le patois et d'universaliser la
langue française* of 1794,[85] was very influential throughout the nineteenth
century and had been internalized by the Franco-Jewish elite. The Alliance,
together with most European *maskilim,* shared the view of Grégoire that
Yiddish was an *"espèce d'argot,"* a *"jargon tudesco-hébraïco-rabbinique,"*[86] a
relic of the past that had to be discarded.

Similarly, for Félix Bloch, Yiddish was an "abominable Polish jargon,"[87] a
judgment that many Alliance teachers did not hesitate to make on their own
mother-tongue, Judeo-Spanish. For Navon, the Judeo-Spanish sentence was
"lame," the language "miserable" and "mean."[88] It was the tongue "of our
ancient persecutors" and had to be abandoned.[89] It is striking that this appears
to have been a sentiment that was shared by most of the leadership of Turkish
Jewry. Precisely at a time when there was an explosion in Judeo-Spanish
literary and journalistic activity,[90] the consensus of most Jewish public figures
expressing themselves through the Judeo-Spanish press and actively involved
in the Judeo-Spanish renaissance was that the language had to be abandoned.
It was considered anomalous, unsuited to the needs of modern civilization,
and almost unpatriotic.[91]

The Alliance did its best to undermine the language. By the early 1880s,
just like the *instituteur* in France who punished students who spoke *patois,*[92]
some of its teachers were already fining students if they used Judeo-Spanish in
the schools.[93] In 1884, the Central Committee formally banned its usage in all
its educational establishments.[94] It is doubtful whether this was ever really
implemented. As Hebrew and religious instruction were given by local rabbis
who used Judeo-Spanish as a teaching medium, its presence in the schools
continued. But by frowning upon it and discouraging its usage as much as

possible, the Alliance institutions contributed to its delegitimization in the eyes of the people. Nevertheless, the language survived for a long time. As one of the foes of Judeo-Spanish, Moïse Fresco, put it, French was like a "gala dress" while Judeo-Spanish was "the old, comfortable dressing gown."[95]

The question that remained on the agenda from the 1880s onward was the place to be given to Turkish in the school curriculum. According to the official view of the Alliance, a good knowledge of the language of the country was an absolute necessity if the Jews were to deserve their emancipation. It was a moral imperative for the Jews of Turkey to learn Turkish.[96] Furthermore, its knowledge was indispensable for social advancement, as many careers in the civil service would then become more open and accessible to the Jews. The Alliance had been shocked to see that it had been very difficult to find a Jewish leader of any stature who could speak enough Turkish to become a member of the Council of State in 1876 when the abortive first Turkish constitution was put briefly into effect.[97] For many an Alliance teacher, the example of the Armenians who had advanced in the Ottoman administration because of their intimate knowledge of Turkish was one that had to be emulated by the Jews.[98] The Central Committee inquired several times as to how to train Jews to become civil servants,[99] but no adequate means were found.

Turkish had been present in the Alliance schools from the beginning. It was taught for two hours per day in each class in the boys' schools, though initially not at all in those of the girls.[100] All the teachers agreed that it was taught badly. There were no teachers to be found who had been trained to teach the language properly,[101] a point mentioned again and again in the Alliance correspondence.[102] By 1887, it appeared that the organization was resigned to the fact that it was impossible to teach Turkish well in its schools.[103]

That there was a shortage of good teachers and no established method to teach Ottoman Turkish appears indisputable. The language deemed necessary to obtain posts in the Ottoman civil service was a highly stylized and complex hybrid of Turkish, Arabic, and Persian, and was inaccessible to the majority of the population. It was not the kind of language that could be taught adequately in an elementary school. Most Jews knew a minimal Turkish that was sufficient for day to day trade and commerce, but very few commanded the official language.

In addition to those who thought that the learning of Turkish was of vital importance, there were many Alliance teachers who remained convinced that it would be of limited benefit for the students. Jules Dalem, the director in Galata, writing in 1882 complained that Ottoman was more like a "hieroglyphic science" than a language. It had been taught in some Jewish schools for the past twenty-five years but had not yielded any results. The Ottoman authorities did not care whether it was taught or not.[104] For Moïse Fresco, the importance of Turkish was exaggerated, since very few students could possibly be interested in a career in the civil service, and Turkish was useful only for that purpose.[105] In fact, after a visit to Istanbul, the Secretary General of the Alliance, Isidore Loeb, himself became convinced that Turkish was of very limited use for the Jews of Turkey and suggested that it not be taught in the schools.[106]

These attitudes reflected the social reality of the Ottoman Empire where for centuries each religious and ethnic group had led a separate existence. The complex Ottoman social mosaic did not require a unitary language for all the inhabitants of the Empire. Unlike the Western nation-state, there was no national language, only the *lingua franca* of the ruling elite, Ottoman, which itself was substantially different from the language spoken by the Turkish masses.

This began to change only toward the end of the nineteenth century, both as a result of Westernization and the pressure on the state to stem the tide of the many nationalisms that threatened its very existence. Turkicization was adopted as state policy under the Young Turks. But already toward the end of the nineteenth century, the authorities began to put increasing emphasis on the control of the foreign schools and on the spread of Turkish among the non-Muslims of the Empire, as will become clear below.

The late 1880s and the 1890s saw the emergence of the language question for the Jews. The Chief Rabbinate transformed in 1887 a *Talmud Torah* in Istanbul into a school called *Şule-i Maarif,* where the language of instruction was Turkish.[107] Though the establishment functioned erratically, it survived and had 151 students in 1904.[108] The state passed a decree in 1894 making the teaching of some Turkish compulsory in all non-Muslim schools and began to send them Turkish teachers paid by the government.[109] The Jews and the Alliance could not remain insensitive to this development. The hours devoted to Turkish were increased in many schools.[110] The newspaper *El Tiempo,* under the editorship of David Fresco, was relentless in propagandizing for the spread of the use of Turkish among the Jews of Turkey.[111] The Chief Rabbinate created a commission to oversee the ways in which Turkish could be introduced into the *Talmudei Torah,* and many of these institutions began to teach a few hours of Turkish per week.[112] Some Jews publicized this development in the Turkish press in response to criticisms that Jews were not doing enough to learn Turkish.[113]

The Young Turk revolution of 1908, which abolished the last inequalities between Muslims and non-Muslims and which instituted universal military service, increased substantially the demands for more Turkish in the schools. All the Alliance teachers pointed out the new possibilities now open to the Jews in the civil service.[114] The Central Committee was quick to respond, and in a new circular, increased the hours of Turkish studied in each class.[115] There were by now better teachers of Turkish available, and the aim was to direct the best students to pursue the rest of their secondary education in government schools, a route which began to be taken by some graduates of the Alliance institutions.[116] Nevertheless, apart from the increase in the hours devoted to Turkish, the organization undertook no major changes in the curriculum. The state did not impose Turkish as the language of instruction in the schools of the *millets.*

The practical difficulties in teaching Turkish notwithstanding, and in spite of a genuine appreciation of Turkey's treatment of the Jews, the truth was that the Alliance never intended to give Turkish pride of place in its program. The Secretary General's reply to a teacher's observation that Turkish Jews had to be initiated into Turkish civilization is revealing in this context. "You speak of Turkish civilization. Have you reflected on the unconscious irony of this reflection?"[117]

Its ideology of emancipation which was predicated upon the transformation of the Jews into good citizens wherever they lived should have led the Alliance to adopt the language of the country as the language of instruction in its schools. However, in the Middle East, the organization was caught in a contradiction in the matter. The Alliance was, after all, a product of the triumphalist West in the age of imperialism. According to it, there was only one civilization and that was the Western, especially the French one. Within this perspective, Turkish culture had to evolve further before it could be considered "civilized." In the meantime, Turkish Jews could be "regenerated" only through French.

It was therefore natural that French would remain the medium of instruction in the Alliance schools. French was the civilizing language par excellence.[118] It was "the language destined to propagate far and wide the genius of the country which has done most for the liberty of conscience and whose most liberal tendencies [were] personified in the Alliance."[119] Hence French instruction formed the base of its educational system. Apart from the hours devoted to Hebrew, Turkish, and in some schools to one other European language, the rest of the subjects from natural sciences to geography and arithmetic were taught in French which the students had begun to learn from the moment of their arrival at school in the lowest grades.[120]

The popularity of the schools in the localities had less to do with moral benefits to be derived from them and more with practical considerations such as the chance to acquire French. By the last quarter of the nineteenth century, the latter had become the *lingua franca* of the Levant. The Ottoman state favored it above all other foreign languages and made it part of the curriculum of its premier educational establishments.[121] French schools, mostly missionary institutions, dotted the Eastern Mediterranean.[122] It was the language that was used in most of the trade and commerce transactions with the West. If the Jews were to advance up the social ladder, a knowledge of French was imperative.

The Alliance railed against the tendency of the local populations to think of its institutions as language schools.[123] Nevertheless, its more lofty aims of moralizing did not exclude a pragmatic approach to the education provided in its establishments. As one school director put it, "one [could] hardly be in harmony with these excellent maxims [about regeneration] when the stomach cries famine. . . ."[124] The Central Committee was aware that the instruction received in these establishments was likely to be the only one that the students would receive and tried as much as possible to provide them with some practical skills. It reminded its teachers again and again not to spend too much time on irrelevant subjects such as French history or ancient mythology. It was better to give the students some useful ideas about the production of wheat, cotton, or oil.[125] Many of the Alliance schools in the major centers began to establish in the late 1880s additional classes to study subjects such as accountancy.[126]

As German influence began to increase in Istanbul in the 1890s and trade with Germany became more and more important, there began to surface increasing demands for the teaching of German. French remained indispensable, but for competition in the marketplace, German was also becoming necessary.[127] The Alliance already subsidized the Goldschmidt school in Galata frequented by the Ashkenazim of the city. The program for this institution was different from the other Alliance establishments and the language of instruction was German. Faced with increased demand, the Central Committee introduced the subject in the 1890s to its major Istanbul schools.[128]

The Alliance was worried about the educational impact of the abundance of languages in its institutions. All its schools offered French, Hebrew, and Turkish. Rabbis used Judeo-Spanish during religious instruction and the teaching of Hebrew. In major centers such as Istanbul, German was also taught, and the Izmir school offered English.[129] Some teachers perceived the multiplicity of languages as bad, but nothing could be done to stop it. Commerce was the lifeline of these communities, and the schools would lose their prestige and popularity if they could not supply what was demanded by the local populations.[130]

The profusion of languages in its schools points to an important fact about the Alliance. The local populations were not its captive audience. Moralizing might be seen by the Alliance as crucial to its task of "regeneration." Nevertheless, it was not this aspect of its education that was important for the local populations. The people were first and foremost interested in improving their economic lot. The Alliance provided them with a service that they could not supply by themselves. By the second half of the nineteenth century, the old traditional educational system was in serious crisis in the midst of communal chaos and anarchy. The Turkish state had not yet established an educational infrastructure which the Jews could utilize. It was precisely the task of the Alliance to provide such an infrastructure which at the time, in the light of local and international Jewish and non-Jewish circumstances, was inevitably a French-oriented educational system.

But the instruction given in its institutions was not a carbon copy of the curriculum in France. The Alliance and its teachers were convinced of the superiority of French civilization. French textbooks were used in many of the classes. Nevertheless, with the profusion of languages and the Jewish subjects taught at school and with the extra classes that were added introducing subjects such as accountancy, their physiognomy was quite different from elementary or junior high schools in France. In fact, they had no counterparts in the metropolis. They evolved as a result of a continuous give and take between Paris and the locality.

It was only by being flexible and responding to the needs of the locality that the Alliance could achieve the tasks of moralizing and modernizing. The former was to be performed through the infusion of a moral content into all aspects of education. The latter entailed practical instruction, one that could be of immediate use to the local Jewish communities, which in effect meant the teaching of languages. Ultimately the schools reflected the social reality of the local setting which was not that of a nation-state but that of a declining multi-ethnic, semi-colonized Empire. In this context, except for idioms of religious import, such as Hebrew for the Jews, languages had not yet totally acquired the weight of national allegiance as in the West. There was as yet no one national medium to the exclusion of all others. Languages were perceived first and foremost as practical instruments of communication. Hence the Alliance school became inevitably an emporium of languages.

The Alliance School Network in the First Decade of the Twentieth Century

What percentage of the school age Jewish population did the Alliance reach? To answer this question, it is important to keep in mind the extraordinary development of its school network by the end of the nineteenth and the beginning of the twentieth centuries.

The smaller communities followed in the path of the larger ones in the establishment of the Alliance schools. The same considerations that determined the Central Committee's decision to found new schools in towns like Edirne, Istanbul, and Izmir also played an important role in this context. The organization had to be guaranteed some financial contributions from the locality, especially from local notables.[131]

There was, however, one major difference in the foundation process that set the small communities apart from the larger ones. Unlike the large Jewish centers which in the foundation years had had to communicate directly with Paris, the smaller ones, coming onto the scene much later, first appealed to the school directors in the larger Jewish communities. Alliance directors such as Samuel Loupo of Edirne and Shemtob Pariente of Izmir played an important role in this respect, assessing the situation in the localities and making recommendations to the Central Committee.

Most of the Alliance institutions in the smaller localities with Jewish populations of 1200 to 3000 people were established in the last decade of the nineteenth and the first decade of the twentieth century.[132] Many communities of Asia Minor came to have Alliance institutions of their own.[133] Indeed, this was the heyday of the Alliance in Turkey. By the time of the Balkan Wars of 1912–13, each Judeo-Spanish community in the Ottoman Empire with a population over 1000 had its Alliance schools, usually one for boys and one for girls, or had reformed its educational institutions under the supervision of the organization. In the large Jewish centers of Istanbul, Edirne, and Izmir, the number of students in the schools increased dramatically in the last decade of the nineteenth and the first decade of the twentieth centuries.

The figures in Table 1[134] show great variations from place to place. The 1908

TABLE 1
Number of Students in AIU Schools in the Major Jewish Communities of Turkey

	1879	1885	1891	1898	1908
Edirne					
boys	216	252	452	380	1106
girls	300	254	242	472	551
Istanbul					
Balat b.	180	142	272	309	359
Balat g.	—	137	295	340	352
Kuzguncuk b.	—	157	131	254	178
Kuzguncuk g.	—	—	—	213	201
Dağhamamı b.	75	106	120	—	—
Dağhamamı g.	—	64	126	—	—
Galata b.	135	119	151	215	235
Galata g.	—	169	292	415	671
" Goldschmidt	—	152	143	215	250
Hasköy b.	135	117	241	341	454
Hasköy g.	100	163	320	447	372
Ortaköy b.	—	80	120	—	269
Ortaköy g.	—	93	137	260	215
Izmir					
boys	140	216	283	332	312
girls	100	277	217	278	351
populaire	—	—	—	—	219

SOURCE: BAIU (1879–1908).

figure for the boys' school in Edirne, for example, reflects the fusion of the Alliance school with the *Talmud Torah* following the great fire of 1905 and is therefore exceptionally high. Internal migrations also affected the number of students. The Dağhamamı school for boys on the Asian side of Istanbul was closed in 1893,[135] as the Jews of that quarter were moving to other parts of the city. The school for girls of the same area was transferred in 1895 to the more populous adjacent Kuzguncuk. The latter community, once one of the richest of Istanbul, also began to decline by the 1890s, as the lure of the most Westernized part of the city, Galata, the business center, attracted the Jews from the outlying districts.

The relatively small number of students in the Alliance school for boys in Galata is explicable by the fact that there were many other Western schools, mostly missionary institutions, situated in this area, which continued to be frequented by Jews. The Ashkenazi community of Istanbul, the overwhelming majority of which lived in Galata, had a special Alliance establishment for boys of its own, the Goldschmidt school, built by a donation from Salomon Goldschmidt, the vice-president of the organization. On the other hand, the Alliance institution for girls of the same quarter was especially large, as it was frequented by both the Ashkenazim and the Sephardim of Galata.[136]

The schools of Hasköy and Balat reflected in their sizes the fact that they were situated in the most populous Jewish quarters of Istanbul, while Ortaköy, a much smaller Jewish community, had a smaller school. Nevertheless, in spite of variations, the general trend in all these establishments shows a substantial increase in the number of students in the 1890s. It was in this period that the Alliance became truly established in the Turkish Jewish communities.

By 1911, the last year before the Balkan wars, the Alliance network within the borders of present day Turkey included the following schools:

TABLE 2
The Alliance School Network in Turkey in 1911

Town	Jewish population	Total number of AIU students	percentage of school age pop. in AIU schools
Istanbul	65,000	4634	35
Izmir	35,000	984	14
Edirne	17,000	1704	50
Aydın	3700	351	47
Bursa	3500	287	41
Çanakkale	3000	343	57
Manisa	2100	334	79
Gelibolu	2000	209	52
Tire	2000	229	57
Tekirdağ	1500	174	14
Turgutlu	1200	135	56
Çorlu	1200	148	61
Kırklareli	1200	120	50
Bergama	1200	112	46
Total	139,600	9764	35

SOURCE: BAIU 36 (1911): 86–115. See note 137.

It is difficult to interpret the above data. The figures for the Jewish population in Table 2[137] are taken from the Alliance bulletins and are generally higher than the available documentation from Ottoman governmental sources seems to indicate.[138] Some of the discrepancy is explicable by the fact that the Ottoman figures do not include a breakdown for foreign citizens living within the boundaries of the Empire. Large numbers of Jews in the major centers had availed themselves of the opportunities provided by the capitulations and the "protection" system to acquire foreign citizenship. In Istanbul alone, there were 126,752 foreign citizens in 1899. The figure for the same group in the *vilayet* of Aydın, where the city of Izmir was situated, was 55,805.[139] It is reasonable to assume that a certain percentage of this group was made up of

Jews. Hence, the government figures for the Jews have to be revised upward, especially for the larger centers such as Istanbul and Izmir.

The Alliance figures are approximate ones. Nevertheless, by and large, they come reasonably close to the government figures if the above correction is taken into account. Thus, an attempt can be made to determine the percentage of the school-age Jewish population that the Alliance managed to reach. A circular of the organization in 1904 estimated that, in general, one-fifth of he Jewish population belonged to this age group.[140] The latter was defined by the Alliance as spanning the ages of six to fifteen.[141] Stanford Shaw, working with the government census of 1885, indicates that 10.05 percent of the Jewish population of Istanbul was between the ages of five and ten, and that 13 percent was between the ages of ten and fifteen.[142] Given the lack of birth records and the vagueness with which most of the citizens of the Empire treated the question of age, these figures, which do not include Jews holding foreign citizenship, cannot be taken as hard data but only as approximations. Nevertheless, they seem to tally with the Alliance estimate of 1904 and point to the very high birth rate among the Jews and to the rapid demographic growth seen in the community at the end of the nineteenth and the early twentieth centuries.

Given all these problems, and the lack of reliable statistical data, one can only discuss the general picture. If one assumes that the school-age cohort was 20 percent of the total Jewish population, it is clear that Edirne proved to be the exception for the Alliance in Turkey. It was the only large Jewish community where the organization reached a clear majority of the school-age population. The fusion with the *Talmud Torah* had brought most of the male Jewish pupils of the town into its school. The available data as shown in Table 2 suggests that the Alliance schools in the smaller communities had the same success. They often became the only institutions of Jewish education in the smaller locality, and most of the school-age children received their education there.

Istanbul and Izmir do not demonstrate the same pattern. Even if one amends the number of Jews in Izmir to about 25,000, as the government statistics indicate[143] (this excludes the Jews with foreign citizenship), only around 20 percent of the school age population would have been studying in Alliance schools there in 1911. The situation in Istanbul appears slightly better, with 35 percent of the school-age cohort receiving its elementary education in the Alliance establishments.

The figures for Istanbul and Izmir are not surprising. These cosmopolitan cities had a number of European schools, missionary or otherwise, which attracted large numbers of Jewish children. For example, in 1906 there were 490 Jewish students in English Protestant schools in the Hasköy quarter of Istanbul.[144] In 1908, for which statistics are available, 491 Jewish students in Istanbul were attending French schools subsidized by the French government. Of these, 245 were in secondary schools.[145] In 1912, French schools in Izmir had 166 Jewish children.[146]

It is unfortunately impossible to have a complete breakdown of the Jewish student body of Turkey according to type of institution frequented. One missing link is the number of Jews in Turkish schools. The available Ottoman statistics make a distinction between Muslims and non-Muslims in the educational data without any further specifications about the composition of the non-Muslim group.[147] Furthermore, a close analysis of the data makes it abundantly clear that it is not too reliable, as many Jewish schools whose existence is well attested by the Alliance archival documentation are missing in the official statistics which were supposed to list all the educational establishments in the Empire.[148]

On the whole, non-Muslims did not attend Turkish schools in large numbers.[149] In 1895, the only date for which statistics are available, 80 non-Muslims were to be found in state and Muslim elementary schools throughout the Empire, with a further 5106 attending state secondary establishments.[150] These numbers are dwarfed next to the 317,089 in the *millet* elementary schools, the 76,359 in the *millet rüşdiye* schools, and the 10,720 in the *millet idadi* schools.[151] Jewish sources, whether the Judeo-Spanish press or the correspondence of the Alliance teachers, all meticulous observers of the Jewish educational scene, make it quite clear that the number of Jews in Turkish schools of all levels was very low. For example, not a single graduate of the Alliance school for boys in Izmir in 1912 continued his education at a Turkish institution of secondary instruction.[152] The question of learning Turkish for the Jews was fuelled precisely by the lack of a real Jewish presence in Turkish establishments. Although the revolution of 1908 brought an increased Jewish attendance in the latter, especially in the secondary level, these schools provided a serious challenge neither to the Alliance institutions nor to the foreign establishments. Non-Muslim mass educational systems continued to attract the overwhelming majority of the non-Muslim students.

In the Jewish context, the *Talmudei Torah* continued to maintain an uneasy coexistence with the Alliance schools in the first decades of the organization's existence. Echoing European *maskilim*, the Alliance teachers were highly critical of the traditional *Talmudei Torah* and lambasted their unsanitary conditions, their "fossilized" teaching by rote, and their lack of opening to the outside world. At the beginning, the aim of the Alliance had been to take over the *Talmudei Torah,* to merge them outright with its own schools. However, this did not prove realistic, as the rabbinate was loath to give up control of these institutions. Instead, the organization turned its attention to instituting reforms in these establishments such as the teaching of French and the introduction of new topics like Jewish history and arithmetic.[153]

The 1890s proved to be a crucial decade in the implementation of these reforms. The growing popularity of the Alliance schools and of the teaching of French led to the weakening of the resistance of the rabbinate. The Chief Rabbis of the cities of Edirne and Izmir asked the organization to send instructors to teach French and other secular subjects in the communal *Talmudei Torah*.[154] These teachers reformed the curricula of the latter to resemble as much as possible those used in the Alliance establishments. In 1898, the Alliance reorganized the small *Talmudei Torah* of Izmir into one *populaire* school for the education of the poorest elements of the population.[155] The great fire of 1905 in Edirne, which destroyed a large part of the Jewish quarter of the town, including the Alliance institution for boys, led to the outright merger of the already reformed *Talmud Torah* with the Alliance school. The new establishment, with 1250 students, became the largest school in the network. With the merger, the traditional education system disappeared altogether in Edirne.[156]

The process of the transformation of the *Talmudei Torah* in Istanbul was more protracted and complicated, reflecting the communal anarchy in the city. However, during the twentieth century, most of these instutions also began to emulate the programs of the Alliance schools.[157]

The Alliance directly reached a minority, albeit a substantial minority, of the school-age Jewish population in Turkey, especially in the large centers. Traditional education, though eclipsed by the Alliance and altered under its influence, still maintained a foothold. However, although the *Talmudei Torah* had survived into the twentieth century, the largest and most significant of them had undergone major changes either through adopting the curriculum of the Alliance or through coming under the direct control of the organization.

The Alliance was particularly significant in the education of Jewish girls. The latter received no instruction in the traditional system. While they were absent in the *Talmudei Torah,* they represented more than half of the student population of the Alliance schools. The education of girls by the organization hence constituted a very important development for the Jewish communities of Turkey.

By World War I, the Alliance institutions had come a long way from their rather halting beginnings. The organization had come to dominate Jewish education, providing a standardized instruction for the masses in the overwhelming majority of the Turkish Jewish communities. Even in towns like Istanbul and Izmir where many Jewish children did not attend its institutions, it was responsible for the education of a substantial proportion of the school-age population. Having succeeded in taking over many of the communal *Talmudei Torah* or influenced them to copy its own programs, the Alliance had become the single most important force in the field of mass Jewish education. There were many Jewish children who attended non-Jewish schools. Many received no instuction whatsoever. But there remained few *Jewish* institutions of education which had not entered the Alliance network or had not been directly influenced by the education provided in its system.

Istanbul (Galata). A class from the Alliance school for boys, end of the nineteenth century. (Note: All photographs reproduced here are from the AAIU and are used with their permission.)

Istanbul (Galata). A class from the Alliance school for girls, end of the nineteenth century.

Izmir. The Alliance school for boys, gymnastics class, end of the nineteenth century.

Edirne. The Alliance school for boys, 1904.

Agricultural school *Or Yehudah,* 1910.

Alliance school, Aydın, 1914.

Çorlu. Orphans in the Alliance school, 1921.

Izmir. Alliance school for girls, exhibition of needlework done by students, June 1926.

V

THE ALLIANCE SCHOOLS AND JEWISH SOCIETY IN TURKEY

The Alliance was greatly concerned about the precarious economic condition of the overwhelming majority of Eastern Jewry. It soon realized that the educational work of the schools had to be complemented by other means to improve the lot of the masses.

Vocational Training

An important aspect of the eighteenth- and nineteenth-century *maskilic* critique of traditional Jewish societies, whether in the East or in the West, concerned the lopsided nature of Jewish social structure, with its lack of real "productive" trades and its concentration in petty trade and commerce. The Alliance fully shared this critique influenced by physiocratic economic theory and echoed by Dohm and Grégoire in the late eighteenth century. In fact, the transformation of Jewish social structure was one of the most important of the goals of the program of "regeneration" adopted by the Franco-Jewish elite in the first half of the nineteenth century.[1] The Alliance reproduced the project outside France and embarked upon an ambitious program of "productivization"[2] in areas where its schools were concentrated. The aim was to instill the love of manual labor and introduce new artisanal and agricultural trades to the Jews of the East in order to transform the socioeconomic profile of the Jewish communities.

Apprenticeship Programs for Boys

An Alliance vocational training system was first proposed in 1872 by David Cazès, when he was the director of the school of Volos. Cazès showed himself sensitive to the plight of the Jewish poor. The central problem facing the Jews of the East was, according to him, the deep economic misery in which they found themselves.[3] He was dissatisfied with the fact that once they left school the students continued to hold the same sort of jobs as their fathers and hence reproduced the same social ills by concentrating on unstable and precarious trades such as peddling. To change the situation, he suggested an apprenticeship system that would consist of placing the students as apprentices with artisan masters in town. The school director would oversee the work of these apprentices, visit them in their workshops, and continue their education by giving lessons to them before and after work.[4] Having received the consent of the Central Committee, he inaugurated the first Alliance apprenticeship project by placing eight students with artisans in Volos in 1872.[5] The same system was put into operation in Tangiers in 1873[6] and soon came to be part of the activities of the Alliance wherever it maintained a school.

The economic state of the Jewish masses in Turkey was dire indeed. David Cazès reported in 1873 that out of 3500 Jewish families in Izmir, 1000 were entirely destitute and survived through begging.[7] Misery had become "chronic" in Edirne, where there were "thousands of men without any regular means of subsistence: beggars, smugglers, porters, peddlers of fruit and vegetables. . . . "[8] As late as 1900, half of the parents of the 600 students in the Alliance school of Balat, in Istanbul, eked out a miserable livelihood. They were porters, day-laborers in workshops making cigarette papers, servants, window cleaners, rowers of boats on the Golden Horn, fishermen, etc. They earned 3 to 10 *kuruş* for a day's work of twelve to fourteen hours.[9] Something clearly had to be done to improve the lot of these Sephardic *Luftmenschen*.

For the Alliance, it was schools that were to play the central role in the "regeneration" of Jewish society as a whole. But their impact could be felt only in the long term, when their graduates would come into their own. The aim of the apprenticeship program was to yield direct results in the short term by imparting artisanal skills to a specific sector of Jewish society, the poor. Many members of the Central Committee, especially Narcisse Leven, the future president of the Alliance, were already involved in the vocational training of the Jewish poor in France through the work of the *Société de patronage des apprentis et ouvriers israélites de Paris* founded in 1853.[10] The apprenticeship system adopted by the Alliance was patterned after the one operated by this society. In line with the private philanthropic schemes adopted by the French bourgeoisie and the Church in the nineteenth century to train the poor in useful trades,[11] consistories and Jewish philanthropic societies were deeply involved with providing training in skilled manual trades to the Jewish poor.[12]

The apprenticeship system constituted for the Alliance "the indispensable logical continuation of the school."[13] The aim was to "train workers who can earn a living with manual labor and to remove the maximum number of young people from the practice of petty trade which is so unstable, so precarious and so little respected."[14]

Poor students of the school, preferably those who were fourteen to fifteen years old, were placed as apprentices with masters for three to four years. The director of the school or a committee composed of people from the locality oversaw the working of the system. The apprentices, and sometimes the employers, were given a monthly salary. The director withheld one-third or half of it, thus maintaining a sort of savings account to be used by the apprentice to buy the necessary tools to practice his trade at the end of the training period.[15]

The moral education of the apprentices was not forgotten. Alliance teachers gave them night and weekend courses on subjects such as Jewish history, accounting, arithmetic, geometry, and drawing. The moralizing so dear to the Alliance's heart was all the more important, as the apprentices were not in a school but were thrown among all the bad influences of the workplace. A. H. Navon summarized well this aspect of the Alliance's work in 1899:

> We must teach [the apprentices] a little reading, a little arithmetic, to make them, through examples taken from history, learn to love manual labor, labor which they hear denigrated all around them, to practice economy, sobriety, order, the principal virtues of the worker and to elevate . . . their soul above the moral state in which they grew up. This is how I understand our mission. . . .[16]

The aim was nothing less than the creation of a moral, upright, industrious Jewish artisanal class.

There had been some previous attempts among Turkish Jews to create an apprenticeship system to teach manual trades to the poor. In Istanbul, a society called *ha-Pe'ulah* (Work) was trying to apprentice orphans in 1867.[17] Also in the 1860s, a charity society had founded a trades school in Izmir which had folded because of a lack of funds.[18] With the coming of the Alliance, these societies left the field to the organization. Initially, they contributed some funds to the Alliance apprenticeship committee in Istanbul,[19] but soon faded from the scene. As in so many other fields, local effort was eclipsed by that of the Alliance.

The school director in Izmir alone supervised the Alliance apprenticeship organization in the city, in spite of promises of support from the community.[20] The situation in Edirne was different. There, Abraham Danon, a noted *maskil*, had been involved right from the beginning, preaching in favor of manual labor as early as 1878.[21] Danon deemed vocational training to be of the greatest import for the transformation of Jewish life. The society that he created in 1879, the *Dorshei ha-Haskalah* (Seekers of Enlightenment), took over the direction of the apprenticeship program of the Alliance school in Edirne and created a sub-society called *ha-Pe'ulah* (Work) to supervise it more closely.[22] Frictions between it and Samuel Loupo, the Alliance school director, led in 1897 to the takeover by Loupo of the apprenticeship program, since Abraham Danon was fully occupied with the Rabbinical Seminary.[23] From this date on, the program was directed exclusively by the director in Edirne.

Predictably, the situation in Istanbul was much more complicated. In 1878, local *Francos* such as Salomon Fernandez, Eliezer de Castro, and Leon Piperno, all members of the Alliance Regional Committee, had taken the apprenticeship program under their wing and had created an apprenticeship committee.[24] For a few years they had complete freedom over it, using the yearly Alliance subventions as they saw fit. Lack of concrete results led to the appointment of an Alliance teacher, a Mr. Hamouth, as the overseer of the program for all Istanbul.[25] In spite of frictions between him and the committee, Hamouth remained supervisor until 1895 and was instrumental in the creation of a joiner's-cabinetmaking workshop in Balat in 1889 for the training of apprentices.[26] After his departure from Istanbul, an Alliance director, usually either that of Balat or of the Hasköy schools, directed the apprenticeship organization of the city.

What was the result of the Alliance's vocational training schemes? The data collected at the turn of the century by the directors sheds important light on the question. This has been published and analysed elsewhere,[27] and only a brief summary will be given here.

In Edirne, 194 apprentices had participated in the Alliance program between 1878 and 1900. Forty were still apprentices at the time of the inquiry in 1900. Of the remaining 154, 21 had abandoned the program while still apprenticed, while 37 were not employed in the trades that they had been taught. The loss to the program was, then, in the range of 40 percent. Sixteen of the remaining were no longer in Edirne but were employed in the surrounding smaller communities. Hence only 80 Alliance-trained artisans remained in Edirne. Including this figure, in 1900 there were a total of 597 Jewish artisans in the town out of a total Jewish population of about 15,000.[28]

According to the statistics compiled by the Alliance school director, tailors constituted 20 percent of the total Jewish artisanate of Edirne, masons 10 percent, confectioners 9.3 percent, and tinsmiths 7.5 percent. If one adds to these the cheesemakers, tavernkeepers (the latter given the rather grand title of *restaurateur* by the director), and "distillers," put under the rubric of "artisan," it becomes quite clear that the majority of this class was made up of semi-skilled workers.

In contrast, even though one-fifth of the Alliance trained artisans were tailors and cobblers, the rest were all in highly skilled trades. The statistics indicate that the Alliance was responsible for the introduction of many such trades to the Jewish community. The only Jewish cabinetmakers, watchmakers, gilders, cartwrights, blacksmiths, joiners, coopers, typographers, mechanical metal forgers, and cutlers in Edirne were the products of the Alliance apprenticeship system.[29] These were entirely new trades for the Jews of the town.

In Izmir, by 1899, 40 percent of those who had begun the apprenticeship program had abandoned it before finishing. Of those who had finished, 95 percent pursued the trades taught to them, reflecting the greater opportunities available to skilled artisans in a large burgeoning port city as opposed to declining, land-locked Edirne. The number of fully trained artisans who were the products of the Alliance program was 119, forming almost one-eighth of the total of 893 Jewish artisans in Izmir. The total Jewish population was about 20–25,000.[30]

The skewed composition of this class in Izmir is very much in evidence in the statistics of 1899. More than half of it was composed of tailors, cobblers, and repairers of sacks. As in Edirne, semi-skilled trades predominated. The Alliance apprenticeship program contributed here too to the diversification of trades, with new skills introduced to the Jewish community for the first time. The only Jewish coopers, woodcarvers, plumbers, mechanics, coachbuilders, and bronze-smelters in Izmir had all gone through the Alliance apprenticeship program. Furthermore, the majority of the Jewish blacksmiths, typographers, metal-turners, carpetmakers, and photographers were also its products.[31]

Nevertheless, the results do not appear to have fulfilled the expectations of the Alliance. The apprenticeship programs did lead to the training of a certain number of Jewish skilled artisans, especially in new trades for the community. However, with a 40 to 50 percent drop-out rate out of a pool of apprentices that was not too large to begin with, the numbers trained by the programs were too limited to affect the profound transformation of the Jewish social structure so desired by the organization. In the end, each new Alliance-sponsored skilled trade was practiced by only one to four Jews in Edirne and Izmir. Furthermore, mistakes had been made in the earlier years and resources wasted by admitting semi-skilled trades, such as tailoring, to the apprenticeship system. The small nucleus of skilled artisans trained with the help of the Alliance was an important group in each of these communities. Nevertheless, their impact on Jewish social structure remained limited.

In Istanbul, the apprenticeship program appears to have functioned badly. In 1899, only 108 out of 325 who had attended it remained in their trades. The loss to the program was around 67 percent. Of the sixteen placed as apprentices with blacksmiths, only one was practicing the trade that he had learned. Only two out of fifteen apprentices in engraving, one out of nine in foundry work, two out of ten in bookbinding, and five out of twenty-one in carpetmaking were working in their trades.[32]

Unfortunately, the archives for Istanbul do not permit a comparison with the rest of the Jewish artisanate of the city. Nevertheless, given the very large number of the totally unskilled Jewish poor in Istanbul and the very small number of artisans trained with the help of the Alliance, it is not difficult to reach conclusions about the results of the apprenticeship organization there. Even though the latter had introduced some new skilled trades, its impact on the social structure of the Jews of Istanbul in general and on the Jewish artisan class of the city in particular appears negligible.

The Alliance set up inquiries at the turn of the century which revealed that there were serious problems with the apprenticeship programs in general. The results appeared all the more limited given the large sums of money spent on subsidizing the apprentices. In Izmir, the Alliance had spent 105,980 francs for this purpose by 1897.[33] Istanbul had cost it over 200,000 francs by 1899.[34] In 1900, the Central Committee asked the director of its trade school in Jerusalem, Albert Antébi,[35] to investigate the causes of the relative failure of its programs.

Antébi identified several factors. The apprentices preferred easy trades such as tailoring, which were oversubscribed and hence not very lucrative. They suffered from a lack of capital at the end of their apprenticeship period and could not set up shop, and they were in general cast adrift after they finished their training, with no further interest shown them by the Alliance. The fact that they would not work on Saturdays gave an unfair advantage to their competitors. They were badly taught by master artisans, often Christians, who did not want to create rivals. The high level of unemployment in Turkey and the backwardness of industry constituted an important hindrance to the spreading of skilled trades among the Jews.[36]

An elaborate report prepared by A. H. Navon, then the director of the Balat school and supervisor of the apprenticeship program in Istanbul, highlighted the same factors. Of all the Alliance teachers in Turkey, Navon was the one most concerned with the moralizing task of the organization, much to the approval of the Central Committee, who was to make him the director of the *Ecole Normale Israélite Orientale* in 1911. Here, too, his moralizing impulse was in evidence. According to him, the parents did not show good will and tried to push their children into easy trades along familiar paths. The "apathy," "skepticism," and "egotism" of the youth and their concern with short-term gain made them detest manual work. Moral education could not be developed properly in the apprenticeship program in Istanbul because of the squabbles between the man in charge of the program and the apprenticeship committee.[37]

Navon suggested a series of reforms to remedy the situation. The best students in the Alliance schools had to be encouraged to go into the apprenticeship scheme, with only those who had reached the upper two divisions of the schools to be admitted. A scale had to be prepared regulating the number of years required by each trade. The salaries to be paid to apprentices had to vary according to the value given to each trade by the Alliance. Special attention had to be given to finding good master artisans to train the apprentices, and if none were to be found in Turkey, they were to be brought from abroad. The experience in Istanbul had proven that the creation of special workshops for the apprentices was too costly and was a policy that should be abandoned. Most importantly, the moral education of the apprentices had to be given great emphasis by revitalizing the night courses.[38] Navon suggested sweeping changes in the curriculum of the Alliance schools to highlight the importance of manual labor. The school had to become the "antechamber of the workshop. . . ."[39]

Antébi approved the reforms suggested by Navon. He also stressed the need to recruit apprentices from the best students of the Alliance schools who had reached at least the upper two divisions and suggested that apprentices should not be encouraged to choose "easy trades."[40]

The section on the apprenticeship organizations in the *Instructions générales pour les professeurs* published in 1903, took note of some of these recommendations. However, it made no mention of the level of studies that the student had to have reached before being admitted to the program.[41] On the other hand, the *Instructions* made quite clear which trades were to be discouraged and which encouraged. There were to be no apprentices placed with tailors, cobblers, hatters, or silversmiths, trades which were practiced by too many Jews already. Hairdressing, confectionery, tinsmithing, and pharmacy were excluded from the list of subsidized trades, as these were not considered serious occupations. The trades most highly recommended were those of locksmith, coppersmith, farrier, blacksmith, cabinetmaker, carpetmaker, cartwright, mason, and saddler.[42] The Alliance emphasized the apprenticeship in highly skilled trades over all others.

The greater stress put on the apprenticeship system and the closer controls exercized over it by the school directors after the inquiry of 1900 improved the results. A report compiled in Edirne in 1912 reveals that of the eighty-six who had been apprenticed in the eight years between 1903 and 1911, twenty-one had abandoned the program before finishing.[43] The sixty-five artisans who were earning a living from the skills acquired through the program in this period included sixteen joiners, cabinetmakers, and turners, eight house-painters, three chestmakers, eight blacksmiths, six stovemakers-tinsmiths, nine metal casters, three mechanics, six cartwrights, three brushmakers, two carpenters, and three carpetmakers.[44] The implementation of the Alliance's desire for a greater emphasis on apprenticeship in skilled trades is again in evidence in the list. Nevertheless, echoing Antébi's claim in a report on Edirne in 1900,[45] the school director of the town pointed out that none of these artisans were great masters of their craft and more often than not produced mediocre work compared to their Greek, Armenian, and Turkish competitors.[46] Many of them just managed to earn a living from their trades.[47]

Comparable statistics for the post-1900 period are missing for Izmir and Istanbul. A list compiled in 1906 giving the results of the apprenticeship program in Izmir between 1896 and 1906[48] is of limited use, as it overlaps with the list composed in 1899 discussed above. Nevertheless, here too the evidence points to an increase in the number of apprentices in highly skilled trades and the phasing out of trades such as that of tailor and cobbler.

The only statistics that are available for Istanbul are the ones provided by Galanté in his history of the Jews of Istanbul.[49] Basing his work on the archives of the Alliance apprenticeship program in Istanbul, which are now lost, Galanté claims that it had trained 572 artisans by World War I. However, the figure does not indicate what percentage of these were actually practicing their trade. There is no reason to believe that the rate of loss to the program had diminished dramatically. As mentioned above, 325 of the 572 had been apprenticed before 1900, with only 108 remaining as artisans by that date. Given the trends of the apprenticeship programs as a whole, it would be reasonable to assume that this number had increased probably to about 250 by 1914.

Other towns such as Bursa, Aydın, Manisa, and Tekirdağ where there were Alliance schools also established apprenticeship programs. However, these were much smaller in scope than the ones in the large centers and the number of trades that could be taught was severely limited. The lack of statistics for these communities makes it impossible to analyze their rate of success. Judging the case of one community, that of Demotica, where some data is available, the programs were not very successful in the smaller centers.[50] The problems that plagued the larger communities did not spare the smaller ones where artisanal skills were in short supply to begin with.

Taking the apprenticeship programs in Istanbul, Edirne, and Izmir as a whole, it becomes quite clear that the Alliance's contribution to the creation of a Jewish skilled artisan class in Turkey yielded limited results. The results were not commensurate with the effort and fell far short of the aim of developing a Jewish artisanal class. The organization did contribute to the introduction of relatively new skilled trades to the Jews, trades involving metals and wood, which had gained importance at the time because of mass imports of finished products from the West. But it did not effect a profound transformation of the socioeconomic profile of the Jewish poor in Turkey.

Three factors played an important role in the relative failure of the apprenticeship program. The precarious economic situation of the Ottoman Empire, bankrupt and indebted to the West, did not create the positive local circumstances that would have allowed such an ambitious program to succeed. The whole area of handicrafts was marked by a deep decline in the nineteenth century, especially after the Anglo-Turkish commercial convention of 1838, which had led to the flooding of local markets by imported goods.[51] Artisanal trades did not constitute the most secure occupations in the Ottoman Empire.

The ethnic division of the marketplace also created serious problems. Local guilds, made up mostly of Greeks and Armenians, did not favor the teaching of artisanal skills to Jews and harassed those who took Jewish apprentices. Certain trades, such as tannery and saddle making, were not open to the Jews in Izmir.[52] On the other hand, tailoring in the capital was predominantly in the hands of Ashkenazi Jews.[53] The Alliance sometimes tried to find a solution to the problem by sidestepping the locality and sending students to the trade school it had established in Jerusalem, hoping that they would come back and practice their trade in their communities of origin. However the numbers involved were very small, and most chose to emigrate upon the completion of their studies, usually to the West.

But, most significantly, it proved impossible for the Alliance to convince sufficient number of students in its schools, and their parents, to favor the apprenticeship program. Most of those who entered it did so for the wages that the Alliance offered and left as soon as a better alternative was found. There was no real incentive to become an artisan, in spite of the glorification of manual labor taught to the students. The trades introduced were too new, their future too uncertain, to attract large numbers. Furthermore, there was no artisanal tradition, no artisanal culture among Turkish Jewry to provide legitimation and status to highly skilled manual labor.

In retrospect, it is clear that the Alliance made a mistake in limiting access to its vocational programs only to the students of its schools. The real *clientèle* of the Alliance for the apprenticeship program was outside, in the many hundreds of youths who for one reason or another did not attend its establishments, received only a very limited education elsewhere, and were entirely devoid of skills to gain a livelihood. The obsession with moralizing which was supposed to have prepared only the students of its schools for the life of a moral and industrious artisan, made the Alliance exclude those who, unexposed to its lofty message previously, were then considered unlikely to reap the benefits of a skilled trade.

These contradictions sprang from the fact that the Alliance never clearly defined the *practical* aims of its schools. Its moralizing rhetoric obscured close analysis of local circumstances. It obviously wanted the students of its schools to go on to earn a decent living and took for granted that the learning of French, arithmetic, and other practical subjects would achieve this goal. But it saw as its central task the transformation of the dress, custom, mores, and way of life and way of thought of the local populations through the Westernizing action of its establishments. The practical benefits to be derived from Westernization were left unclear. At the same time, it attempted to determine part of the outcome by grafting onto its school system an apprenticeship program informed by current European bourgeois notions about the means to be used to improve the state of the poor. The Alliance's views could not but reflect the central paradox of the dominant nineteenth-century European educational ideology which combined the belief that education opened all doors and then attempted to guide the poor through only rigidly defined passageways.

Vocational Training for Girls

A few years after the establishment of the apprenticeship program for boys, the Central Committee decided to institute workshops in many schools in which girls would be taught trades. Given the great importance with which the question of morality was treated by the Alliance, it was natural that it did not favor apprenticing girls in town where they could be exposed to "negative" influences. Instead, workshops teaching dressmaking, sewing, embroidery, laundering, ironing, and weaving were created at the schools where the director could exercise direct control. Only the students who were aged between twelve and fourteen and had been studying at the Alliance school were to be admitted to the program which was to last for three years.[54]

As in France, needlework had been part of the curriculum of the Alliance schools for girls from the beginning. The vocational training program sought to give the poorer girls a skill which they could eventually use to supplement their future husbands' earnings. The goal was defined, as always, in moralistic as well as practical terms:

> . . . primary instruction cannot alone assure for girls a livelihood, and given the habits of laziness and indolence of the Oriental woman, it was particularly

urgent to provide her with a trade which, by allowing her to contribute to the upkeep of her future household, will give her more authority within the family, and more confidence in herself.[55]

The first workshops for girls were established in Galata (Istanbul) in 1882,[56] and were followed by workshops in Edirne, Izmir, and other quarters of Istanbul from 1884. Between fifteen and thirty girls were admitted to each of these every year. However, it soon became clear that none of them was yielding the expected results. There was resistance to the specialized nature of the training provided, most parents insisting that their children learn only the sewing which could be useful at home.[57] The workshops in Edirne were difficult to manage and were reorganized in 1887.[58] The director of the Galata school attempted to transform the workshop into a sewing room for the school in general, an idea that was angrily rejected by the Central Committee, which insisted that it did not want to train amateurs but real professionals.[59]

By 1889, the Central Committee was complaining that none of the workshops was working well.[60] There was little improvement over the years. In 1899, only a very small number of women trained in the workshops were using their skills to earn a living in Hasköy, as there were too many dressmakers in the area.[61] In 1905, the workshops in the Balat schools were closed, as they had not given any appreciable results. The Central Committee decided that such an establishment could not succeed there.[62] Their results were none too brilliant in Izmir, according to a report of 1909.[63] In a frank letter to the director of the Edirne school in 1910, the Central Committee conceded defeat and instructed him not to create new workshops, as they had not proved to be successful in general.[64]

The lack of statistics comparable to the ones available for the apprenticeship program for boys makes it impossible to discuss with any precision the results of the vocational training of girls in Turkey. The general comments from the directors and the Central Committee referred to above make it amply clear that the outcome of the training fell far below expectations. The only thorough study of an Alliance school for girls,[65] that of Galata, corroborates this conclusion. The Alliance had somehow unrealistic expectations about the possibilities open to female labor in Turkey, even in the most Westernized areas such as Galata. Even the girls who could work stopped doing so once they were married. Those who wanted to work preferred to be employed as governesses, teachers, and secretaries, or as sales assistants in the European shops of the Galata quarter.[66] The school was far more effective than the workshops in providing the skills necessary for this kind of employment which was just beginning to attract Jewish girls.

The Alliance did not gauge correctly the social aspirations of the local population. The Jewish poor did not look favorably upon manual labor. It was not the workshops but the schools themselves which were seen by the local populations as a means of upward social mobility, of moving upward on the ladder of status. As the school director in Galata commented, "the Spanish

[Sephardic] mothers believe that once a young girl has attended a school, she can no longer become a laundress, an ironer, a maid, [or] a cook. . . ."[67] No amount of moralizing, of lauding the virtues of manual labor, could alter this attitude.

Agricultural Training

Agricultural training formed an important part of the Alliance's activities. It saw the return of the Jews to the land and to the practice of farming as an integral part of the work of "regeneration." This concern had prompted the Alliance to create the agricultural school of *Mikveh Yisrael* (hope of Israel) near Jaffa in Palestine in 1870,[68] where students were to learn the latest agricultural techniques and acquire all the skills necessary to become farmers. A few students from each Alliance school in the Middle East and North Africa were sent there every year to receive training together with students originating from Palestine.

The number of students at *Mikveh Yisrael* grew considerably with the onset of mass emigration from Russia at the end of the nineteenth century.[69] Agricultural training moved even higher up the agenda of the Alliance with the creation of the Jewish Colonization Association in 1891 by Baron Maurice de Hirsch, who wanted to direct the emigrants toward settlement on land in Argentina and elsewhere. The new organization shared the same president with the Alliance, Narcisse Leven, and closely coordinated its action with the older body.[70] It had now become imperative to train Jews in agriculture so that they could make a success of farming in the new areas that they settled. Apart from increasing the number of students in *Mikveh Yisrael* to improve the situation of the new arrivals in Palestine, the Alliance created a second agricultural school in Djedeida, in Tunisia in 1895.[71] The new institution was designed to give an impetus to the movement toward agriculture among the Jews of North Africa.

The Alliance also attempted to introduce agricultural training in Turkey. In 1887, some Russian Jewish refugees, seventeen families in all, had settled near Aydın in Asia Minor and had tried to engage in agriculture.[72] When they ran into difficulty, the Alliance had helped them financially but could not alleviate their distressed economic situation. By 1890, most of these settlers had left.[73] The episode highlighted the poor agricultural skills of the Jews. The school director of Izmir, Shemtob Pariente, had followed the fortunes of the settlers very closely. He wanted to direct some of the students of his school toward agriculture. Upon his initiative, the organization bought, with the financial help of Baron de Hirsch, a farm in Burnabat, near Izmir, in 1890.[74] A few students of the Alliance school in Izmir were sent there to be "apprentice farmers" under the direction of some graduates of *Mikveh Yisrael*. However, the experiment was short-lived. The land which had been bought proved to be of bad quality and was abandoned in 1895.[75]

But the Alliance had become convinced that a farm school modelled after

Djedeida in Tunisia would be beneficial in Turkey. In 1896, Jacques Bigart, the Secretary of the Alliance, authorized Gabriel Arié, the director of the Alliance school in Izmir, to explore the possibilities of buying a farm in Asia Minor.[76] Upon his advice, the Jewish Colonization Association bought a farm of 2587 hectares near Aydın, where the few Russian Jewish settlers had remained, and transformed it into an agricultural school called *Or Yehudah* (the light of Judah) in 1900.[77]

As the institution was directed by the Jewish Colonization Association, its history does not fall within the scope of this study. Suffice it to say that the Alliance maintained a great interest in its fortunes and used its own personnel to inspect it periodically. In the first years, there were thirty to thirty-five students in the school, pursuing a program of study and practice lasting for three years.[78] One-third to one-half of the student body was recruited from Rumania, and the rest were Jews from Asia Minor.[79] By 1908, the number of students in the school had been increased to fifty.[80]

As far as Turkey was concerned, the Alliance's efforts to direct the interest of the local communities toward agriculture did not achieve much success. There is no evidence to suggest that the Turkish Jewish graduates of *Mikveh Yisrael,* Djedeida, or *Or Yehudah* engaged in agriculture in Turkey. The numbers who received agricultural training were too few, the local conditions were too difficult to make agriculture an attractive occupation. The Jews remained an overwhelmingly urban population, with trade and commerce constituting the means of livelihood for the majority.

The Social Impact of the Schools

Given the lack of precise statistics about the social structure of Turkish Jewry in the second half of the nineteenth and the first decades of the twentieth centuries, it is impossible to conduct a numerical analysis of the contribution of the Alliance schools to the changes it underwent. Nevertheless, the data to be found in the Alliance archives do suggest certain trends.

It is obvious that in the first decades, the Alliance establishments could reach only a small minority of the Jewish school-age population. The constituency increased considerably with the gradual expansion of the number of schools. As discussed previously, by 1911 the majority of the Jewish school-age population was attending Alliance institutions in Edirne and in all the smaller Jewish communities. In Istanbul and Izmir, on the other hand, success was more uncertain, with one-fifth to one-third of the school-age cohort enrolled in the schools. As the combined Jewish population of these two cities made up more than three-fourths of all Turkish Jewry, it becomes quite clear that at the height of its expansion, the Alliance reached a minority, albeit a substantial minority, of the total number of the school-age Jews of Turkey.

What was the social composition of the Alliance student body? This varied according to time and place and reflected the surrounding Jewish society.

There is no doubt that the economic situation of the majority of the families of the students was precarious at best. Nevertheless, there were some variations. Initially, the Galata schools in Istanbul, operating in the European quarter, attracted a relatively wealthier student body than those in Balat and Hasköy, and yielded better results too.[81] The Kuzguncuk area, on the Asian side of Istanbul, had traditionally had a more well-to-do Jewish population, a fact reflected in the statistics sent to Paris by the directors of its Alliance institutions. Of the families of the eighty-seven Jewish students (there were four Greeks and eight Armenians at the school) registered in the boys' school in 1896, fifty (57.5 percent) were termed "very well-to-do" and "well-to-do," while the rest were qualified as "poor" or "very poor."[82] In contrast, thirty-six of ninety-three Jewish families (38.7 percent) whose daughters were attending the girls' school were termed "well-to-do" whereas the rest were "poor."[83] It is not clear what criteria were used to determine these categories. They do indicate that even in the same quarter, the social composition of the schools could vary considerably.

The students who attended the Alliance schools had to pay a monthly fee according to the means of their parents. Initially, the fee could range from 5 to 75 kuruş a month (1.05 francs to 15.75 francs).[84] This becomes more meaningful if one takes into consideration that 75 kuruş represented in 1897 the average weekly wage of a sales assistant in a shop in Istanbul after many years of service.[85] A large number of students were admitted every year free of charge, as their parents were considered too poor to pay even the lowest fee. Until the first decade of the twentieth century, there were, in general, more students admitted free of charge than those who paid a fee. In 1895, the Central Committee decided to have even the poorest pay a symbolic sum every month,[86] as this was supposed to teach the moral lesson of contributing to one's own betterment. The number of those admitted free of charge was cut substantially in the first decade of the twentieth century.

The statistics on the number of students who did or did not pay a fee are of limited use, as they do not indicate the actual fees paid. As one report indicates, the great bulk paid very little,[87] and it would be misleading to assume that the actual fact of paying is an indication of economic position. All the available information suggests that, on the whole, the Alliance school network constituted a mass educational system in which the majority of the students paid symbolic sums as fees or nothing at all. The school network was not necessarily for the indigent, as it did include students from relatively better-off families. Nevertheless, reflecting the social reality of Turkish Jewry, the majority of its students came from poor families.[88]

This is further illustrated by the few statistics compiled by the more enterprising of the school-directors. In 1895, out of a total of 306 fathers of the students of the Alliance school in Izmir (thirty students were orphans), seven (2.28 percent) were merchants who were qualified as "notables," sixty (19.6 percent) were brokers and money-changers, forty-one (13.3 percent) were tailors and other artisans. Eleven rabbis, four beadles, three teachers, and twenty employees represented the "tertiary sector" (12.4 percent). Thirty-five were unemployed (11.4 percent). The remaining 125 (40.8 percent) were engaged in small-scale buying and selling, peddling, and other commercial activities.[89] The relatively well-to-do among these families came from the rank of the merchants and brokers. The economic situation of the overwhelming majority left much to be desired. The Balat school in 1900 presented the same picture, with more than half of the parents of the 600 students registered at the school eking out a miserable livelihood in unstable occupations.[90]

Poverty constituted the principal reason for the early departure of students from the schools before completing the full program. This was a constant source of complaint for the directors who bemoaned the fact that the very group that the institution was designed to educate escaped its influence due to economic necessity. The lowest classes of the schools were especially porous, with a constant movement of students in and out every few months. The average length of stay in the school could vary from quarter to quarter in the same city. For example, the students who left the Ortaköy school in Istanbul during the course of the 1883–84 academic year had spent an average of 1.4 years there.[91] In the same year, the figure was 3.4 years for the Galata school.[92] Galata had a relatively wealthier population which could afford to leave its children in the school longer than in Ortaköy.

The Izmir school was constantly plagued by the rapid turnover in its population. In 1880–81, the average stay was 29.4 months,[93] the figure increasing to 3 years by the academic year of 1895–96.[94] The Edirne school was more successful in this respect, with students staying an average of 3.5 to 4 years at school as early as 1888–89. Fifteen out of a total of eighty-three (18 percent) left that year having spent 5 or more years at the school.[95] Of course, not all departures meant that the students had stopped their education. As will become clearer below, many attended other schools, especially from the 1890s onward. The incomplete nature of the statistics available renders it impossible to establish a precise breakdown of the subsequent activities of all the departing students. Still, it is evident that a substantial number of those who left after only a brief period spent at the school joined the ranks of the hundreds of Jewish shopboys and peddlers in the teeming cities of Turkey. The influence of the Alliance on this group did not go beyond the teaching of reading and writing, and the rudiments of arithmetic and of French.

A continuous set of statistics about the destinations of the students leaving the Edirne school during the ten years between 1895 and 1905 provides ground for further analysis.

As Table 1[96] indicates, of the 623 students about whom there is definite information, 44.1 percent continued their education in other institutions, while 55.9 percent entered employment. Most of those who continued in Alliance institutions and in non-Jewish schools (25.7 percent) received some form of secondary or professional education. A significant minority of the total, 18.4 percent, went to the local *Talmud Torah* or to another small religious school. This high number is due to the fact that it had become a custom

TABLE 1

**Careers chosen by students of the Edirne Alliance school for boys immediately
after their departure from school, 1895–1905**

continued education in other Alliance institutions in Turkey, in Paris or in the Alliance agricultural schools:	61
continued to attend other Jewish schools such as the local *Talmud Torah:*	115
continued to study in non-Jewish schools in Edirne or outside:	99
employees in town:	28
apprentice artisans and other jobs involving manual labor:	166
employed in trade and commerce:	154
no information available:	151
emigrated from Edirne:	91
deceased:	5
total:	870

SOURCE: AAIU, France XVI. F. 27. See note 96.

for many parents to switch their children between the *Talmudei Torah* and the Alliance schools every year, depending on their financial resources and the amount of free clothing and food distributed by the community to the *Talmud Torah*. In fact, many who came to the Alliance school had already spent several years in the *Talmud Torah*. They went to the Alliance establishment for a short time to acquire the rudiments of French and then would go back to the *Talmud Torah* until old enough to earn a living. Whether the Alliance liked it or not, many parents did treat its institutions as language schools.

A large number of the students going on to apprenticeship in artisanal trades (26.6 percent) were encouraged to do so by the Alliance. The bulk of these had left the school to become part of the organization's apprenticeship program, even though a substantial percentage would drop out eventually. A majority of those who went into jobs involving trade and commerce had not completed the full cycle of education in the Alliance school. Of the 120 who were in this category up to 1903, thirty-four (28.3 percent) were graduates of the upper division of the Alliance school. The rest had left the school from the lower divisions.

Those who had studied in the school for five or more years and were the graduates of the upper division constituted 17 percent (126) of the 728 who had left the institution between the years 1895 to 1903 for which precise data are available. Forty-two of these 126 (31.7 percent) continued their studies in the Alliance *Ecole Normale* in Paris or in the Alliance agricultural schools, twenty-three (18.2 percent) attended further secondary and higher education establishments in Turkey or in Europe, and thirty-four (26.9 percent) were involved in trade and commerce in town. The rest had left town and no further information is available on them. Presumably many were also continuing with their studies.

It is important to note that these statistics provide information about the path taken by the students only in the first year subsequent to their departure from the school and do not constitute a clear guide to their future activities. Nevertheless, they do indicate certain trends. As can be expected from a mass-education system in an underdeveloped economy, the majority of the students were at school to acquire the rudiments of reading, writing, and arithmetic, in this case in French, and after a relatively brief stay at the school would enter the market place to try to earn a living. By the turn of the century an elite composed of about one-fifth of the students completed the cycle of studies.

It was this group which could take full advantage of the education provided by the Alliance. For many, the organization itself had become an avenue of social advancement. By 1900, fifteen graduates of the Edirne school for boys, founded in 1867, had become Alliance teachers, and there were seven who were studying at the Alliance *Ecole Normale* in Paris to join the ranks of the Alliance teaching corps.[97] Others had chosen different routes. Twenty were pursuing university studies in Paris and Istanbul, ten had become teachers, three doctors, two judges, one an engineer, one a lawyer, one a pharmacist, two were civil servants, and about thirty had become merchants and bankers.[98] Those who were able to finish the full cycle of studies in Alliance schools did find it relatively easy to find jobs and advance socially and economically, as was noted by directors.[99]

Statistics comparable to the ones available for Edirne are unavailable in the case of the other schools. The lists compiled by the directors in Izmir, Istanbul, and the small towns do not span several years and are of limited use. However, the reports make it amply clear that in the earlier years of the Alliance, small-scale trade and commerce constituted in all the cities almost the only avenue chosen by the graduates of the upper divisions upon their departure from school.[100] This had begun to change by the last decade of the nineteenth century with the majority of those who had finished the program of studies continuing with their education elsewhere. The latter trend became an established pattern in the 1880s in Istanbul and in the late 1890s in Edirne and Izmir. For example, in the latter city, of those who left the school in the academic years of 1896–97, 1898–99, and 1900–01, 28.6 percent were continuing their studies in non-Jewish schools, most of them in institutions of secondary education,[101] a rate 10 percent higher than in Edirne.

This development pointed to the gradual improvement of the economic situation of many sections of Turkish Jewry. A Jewish middle class had come into being toward the end of the nineteenth century, which owed its existence mostly to the start that it had been given in the Alliance schools. Increasing numbers of Jews, almost all of them Alliance graduates, had begun to receive further and higher education. The trend was most pronounced in Istanbul, where there were greater possibilities for further education and social advancement than in the provinces. In contrast to the very few Jews who attended the Imperial *Lycée* of Galatasaray (with French as the language of instruction) during its early years in the 1860s and 1870s, there were fifty-four graduates of the Alliance schools in Istanbul studying there in 1887.[102] Of the graduates of the Camondo school, which had been founded in 1854 by Albert Cohn and which followed a program similar to that of the Alliance (it was directed by Félix Bloch), nine had become doctors by 1890, fifteen were teachers, fifteen were studying in the medical schools in Turkey and abroad, and eight had become civil servants.[103] By the first decade of the twentieth century, increasing numbers of Jews in the liberal professions and in large-scale trade and commerce were to be found in the major cities. In 1925, the journal of the order of *B'nai B'rith* in Istanbul reported that 60 percent of the well-to-do Jews in the city were Alliance graduates.[104]

The emergence of such a class created some new problems for the Alliance. Initially, the instruction provided in its institutions was seen as quite sufficient, especially for the purposes of trade and commerce, and there were no complaints about the program. As the aspirations of this class increased, so did its expectations from the schools. As early as 1885, there began to increase pressure on the Galata school to institute more advanced courses where accountancy would be taught, and the director increasingly expressed the opinion that there was a need for an Alliance institution of higher education in Istanbul.[105] Accountancy classes had been added to the curriculum of the school by 1890, and German was now taught as a second European language. The same pressure for an added class where accountancy and other subjects useful for commercial occupations would be taught was also in evidence in Izmir by 1895.[106]

By the early twentieth century, the wealthier elements had begun either to abandon the Alliance schools altogether and send their children to non-Jewish European establishments, whether missionary or not, or were keeping their children for shorter periods in the Alliance schools before sending them to European institutions.[107] The migration of the wealthier elements from the outlying quarters of Istanbul, such as from Hasköy to the district of Galata, compounded the trend in Istanbul. Most Alliance schools in these quarters were catering almost exclusively to the poor and the very poor by 1914.

The Alliance was caught in a bind by this development. It had itself contributed to the emergence of a middle class in Turkey which was more numerous than the old tightly knit elite of *Francos* and other notables of the 1860s. By the first decade of the twentieth century, the aspirations of the new group had outstripped what the Alliance was prepared to provide. There were thousands of poor Jews in Turkey, and they still constituted the main constituency of the Alliance. The Central Committee remained transfixed by the plight of the poor and stuck to the original program of the schools, with minor modifications such as the introduction of German and accountancy classes. The Alliance institutions preserved the character of elementary-cum-junior high schools.

In retrospect, it is clear that the failure of the Alliance to initiate moves for a Jewish institution of secondary education in the capital was politically a grave mistake. The ideological prism through which the Alliance perceived Eastern Jewry was ill-suited to the needs and aspirations of its most dynamic sectors in the twentieth century. The new middle class had a different agenda. In the sphere of instruction, it included the demand for further education for its youth.[108] With little done by the Alliance in this domain, the middle class drifted elsewhere and was lost to its influence. When a Jewish *lycée* was finally created in Istanbul in 1915, it was under the auspices of the local chapter of the *B'nai B'rith*.

What conclusions can be drawn about the impact of the Alliance on Jewish society in Turkey? The lack of statistical studies on Turkish society and economy in the late nineteenth and early twentieth centuries and the lack of thorough statistics in the Alliance archives renders a quantitative answer impossible. Only the major trends can be identified. The vocational training schemes established by the Alliance through its apprenticeship program and agricultural school had a limited impact. They did introduce certain new artisanal trades to Turkish Jews, but could not "productivize" the poor, could not create an artisanal class that could live off its manual labor. Artisanal labor was not lucrative in a semi-colonized society flooded by cheap finished products from the West, the ethnic division of labor did not create room for the Jews, and the resistance to skilled manual work was too ingrained to allow this avenue of social change to produce substantial results.

The central thrust of the Alliance's work in Turkey remained its schools. These fulfilled several functions. Over a period of fifty years, they provided the only standardized mass educational system dispensing an elementary and secondary instruction in the three R's in French to the Jews of Turkey. From modest beginnings, they eventually reached a public composed of over one-third of the total school-age Jewish population in Turkey by the end of the first decade of the twentieth century. The majority of those who attended acquired the skills of reading, writing and arithmetic in French, and, in the case of the boys, entered the market place directly from the school before finishing the full cycle of studies. By the turn of the century, a significant minority, about a fifth to a third of those who attended the schools, finished the full program and went to further education either in Turkey or in Europe or entered local businesses at the end of their studies. It was on this group that the Alliance left its most direct imprint.

The schools did not operate in a vacuum. The economic and social reality of the surrounding society shaped their action and determined their impact. Like all institutions of education, the Alliance establishments played a double role. On the one hand they were agents of social change, and facilitated the upward mobility of the students by the very skills that they imparted. This was particularly significant at a time of rapid change brought about by the increasing Western presence in the Ottoman economy and society. On the other hand, the schools reproduced the inequalities of the societies they operated in. The wealthier students always had a head start over the poor and could benefit more from these institutions by studying longer and by continuing their education after graduation which in return brought greater economic opportunities.

The Alliance's perception of education as an agent of radical social transformation was overly ambitious when analyzed from the economic point of view. The school could not be a panacea for all the social ills that plagued Turkish Jewry. There were too many independent variables that the Alliance could not control. The state of the Turkish economy, the nature of its relationship with the industrialized West, the rivalry between the different ethnic groups of the Ottoman Empire, the opportunities available in given locales were all factors which were beyond the reach of the organization and yet affected profoundly the economic state of Turkish Jewry.

Nevertheless, even if the work of the Alliance was one of many factors that contributed to the transformation of the economic condition of the Jewish masses, it did provide skills which were crucial for the social advancement of increasing numbers of its graduates. As many a school director pointed out, the proficiency of Alliance graduates in French opened many paths in the world of business.[109] In the context of the Westernization of the Ottoman Empire, of increasing Western penetration of the local economy, the West had become the central frame of reference and Western languages indispensable for moving up the social ladder.[110] The increasing demand for the teaching of German as well as French in the schools in Istanbul at the turn of the century illustrates the utilitarian perspective in which the local population saw the whole enterprise of education and the importance it attached to the learning of European languages. Ultimately, the education provided by the Alliance constituted a crucial factor in the making of a Francophone Jewish middle class in Turkey.

There is no doubt that modern schooling established by the organization also contributed to the process of secularization of the community. The erosion and, in many cases, the total elimination of the traditional education system led to a considerable weakening of the institutionalized transmission of traditional culture. Whereas in the *meldar* or in the *Talmud Torah*, education had been an exclusively religious affair, in the Alliance school it was mainly secular in character. The few hours devoted to Hebrew and religious instruction during the week could not compensate for the fact that these had lost the primacy that they had enjoyed for centuries. The place of religion, ubiquitous and all-encompassing in the traditional education system, had contracted to that of a topic covered like all others in the Alliance schools.

The "traditional" education system imparted above all a *praxis* that ensured the vertical transmission of verities good for all times and places. The "modern" one conferred skills that were horizontal in nature, designed in theory to render the individual a useful and productive member of his or her society. Of course, in practice, modern education often still acted to reproduce the dominant values in society and to integrate the individual within a particular social structure.[111] Nevertheless, dispensing both social and intellectual skills, it had an open-ended aspect that could also act as an agent of liberation by supplying the tools for the maximization of the potential of the individual. As Giroux observes, "modern" education can be both an agent of transformation, bringing with it the possibility of emancipation, and a medium of social integration.[112]

Hence, the destruction of the traditional Jewish education system in Turkey in the second half of the nineteenth century and its replacement by a modern European one constituted a major turning point for Turkish Jewry. It weakened the chain of transmission of the past and contributed to the secularization of large sections of the community. It introduced a hitherto unseen fluidity in Jewish society, offering a range of social and cultural possibilities that could be taken in numerous directions by the individual Jew.

The spread of French among the Jews and the familiarization with Europe acquired on a mass basis in the schools, gave rise to a growing orientation toward the West among an increasingly large section of the population. The directors reported from all the Jewish centers that customs and habits were being transformed and there had been important changes in the way of thinking, of speaking, of dressing, in short, in the way of life as a whole.[113] The Europeanization of day-to-day life was perhaps one of the most visible results of the new education. Names were a good barometer of change: "One would be loath today to be called Mossé, Chabetai, Calo, Simbul . . . [instead] one is called Moïse, Charles, Caroline, Eugénie. . . . "[114] The growing use of French at home among graduates of the Alliance schools, and the relative eclipse of Judeo-Spanish was noticed as early as 1887.[115] The language began to exercise a tremendous influence upon Judeo-Spanish, with many loan words transforming the very nature of the language itself.[116]

It was precisely the introduction of French into the cultural profile of Turkish Jewry which was the most significant and long-lasting consequence of the action of the Alliance in the area. Beginning with the late 1860s, three generations of Turkish Jews slowly adopted and adapted French into their day to day existence. The process of cultural change went through several stages to end up in a classic case of "biculturalism" identified by the anthropologist Robert L. Bee.[117] French and Judeo-Spanish coexisted side by side for the newly Francophone middle class. Indeed, French became the central referent for culture and prestige for the whole community.

A hierarchy of languages had established itself by World War I. French was the language given the greatest value, the language of culture and civilization. This paralleled its prestige among the Westernizers in Ottoman officialdom. Judeo-Spanish was the language of the home, of the domestic culture, of the inner traditional world of Turkish Jewry. Like in all Jewish communities, Hebrew continued to be significant as the sacral language. And Turkish was used in a limited way by the male section of the population for the strictly utilitarian purpose of the give and take with the surrounding society. This hierarchy of languages and cultures, a situation of "diglossia" where languages fulfill certain distinct cultural functions and are used according to circumstance,[118] was to last for Turkish Jewry well into the twentieth century.[119]

With the opening of the Empire to the West, some degree of Westernization of the Jewish community would have occurred even if the Alliance had been absent from the scene, especially in cosmopolitan cities such as Istanbul and Izmir. However, it was the mass educational system established by the Alliance which gave the process of Westernization a definite direction toward a French–Judeo-Spanish biculturalism. Unlike West European Jewry, "modernization" for Turkish Jewry did not lead to the adoption of the culture and language of the surrounding society but resulted in an increased orientation toward a distant civilization. Largely as a consequence of the work of the Alliance, French culture, not the Turkish one, became the culture of reference of an increasingly polyglot Turkish Jewish community.

VI

THE ALLIANCE AND THE EMERGENCE OF ZIONISM IN TURKEY

The Alliance at the Summit: 1908

By the time of the Young Turk revolution of 1908, the Alliance had reached, from the institutional standpoint, the height of its power in Turkey. Not only did it exercise a quasi-monopoly over the field of Jewish education through its school network and its effective control of the major *Talmudei Torah,* but it had created a series of ancillary organizations to supplement the work of its educational establishments.

In Edirne, the school director organized in 1890 a reading club, the *Cercle Israélite,* composed of the graduates of the Alliance institutions in Edirne.[1] The club occupied itself with philanthropic activities in the town, collected money for the poor students of the schools, and sponsored theatrical productions in French and in Judeo-Spanish.[2] By 1898, it had become the most important Jewish association in Edirne, subscribed to French, Hebrew, and Judeo-Spanish newspapers, and had built a lending library of 1000 volumes.[3] An Alliance alumni association came into being in Izmir in 1895 which created its own *Cercle Israélite* in 1897 and was also active in the field of philanthropy.[4] The Central Committee saw in these organizations effective tools for bringing together the graduates of its schools and for continuing to expand its sphere of influence over the generations that had passed through its institutions. In 1898 it sent a circular to all the directors, encouraging them to create such bodies in the towns where they had not yet come into existence.[5]

At the turn of the century, the directors in Edirne and Izmir also established mutual aid societies for the Jewish artisans of the two cities. The members contributed each week to a fund which was then used to help them at times of unemployment and illness. By 1903, one-third of the Jewish artisanate in Edirne was enrolled, and the society ran a cooperative grocery store and engaged the services of a permanent doctor. Weekly lectures by the school director on topics ranging from the virtues of manual labor to the heroes of Jewish history complemented the practical side of the organization with the moral one deemed so indispensable.[6] The Izmir society, put under the aegis of the alumni association, led a more ephemeral existence, but nevertheless did manage to organize some artisans, to help them find jobs, and to provide assistance at times of distress.[7]

Alliance-sponsored reading clubs, alumni associations, and mutual-aid fraternities provided new associative frameworks for the young generation. Coexisting side by side with many traditional philanthropic organizations such as the ones for the clothing of the poor, for the visiting of the sick, for the supporting of the *Talmudei Torah,* and often replacing them, the Alliance societies based on Western models contributed to the Westernization and secularization of the associative life of Turkish Jewry.[8]

In many towns, the schools constituted centers from which radiated the action of the Alliance to influence several aspects of Jewish communal existence. Izmir provides a good case in point. In the twenty-five years since the coming of the organization to the city in 1873, it had created one school for boys, one school for girls, one kindergarten, one coeducational school in the suburb of Karataş, two "popular" schools resulting from the merger of several small *meldars,* two apprenticeship programs, one dressmaking workshop for girls, one alumni association with 300 members, one reading club, and one mutual aid society for artisans. One of the teachers sent by the school directed the *Talmud Torah.* The Alliance schools were deeply involved in philanthropic activities. They provided thirty to forty thousand free meals a year to the poor students and were directly involved with the administration of the Rothschild hospital that had been in existence since the 1850s.[9]

A similar expansion of the Alliance's influence characterized the evolution of its work as a whole in Turkey. The society arrogated to itself many of the functions which the conflict-ridden, bankrupt and atrophied local communal institutions were no longer fulfilling. It offered an alternative avenue of social action and reform, and its infrastructure came to constitute almost a surrogate Jewish community. By the first decade of the twentieth century, its establishments were ubiquitous in the Turkish Jewish landscape. But, to use terms that have been employed by Michael Graetz in a different context,[10] it was the election of Haim Nahum to the Chief Rabbinate after the Young Turk revolution of 1908 that marked the final transition of the Alliance from the periphery to the center of the ruling elite of Turkish Jewry.

The highest echelons of the Turkish rabbinate in the provinces had already entered into a close relationship with the Alliance. The son of Samuel Geron, the Chief Rabbi of Edirne, had been educated in the local Alliance school and was accepted to the ENIO in Paris in 1893 to receive training to become an Alliance teacher.[11] The grandson of Abraham Palacci, the Chief Rabbi of Izmir, had also gone through the same process and had become an Alliance teacher in 1895.[12] In 1913, an Alliance graduate, Rabbi Nissim Danon, became the Chief Rabbi of Izmir.[13]

The rabbinate in Istanbul proved to be less open to the influence of the organization. Closely allied with the Hamidian regime, the Chief Rabbinate had become increasingly inefficient and corrupt. The acting Chief Rabbi, Mosheh Halevi, who occupied the position for thirty-five years without a formal appointment, was under the thumb of a few highly placed Jewish notables who prevented the regular functioning of communal affairs. By the first decade of the twentieth century, this group, called in Judeo-Spanish the *banda preta* (the black camarilla) by its critics, was increasingly drawing fire from the reformers among the young generation such as Abraham Galanté, who attacked it tirelessly in his Judeo-Spanish newspaper, *La Vara,* published in Cairo.[14]

The Alliance steered clear of the Chief Rabbinate, taking great care not to become embroiled in the internecine quarrels of the Istanbul community. But it was well aware that the reform of communal affairs was, in the long run, of great importance for the future of its institutions in Turkey. The *consistoire* model in France, entrusted with the task of the "regeneration" of French Jewry, was never far from the mind of its leadership. The latter saw the establishment of a rationalized and well-structured communal administration in Turkey run by an enlightened rabbinate and laity as the indispensable complement of its work in the transformation of Turkish Jewry.

By the turn of the century the organization began to plan for the eventuality of the replacement of the acting Chief Rabbi, who was already very old. It carefully groomed its own candidate for the post. Its *protégé* was a young man, Haim Nahum. The Alliance Central Committee in 1892 took under its wing the young Nahum who had received a traditional Jewish education as well as secular instruction in a Turkish *lycée*. It brought him to Paris where he studied at the Rabbinical Seminary as well as in various institutions of higher education. Upon graduation, he returned to Turkey in 1897 and was appointed to teach at the newly opened Alliance Rabbinical Seminary in Istanbul and in two other Alliance establishments in the city.[15]

From the tenor of the correspondence between him and Jacques Bigart, then secretary general of the Alliance, it is clear that the organization had earmarked him as a future Chief Rabbi of the Ottoman Empire. His ascent was steady. In 1899, he was appointed secretary of the administrative council of the Istanbul community, a development which delighted the Alliance.[16]

Nahum's moment of opportunity came with the Young Turk Revolution. Mosheh Halevi, closely associated with the Hamidian regime which had now been overthrown, was forced to resign, and the administrative council of the Jewish community chose Nahum to replace him as the acting Chief Rabbi.[17] A bitter campaign for the election to the Chief Rabbinate followed in which he was pitted against his father-in-law, Abraham Danon (Nahum had married his daughter Sultana, who was an Alliance teacher), who had also announced his candidacy for the post. Some Orthodox congregations in Germany sent letters to Istanbul opposing Nahum's candidacy, accusing him of being too liberal in matters of religion, adding fuel to the polemics that became the hallmark of the Judeo-Spanish press now freed from the stranglehold of Hamidian censorship.[18] Nevertheless, in the end, the years of careful cultivation of the important personalities in influential positions paid off, and Nahum was elected on January 24, 1909 to the Chief Rabbinate of the Ottoman Empire.[19]

The Alliance was caught by surprise by the Young Turk Revolution and its consequences. It had anticipated a much more gradual rise to power for Nahum and was afraid that in the case of a counter-revolution or a return to power of the conservatives in Turkey, he and the institution of the Chief Rabbinate would be put in a very vulnerable position. Consequently, it thought that Abraham Danon, the director of the Rabbinical Seminary, less associated with the revolution, would stand a better chance of survival as Chief Rabbi if reaction set in.[20] But after this initial hesitation, it showed itself overjoyed by the success of Nahum. Congratulating him upon his initial election as the acting Chief Rabbi, Bigart could not help adding that the Central Committee considered his victory also a victory for the Alliance.[21] Nahum's opponents accused him of being too much of an *Allianciste,* a charge which, as he wrote to Bigart, he considered an honor.[22] Bigart's letter of congratulation written one day after Nahum's final election summarized well the Alliance's attitude toward his triumph:

> Your victory is so fine and so complete . . . your success is that of the liberal circles, in the French meaning of the term. The Alliance partakes in your victory, as, almost in spite of herself, it has been shown to be in solidarity with you . . . let us accept this outcome.[23]

The organization had come a long way in Turkey since its hesitant first steps in the 1860s. The Chief Rabbinate was now occupied by a man who owed his higher education and rise to power to a large extent to the Alliance, who prided himself on being an *Allianciste,* who had, on a previous occasion, declared to Bigart that there was "between me and the Alliance a moral contract which unites us."[24]

The election of Nahum inaugurated the rise to power of the *Allianciste* notables within the community. This secular elite finally had come into its own. The liberal atmosphere brought about by the Young Turk Revolution had led to the eclipse of the more conservative elements within. The small cabal that had run the affairs of the Chief Rabbinate had now been displaced from its position of power and authority.

The conflicts within the community in the years 1858–65 had ended in a stalemate between the reformers and the traditionalists that had paralyzed communal affairs for decades. The conservative Hamidian state had not pushed for a rationalization of the administrative system of the Jewish *millet.* The 1865 statutes for the community had been ignored, and no Chief Rabbi had been formally appointed. Mosheh Halevi had ruled as acting Chief Rabbi only. In fact, Haim Nahum was to be the first and last Chief Rabbi ever to be appointed formally under the provisions of the 1865 statutes. In the context of the paralysis in communal administrations, most of the reforming impulse of the community had coalesced around the work of the Alliance in Turkey, which had provided an alternative base of power and influence, albeit under strict and often rigid control from Paris. With the wind of liberalism blowing from the Ottoman state itself, the reformers could now surface and take over the communal administrations. The Alliance could look forward with confidence to the reorganization of the Jewish communal bodies under the leadership of Nahum and the notables and to the effective support for its schools from the institution of the Chief Rabbinate.

The revolution of 1908 led to the legal emancipation of all the non-Muslims of the Empire, removing their last surviving disabilities. After 1909, all non-Muslims were liable to conscription, and the exemption tax (the *bedel-i askeriye*) was abolished. The tax had been a revamped version of the old poll-tax paid by the non-Muslim communities until the Reform Decree of 1856. Classic legal emancipation, on the Western model, appeared to have arrived in Turkey.

The Young Turk revolution was received with jubilation by the Jewish communities of the Empire,[25] with high expectations about new opportunities for Jews in all areas of public life in Turkey.[26] There emerged a great demand for education in Turkish.[27] The Alliance increased the number of hours of the language taught in its schools, since it too had great expectations about the consequences of the revolution for the future of Turkish Jewry and took credit for having prepared it for the era of liberty that had arrived:

> The work of education of the Alliance . . . has prepared the Jews to take part in the new political organization of the country. It is from the school of the Alliance that numerous generations have drawn the sentiments of gratitude, devotion and affection for Turkey.[28]

It recognized in the ideas of the revolution a kindred spirit. Bigart put it thus: " . . . one can say that the Turkish revolution is like a triumph of our ideas, so moderate but so liberal, and inspired by the love of the public good."[29]

Now that all barriers that had prevented full emancipation had been removed and despotism overthrown, the work of the Alliance appeared vindicated. Most of the Jewish communities were administered by its graduates. Three of the four Jews in the new Ottoman Chamber of Deputies, Carasso, Faraggi, and Masliah, were graduates of its schools.[30] Furthermore, some Turkish deputies such as Rıza Tevfik Bey, a poet and a philosopher, had also studied in Alliance schools.[31] Talat Paşa, one of the most important leaders of the Committee of Union and Progress, had taught Turkish in the Alliance school in Edirne and had been instructed in French by the daughter of the school director there.[32] The organization now had good friends in high places. It had contributed largely to the emergence of Westernized elements within the Jewish community which could participate in the political process of the country. Its task of preparing Eastern Jewry for the benefits of emancipation appeared to have borne fruit. But as it was to discover soon, the new situation in Turkey also inaugurated the period which saw the emancipation of important sections of Turkish Jewry from its own tutelage.

The Emergence of Zionism in Istanbul

The revolution brought in its wake freedom of the press and the removal of restrictions on political activity. Many currents of opinion that had been muffled by the tight control and censorship of the old regime now rose to the surface. The Jewish community was not immune to this development. An important political ideology to emerge among Turkish Jewry, mostly in the capital (but also in Salonica), was Zionism, which developed into a full-fledged movement and threatened the very existence of the Alliance institutions.

The standard interpretation, fostered by the apologetic writings of Abraham Galanté during the first decades of the nationalistic Turkish republic and later taken up by Western historians, has been that Zionism met with no response from Turkish Jewry and remained an exclusively "foreign" import.[33] Although there is truth to the suggestion that the impulse for Zionism came from abroad, developments after 1908 in Istanbul indicate that the degree of local support for the movement was much more significant than hitherto believed. It is impossible to enter into the details of the history of the Turkish Zionism here. Only those aspects of its development which affected the Alliance in Turkey will be analyzed in full.

There is no doubt that Zionism was little known among the Turkish Jewish masses before 1908. News filtered through the Zionist Judeo-Spanish press of Bulgaria, which was available in Turkey. David Fresco, the editor of *El Tiempo* published in Istanbul, engaged in fierce attacks against Bulgarian Zionists in the columns of his paper in 1898 and 1901.[34] Nevertheless, Zionism became a burning issue in Istanbul only after 1908.

In parallel with Herzl's abortive attempts to negotiate the fate of Ottoman Palestine with the Sultan, major currents within the World Zionist Organization had always believed that Istanbul held the keys to Palestine. However, nothing of substance could be achieved under the Hamidian autocracy. The Revolution of 1908 changed the situation. A Zionist representative, Dr. Victor Jacobson, arrived there in the autumn of that year, ostensibly as the head of the Anglo-Levantine Banking Company, a subsidiary of the Zionist Anglo-Palestine Company. In reality he came to explore contacts with influential personalities in the capital and to further the cause of Zionism through links with the government.[35] Scholarly literature has documented well the relationship between the officials of the Zionist Organization and the Turkish government, and the government's steadfast opposition to the Zionist endeavor in Palestine.[36] It is only recently that attention has been paid to the impact of the activities of the Zionists on the local Jewish population.[37]

Upon arrival, Jacobson immediately launched a campaign to propagate the ideas of Zionism in Istanbul. The Zionists created two newspapers, *ha-*

Mevaser in Hebrew, and *Le Jeune Turc* (previously *Courier d'Orient*) in French and succeeded to gain two others to their cause through subsidies, *El Judio* publishing in Judeo-Spanish, and *L'Aurore* in French.[38] Istanbul (and Salonica) became a major center of Zionist activity, the provinces remaining relatively quiescent.

The Ashkenazi community of Istanbul proved ripe for the message of the new movement[39] and gradually increasing numbers of Sephardim, especially the youth, were also won over. Gymnastic clubs such as the *Makabi* provided an organizational base to win new adherents to the cause.[40] Violent polemics between the Zionist *L'Aurore,* directed by Lucien Sciuto, a graduate of the Salonica Alliance school,[41] and *El Tiempo,* directed by David Fresco, a member of the Alliance Regional Committee,[42] became an almost daily occurrence between 1909 and 1911, going as far as Sciuto being taken to court by Fresco for defamation of character in 1911.[43] The Alliance teachers grew increasingly pessimistic, bemoaning the inroads made by Zionism among the masses.[44] In 1911, Isaac Fernandez, the president of the Regional Committee, reported to the Alliance that "90 percent" of the youth had become Zionist.[45] Haim Nahum also became the target of attacks in the press, especially after his resignation from the *Makabi* club in 1910, of which he had been an honorary member. The resignation was provoked by the increasing attacks of the Zionists against the Alliance.[46]

After 1911, the administrative council *(Meclis-i Cismani)* of the community came to have increasing numbers of Zionists in its ranks.[47] Through deft electioneering, Zionists managed to gain majorities in the communal councils in 1913 and 1914.[48] Although this does not prove that the majority of Istanbul Jewry had become Zionist, as these were not mass-based elections, it does indicate that the movement, well-organized and well-directed, had become an important force, not limited to a few foreigners but espoused by many Turkish Jews. With its clever utilization of the press and of the numerous clubs that sprang up in the capital, Zionism was a force to be reckoned with in the years between the Young Turk revolution and World War I.

It was inevitable that the Alliance, the very incarnation of the ideology of emancipation with its strong views on the integration of the Jews in the countries they lived in, would become a target for all those who upheld an ideology of Jewish nationalism. The organization, bitterly opposed to Zionism, constituted a major bulwark against the movement in France and in Europe. In return, it was attacked by Herzl and by the official Zionist organ, *Die Welt.*[49] A conflict in 1911 between the German membership of the Alliance, organized into an umbrella organization called the *Deutsche Konferenz- gemeinschaft,* and Paris over the reelection of Salomon Reinach to the Alliance Central Committee, provided further ammunition for the Zionist publicists. Reinach, the famous archeologist and colleague of Leven and Bigart, had made several public anti-Zionist comments and had also belittled certain aspects of traditional Judaism in some of his publications. The Zionists did their best to have him defeated. Until then, elections to the Central Committee had been quiet affairs, the list suggested by the Central Committee being accepted by the membership without any opposition. The polemics that surrounded the 1911 elections were so serious that the Alliance mobilized all its efforts by appealing to some of its school directors to propagandize in Reinach's favor. It succeeded in bringing about his reelection. It then changed its statutes, abolishing elections to the Central Committee and instead instituted cooptation of new members by the already existing Committee.[50]

The conflict in the international arena had its counterpart in Istanbul. Until the end of 1909, the leading Zionist newspaper, *L'Aurore*, refrained from directly attacking the Alliance. However, other Zionists in the Jewish quarters of Istanbul increasingly began to express criticism of the programs of the schools for devoting too many hours to French and too little to Hebrew.[51] The *Makabi* clubs gained real popularity, reaching a membership of 2000 before World War I.[52] They propagandized openly against the Alliance.[53] A Zionist society, the *Bnei Yisrael*, was founded in Hasköy with links with the *Makabi*, and coordinated attacks on the Alliance school there.[54] Zionists increasingly flirted with the traditionalist rabbinate and used the synagogues as bases to recruit for their cause among the more conservative elements of the population. The administrative council, still *Allianciste* in 1909, tried to put a stop to this development by forbidding political meetings in the synagogues and by limiting the giving of sermons to the students of the Alliance rabbinical seminary.[55]

However, the real conflict erupted over the creation of an Alliance Alumni Association in Istanbul in 1910. The Regional Committee made an appeal for the foundation of such a society, as Istanbul was the only major city without an Alliance alumni group. In the general assembly of the Alliance graduates which met in March 1910, the Zionists and the anti-Zionists split into two hostile factions. It appears that the Zionists among the graduates came to the meeting well prepared, with a definite program. The conflict was ostensibly over the wording to be used to delimit the aim of the society. The *Allianciste* faction defined this as "improving the state of Ottoman Jewry by creating a meeting center and by developing among the Jewish youth ties of friendship and solidarity."[56] The Zionists wanted to add the following sentence: "To bring about, every time that events warrant it, a movement of solidarity among the Jewish population with our coreligionists of whichever country where they suffer because of being Jewish *(en leur qualité d'israélite)*." The maneuver was no doubt a clever, calculated move on the part of the Zionists, as solidarity with those "suffering for being Jewish" was the wording used by the Alliance in its famous manifesto of 1860 and had been included as the second clause of the first article of its statutes.[57] The *Alliancistes* could not object to it on ideological grounds and had to fight a rearguard action by arguing that this was not the task of an alumni association.

It is clear that the conflict over the definition of the aims was just a smokescreen that hid the real struggle over control of the nascent organization. In the end the *Alliancistes* seceded and formed the *Amicale*, which had the support of Paris and of other Alliance alumni associations in the provinces. All attempts at reconciliation between the two groups proved fruitless.[58]

Significantly, the Zionists called their Alliance alumni group the *Agudat Crémieux*[59] (The Crémieux Union) after the most famous president of the Alliance. One of the Zionists' favorite criticisms of the organization was that it had been originally on the right path while under the leadership of people like Crémieux and Netter, the founder of the agricultural school *Mikveh Yisrael* in Palestine, working for the "national regeneration" of the Jewish people, but its true aims had been perverted by their successors who had transformed it into a tool of French interests. This was a line of attack which was constantly repeated in the official newspaper of the Zionist Organization, *Die Welt,*[60] and became the *leitmotif* of *L'Aurore*'s criticisms of the Alliance.

The Central Committee's rejection of an appeal by the *Makabi* to be allowed the use of the Alliance Balat school building for its activities, and the *Amicale* affair, enraged Lucien Sciuto, the editor of *L'Aurore*.[61] He had already suggested in the columns of his paper that the Alliance had to renew itself, to issue a second appeal, like the famous one of 1864, making Hebrew the language of instruction in its schools.[62] According to him, the Zionists were better interpreters of the true spirit of the Alliance than its current leadership,[63] who had transformed the organization into an *"Alliance assimilatrice française."*[64] The main aim of the Zionists appeared to Hebraize the education dispensed in the Alliance schools and to weaken the position of the organization in all levels of Jewish communal life. For this purpose, Zionist newspapers such as *L'Aurore* gave wide publicity to the activities of rival organizations like the *Hilfsverein der Deutschen Juden,* which had begun to subsidize two *Talmudei Torah* in Istanbul after 1908 and was supported by the local Ashkenazi community.[65]

David Fresco, the editor of *El Tiempo,* emerged as the leading anti-Zionist in the *Allianciste* camp. He used his newspaper to hound the movement in all its manifestations to such an extent that he appeared to the Zionist leadership as the major orchestrator of an Alliance campaign of vilification against them.[66] Fresco collected several of his anti-Zionist articles in *El Tiempo* into a pamphlet which he published in Judeo-Spanish and French in 1909. The pamphlet, entitled *Le Sionisme,* summed up the position of the anti-Zionists and represented the views of the *Allianciste* faction among Istanbul Jewry.

Zionism, according to Fresco, was nothing more than a new form of false messianism, like the Sabbatean movement of the seventeenth century. It ran counter to the liberal and rationalistic impulse in human history to which Judaism had been a major contributor. The emancipation of the Jews and their assimilation into the surrounding populations had inaugurated a new era in human history which would see the final disappearance of antisemitism, a remnant of the Middle Ages. It was incumbent upon Turkish Jews to move in step with the new era of freedom ushered in by the revolution of 1908, adopt Turkish as their mother tongue, and work for the good of the Ottoman motherland.[67]

This classic liberal anti-Zionist stance, informed by the ideology of emancipation, acquired a particular urgency in the Turkish context by conjuring up the spectre of treason that Zionism was supposed to imply. What was particularly problematic about Zionism in Turkey was the fact that unlike anywhere else, it concerned an area, Palestine, that was an integral part of the state in which the movement itself was operating. Fresco was very conscious of this fact and had no doubts about the insincerity of the recent Zionist declarations repudiating all interest in an independent Jewish state in Palestine and demanding only a Jewish homeland under the rule of the Sultan. For him, the aim of Zionism remained political independence for a Jewish Palestine. And Palestine was not some distant land but a part of the Ottoman Empire. Zionism, therefore, could easily raise questions in the minds of the government about the loyalty of its Jewish subjects:

> Ottoman Jew[s], can you imagine the scope of the disaster that would befall the Jews of [this] country if our compatriots, and especially our Muslim compatriots which make up the majority, became convinced that the Ottoman Jew is not attached to his motherland, that he runs after another ideal, that he dreams about the creation of a Jewish state to the detriment of Ottoman national unity?[68]

Fear remained a powerful factor in the anti-Zionist position taken by the Chief Rabbi and the leading notables, as well as the Alliance representatives in Turkey.[69]

Fresco's writings drew a response from no less a person than Nahum Sokolow who, in a pamphlet translated and published in Judeo-Spanish in 1910, defended Zionism by showing that it was not at all unpatriotic and questioned the sanity of Fresco.[70] The press war became particularly bitter after Fresco published a violent attack on the *Makabi* in *El Tiempo,* which was followed by Haim Nahum's resignation from his honorary membership in the club.[71] From then on, Nahum was attacked directly for being an *Allianciste* and a puppet in the hands of David Fresco.[72] Friction in Istanbul became so intolerable that the leadership of the Zionist movement wrote directly to the Alliance in Paris, calling for an official truce, a move rejected by the Central Committee, which announced that it had not started the fight and it could not control what was happening in the city.[73]

Conflicts between the communal administrations and Haim Nahum, between the Ashkenazim and the Chief Rabbinate, between the Zionists and the anti-Zionists paralyzed all communal affairs. While the war years brought a relative calm, the Armistice brought the old conflicts back to the surface. The Balfour Declaration gave a new zeal to the local Zionists, who could attract more people into their ranks now that the dream of "a National Home for the Jews" was realized. Furthermore, the very future existence of Turkey as an independent state appeared to be in doubt. Inspired by the Wilsonian ideals of autonomy for minorities, the Zionists were active in the creation of a Jewish

National Council in Istanbul in 1918 to take over all communal administrations.[74] The Chief Rabbi Nahum, against whom this *coup d'état* had been intended, succeeded in disbanding the council in 1919.[75] Nevertheless, the Zionists dominated the communal administrations between 1920 and 1922.[76] The *Fédération Sioniste d'Orient* created in 1919 recruited 4000 members in Istanbul.[77] Other Zionist organizations also attracted increasing numbers in the capital and in provincial cities such as Edirne.[78] The attacks on the Alliance continued in the Zionist press.[79] Finally, the advent of the new Turkish Republic drove Zionism underground and removed it from public view.

The expectation in 1908 on the part of the Alliance of sweeping reforms in the Istanbul communal administration and the restructuring of the Jewish *millet* did not materialize. The emergence of an ideological opposition caught the organization by surprise and put it increasingly on the defensive. As long as Nahum was in power, the Alliance could be certain that the attacks on it could be neutralized, as it was the Chief Rabbi who had the real executive power in the community. And indeed, the schools were thus able to function normally. But this was small consolation for an organization which had expected that its troubles in Turkey would be over after the replacement in 1908 of the old guard at the helm of the Jewish community. The Alliance was still in an unsurpassed position in the field of Jewish education in Turkey. But by 1914, it no longer commanded the allegiance of important sectors among the secular elements within Turkish Jewry.

The Coming of Age of Turkish Jewry

Although the Alliance was not facing a comparable conflict in Edirne and Izmir, its position among Turkish Jewry as a whole was in danger of being eroded by the situation in Istanbul, not only the capital of the Empire, but also the real center of power of the Jews of Turkey. There were many graduates of its schools, especially among the notables, who stood by the Alliance. But many of its fiercest opponents were also graduates of its institutions. The teachers pointed out with great bitterness that all of the leading anti-*Alliancistes* were themselves the products of the Alliance.[80] A majority of the membership of the Zionist *Makabi* club was composed of Alliance students. The *Agudat Crémieux* had been created by the Zionist alumni of the Alliance schools. Sciuto, the editor of *L'Aurore,* was an Alliance graduate.[81] So was Nessim Rousso, the secretary of the Ministry of Interior, and a leading Zionist and opponent of Nahum.[82] David Elnekave, the editor of the Zionist *El Judio,* had been a student in the Alliance Rabbinical Seminary in Istanbul and had been taught by Nahum himself.[83] Significantly, the two leading Zionist newspapers in the city, *L'Aurore* and *La Nation* published in French, and their audience was the Francophone class that had come into existence as a result of the activities of the Alliance. Sam Hochberg, a leader of the Zionist movement in Istanbul, and Jacques Loria, the editor of the Zionist *La Nation* after

World War I, were both ex-directors of Alliance schools.[84] Though these two were exceptions, as most Alliance teachers remained loyal, they epitomize the erosion of the position of the organization in Turkey.

It is evident that sections of the mass following of Zionism in Istanbul were composed of individuals that had hardly been touched by the educational activities of the Alliance. Often poor and uneducated, many gravitated toward an anti-establishment movement that promised change in communal affairs and the imminent dawn of better days.[85] But it is also true that substantial elements among the Zionists, especially among its local Sephardic leadership, were composed of Alliance graduates.

As Giroux argues, while the modern educational process reproduces dominant social values, it can also be remarkably open-ended in its outcome. Modern schooling acts to mould and socialize the student according to distinctly ideological criteria, but it can also create sites of contestation where many of the recipients of the instruction can turn their newly acquired tools toward directions never intended by the dispensers of the education.[86] The latter situation was in evidence in the case of many nationalist elites in colonial contexts who clashed with the colonial power that had educated them. It was also the case with many graduates of the Alliance schools.

Teachers in the 1890s and early 1900s already identified the fact that the organization was losing some of its influence over the new middle class, especially in Istanbul. Many Turkish Jews were no longer satisfied by the very insignificant role assigned to them by the Alliance Central Committee in the running of its schools. The local committees, or school committees which were supposed to support the activities of the Alliance and have a say in the day-to-day administration of its institutions, had never functioned properly. The directors were jealous of their prerogatives and did not want to share power. So, with a few exceptions as in Galata where a school committee composed of the leading Istanbul notables, *Francos* or otherwise, had been in continuous existence since the 1870s, most schools were directed by the Alliance personnel under the strict supervision of the Central Committee. By the twentieth century, most committees had either been disbanded or were moribund.

The Alliance had always enjoyed a strong relationship with the notable class in Turkey. The Regional Committee, the preserve of the *Francos* under the leadership of first Salomon and later Isaac Fernandez, though never functioning on a regular basis, had been important for the Central Committee in its dealings with the communal organizations. The school directors had courted the notables over questions of money and had relied on them to neutralize any threat from the rabbinate. But the notables had not been directly involved with the running of the Alliance institutions. Neither the Central Committee nor the directors were prepared to compromise the total independence of the Alliance. Even though the organization had to satisfy the wishes and needs of the locality, Paris had always enjoyed a great freedom of action in the way it went about responding to local demands. A partnership between the locality and the Alliance was indispensable for the survival of its institutions. But this was an unequal partnership at best, with the Central Committee firmly in charge, and Eastern Jewry very much a weak, junior partner in the Alliance enterprise.

As several generations educated in the Alliance schools, fully cognizant of developments in Europe, came into their own, there began to emerge increasing signs of resentment of the great degree of centralization of the Alliance, of the paternalism that marked the relationship between Paris and the locality. Criticism of the curriculum of the schools began to appear in the Judeo-Spanish press in the 1890s and early 1900s.[87] Letters to the Central Committee from local personalities began to change in tone, no longer petitioning humbly the august body in Paris, but making outright demands and sometimes lashing out in fury at the inflexibility of the leadership of the Alliance. This is well illustrated in the bitter letter written by Jacques Danon, an Alliance graduate and a leading figure in the Alliance local committee and the *Cercle Israélite* in Edirne. Writing to Jacques Bigart, the general secretary of the Central Committee in 1903, he protested the Alliance's refusal to listen to his criticisms of the way Samuel Loupo, the director, was running the Edirne school:

> I ask a favor, please consent for five small minutes to consider the humble peasant of the banks of the Tunca and the Maritza [rivers which met in Edirne], the barbaric "Turk" who carries the name of Jacques Danon, as the equal, or better than that, as the comrade of Monsieur Jacques Bigart, the dweller of the "City of Light" *(la Ville lumière)*, the all-powerful general secretary of the Alliance Israélite Universelle.[88]

He went on to criticize the curt way in which the Secretary responded to letters sent from Edirne and demanded some explanation as to how decisions affecting the school were reached in Paris. To him the Alliance appeared to be saying:

> Jews of Turkey, you have the misfortune of being poor and miserable, generous men have given us the mission of coming to your aid, but in return we demand from you that you make the sacrifice of leaving in our hands your dignity [and] all your aspirations of being free men. . . .[89]

This language, coming from the "progressive" camp in Turkey supposed to be friendly to the Alliance, was entirely new.

It had been preceded by a critique of the Alliance curriculum written by the future historian of Turkish Jewry, Abraham Galanté, and published in the *Archives Israélites* of 1901 and 1902. According to Galanté, it was indispensable to teach more Turkish in the schools. But more significantly, local committees had to be revived so that local populations could have a say in the running of the Alliance institutions. When similar appeals that he had made from the island of Rhodes met with no response from the Alliance, Galanté was bitter. He accused the Central Committee of having nothing but contempt for "the grievances of a Turkish Jew, a savage!"[90]

There is a direct continuity between the revolt against the paternalism and centralization of the Alliance, already in evidence before 1908, and the attitude seen in the Turkish Zionist press after the Young Turk Revolution. The secretary general, Jacques Bigart, by all accounts a cold and authoritarian figure, and an ardent anti-Zionist, was a favorite target. He was accused of feeling contempt and disgust at "Orientals,"[91] of "hating certain Turkish cities and personalities."[92] The same ironic and bitter language was very much in evidence. The Alliance treated Turkish Jewry with condescension. "[Turkish Jews] are only Orientals, while the secretary and the vice-president of the Alliance are, by the virtue of their office, the dispensers of light emanating from the great City of Light itself."[93]

The creation of local lodges of the international *B'nai B'rith* order in Istanbul, Izmir, and Edirne in 1911 gave a further institutional expression to the growing independence of Turkish Jewry from the tutelage of the Alliance.[94] Grouping some of the leading members of the Jewish bourgeoisie, whether Sephardic or Ashkenazic, the lodges were philanthropic organizations designed to coordinate the charity and mutual help activities within these cities. They became particularly active in helping the needy among Turkish Jews during the Balkan wars of 1912–1913 and during World War I.[95] They soon became influenced by the activities of the many Zionists who joined the organization and who were successful in using it as yet another base of agitation against the Chief Rabbi Nahum.[96]

When the forced closure of many foreign institutions of secondary institutions—upon Turkey's entrance into World War I—threatened to leave many Jewish students without schools,[97] the Istanbul lodge created a Jewish *lycée* in 1915, the first such Jewish institution in Turkey.[98] The *lycée* taught in French and filled an important gap in the Jewish educational system. The Alliance had resolutely refused to concern itself with secondary education, arguing that it had to look after the interests of the thousands of poor Jewish youth who were not receiving any instruction whatsoever. This answer was no longer satisfactory for those elements of the new middle class who wanted to provide a more complete education for its children and had been obliged to send them to foreign, often missionary, establishments.

The president of the Istanbul lodge, as well as of the XIth District of the *B'nai B'rith* order that encompassed all the Levant, was none other than Joseph Niégo, who had been the director of the Alliance agricultural training school at *Mikveh Yisrael* in Ottoman Palestine and who now represented the Jewish Colonization Organization in the Ottoman Empire, a society with very close links with the Alliance.[99] A trusted friend of the Central Committee, he also enjoyed close contacts with the Zionists.[100] He vented the frustration of many a communal leader vis-à-vis the Alliance in the foundation speech of the lodge of Istanbul in 1911. He expressed admiration for the extraordinary work of international Jewish organizations but at the same time, in a thinly veiled allusion to the Alliance, criticized "some of them" for considering "us Jews of the East as minors in order to hold us under their tutelage, while the *Bene Berit* [his spelling] organization declares us independent adults."[101]

The lodges of the *B'nai B'rith,* all acting independently from any centralized body, went from strength to strength in Turkey in the years following World War I. By the early 1920s, they held all communal affairs in their hands.[102] They gave the local Francophone Jewish bourgeoisie a base which the Alliance local committees, under the rigid paternalist rule of Paris, were not capable of doing. Even the greatest defender of the Alliance in Turkey, the journalist David Fresco, recognized the fact that while a member of the Alliance was supposed to pay his dues and let Paris take care of everything, the *B'nai B'rith* lodges were centers of extraordinary activism and enterprise in local communal affairs.[103] Between 1908 and the early 1920s, the Alliance network had been dethroned from its position at the center of communal dynamism among Turkish Jewry by the class that it itself had brought into being.

The trends that explain the success of the local *B'nai B'rith* lodges on the institutional and communal levels are also in evidence in the political and ideological rallying of many Alliance graduates to Zionism. For many, the latter supplied a highly ideological medium to channel a reservoir of resentment that had developed over the years. It was a declaration of independence from Paris, an attempt to prove the coming of age of Turkish Jewry. Indeed, whatever the fervor with which convictions were held, it is impossible not to see a certain degree of calculated instrumentalism in the rallying to the banner of Zionism, as a means of bringing the all-powerful Alliance to its knees. Commenting on a conflict in Monastir in Macedonia in 1911 between Paris and the local Alliance Committee, Sciuto, the editor of *L'Aurore,* suggested that the Jews of Monastir invite the *Hilfsverein,* the rival of the Alliance. "The Alliance feels a strong jealousy toward the *Hilfsverein,* Monsieur Bigart would submit like a lamb."[104] This proposal for a playing off of one Western Jewish organization against another to obtain maximum satisfaction for the locality is very revealing. Zionism could be an abstract ideology of Jewish nationalism without many practical consequences. But in the local context, it was the rallying call of all the "outs" against the "ins," of the younger generation against the older, a means of ending the rule of the old oligarchy in the community, a call for the democratization of the political process.

The Alliance, the 1848 republicanism of its founders notwithstanding, had become deeply conservative by the twentieth century and was steeped in the politics of notables, used to working behind the scenes with a few influential individuals. It was now part of the Jewish establishment, and had itself become the Jewish *ancien régime.* The democratization of its institutions called for by the Zionists, the opening up of its local committees, would have meant sharing power with the locality to a degree hitherto unknown in the annals of the organization. The Central Committee opposed this development steadfastly in all the areas where it had schools. Turkey was no exception.

However, the ideological appeal of Zionism for Turkish Jewry should not be ignored. The situation in the Levant in the first decade of the twentieth century was ripe for a nationalist movement among its Jewish communities. The Judeo-Spanish *Kulturbereich,* till then a unit within the confines of the Ottoman Empire, had seen the world it had known for centuries crumble away. Ottoman rule was being replaced by new nation-states. Serbia was the first such state with a sizeable Judeo-Spanish population to break away from the Empire in the early nineteenth century. It was followed by the rise of Bulgaria in 1878, with a much more substantial Sephardic community. Salonica was to fall under Greek rule in 1912. The opening up to the West of the Ottoman state, the penetration of European imperialism, the examples of Greek, Armenian and other nationalisms all led many Turkish Jews to rethink traditional political categories.

The concept of the separate Jewish "nation (denoted by the same word in Judeo-Spanish)," called the Jewish *millet* in Turkish by the nineteenth century, had been an important entity in the Ottoman Empire, whether *de facto* or *de jure*. It had constituted the central frame of reference in all questions of identity and had been legitimized for centuries by the Ottoman state. With these antecedents, and in the context of an Empire in its last years, an ideology of Jewish nationalism did not need much belaboring to appeal to some Turkish Jews. By asserting that the Jews constituted a "nation" like all others, it appeared to reformulate in a modernized form the traditional category of the Jewish *millet* in the Middle East. The sense of a corporate Jewish community, unlike in Western Europe where it had been dismantled long before the arrival of Zionism, was still, like in Eastern Europe, a living reality in Turkey when Zionism became a burning issue.

Like many Zionist movements elsewhere, there is little evidence to suggest that Turkish Zionists were very concerned in the emigration to Palestine. In the local context, Zionism stood for a Jewish nationalism aiming at cultural revival. This implied the "nationalization" of Jewish education and the adoption of Hebrew as a living "national" language. Ultimately, it stood for the modern legitimation of the Jewish "nation" as the primary source of identity for Turkish Jewry.

The ideology of emancipation, central to the world view of the Alliance, exercised an appeal on some Turkish Jewish intellectuals such as Abraham Galanté, Moïse Kohen (alias Munis Tekinalp), and others who greeted the Young Turk revolution with great enthusiasm and who were to participate in the political life of the country.[105] However, it is significant that its appeal was limited to certain individuals and that their constituency was not a Jewish one. Unlike Zionism, Turkish politics did not attract the participation of large numbers of Jews. In spite of the writings of a few intellectuals, there did not emerge an organized political movement among them which sought to spread Turkish nationalism among the Jewish masses or to actively involve them in the political process in the country.

The Alliance itself played a complex, dialectical role in the emergence of

Zionism among some of the graduates of its schools. By infusing a great degree of Westernization into the life of Turkish Jews, it put them into direct contact with the currents of opinion in world Jewry. It gave Turkish Jewry the tools to forge new links with modern political ideologies. The ideology of emancipation that it espoused had been shaped by the Jewish experience in the modern West-European nation-state. This ideology, which emphasized the abstract virtues and duties of citizenship over and above ethnic-religious affiliation, had little chance of mass acceptance in the context of a crumbling Empire where such an identity, instead of weakening, was gaining new life under the influence of modern nationalism.

In its institutions, the Alliance familiarized Turkish Jews with the Western model of emancipation, a development which also increased their consciousness about the local conditions which fell far short of that model. The revolution of 1908 had come too late to make a fundamental difference and had not had time to alter the place of the Jew in the Ottoman polity. The Ottomanist agenda of creating a new nation composed of all the groups that lived in the empire had collapsed under its own contradictions and was now increasingly replaced by a more exclusivist Turkish nationalism. The institution of the *millet,* its autonomy much eroded by the Ottoman state, had nevertheless survived as a separate entity. Given the difficulties of implementing the Western route of emancipation and its accompanying *state-imposed* "regeneration" in the context of the multi-ethnic, semi-colonized Ottoman Empire, many Alliance graduates drew nationalistic conclusions which had not been foreseen by the organization. These conclusions were also reinforced by the message of a secular Jewish solidarity taught in the schools. A perspicacious French consul, writing about the spread of Zionism among the Jews of the East in 1911, put it succinctly: "The nobility of sentiments [of the leaders of the Alliance] have hid from them certain social realities. They did not realize that by favoring the birth of principles and ideas of a Hebraic nationalism, they would give rise to new aspirations. . . . "[106]

For many such as Lucien Sciuto, the activities of the Alliance and the message of Zionism need not be contradictory. There were two forces of Jewish emancipation. The first worked by "raising us through instruction," the second, "renewed us by national sentiment." The first "wrested us from intellectual obscurity, as the other attempts to wrest us from national humiliation."[107] "Regeneration," the ideal of the Alliance, had undergone a metamorphosis, and had become "national regeneration." In spite of itself, the Alliance's work constituted an important catalyst in this development.

The Response of the Alliance to Zionism

Three factors shaped the Alliance's response to Zionism: its ideology, its direct experience of Zionist agitation against its schools in Bulgaria, and its fears of alienating the Turkish government.

The ideology of the Alliance diverged considerably from that of the Zionists. The organization was passionate in its belief in the importance of the emancipation of the Jews wherever they lived and saw it as its central task to help the Jews achieve equality with their fellow countrymen throughout the world. In this it reflected the mid-nineteenth-century optimism of Western Jewry. It saw antisemitism as a throwback to the Middle Ages and was never in doubt about the ultimate victory of the principles of emancipation. Zionists, on the other hand, believed that emancipation was an illusion and that antisemitism could not be eradicated. Furthermore, the naive faith in emancipation and in its benefits would lead to increasing assimilation and to the eventual disappearance of the Jewish people as a distinct entity.

This fundamental ideological chasm could not be bridged, some points of contact notwithstanding. The Alliance's motto was that of Jewish solidarity, of union among the Jews tied together by a common religious and moral tradition. The Alliance was not, as the Zionists were to claim, just a philanthropic organization, and its political program did call for international Jewish mobilization, an idea not alien to the Zionist canon. Furthermore, the Alliance had been the first Jewish organization to concern itself with the "productivization" of Jewish life in Palestine, founding there the first agricultural school, *Mikveh Yisrael,* and the first trade school. But its "Palestinophile" stance certainly did not envisage a Jewish political presence, nor massive immigration, as the land was considered too poor to support large numbers of people. This, of course, was anathema to the Zionists.

But the clash was not confined to the level of abstract ideology. The Alliance was the *doyen* of international Jewish organizations. The Anglo-Jewish Association and the *Israelitische Allianz zu Wien* were sister societies which worked closely with it. The Alliance's position of leadership in the Jewish world was gradually eroded toward the turn of the century with the emergence of the Zionist Organization and the *Hilfsverein der Deutschen Juden* which were completely independent and acted directly against its interests. Part of the Alliance's opposition to Zionism should be seen in the context of its trying to defend the status quo in the Jewish world where it had become used to primacy in the international scene.

It is possible that the conflict with the Zionists might have been more muted if it had remained in the sphere of high politics and ideology. However, it was Zionist politics in practice, in the localities where the Alliance had a considerable stake in numerous institutions, which added a degree of bitterness to the quarrel which would take years to heal. Historians have practically ignored the fact that it was in Bulgaria, and not in Palestine, that the Alliance-Zionist clash on this level erupted first. It was the experience of Bulgarian Zionism which marked deeply the attitude of the Alliance.

The reasons for the emergence of Zionism as a mass movement among the Jews of Bulgaria and its extraordinarily successful culmination in the emigration of the whole community en masse to the state of Israel after World War II (the only community to do so as a whole of its own volition) appear extremely complex and await scholarly treatment.[108] The traumatic transition after the Russo-Turkish war of 1878 from centuries of Ottoman rule to the new Bulgarian one, the militant nationalism of the new state, the strategic position of the community living in a border area between the Ashkenazic and Sephardic worlds open to influences from both sides, were all significant factors in this development.

As early as 1895, long before Herzl came onto the scene, the directors of the Alliance schools in the Bulgarian communities were already noting increasing *Hovevei Zion* (Lovers of Zion) influence among the youth, with several Palestine colonization organizations forming in cities such as Sofia, Philippopoli, and Phlevna.[109] The same press wars that would erupt over a decade later in Istanbul were already in evidence in 1895 in Philippopoli, with the charismatic Marco Baruch emerging as a leading Zionist propagandist. The Alliance school director of the town was quick to call him "a kind of a maniac, an escapee of Bicêtre [the famous insane asylum in Paris]."[110]

Inevitably, the Alliance schools became involved in the conflicts. Zionists accused them of being too French, of making Jews too submissive to the authorities.[111] This was the first time that the schools were attacked by Zionists anywhere and Secretary General Bigart's reaction set the tone of the Alliance's response throughout the Sephardic world in the next two decades. Zionism was "a movement which appears to us as neither suitable for the interests of Judaism, nor to its actual needs; it is ill-timed, it is nothing more than an attempt to plunder those who possess a little and those who possess nothing. . . ."[112] He wrote to another director:

> This agitation is extremely disreputable in all the countries in which the Jews enjoy the same rights as their fellow citizens, and is particularly dangerous in Bulgaria where the ideas of tolerance and of civil and political equality remain only on the surface and have not been able to penetrate the way of life of the masses. That the Jews, in a far distant future, could reconstitute themselves into a nationality is conceivable, even if we do not share in this desire, but the talk of this project in the present is . . . [nothing but irresponsible] . . . It is revolutionary socialism—a big word, but in my opinion a totally exact one, that makes its entry into Judaism in this special form. If it is not checked, one will perhaps soon see a general outcry on the part of the poor Jewish class against the rich.[113]

This statement by Bigart highlights the three constants in the Alliance's perception of Zionism, that it was utopian, that it would jeopardize Jewish emancipation and increase antisemitism, and that it was a radical movement which upset the status quo.

The latter judgment appeared to be vindicated when, in the next few years, the old notables who had controlled communal affairs since Ottoman times came under increasing fire from the Zionists and, under conditions of universal suffrage introduced by the Bulgarian constitution, were defeated in many cities.[114] The Zionists benefited from the democratization of the political process in these communities where the classic form of rule had been oligarchic and became the favorites of the dispossessed classes.[115]

Soon, Zionists took over most of the Alliance school committees, now compulsory institutions under Bulgarian law.[116] In a Zionist congress taking place in Philippopoli in 1899, severe attacks were directed against the Alliance, and the school director was asked to make Hebrew the language of instruction in the school and not to teach French until the upper division.[117] The Alliance was helpless to stem the tide of similar demands in other Bulgarian cities but refused to budge and to make any concessions.

In 1903, the Zionists openly threatened the Alliance with expulsion from Bulgaria. The Bulgarian Zionist Central Committee in a vitriolic letter written to Paris in 1903 accused the organization of "assimilationist" and "anti-nationalist" activities and of being the "organizers of French influence in the Orient."[118] Echoing the theme of independence from Paris that would emerge in Turkey a few years later, in the same context, they added: "We are sufficiently grown up to do without your tutelage . . . If you do not want to leave of your own volition, we will send you away by force."[119] And indeed, the Zionists literally expelled the Alliance from all but two Bulgarian Jewish communities by 1913.[120] This was an unprecedented development in the history of the organization and would not be paralleled anywhere else. The first encounter between the Alliance and Zionism on the local level did not augur well for the future and made the Alliance exceptionally nervous about the spread of the movement elsewhere.

In a letter written in 1908, the Alliance defended its decision not to allow Zionists to use its school building in Varna for their activities in the following way: "You do not ignore the sentiment of hostility that Zionism inspires in the Ottoman government, and we do not want it to believe that our buildings serve as meeting centers for the propagandists of the doctrine."[121] This supplies the key to an important factor that contributed to the Alliance's hostility to Zionism, the fear of alienating the Ottoman government.

The bulk of the organization's schools were in the Ottoman Empire. It had created important institutions like *Mikveh Yisrael* and the Jerusalem trade school in Palestine. It had closely monitored Ottoman moves to restrict Jewish immigration to the Holy Land since the 1880s. The presidents of the Regional Committee in Istanbul, Salomon and Isaac Fernandez, kept the Alliance informed of every change of mood of the Porte, from its reactions to Oliphant's proposals for Palestine[122] to the decision in 1896 not to allow Jews to buy land there.[123] Isaac Fernandez laid the blame for the latter development squarely at the door of Herzl and the agitations of the Bulgarian Zionists.[124] Together with many Alliance teachers, he warned repeatedly of the dangers of Zionism for Turkish Jewry.[125]

The Alliance was genuinely pro-Turkish. It always lauded the very humane treatment of the Jews by the Ottoman governments and compared it with the barbaric policies of "Christian" Russia.[126] True to the spirit of its ideology of emancipation, it tried to foster patriotism for Turkey in its schools in the Empire. In 1892, it delegated its Regional Committee to convey to the Sultan the sentiments of gratitude of world Jewry on the 400th anniversary of the arrival of the Sephardic exiles in the Ottoman Empire.[127] It reacted favorably to the plans of conscription of Jews in 1893,[128] and was satisfied when this became a reality after 1909, viewing it as a normal duty of all citizens.[129]

Nevertheless, in spite of its pro-Turkish attitude, the organization could not escape the suspicion with which all foreign organizations were viewed by the Turkish government in the second half of the nineteenth century. The period saw a massive increase in the number of schools created by foreign missionary organizations and by the non-Muslim communities of the Empire.[130] Turkish attempts to limit or control the activities of these schools which maintained complete independence from Istanbul and taught whatever they saw fit, were continually hampered by the action of foreign powers. The capitulation treaties[131] gave virtually limitless rights of "protection" to Western powers which used and abused these rights to further their own interests. There was a great deal of resentment in the Porte at this interference, resentment which contributed to the opposition to Zionism which was seen as creating yet another avenue for foreign meddling in Turkey's internal affairs.[132]

The Alliance could not escape the fact that it was a "foreign" organization in the eyes of the Turks. It was usually left alone, as the Jews were not considered a threat until the rise of Zionism. Nevertheless, with the emergence of the issue of Jewish immigration into Palestine in the 1880s, there began to appear indications that the Porte was growing suspicious of its activities. The Jewish doctor of the Sultan, Elias Paşa, did not come to the festivities in Istanbul on the twenty-fifth anniversary of the foundation of the Alliance in 1885, because of the Sultan's belief that the Alliance was encouraging Jewish immigration to Palestine.[133] Isaac Fernandez mentioned in 1898 that his friends at the Porte advised a clear public statement against Zionism on the part of the Alliance,[134] advice which does not seem to have been acted upon by Paris. In 1901, during a discussion at the Council of State on the question of the authorization to be given to legalize the agricultural school *Or Yehudah,* several members of the Council accused the Alliance of having political aims.[135] One of the reasons given for the rejection by the Porte in 1907 of Jacob Meir as Chief Rabbi of Jerusalem was that he was associated with the Alliance.[136]

In spite of the great degree of independence enjoyed by the organization until 1914, it had become well aware by the turn of the century that as a foreign institution it had to tread very carefully in Turkey. Given the Turkish suspicion of all foreign groups and organizations in a new climate of nationalism, and the particular suspicion with which Zionism was treated at the highest levels of power, it appeared doubly imperative to the Alliance to distance itself as much as possible from the movement. Apart from its own ideological inclinations, and the bitter taste left after the *débâcle* in Bulgaria, it had too much at stake in the Ottoman Empire to risk being tarred with the Zionist brush.

This attitude was in evidence throughout the Alliance's dealings with the Zionist movement in Turkey. Fernandez had warned the Alliance of the dangers of Zionism for the Jews of Turkey as early as 1897.[137] Then followed a mysterious correspondence between the Central Committee and the Porte on the question of Zionism. The only trace of it left in the archives is the mention made by Fernandez that he had forwarded a letter sent by the Alliance to the first secretary of the Sultan and to the grand vizir.[138] Presumably it was some sort of assurance that the Alliance had nothing to do with the Zionist movement.

The tactic adopted by the Alliance as an organization in the face of Zionism in Turkey was public silence. The Central Committee continually refused the advice of its friends to go on the attack and to subsidize a newspaper in French that would oppose the Zionist *L'Aurore*.[139] It even refused to allow the *Amicale,* its alumni association in Istanbul, to install gymnastic equipment in its school buildings to draw the youth away from the Zionist *Makabi,* which had become very popular among Alliance students. It also refused to subsidize the buying of a new building for the *Amicale*.[140] The same policy was adopted in Salonica where similar conflicts between the Zionists and the anti-Zionists were taking place.[141]

The Alliance preferred to leave its position on Zionism ambiguous in the Jewish world and did not want to alienate some of its membership. Furthermore, it did not want to fuel further the polemical fires. In contrast to its early years, when it had shown a particular agility in using the press for propaganda purposes, the *grande dame* of Jewish organizations, after close to half a century of existence, had become set in her ways, had lost a certain *élan,* had become too much part of the establishment in the Jewish world to stomach active participation in a press war.

There was one occasion when the Alliance broke its silence, and it was, significantly, during a meeting with a Turkish parliamentary delegation in Paris in 1909. The delegation, headed by Dr. Rıza Tevfik Bey, deputy for Edirne, himself a graduate of an Alliance school, made a courtesy call to the Central Committee in Paris on July 15, 1909. In the course of the conversation, after expressing his great sympathy for the Alliance, Rıza Tevfik Bey indicated that

> it would be prudent not to encourage this (Zionist) agitation. Turkey intends to keep its doors open to all the persecuted . . . [but] it would not tolerate a movement which would end up by creating a Jewish Question [in Turkey] which does not exist at present, and that it is in the interest of the Jews not to bring it about.[142]

Narcisse Leven was reported to have answered by stating that this conformed totally to the views of the Alliance "which has always intended to remain an outsider to Zionism and has avoided encouraging it from any direction."[143] The publication of the exchange in the bulletin of the Alliance was a relatively discreet way of making the Alliance's position clear. Nevertheless, Leven's statement was given wide publicity in the European and Jewish press.[144] The Zionist press and publications were, in future years, to put Rıza Tevfik's words in Leven's mouth so that it appeared that it was Leven who had warned the Turkish delegation that Zionism threatened to create a Jewish question in Turkey.[145]

Apart from this episode, the Central Committee maintained a public silence on the question of Zionism in Turkey (though individual members of the Central Committee did make occasional anti-Zionist comments in public). Privately, it had a more interventionist policy, relying on Haim Nahum to carry on the anti-Zionist fight. When Nahum became discouraged by the Zionist agitation against him in 1909 and began to talk about resignation, it was Bigart who tried to lift his morale. He then made the extraordinary suggestion that Nahum use some of his contacts to have a non-Jewish deputy ask in Parliament for the government's opinion of Zionism in order to elicit a firm anti-Zionist statement, and offered his help to find funds if it were necessary.[146] It was Bigart's theory that a governmental statement of opposition to Zionism would dampen the agitation among the masses. Nothing seems to have come out of the plan in the short term. Bigart returned to the charge a year later, encouraging Nahum to adopt a more activist anti-Zionist stance and encourage a minister who was his friend to make anti-Zionist statements in the Chamber of Deputies.[147] These suggestions do not appear to have been implemented. Nahum was increasingly in conflict with the communal administration, and any leak that might have followed his acting upon Bigart's advice would have destroyed his political career for good. Although 1911 was to see two great debates in the Ottoman Chamber on Zionism,[148] there is no indication that they came about because of Nahum's following the advice of the Alliance.

What is extraordinary about the plan of Bigart is that it was a remarkably foolhardy suggestion coming from a very conservative man. Zionism was indeed a sensitive topic, and the Alliance was right to fear that in the climate of injured Turkish nationalism in the twilight years of the Empire it could lead to the rise of antisemitism. Yet it appears that Bigart was sufficiently consumed by anti-Zionist emotion to throw caution to the winds. Anti-Zionist statements in the Chamber were bound, as they did in 1911, to spread distrust of the Jews among the Turkish public at large. The Empire was threatened by rampant nationalisms from all sides. It did not require much to add the Jews to the list of distrusted nationalities. Bigart's plan would have contributed directly to what the Alliance feared would be the inevitable consequence of Zionism, the emergence of a Jewish Question in Turkey.

This uncharacteristically adventurous and ill-advised move by Bigart is best interpreted in the light of the mood of desperation that seems to have been created in the Alliance headquarters in Paris by the hostile propaganda and politics that had emerged in the Jewish communities of the Levant. None of the reorganization of the communal administrations so ardently anticipated in

1908 had come about. The Alliance schools were threatened from all sides. The Bulgarian precedent constituted a chilling reminder of what could happen if Zionism were not checked.

Faced with all these problems, the Alliance engaged in some rare soul-searching in 1910–11. Responding to an Alliance teacher who had sent a report on how Zionism was transforming Turkish Jewry, Bigart was pessimistic:

> If Turkish Jewry allows itself to be overtaken by this gangrene, it would prove that our system of education has not been good, has not created the mentality that we wanted to impart.[149]

Elaborating on the same theme a few months later in a letter to Fernandez, who had stated that 90 percent of the youth was now Zionist, Bigart was even more categorical:

> [If this were true, it would be] a total condemnation of all our system of education. We do not have the pretension to reproach for this failure of our efforts of thirty years the versatile character or the weakness of intelligence of the Jewish population of Constantinople; it appears to us as more logical to accuse our incomprehension of the real needs of the youth. The conclusion would be the total modification of our program of action or the renunciation of the prolonging of an attempt which has failed so badly . . . [there will be] no concessions to this utopian doctrine; it will remain for us to envisage coldly the possible closure of some of our schools in Istanbul . . . [150]

Nevertheless, the Alliance remained steadfast in its opposition. This continued even after the Balfour Declaration. Its president, Sylvain Lévi, became notorious with the anti-Zionist speech he made during the debate on Palestine held by the Supreme Council of the Allies in 1919 in which he rejected most of the Zionist arguments.[151] The organization would change its stance only after the Holocaust and the establishment of the state of Israel in 1948.

Its only concession in the schools was to increase the hours devoted to the study of Hebrew in 1920.[152] But soon, the new republic terminated the question of Zionism in Turkey as well as putting an end to the Alliance schools within its borders.

The Alliance still had many friends in the Turkish Jewish community, and an elite which, even if quite independent from the Alliance, bore its strong imprint. Nevertheless, by World War I, the trend away from the Alliance had become unmistakable. Its tutelage of Eastern Jewry no longer carried the same clout, or enjoyed the same popularity. New forces had emerged, and the Alliance, whose world view was still fixed within the parameters of the experience of Jewish emancipation in Western Europe a century earlier, was slowly but surely left behind.

VII

BETWEEN FRENCH IMPERIALISM AND TURKISH NATIONALISM
THE END OF THE ALLIANCE IN TURKEY

The Alliance and French Interests in the Levant

There is no doubt that the Alliance played a particularly important role in propagating French language and culture among the Sephardim of the Levant. However, the nature of its ties with France and the evolution of its official relationship with the French foreign ministry defy a simplistic identification of its interests with that of French policy in the Middle East in the second half of the nineteenth and early twentieth centuries. The real picture was considerably more complex and can be understood only in the context of French cultural politics in the Levant.

The *mission civilisatrice* which was such a hallmark of French imperialism had always attached great importance to the work of French schools overseas. French values, deemed to be the finest expression of civilization, could be expressed best by the French language as propagated by the French school.[1] In the words of Aulard, the famous historian of the revolution of 1789, these schools taught "our language, our genius, the spirit of France herself, the ideas of justice and fraternity between individuals and peoples."[2] They were the guardians and champions of the French nationality. By the turn of the century, it was taken as axiomatic among official and intellectual circles in Paris that it was a patriotic duty to "extend the frontiers of the French language to where they did not coincide with [French] political frontiers."[3]

The ideology of French linguistic expansion could combine the most lofty rhetoric about equality and fraternity with the most self-interested economic and political considerations. A member of the *Alliance française,* an organization founded in 1883 to encourage the spreading of the French language throughout the world, put it in a nutshell at a speech at Rheims in 1891: "The French language gives French habits, French habits lead to the buying of French products. He who knows French becomes a client of France."[4] In the same vein, Delcassé, the French minister for foreign affairs, expressed in 1902 his belief that "[h]e who speaks French in the Orient is not far from thinking in French and acting in French and finds himself quite naturally oriented toward France, whether for his moral aspirations or for his material needs."[5] This rather naive faith in the powers of the French language contributed to the perception of the French school abroad as the perfect agent of cultural, political and economic penetration.

Nowhere did the politics of schooling become such an important issue for the French as in the Middle East. The latter was a region where France had no formal colonies, and it was hoped that French culture would become a powerful tool for French interests. Until the 1880s, French schools in the area had grown on their own, supported by the Catholic religious orders which had founded them, with occasional aid from the French government. The state welcomed the beneficial effects of the dissemination of the French language that it assumed ensued from the work of these institutions. It protected them in the Ottoman Empire under the capitulation treaties which had made France the traditional protector of the Catholics in the Levant[6] but did not concern itself too much with their actions.[7]

From the 1880s, benevolent passivity gave way to active interest and intervention. This was directly related to the weakness of the Ottoman Empire after its defeat by the Russians in 1878 and the need to secure as large a *clientèle* as possible for France in the face of growing competition from other powers for influence in the region. The French near monopoly of Catholic education was also now threatened by the spread of Italian schools and the work of Anglo-Saxon and German missions. As a result, state subsidies to French language schools went up from 600,000 francs per year in the 1880s to 800,000 in 1900 and to 1,270,000 francs in 1914.[8] The schools gained even further importance in the eyes of the policy makers at the *Quai d'Orsay* when France's traditional protectorate of the Catholics in the Levant under the capitulatory regime ended formally with the breaking of French diplomatic relations with the Vatican in 1904.[9]

In the first years of the twentieth century, internal French political turmoil surrounding the issue of Church and State spilled over into cultural politics in the Middle East. The overwhelming majority of schools subsidized by the French government in the region were missionary establishments, and the contradiction of Republican France represented abroad so heavily by Catholic institutions bothered many an anticlerical. The *Quai d'Orsay* came under increasing attack for its subsidies to these schools.[10] An independent organization, the *Mission laïque,* was founded in 1901 to create more secular establishments. It set up important *lycées* in Alexandria, Beirut, and Salonica.

Sticking to Gambetta's dictum that anticlericalism was not an article for export, the *Quai* defended the use of missionary schools for French interests in the Levant saying that harm would follow from their precipitate closure.[11] To please the anticlericals, it did increase the subsidies to newly founded secular French institutions in the Middle East.[12] But it remained committed to the continuation of the missionary establishments.

France still had an unsurpassed position in the educational field in the

Middle East, its fears of the activities of its rivals notwithstanding. According to the archives of the French Ministry for Foreign Affairs, there were 95,160 students in French-subsidized educational institutions in the Levant in 1910. (The term "Levant" was used to cover the area including the Ottoman Empire, Egypt, Persia, Bulgaria, and Greece.) Of these students, only 6409 were outside the Ottoman Empire and Egypt. Catholic religious orders were in charge of the education of 87,126 out of the total of 95,160. The overwhelming majority of the students were in elementary schools.[13]

Who attended the schools where French was the language of instruction in the Levant? Jacques Thobie has broken down the figures for the student body of these institutions in the Asian parts of the Ottoman Empire according to religious and ethnic groups, basing his study upon a 1912 account by Maurice Pernot, one of the editors of the *Journal des Débats* and a member of the *Comité des intérêts français en Orient*.[14] These figures approximate within 5 to 10 percent with those of the *Quai d'Orsay*.[15] Thobie's study is based upon 55 percent of the total student body, many schools not having supplied the relevant information, but nevertheless provides a good indication for the general trends. His findings reveal the following: In 1912, 44 percent of the student body in these institutions, *whether subsidized by the French government or not,* were Catholics, 26.8 percent were Jews, 22 percent were Greek Orthodox and Gregorian Armenians, 6.5 percent were Muslims, and 0.3 percent were Protestants.[16]

As Thobie demonstrates, the Greeks and Armenians seem to have constituted roughly the same proportion of the school population as of the general population. The Catholics are largely overrepresented and Muslims largely underrepresented.[17] This is not surprising, as the great majority of these establishments were Catholic institutions and the majority of Muslims were loath to attend Christian schools. But the Jewish share appears unusual—3.5 percent of the general population and 26.8 percent of the student population in French language institutions—until one realizes that the overwhelming majority of these students were in Alliance schools. If the figures for the Alliance institutions are not taken into account, the Jewish share falls to only 3.7 percent of the total.[18]

I have done further computations, breaking these figures down according to the major cities. The results are quite revealing. If one includes the number of students in the Alliance schools, the Jews in 1911 constituted 58.7 percent of the student population in all the schools where French was the language of instruction in Istanbul, 58.1 percent in Baghdad, 43.6 percent in Izmir, and over 20 percent in all other major towns of the Asian possessions of the Ottoman Empire and Egypt.[19]

The figures for Salonica and Edirne, towns in the European areas of the Ottoman Empire, were not included in Pernot's study. But they are available for 1909 in the *Quai d'Orsay* archives and they show the same trend even more strongly. If one adds the number of students in the Alliance schools to the total figure for the students in establishments in these two towns where the language of instruction was French, it emerges that 79.2 percent of the total in Salonica and 85 percent of the total in Edirne were Jews.[20]

Therefore the Jews emerge as a significant element in the Francophone phenomenon in the Levant on the eve of World War I. Like the Maronites in Lebanon, but for entirely different reasons, they were one of the few autochthonous groups in the Middle East for whom French had become indisputably the language of instruction for mass education. It is evident that this was entirely due to the work of the Alliance Israélite Universelle.

Hence, one would assume that the *Quai d'Orsay* saw the Alliance as a natural ally of its politics of linguistic expansion and therefore actively assisted it. Surprisingly, this was a late development. Both the *Quai d'Orsay* and the Central Committee took the international nature of the Alliance very seriously. Only the *Ecole Normale Israélite Orientale* was registered as an official body in Paris. The Alliance, as an institution, had no legal French status. As a result, in the first half century of its existence, it asked for and received no subsidies from Paris and was not officially protected under the capitulatory regime by the French government in the Levant, only benefiting from unofficial protection when the need arose.

In the first years of the Alliance's existence, when it was wary of various threats to its schools, it had clearly wanted to have the guarantee of French consular protection if the need arose. In the words of Charles Netter writing about the Tetuan school in 1862, "[i]n these barbaric countries, it is necessary for all men, for all institutions to be protected by a European government, otherwise nothing stable can be established. . . ."[21] Nevertheless, it sought no blanket protection from the French government. The French foreign ministry responded to individual appeals from the Alliance in specific cases and gave instructions to the French consuls concerned to help schools as problems arose. Hence, Foreign Minister Marquis de Moustier instructed the French consul in Jerusalem (on 17 April 1868) "to give, if there is any need, and in a way that you judge proper, your official help to the Jewish school founded (by M. Krieger) in Jerusalem."[22] In 1879, the Alliance asked Foreign Minister Waddington to "transform into a regulation" *(règle de conduite)* the protection that had been given on a "spontaneous" basis to its schools by the French consuls in the Ottoman Empire.[23] Responding in the affirmative, Waddington instructed the French Ambassador in Istanbul to give help to the Alliance schools and to their teachers.[24]

But it appears that this circular remained without much force. The French consuls might attempt to help if the need arose, but since the Alliance was not registered as an official French body, they could not, and did not want to, claim a juridical right of protection. The Alliance was well aware of the fact. Responding to a move by Pariente from Izmir in 1892 to clarify the status of its schools with the French consulate there, the Alliance made it clear that it believed that "neither the French embassy in Constantinople nor the ministry [in Paris] will consent to place the schools under French protection."[25]

Some French consuls in Turkey took an interest in the local activities of the organization. In 1869 and in 1870, the consul in Edirne wrote glowing letters to the Alliance, congratulating it on the work of the school.[26] Writing to Félix Bloch, he expressed satisfaction over the fact that by teaching French, the school was "serving our interests [by helping in] the moral conquest of the country."[27] Very often, a newly arrived consul would discover the Alliance schools with great surprise and would express his amazement at their splendid work in spreading the French language.[28] One consul put it thus: "It is perhaps sad to say, but it is irrefutable that it is these unfortunate Jews whom the whole world persecutes who are doing most in the town to propagate our language and approach our civilization."[29] But this did not find an echo at the *Quai d'Orsay.*

Occasionally the French representatives, along with other consuls, would attend the ceremonies marking the end of the school year when prizes were given to the best students. But their role was limited to showing a French presence in these occasions. The Alliance simply did not figure among the preoccupations of the French foreign ministry. In all the consular correspondence between Izmir and Paris between 1873 and 1895, there is not a single mention of the Alliance institutions in the town,[30] even though the Alliance archives reveal that the consuls did occasionally have contacts with the schools.[31]

In fact, it is quite clear that the French foreign ministry neglected the organization in the Levant and was very often ignorant of its activities there until the first decade of the twentieth century. Many Alliance teachers complained bitterly about the lack of interest shown by the French consuls in their work, especially in the large towns of Turkey like Istanbul.[32] They commented on the excessively clerical orientation of both the French diplomatic corps and of the expatriate French communities in the Levant.[33] Indeed, the French were first and foremost interested in their protectorate over the Catholics. The fact that French was the language of instruction in the Alliance schools was mentioned by the consuls to Paris, but their main preoccupation was to protect and further the activities of the missionary establishments.

The situation differed markedly in North Africa where France exercised direct influence in Tunisia and Morocco and where there was no native Christian population on whom it could make any claims. The Alliance emerged from the beginning as an important interlocutor for the French vis-à-vis the local Jewish communities. The latter could be useful for France as intermediaries in the localities, as well as a force which would support its interests. The Central Committee also, while always trying to maintain an independent line, was not loath to work closely with the French in North Africa, as it saw the future of the area and of its Jews as inextricably linked to that of France. In a colonial context, the colonial power was the major referent for the Alliance, and there was never any doubt in the mind of its leadership that the organization and the Jews of North Africa would benefit from a close association with the metropolis.[34]

But the situation in the Levant was completely different. There France relied on local Catholics for spreading its influence. And for the Alliance, power in the area still rested with the Ottoman Turks, weakened though they were. It did not expect France to exercise direct political control and did not assume that French interests and those of Ottoman Jews were identical.

Hence, the Central Committee was not dissatisfied with the neglect of the schools in the Levant by the *Quai d'Orsay*. It was very careful not to alienate the Ottoman government under whose jurisdiction most of its institutions operated. Fernandez had advised it that the Waddington circular of 1879 had caused displeasure at the Porte and that any intervention by the French embassy on behalf of its schools would do more harm than good.[35] Consequently, it never invoked the Waddington circular in its dealings with the Turkish authorities. Significantly, the Alliance schools were not included in the 1901 list of protected institutions compiled by the French embassy. The list was accepted by the Turks after the Mytelene incident when the French occupied the Aegean island to force the Turks to accede to their demands for the reaffirmation of their protectorate over the French schools under Ottoman rule and to abolish new taxation measures that had been proposed for these institutions.[36] Responding to Fernandez's apologetic letter that he had not known of the Central Committee's intentions over the matter and had therefore not been able to intervene in time at the French embassy, Bigart made the position of the Alliance clear:

> . . . [the Central Committee] is not at all upset about the fact that our schools have not been included in the list of the schools protected by the French embassy which has been submitted to the Porte. Our schools are not French schools, and except for small local problems, we have never had anything but praise for the attitude of the Ottoman civil servants toward our institutions. If the circumstances require it one day, we could perhaps remind the French Ambassador in Constantinople of the circular of his predecessor. But for the moment, it is much to our advantage not to mix up our establishments with the schools placed under the direct control of the embassy.[37]

The Alliance wanted both not to alienate the Turks by becoming associated with the hated capitulations and to maintain absolute independence from the French foreign ministry.

The latter sentiment was put in sharp relief by the Alliance response to the news in 1908 that there were proposals for some of its teachers to receive decorations from the French embassy for services rendered to the French language. They would be happy to see their teachers decorated:

> . . . but here we will not take any steps with the ministry. At the ministry they would perhaps grant us a few centimeters of ribbon . . . but they would then think that they had done a lot for the Alliance. We prefer not to owe anything to the ministry in order to keep our freedom of action. . . .[38]

Whether in its interaction with the Turkish government, with the local Jewish populations, with the Zionists, or with the French authorities, the Alliance always guarded jealously its independence and freedom of movement.

It also kept an eye on the Jewish world by doing its best not to appear to be too associated with France. It was very strict with its teachers who were sometimes overzealous in their relations with local French representatives. It forbade them from becoming members of the local *Alliance française* chapters. It was furious when Nissim Behar, the director of its school in Jerusalem, asked for a subsidy from the *Alliance française* in 1886. Loeb reprimanded Behar severely: "The Alliance Israélite Universelle is an international organization, and your demand threatens to compromise us with our German, Italian, etc. members. And all this for 1000 francs!"[39] When Bloch had proposed preparing the best students of the schools in Istanbul to take the examination of the *brevet de capacité* given in the French embassy, Loeb's refusal was as categorical: "The Alliance is an international organization and not a French one, and our members abroad might find it singular that we direct the education of our students, even of only a few among them, toward examinations . . . which are purely French."[40] Even though the decision making leadership of the organization was exclusively French and the schools used French as the language of instruction, the Alliance had claims to represent the entire Jewish world and could not afford to be seen as too closely allied with French interests.

It was the emergence of Zionism in the East that led to a change of attitude at the *Quai d'Orsay* toward the Alliance in the Levant. This development drew the attention of the French consuls and of the foreign ministry to its work and to the discovery and recognition of its very significant achievements in the teaching of the French language. The letters to Paris from the consuls in the Levant in the first decade of the twentieth century are full of references to the Alliance and to its struggle with the Zionists.[41] The French were hostile to Zionism for their own reasons, as in the event of a breakup of the Ottoman Empire, they had their own designs on Greater Syria, *la Syrie intégrale,* which included Palestine.[42] But while Zionism as a political movement was dismissed by the French as utopian and unlikely to succeed, it was taken much more seriously, especially outside Palestine, once it was realized that its attacks upon the Alliance were also attacks upon the privileged position enjoyed by the French language among the Sephardic communities of the Levant. Hence, the position emerged that a weakening of the Alliance was against French interests.

Furthermore, France was increasingly on the defensive in the Middle East by the turn of the century and was searching for new allies. If for the rather right-wing *Quai d'Orsay* anticlericalism was not an article for export, neither was antisemitism in the newly straitened circumstances in which it found itself in the Levant. Its traditional protectorate over the Catholics was coming to an end, and Germany, a relative newcomer to the Middle East scene, had made great strides in extending its influence at the Porte. It is in this context that one sees the development of the myth of Zionism as a "German" phenomenon, as a German ploy to weaken France's interests in the region.

The first report about the Germanic affinities of Zionism came from the French consul in Jerusalem in 1900, who commented that "in a general way, Zionism, whether by a secret affinity as yet ill-defined or by considerations of self-interest . . . appears as a new form of German expansion."[43] When, in 1901, the *Hilfsverein* was founded in Berlin by German Jews to establish German schools in the Middle East and soon started to compete directly with the Alliance, the conspiracy picture became quite clear. The *Hilfsverein* and Zionism were two sides of the same coin. Both aimed at the spreading of German influence. By 1904, observing the struggle between the Alliance and Zionists in Bulgaria, Paris had reached the conclusion that Zionism in that country had a "clearly German character and was looking for help to the *Hilfsverein.*"[44] The old benign neglect of the Alliance could be maintained no longer.

The man who was responsible for alerting Paris to the necessity of drawing closer to the Alliance was Boppe, the French consul of Jerusalem and a close friend of Albert Antébi, the colorful and controversial director of the Alliance Jerusalem school. In a long report written in 1903, commenting on the Zionist congress of that year, Boppe gave a fascinating interpretation of the Jewish world as he saw it. There were two groups, the Ashkenazim who lived in Slavic and Saxon countries and the Sephardim who had maintained the

> imprint of the Latin idea *(idée latine)*. . . . The Jews of the South have kept from the countries they once inhabited the tolerance, the gentleness *(douceur)* of belief, the love of the good life, the indolence and submission to public power. . . . The Ashkenazim . . . the Jews of the North, [are mostly] Orthodox and are the main defenders of the Mosaic dogma. [They are characterized] by a cold-bloodedness, endurance, and suppleness which has enabled them to be placed in the first rank.[45]

The Alliance had the greatest influence among the former, and the *Hilfsverein* and the Zionists among the latter. He then went on to laud the work of the organization and the services that it had rendered France by its dissemination of the French language. He continued by pointing out that the Alliance

> . . . now faced by attacks from the Zionists and the *Hilfsverein,* whether she wants it or not, has become a real French organization by her propagation of our language, and by its constant diffusion of our spirit, ideas and methods. All the Jewish societies have become nationalized and now serve, in the accomplishment of their philanthropic missions, the cause of the countries they spring from, [and are] supported officially or unofficially, by their governments . . . The attitude of

other powers has, at present, rendered it a necessity to bind [the Alliance] more intimately to our cause by granting her official protection. . . . [46]

Paris acted upon this remarkable report and asked for further information about the organization from other consuls in the area and directly from Leven himself.[47]

In 1904, France intervened in favor of the Alliance at the Porte for the first time, over the question of the registration of its trade school in Jerusalem directly in the name of the organization. The president, Narcisse Leven, taking advantage of the new official French interest in the Alliance, had informed the *Quai d'Orsay* about a Turkish law which required the registering of its schools under the name of members of the Central Committee and other individuals and that it caused the organization to pay unnecessary taxation. He solicited the help of the Foreign Minister in changing the registrations to the name of the Alliance with priority to be given to the case of the Jerusalem school. In the meantime, the consuls had informed the *Quai* that the Porte had allowed the Evelina de Rothschild school in Jerusalem to be registered under the name of the Anglo-Jewish Association in violation of the law which forbade registration under the name of organizations. The French intervened in favor of the Alliance and were adamant in insisting upon equal treatment for a "French society," as it was put in a *note verbale* delivered to the Porte,[48] the first time since the foundation of the organization that it had been referred to in these terms by the French foreign ministry. The Turks opposed the move at first but finally acceded to the demand in 1908.[49]

The growing tendency at the *Quai* to think of the Alliance as a French organization had been fuelled by the first concrete Franco-Alliance collaboration against the Zionists in Bulgaria in 1903–1905. In spite of the active support of the French consul, the organization had been forced to abandon its school buildings in Philippopoli to the Zionists and was gradually forced to close most of its schools in the country. This was taken by the *Quai* to be a defeat for the French language, and it hardened its anti-Zionist resolve.[50]

In 1907, Boppe was *Chargé d'Affaires* in Istanbul and, developing the line which he had at first adopted in Jerusalem in 1903, suggested a much warmer attitude on the part of the *Quai* toward the Alliance:

> . . . we have not always shown to the majority of these schools the interest which they merit. The embassy has benefited from the support of these schools in Constantinople, Syria, Palestine . . . without their having, so to speak, asked for anything in return . . . the Alliance has succeeded in improving in many regions of Turkey the moral and material state of a great number of its coreligionists. [It is now decreasing its subsidies] and wants the local committees to find local sources of funds . . . I fear that if we continue to observe toward the establishments of the Alliance the same reserved and almost indifferent attitude which we have shown in most of the towns of Turkey, some of the local committees might be led to diminish the hours devoted to French . . . and other

governments who try to oppose the propagation of our language in the Orient might give subsidies. We should encourage these committees, but prudently, since they are Ottoman schools.[51]

He suggested that more acts of friendliness be shown toward the teachers, more visits by the consuls to the schools, the distribution of prizes at the end of the year, the granting of decorations to the most important Alliance educators.[52] The suggestions were adopted in their totality by the *Quai* and relayed to the embassy in Istanbul who then informed all the consuls of the new disposition toward the Alliance. Significantly, prudence was urged again, and the consuls were asked not to lose sight of "the particular situation of the Jewish schools which are under the jurisdiction of the Imperial [Ottoman] authorities. . . ."[53] The new circular was a revamped version of the one issued by Waddington in 1879 and was much more positive toward the organization, granting it a French naturalization of sorts. Nevertheless, France could still not formally protect the Alliance institutions as they were not juridically French entities.

Under the new dispensation, in 1908 the French Embassy in Istanbul decorated many Alliance teachers and awarded them *palmes académiques*.[54] The years after 1908 saw much closer contact between the French authorities and the Alliance personnel in Turkey. The reaction of the Central Committee to these developments was cautious. It affirmed again and again its stand that its schools were Ottoman institutions, and that they had only a "moral link" with France.[55]

On the other hand, it also welcomed the new French interest, as long as it was discreet and did not jeopardize its position vis-à-vis the Ottoman state. The Alliance was not loath to use arguments designed to appeal to the *Quai d'Orsay* when help was needed. In this period it started to increase its appeals to the French government. It asked for the formal protection of its schools in Persia, pointing out the great services the Alliance rendered to France by spreading the French language and ideas.[56] When it wanted France to intervene strongly in a direction which it saw as beneficial to its interests, it tried invariably to highlight the benefits derived by France from its activities. In 1912, to influence France to act against a possible annexation of Salonica by any Balkan state which could endanger its institutions in the city by nationalizing them, it pointed out that "wherever the Alliance creates a school, there comes into being a small home of French culture."[57] If the *Quai* wanted to use the Alliance for its own purposes, the Alliance was, in turn, not above reciprocating in kind. However, in this case, its proposal for turning Salonica into a free port, as the Jews of the city wished, was not in the end supported by France which, significantly, did not believe that the Alliance would be able to resist the Zionists there. And if the Zionists gained control, than Salonica would turn into a center of German and Austrian influence.[58] The myth of the German links with Zionism could affect even an important policy decision such as this.

The Zionists and the *Hilfsverein* often acted in tandem in the localities to dethrone the Alliance from its position of preeminence, and they had cordial relations on the official level[59] until the great crisis of 1913 over the language of instruction to be used in the future Haifa *Technicum* to be founded by the *Hilfsverein*. The Alliance, however, believed that the *Hilfsverein* and Zionism were two sides of the same medallion. Antébi, who might have originally planted the idea in the head of the French consul in Jerusalem, spoke frequently in his letters of the machinations of the *siono-Hilfsvereinistes* and the *germano-sionistes*.[60] Bigart himself referred to the "*Hilfsverein* and its allies the Zionists" in a letter to Nahum in 1908.[61] In this period, there were many contacts between Bigart, Leven and the *Quai* and one can presume that the perception was mutually reinforced. Suffice it to say that by 1914 both the Alliance and the Quai had the same view of *germano-sionisme*.[62]

Several inroads had been made into the Alliance policy of splendid isolation in the first decade of the twentieth century. The attacks that the Alliance had had to face in many communities of the Levant had obliged it to collaborate more closely with the *Quai d'Orsay*. On the other hand, the *Quai,* also on the defensive, had begun to support the organization, recognizing it as an important ally in its policies of linguistic expansion, and had tried to further its interests as much as possible.

The Alliance policy of maintaining a certain distance from the *Quai d'Orsay* in the Levant, trying to act as independently as possible, and using the support of the *Quai* as an insurance policy only when it encountered problems, lasted for close to half a century and was on the whole successful. The fact that it took great care that its schools not be perceived as French institutions by the Turks, and its reluctance to invoke French protection for these establishments, proved beneficial when World War I broke out. The Ottomans and the French were now formally at war. The Alliance schools, upon the intercession of the Chief Rabbi Haim Nahum, were declared Ottoman communal institutions and allowed to function freely, while all the establishments formally protected by France were closed.[63]

The war years were hard ones for the Alliance network in Turkey and elsewhere. Communication between the Central Committee and the schools was cut to a minimum and could be maintained intermittently only through intermediaries in neutral countries. The Turkish government did not touch the schools which benefited from the protection of Chief Rabbi Nahum, who had a close relationship with the leadership of the state. Most schools managed to function normally. They experienced, however, considerable economic hardship, having to rely increasingly on local sources of financial support as well as on funds sent by the American Joint Distribution Committee to alleviate the economic misery into which the war and conscription plunged many a Turkish Jewish family.[64] Still, the schools, teaching the language of a belligerent enemy country, survived the war remarkably well.

The Central Committee managed to send funds to some of its institutions though Salonica, Cairo, Geneva, and Bucharest throughout the war years.[65] It was authorized to do this through the *Quai d'Orsay*'s intervention with the appropriate authorities in France. In the words of the *Quai*, the Alliance "had become more and more a real French society"[66] and served French interests abroad.[67] Furthermore, the Alliance intervened and succesfully prevented the deportation of thousands of Ottoman Jews who had emigrated to France but who had not yet become French citizens. Its arguments that this population was overwhelmingly pro-French as a result of the education it had undergone in its schools proved to be convincing. The Interior Ministry created a special category of *protégés* called *"israélites de Levant"* and entrusted the Alliance with the task of identifying and delivering certificates to Jews of the Ottoman Empire who had settled in France.[68]

The close collaboration between the organization and the *Quai d'Orsay* became a daily reality through the war. Leading members of the Central Committee such as Jacques Bigart, Sylvain Lévi, and Eugène Sée were among the founders of the *Comité français d'information et de propagande auprès des Juifs neutres* designed to influence Jewish public opinion in neutral countries, especially in the United States, in favor of the Entente.[69] Neither the *Quai* nor the Alliance were favorably impressed by the Balfour declaration. Sylvain Lévi, then vice-president of the organization, was sent by the *Quai* in the spring of 1918 as part of the commission to study local conditions in Palestine and report to the government. Lévi, though impressed by the transformation of the country, remained steadfast in his opposition to any of the political manifestations of Zionism, a position he made amply clear in his famous negative declaration after the war during the debate by the Supreme Council of the Allies on Palestine in 1919.[70]

The new closeness between the Alliance and the *Quai d'Orsay* found its concrete expression when the organization as a whole began, for the first time, to receive subsidies from the French government in 1920. In that year, it was allocated 1,500,000 francs and subsidies continued regularly thereafter.[71] The independence of the Alliance from official French policy had, by then, become only a relative affair.

The situation in Turkey in the years after the war also followed the same pattern. The French high commissioner in Istanbul adopted a very protective stance vis-à-vis the local Alliance schools. Abraham Benveniste, the director of the school for boys in Galata, had frequent meetings with officials in the French embassy from 1919 through 1922, giving detailed reports on the political situation within the Jewish community.[72] The High Commissioner was concerned with the inroads made by Zionism and to forestall attacks recommended a more supple policy to the Alliance of partial reconciliation with the movement through increasing the hours of Hebrew taught in the schools,[73] advice which appears to have been followed.[74] The concerns over the dethronement of French as the language of instruction for the Jews remained uppermost in the minds of French officials in Turkey. The embassy and the consulates in the various cities began to give regular subsidies to local Alliance schools after 1920 over and above the sums received by the Central Committee in Paris.[75]

Developments such as the rise of Zionism and the weakening of France's political position in the Levant had brought about a convergence between French interests and those of the Alliance, a rapprochement that had become even stronger during the war years and the period that immediately followed. However, the organization, still claiming leadership in the Jewish world, did not take the steps to become a formal French institution and still did not put its schools under official French protection. This position had served it well and had saved its institutions in the Ottoman Empire during the war. But it was precisely the fact that the schools were legally Turkish communal institutions that rendered the Alliance and its French protectors helpless in the face of the rising tide of Turkish nationalism that followed the establishment of the Turkish Republic in 1923.

From Empire to Republic: The Alliance Schools in the Age of Turkish Nationalism

In 1882, Jules Dalem, the director of the Alliance school for boys in Galata, writing on the attitude of the state vis-à-vis the educational institutions of the non-Muslim communities, observed that they were "under a regime not of independence but of absolute indifference."[76] It was this indifference that had allowed the Alliance to create its school network in the Empire in the first place. But Dalem's words were fateful ones, as the situation was to change drastically from the end of the nineteenth century.

The Public Education Law of 1869 had contained provisions for the registration and inspection of non-Muslim schools (clause 129), but they do not appear to have been acted upon until 1886, when an inspectorate of non-Muslim schools was created.[77] The new inspectorate inaugurated the beginning of an activist policy by the state. As mentioned above, educational institutions increased rapidly in the reign of Abdülhamid, with the state taking a leading role in their development.[78] This was accompanied by a steady encroachment upon the autonomy and independence of the educational infrastructures of the non-Muslims which, in the atmosphere of exacerbated nationalisms in the region, were increasingly treated with suspicion. In this respect, there is a direct continuity between the policies adopted by the successive governments from Adülhamid through the Young Turk regime to the Kemalist republic.

The Alliance schools were regularly inspected after 1886.[79] The books used in the schools were scrutinized and censored. As the Hamidian regime grew more and more suspicious of all foreigners, censorship increased greatly and was a constant source of complaint by Alliance teachers.[80]

A decree in 1902 banned all Muslims from attending non-Muslim schools.[81]

This affected the few Muslim students who were studying at the Alliance schools. The organization had looked favorably upon the presence of a certain number of non-Jews in its schools, as it thought that this would bring the Jews and non-Jews closer together.

The education authorities increasingly created difficulties for Alliance teachers who were foreign citizens. Moïse Franco, an Austrian subject, was prevented from continuing as school director in Demotica and ran into the same problem in Gelibolu.[82] This became an issue in the provinces with overzealous governors insisting on the letter of the law to make life unpleasant for foreigners. The Alliance tried to cover up the matter as much as possible, as it did not want to draw the attention of the central government to the question.[83] A blanket ban in the Empire on teachers who were foreign citizens would have wrought havoc in its entire system.

The 1908 revolution ended the censorship but only intensified the state's efforts to control the education of all its subjects. The new regime showed itself to be a more aggressive champion of Turkish nationalism than the old one. It increased the numbers of inspections dramatically, especially in the non-Turkish Muslim provinces, such as the Arab ones, and launched a campaign of Turkicization in the educational arena.

However, a new education law that would have put non-Muslim schools under the closer control of the state was postponed due to the fierce resistance of the Greek deputies in the Ottoman Chamber of Deputies who saw it as an outright attack upon the right of the *millets* to maintain their own educational systems.[84] A new elementary instruction law in 1913 reasserted the principle of the state inspecting and controlling the establishment of all private and non-Muslim schools[85] but did not go further.

It is clear that that the state would not long tolerate foreign citizens teaching in Alliance schools. The matter did not become an urgent issue between 1908 and 1914, but the threat was always there. The Alliance schools continued to be inspected regularly, especially in the provinces.[86] The education ministry also imposed its own calendar for the school year. The Alliance had resisted the changing of the time of the summer vacations from its preferred date of the Hebrew month of *Tishri,* the month of the Jewish High Holidays, to that of two months in the summer used as vacation time by other schools. This came to an abrupt end in 1914. The government flatly decreed that all schools had to have their summer vacations at the same time and only upon Nahum's intervention made allowances for the Jewish High Holidays. But otherwise, the Alliance had to conform to the state law.[87]

Furthermore, the organization had an exposed flank which could have doomed its schools in Turkey if the state had chosen to take action. Many of its institutions had not received the necessary permits from the appropriate bodies and were juridically illegal.

Most of the Alliance school buildings had been either constructed or bought by funds from the organization, supplemented by local contributions. Before 1908, the Ottoman law did not allow the registry of properties in the name of organizations. To forestall the possibility that one day the local Jewish communities, in a dispute, could take over these buildings, the Alliance had them registered as the private properties of individual members of the Central Committee, such as Narcisse Leven or Salomon Goldschmidt. This began to be a problem toward the end of the 1880s, with long delays in the registration process because of the Turkish suspicion of foreigners.[88] The organization then switched to using the name of Fernandez, trusted by the Turkish authorities, for this purpose.[89]

Registration as a school would have required express permission in the form of an *irade* (authorization) from the education ministry under clause 129 of the 1869 Public Instruction Law.[90] Through neglect, ignorance, and the fear of long delays because of the cumbersome nature of the Turkish bureaucracy, most Alliance schools were functioning without permits. The authorities did not bother them in their operation, another testimony to the indifference of the state to the educational system of the Jews. Of all the Alliance schools in Istanbul in 1889, only the one for boys in Hasköy had obtained such an *irade*.[91] Usually bribes distributed in the right quarters closed the matter when the question came up.[92] The Alliance did try to get permits for new institutions but the problem persisted for many years and difficulties dogged the granting of *irades*.[93] The organization went through years of delay before obtaining the official permits for the Istanbul Rabbinical Seminary and the agricultural school of *Or Yehudah*. Many of its early institutions remained without the proper licensing.[94]

As the climate of opinion became more nationalistic, the Alliance tried to protect itself. It felt the need for an official document from the state that would recognize the services rendered by the organization for the improvement of education in the Empire. The purpose was to guard against potential attacks on its network of schools under Ottoman rule. Haim Nahum proved to be of great help in this task. He obtained in 1900, after much effort (going seventeen times to the ministry), a formal statement of appreciation of the work of the organization from the education ministry.[95]

After becoming Chief Rabbi, Nahum intervened with the appropriate authorities on all matters concerning the Alliance, on questions such as the recognition of its institutions by the state as junior high schools, which gave the graduates automatic right of entry into the state *lycées*,[96] the allowing of school directors of foreign citizenship already employed in Turkey to continue in their duties,[97] and the exemption of the school buildings from property taxes.[98] Nevertheless, if the Turkish authorities had decided to cause trouble for the Alliance, there were sufficient juridical irregularities in the way the organization functioned in Turkey which could have put it in a very difficult position.

The growing pressures from an increasingly nationalistic state should not hide the fact that the Alliance schools enjoyed, until 1914, a degree of independence that would have been unthinkable for a comparable organization in France and elsewhere in Europe. For all the growing Turkish nationalism in the last years of the Ottoman Empire, Turkicization as a policy was hardly applied to the Jews. From 1894 on, a teacher of Turkish was sent to all non-Muslim schools,[99] but the effort stopped or was stopped by foreign powers there.

In 1914, the Ottoman Empire was a hybrid polity, assuming many of the characteristics of contemporary European nation-states, and yet incapable of implementing a successful policy of "nationalization" and unification of the masses that lived under its rule. The educational system of the Empire, which would have been the site where such unity could be forged, was a patchwork of incongruent autonomous sub-systems, state secular schools, Muslim religious schools, *millet* schools, and foreign schools, all of which coexisted and operated according to different philosophies and outlooks. Considerable resistance from Islamic religious elements to the secularizing attempts of the reformers, and the particularist traditions and aspirations of the constituent ethnic and religious groups of the Empire proved too strong, and Western meddling too powerful, to crown the efforts of modernization and reform with success.

Indeed, Western powers were caught in a dilemma when it came to their interaction with the Ottoman Empire. On the one hand, they offered the path of Westernization as the only possible cure for all its problems. On the other hand, they viewed with much misgiving the consequences of this Westernization: growing centralization, the expansion of an administration increasingly using Western means of organizing, controlling, and mobilizing civil society, which put in jeopardy their interference in its internal affairs. The more the Ottoman state attempted to adopt the policies of a European state, the more it aggravated its frictions with the Western powers, which by then had an enormous stake in the preservation of the status quo of the Empire as a semi-colony.

World War I provided the opportunity to the Ottoman government to end foreign meddling by abolishing the hated capitulations[100] and to take action in areas in which its hands had previously been tied. Soon, it closed all establishments of education belonging to, or protected by, the Entente powers. As mentioned above, the grave danger that this could have posed to the Alliance network was averted when the Chief Rabbi used his influence in high places to have its schools declared communal ones.[101] As Ottoman institutions, they were beyond any danger of closure. However, as a result of financial problems, many of the teachers resigned or were obliged to find additional sources of income.[102] Furthermore, the same problems obliged the directors to allow the local communities and personalities to have a greater role in the day-to-day administration of the institutions.[103] Nevertheless, the schools managed to function more or less regularly throughout the war years.

The state, now unhindered by foreign interference, could proceed with its policy of greater control of private institutions of education as well as of those belonging to the non-Muslim minorities. It passed a new regulation in 1915 which allowed thorough supervision of these establishments. The new regulation also made it compulsory for the schools to teach the Turkish language as well as Turkish history and geography. Furthermore, these subjects had to be taught by Turkish teachers appointed by the state.[104] The logistical problems engendered by the war appear to have prevented the implementation of the regulation, and there is no evidence to suggest that the Alliance schools ever had to fulfill its provisions.[105] Nevertheless, it provided a powerful precedent, and was to be revived by the Republic only a few years later.

The immediate years following the victory of the Entente in 1918 saw the full unhindered revival of foreign educational establishments in defeated Turkey. In the absence of the central government now under allied control, these institutions could proliferate at will and utilize whatever curricula they wished. The Central Committee in Paris also reasserted its control immediately after the armistice and began to guide the Alliance schools again. The schools in Istanbul reverted to their work of the prewar years. However, those Alliance institutions falling under Greek rule in Western Asia Minor as well as in Thrace had to replace Turkish with Greek in the curriculum. This was not a welcome development for the directors, who, together with the bulk of the Jewish population, preferred Turkish rule to that of the Greeks.[106] The longtime economic rival of the Jews, the Greeks were also feared for their antisemitism, as it was the Greek communities that had spawned, year after year, the blood libel accusations that had plagued the Jewish communites of the Levant in the second half of the nineteenth century.[107] The same fears that had been manifest in the Jewish community of Salonica after the conquest of the city by the Greeks in 1912[108] were also in evidence now in Izmir and the smaller centers in Asia Minor. The latter did in fact suffer from considerable harassment in the hands of the occupying Greek armies in 1921–22.[109]

The Turkish war of independence ended with the defeat of the Greeks. The Jewish communities of many towns in Western Asia Minor were caught in the hostilities, and fled to Izmir. The Alliance schools in the towns of Aydın, Turgutlu, Manisa, and Vurla were destroyed, never to open again. The Izmir schools miraculously survived the great fire of 1922 which followed the Greek retreat and the victorious entry of the Turkish troops into the city.

At the time of the foundation of the new Turkish Republic in 1923, the Alliance had twenty-eight schools with a total of 9904 students in Turkey.[110] Lulled by its long experience under the Ottomans, it expected its institutions to continue to function normally under the new regime. It was ill prepared for the ruthless nationalism of the new masters of the country who were determined to put an end to any vestige of foreign presence on Turkish soil.

The emergence of the republican state out of the ashes of the Ottoman Empire after close to a decade of crisis and military combat, beginning with the Balkan wars of 1912–13, radically altered the contours of non-Muslim existence in Turkey. Most of the Armenian community had perished, and the Greeks, with the exception of the Istanbul community, were transferred to

Greece in return for the transfer of most of the Turks of Greece (excluding those in Western Thrace) to Turkey. This meant that outside Istanbul, no significant non-Muslim presence remained in the country.

The modern Turkish nation-state, now divested of its multi-ethnic ballast, could act much more decisively than the ramshackle Ottoman Empire. The bureaucratic military elite, continuing in its ruling role into the Republic, could now take the reforms of the Ottoman period to their logical conclusion, unhampered by foreign intervention. The republican state, like the Western one on which it modelled itself, hence went much further than the Ottoman one. Under its Western-oriented leadership, not only was it concerned with controlling civil society, but it now also wanted to reform it, to "civilize" it, to bring it up to the level of West European societies. The model for the Republic was the French Jacobin state, highly centralized, with no intermediary bodies between the citizenry and the state. It drew upon this Western tradition as well as upon the specifically Ottoman one that stressed the omnipotence of the rulers. Under Atatürk, Turkey saw the separation of religion and politics through the effective disestablishment of Islam, the adoption of Western institutions in all areas of life, the creation of a universal secular education system, and the putting in place of a Republican ideology, populistic nationalism, that acted as an agent of integration and social mobilization.[111]

The Lausanne Treaty of 1923 signed by Turkey and the European states with which it had been in conflict also gave several rights to the minorities remaining in the country. They could continue to operate their schools and teach in their own languages, could not be barred from civil employment, and could regulate matters of personal and family status according to their religious laws.[112] However, the bitterness caused by the years of war combined with the exacerbated nationalism of the period unleashed a wave of xenophobia among the Turks, and the Jews, together with other non-Muslims, soon became easy targets. All non-Muslim employees in public service as well as in companies that had extensive relations with the public sector were dismissed in 1923–24.[113] The public mood was firmly set against "foreign" elements. Some Turkish newspapers charged that the Jews, as well as others, had profited from the war and should now be generous in their financial contributions to the reconstruction of the country.[114]

The Jewish press followed the allegations closely and put up a strong defense, arguing that the Jews had always been strong supporters of the Turks and had themselves suffered much during the war.[115] David Fresco, the editor of *El Tiempo* and a strong Turkish patriot, was particularly bitter over the dismissal of Jews and accused the authorities of contradicting their own principles of equality under the law for all the citizens of the country.[116]

The schools could not remain immune to the reigning atmosphere of xenophobia. Already in May 1923, the Ministry of Education revived the provisions of the 1915 regulations, whereby the teaching of the Turkish language, history, and geography was made compulsory in all the schools of the non-Muslims.

Furthermore, these had to be taught in Turkish by "Turks" appointed by the ministry.[117] It soon became clear that non-Muslims did not qualify as "pure Turks"[118] and hence were excluded from these teaching positions.

The new appointees also posed serious financial problems for non-Muslim schools, including the Alliance ones. They were to be paid by the schools themselves at salaries set by the Ministry of Education, salaries which were higher than the usual ones.[119] The Jewish community made several appeals to the authorities for a gradual introduction of the new regulation,[120] all to no avail.[121] From this time on, the communities and the schools had to find the financial resources to meet the extra cost.

In March 1924, the new regime passed the "Unification of Education" *(Tevhid-i Tedrisat)* law which altered radically the educational landscape of the country. The law prohibited all religious instruction in the schools and closed down the institutions of advanced Muslim learning, the *medreses*. It ended the duality between the secular and religious education systems that had hindered the success of educational reforms under the Ottomans since the *Tanzimat*.[122] The law, together with the expulsion of the Caliph in the same year, underlined one of the fundamental principles of the Republic, that of secularism, and pointed to the disestablishment of Islam to be formalized in 1928.

The radical secularism of the Republic could not yet affect the curricula of the schools of the minorities, as the Lausanne clauses allowed the teaching of religion in these institutions. It was only in 1936 that religious instruction would be banned also in these establishments.[123] However, the new law, rationalizing and streamlining the educational system of the country, served notice of the great degree of control that the state would henceforth exercise on all institutions of education in Turkey.

In early 1924, Alliance directors in the provinces began to report that the Turkish educational authorities were creating problems, refusing to recognize the schools as Alliance institutions, insisting that they be called communal schools.[124] In March 1924, the Alliance schools were ordered by the Ministry of Education to cease all contact with the organization in Paris.[125] Juridically, this spelled the end of the Alliance in Turkey.

The organization could not avail itself of the help or protection of the French Embassy, as it was not an officially French body, and the schools were not French institutions. The latter were, in fact, in a much better position than the schools of the Alliance. An accord of 1921 between the French and Turkish nationalist authorities in Ankara had recognized the right of all French institutions of education in existence before 1914 to continue to operate in Turkey.[126] Though these schools were harassed considerably in the years following the creation of the Republic and had to secularize themselves and obey the same regulations being applied to the schools of the non-Muslim minorities,[127] their legal existence was not challenged by the state.

The Alliance, having no French legal status, could not benefit from the accord. Ironically, its strategy of formal independence from France which had served it so well in the war years when it had been able to continue to operate its schools in Turkey, now doomed it in the new nationalist Republic.

The Central Committee kept silent in the face of the ban on the Alliance. Its hope was to be able to continue its work of schooling under the fiction that the schools were now communal institutions. But a new decree, this time affecting the whole curriculum of its schools in Turkey, rendered such a strategy impossible.

In June 1924, the Ministry of Education presented all Jewish elementary schools with the option of either teaching in Turkish, or "in their mother tongue," which it declared was Hebrew.[128] This was a clever move, as very few Turkish Jews were familiar with Hebrew as a living language and almost all spoke Judeo-Spanish. It is obvious that the decree was intended to displace French from its place as the language of instruction of the Jews of Turkey.

The same requirement from the Greeks and Armenians would not have been problematic, as both minorities used their respective mother tongues, Greek and Armenian, as the language of instruction in their schools. In the case of the Jews, however, Judeo-Spanish had long ago been demoted to the position of "jargon" as a result of the work of the Alliance and would not have been considered in the 1920s as an appropriate medium of instruction by the Jews of Turkey. Furthermore, the state did not appear to recognize it as the mother tongue of the Jews, which, of course, it still was. The Zionist movement could have taken the opportunity of instituting a Hebrew educational system. However, the Republic did not tolerate any nationalist movement within its borders, and Zionism went underground.

Hence the Jewish community took the only option available, the adoption of Turkish as the language of instruction in its elementary schools. Ankara agreed to the appeal made by Jewish communal leaders that the new reform be introduced gradually.[129] A transitional period ended in 1925 when Turkish was introduced progressively each year as the language of instruction for each class beginning with the lowest one.[130] French could be taught in the fourth year, but only as a second language. Since most Jewish elementary schools had only four grades, this meant practically the end of instruction in French. By 1929, these institutions were following the state curriculum, with the exception of a few hours devoted to Jewish religious education. The schools had now been totally nationalized.[131]

The loophole that allowed Turkish citizens to attend foreign schools, such as French ones, was closed at the elementary instruction level in 1931.[132] With the new law, no Turkish citizen could attend foreign elementary schools. The process of the nationalization of the Alliance institutions was part of the larger process of the creation of a unitary national elementary education system in Turkey.

The nation-building policies of the leaders of the Republic, attempting to forge a new state on the French model, could not square well with the existence of minority rights granted by the Lausanne treaty, which allowed non-

Muslims some pockets of autonomy. The relevant clauses of the treaty were renounced by the non-Muslims themselves in 1925–26 under rather enigmatic circumstances that require further clarification. This followed the abolition of the caliphate and of Muslim religious courts in 1924, and the making public of plans to adopt a new legal system modelled on the Swiss, Italian, and German codes.[133] The argument put forth by the official announcements of the leadership of the non-Muslim communities was that since the new legal codes of the state were no longer to be based on Muslim religious law but were to adopt secular Western statutes, then the need had disappeared for them to apply their own separate laws in matters concerning personal and family status.

With these developments, the last vestiges of the old *millet* privileges came to an end. No legal distinctions whatsoever remained in the statute books separating Muslim from non-Muslim. The Jewish as well as the other non-Muslim communities became strictly voluntary confessional organizations.

The Alliance continued to send funds to the schools and to maintain regular contacts with their directors well into the 1930s. It considered them important, as they were still schools for Jews and were, at least until 1936, providing some Jewish religious instruction. However, its hopes for a relaxation of the new regulations were not realized. The state curriculum remained firmly in place. With the introduction of Turkish as the language of instruction in 1925, these schools ceased to be, for all intents and purposes, Alliance institutions.

Many Jews who went on to study beyond the elementary level continued to attend foreign *lycées,* and French remained the language of choice. However, the elementary French mass educational system put laboriously in place by the Alliance since the 1860s came to an end in 1925. It is only after this date that one can speak seriously about the beginning of the process of the Turkicization of the Jews of Turkey.

The Alliance suffered from the contradictions of its ideology. It had greeted the process of reform and Westernization in the Ottoman Empire and in Republican Turkey with great satisfaction, as it held Westernization to be an absolute good. Nevertheless, the organization became increasingly uncomfortable with the consequences of the policies of reform, especially in the field of education, which by their very nature had the potential of severely limiting its own freedom of action. Like the European powers, it held a double standard when facing non-Western societies. It would have accepted the principle of the state deciding on the dates of summer vacations for schools as totally normal and indeed desirable in France, but chafed under this decision when it was applied to its schools in Turkey. Although increasing the number of hours devoted to Turkish, it resisted, in contradiction to its own ideology of emancipation, the proposals to make Turkish the language of instruction and was appalled when this became law under the Republic. And yet, it would have found it inconceivable in France that the Jews should attend schools where the language of instruction was anything but French.

The truth was that the Alliance, a product of its time and place, was convinced of the superiority of European culture and civilization. Turkish would not have been a suitable medium for its program of "regeneration." As far as Turkey was concerned, the Alliance ardently desired the civil and social advancement of its Jews. But it preferred a polity which would not take the Western model to its logical conclusion and transform itself into a nation-state but would rather remain under the influence of European powers, an amalgam of East and West where French would continue to occupy a privileged position. Ultimately such a position which shared the assumptions of the European imperialism of the day was not to remain a tenable one in the age of nationalism in the Middle East of the twentieth century.

The logic of the nation-state had in France for the first time created for the Jews the ideology of emancipation and "regeneration" which aimed at their integration. The Alliance had exported the French-Jewish program of "regeneration" to remake the Jews of the Muslim world in the image of French Jewry. But when adopted in Republican Turkey, and pushed to its logical conclusion, the same logic led inexorably to the closing of the autonomous sphere which had allowed the organization to flourish, and to the end of the Alliance's work in the first modern nation-state to emerge in the Middle East.

CONCLUSION

On the eve of World War I, the bulletin of the Alliance claimed, with a great deal of justification, that "[i]n all of the Ottoman Empire, there is not a single important or middling Jewish community where the action of the schools has not made itself felt. . . ."[1] The Alliance had come a long way in Turkey since its halting beginnings in the 1860s. It had established a major school network and a series of auxiliary bodies and institutions, apprenticeship organizations, reading clubs, alumni associations, mutual-aid societies and the like. Traditional Jewish education, already in economic crisis before the arrival of the organization, had been largely eclipsed by the new system of education it had introduced.

Westernization was on the agenda for the Jewish community from the middle of the nineteenth century onward. The Ottoman state was seeking desperately to reform its institutions to brake the precipitous decline that was threatening its very existence. The West was already an important presence in the economy of the Empire, and it was to take it over almost entirely with the debt administration instituted after the bankruptcy of the state in the 1870s. Adaptation to the new social and economic realities had emerged as a serious issue for a Jewish community whose decline had paralleled the fortunes of the Ottomans.

It was this context which predisposed the local Jewish notables to support the intervention of Western Jewry in the internal life of their communities and the reforms that it attempted to implement. The founding of the Alliance launched in 1860 the organized and institutionalized stage of the intervention that had begun two decades earlier with the activities of Montefiore, Crémieux, and Albert Cohn. The organization succeeded in establishing itself in Turkey precisely because its work fulfilled a need at a particular conjuncture in the history of Turkish Jewry—the need for a European-style education that could adjust the Jews to the new realities facing the Levant in the second half of the nineteenth century.

The traditional education system was unable to compete with the Alliance in this domain. Furthermore, the power of the rabbinate, the main upholder of this education, had been slowly eroded by the action of lay notables and local *maskilim* from the 1850s to the 1870s in all the major communities. The traditionalists at first managed to check the efforts of the reformers but were

slowly obliged to yield in the face of the dire economic situation of Turkish
Jewry. The latter had rendered their opposition particularly ineffective vis-à-
vis an organization such as the Alliance which appeared to promise all the
munificence of fabled Western philanthropy.

The Alliance provided the first mass European-style elementary and lower
secondary education system for Turkish Jewry. Generations of Jews were
educated in its schools. For many, this education remained at a quite rudimen-
tary level, as economic necessity forced the early abandonment of studies. It
did not go beyond the acquisition of the elements of reading and writing in
French and some arithmetic. For a significant number, however, the schools
served as powerful avenues of upward mobility, either by the imparting of
skills useful in trade and commerce or by facilitating further education which
opened up career prospects in the liberal professions. By the twentieth century, a new Jewish middle class had come into being in Turkey, and the
Alliance had played an important role in its making.

It is quite clear that the popularity of the Alliance schools was due to the
fact that they dispensed an essentially European education, and even more
importantly, used a European language as the language of instruction.
French, as the *lingua franca* of trade and commerce in the Levant in the last
decades of Ottoman rule, had become a very important commodity. Economic success depended largely on contacts with the West, increasingly omni-
present in the area, especially in the economic sphere. Such contacts would
have been impossible without the mastery of a Western language.

The schools, and the teaching of French, had an impact on other aspects of
social life. By eroding further the traditional education system, they contributed to the growing secularization of the community. The Alliance was concerned to dispense a Jewish education. But its version of Judaism, highly
abstract and rather aseptic, was far removed from the popular religiosity that
had been all important to the *Talmudei Torah*. In the Alliance schools, religion retreated from the center it had occupied in the traditional system to the
periphery.

The introduction of female education by the organization constituted a
revolutionary development. For the first time in the history of Turkish Jewry,
girls received substantial schooling. There was, of course, no "emancipation"
of women in the modern sense of the word, and very few women graduates
embarked upon independent careers, not an option in the local context of the
time. However, early marriages declined,[2] and the position of the woman
within the household advanced. As some directors observed, men who were
Alliance graduates preferred to marry women who had also attended Alliance
institutions and who knew some French.[3] Education contributed to an equal-
ization of sorts between the husband and wife, though it is clear that this was
only a relative development. Still, the social status of women improved considerably as a result of the schooling they received.

What motivated the organization's work was neither a philanthropic endeavor to improve the economic state of Eastern Jewry nor the propagation of the French language. Both were considered important in their own right but were also seen as a means to an end. That end was nothing less than the "regeneration" of Eastern Jewry. Jacques Bigart, the secretary general, responding to a report in 1899 that some Alliance graduates were disappointed at not finding lucrative jobs immediately after graduation, had said that it had never been the aim of the organization to find its graduates jobs. He added: "We want to form men: that, in a few words, is what our program is all about."[4] "Forming men" indeed supplies the key to the understanding of the ideology behind the organization's work.

The Alliance was deeply rooted in the Enlightenment ideological matrix that had brought about the emancipation of Western Jewry by reconceptualizing the Jew as a "man" first, a universal category, and a Jew only afterward. But for the Jews to be rendered "worthy" of emancipation, they had to be "regenerated," shorn of their particularism and exclusivism and readied to become moral, upright, equal citizens of their respective countries. This Enlightenment discourse on emancipation and "regeneration," deeply internalized by the foremost intellectuals and leaders of French Jewry, had come to constitute the prism through which they viewed all Jews. Those sections of world Jewry which were as yet steeped in the old ways and living far from "civilized" areas where the desired changes had been taking place, had to be transformed in imitation of their more fortunate coreligionists in the West. The French model for the transition of the Jews into the modern world, that in which emancipation and "regeneration" were inextricably linked, had become a normative, and indeed, a prescriptive one for all of world Jewry.

However, the local context made the results of the Alliance's work in Turkey go in a very different direction. Shemtob Pariente, the director in Izmir, pointed out on a visit to Austria in 1884 one great difference between the position of the Jews of Galicia and the Jews of Turkey. "The former, living under the rule of a civilized government, have only to wish it to improve their intellectual level by attending the schools of the state, while, on the contrary, the Jews of the Orient have to wait for everything from the private intiative and the help of their brethren in the Occident."[5] The Alliance established its ambitious program in the East by arrogating to itself the task of the education of the Jewish masses which, as Pariente mentioned, was fulfilled normally by the modern state in the West.

The Ottoman state was, indeed, largely absent from the life of the Jewish communities which lived under its rule. This was noted in 1893 in a remarkable report by Gabriel Arié, the Alliance director of the Izmir school who came from Bulgaria.

> What strikes a Bulgarian when he enters Turkey is, before everything else, the air of freedom that one breathes. Under a theoretically despotic government, one definitely enjoys more freedom than in a constitutional state . . . one al-

most does not feel that there is a government . . . the absence of an irksome
police, of crushing taxation, of very heavy civic duties, here is what the non-
Muslim subjects of the Sultan should appreciate; the Jews in particular, can,
quite justifiably, consider themselves in this country as the happiest among all of
their coreligionists in the world: enjoying all the rights, they have almost no
duties. . . . [6]

However, he went on to enumerate the nefarious consequences of this state of
affairs: it bred an indolence, apathy and lack of moral sense among the Jews
which rendered the moralizing work of the Alliance particularly difficult,
while in Bulgaria, with an activist, interventionist state, the atmosphere was
"healthy" and "moral," and the "regeneration" of the Jews continued rapidly.[7] "There the Alliance has little left to do: in a few years it can (should one
say it should?) discontinue its work."[8]

Indeed, there had been no successful attempt to integrate the Jews or other
non-Muslims into the Ottoman polity. Equality remained mostly on paper.
Until the end, the Empire remained a mosaic of different ethnic and religious
groups, each maintaining its distinctive characteristics. Both the order of
priorities of the Ottoman state, unused to a mobilized civic culture, and
Western interference prevented the creation of a unitary educational system
which would have accommodated all the non-Muslims of the Empire. While
the state began to control the institutions of the latter much more closely at
the end of the nineteenth century, their existence was never questioned. Non-
Muslims continued to attend their own separate school systems. No unifying
ideology could be found to cement these groups together, to supply a centripetal force. Consequently, a separate *millet* identity survived intact for the Jews.

The absence of a "regenerating" Ottoman state which had created the
raison d'être of the Alliance in Turkey in the first place and had provided it
with the freedom to establish its network, also distorted its message. In the
local context, the Jew remained a Jew first, and a "man" second. Universalist
values had not yet penetrated the East, and religion and the ethnic group still
constituted the primary source of identity.

As a result, the ideology of "regeneration," in a context where *millet* identity remained paramount, slipped into a gray area where it facilitated for some
the receptivity to the ideology of "national regeneration" espoused by the
Zionists, much to the dismay of the Alliance. The organization acted unwit-
tingly as a catalyst in this development. By the education it dispensed, it
opened the means of communication to Turkish Jewry with the larger Jewish
world, put it in touch with the broader developments, and made it more
receptive to modern ideologies.

But the flocking to the Zionist movement of many of the graduates of its
schools after 1908 was part of the larger revolt against the society by the very
groups that it had itself brought into being. By the twentieth century, the new
Jewish middle class was chafing under the rule of the notables and had begun
to abandon the Alliance with which the latter were associated. The excessive

centralization, paternalism, and authoritarianism of the organization did not sit well with the new dynamic elements that wanted a greater say in the education of the youth. The instruction received in the Alliance establishments had provided a kaleidoscope of possibilities for social action to increasing numbers. Not all of these were in directions that pleased the Central Committee or the teachers.

The convergence of factors that had brought about an alliance between local elites and the Alliance in the 1860s and 1870s were no longer operative on the eve of World War I. The traditionalists had been relegated to the background as actors in local Jewish politics. Economic conditions had improved for many, and the ever growing middle class wanted to have the upper hand in the running of all the institutions of concern for the community, including the Alliance schools. The latter were still needed, especially when it came to the education of the poor. However, they now had to be under the closer control of the locality. An open clash, whether under the guise of a Zionist takeover of the schools or an eventual expansion of the influence over them by the local chapter of the *B'nai B'rith* order which came to include all the leading personalities among the new Turkish Jewish elite, was preempted by the emergence of the Turkish Republic in 1923.

The conflict with the Zionists had led, by World War I, to a close collaboration between the Alliance and the *Quai d'Orsay,* which was concerned about France's beleaguered postion in the Levant. However, this association was not sufficient to save the schools from becoming effectively "nationalized" by the Republican Turkish state between 1924–1925. Ironically, it was a nation-state that modelled itself closely after the French one which in the end spelled the doom of the Alliance in Turkey. The new regime could not tolerate a section of its citizenry receiving the bulk of its education in schools directed by a foreign organization and teaching in a foreign tongue. The age of nationalism, of an interventionist state that would attempt to "nationalize" its minorities, had arrived with a vengeance in the Middle East.

In spite of its ideology of emancipation, the Alliance remained firmly rooted in the European imperialist context of its first fifty years. Though it wanted to render the Jews everywhere into good productive citizens, it could not accept the fact that the moralizing and "civilizing" necessary for this could be done in any medium outside the French language, following non-French methods. As a result of its activites, the language of instruction for most of the Jewish communities in the lands of Islam became French. In Turkey also, the language came to dominate in the Jewish school system and assumed a position of great prestige for the Jews. Of course, this stature enjoyed by French was also the case among other groups, not least among the highest echelons of the Westernizing Ottoman officialdom. Nevertheless, for no other community in Turkey did it become the language of modern mass education.

The Alliance was hence instrumental in the creation of a Francophone Jewish middle class whose eyes were turned for inspiration not to the local capital, but to the "city of light," Paris. Large sectors within Turkish Jewry became acculturated to a distant civilization. Judeo-Spanish remained the language of the home, though it was displaced by French in many cases, while French became the language of culture. While much fuss was made about learning Turkish, this remained relegated to the background. By the time of the creation of the Republic, very few Jews knew more than a limited vocabulary of Turkish necessary for the world of business.

The place given to French as the language of mass education created a non-integrated polyglot Jewry unprepared for the requirements of the new nation-state. The polyglot orientation of Turkish Jews has survived to this day, in spite of the process of Turkicization begun seriously under the Republic. In many ways, this is a direct legacy of the role played by the Alliance schools in shaping the cultural horizons and value system of the community at a decisive stage in its history.

As a consequence of the activities of the Alliance, like in the case of most Jews in the lands of Islam, but unlike the communities of Western and Central Europe, "modernity" did not come to Turkish Jewry accompanied by acculturation into the dominant culture of its surroundings. The obsession with French delayed or prevented the implementation of one of the key principles of the organization's ideology of emancipation, the integration of the Jews in their respective countries. The distinct path of "modernization" of most of the Jews in Muslim lands led, instead, to their increasing cultural and political dissociation from the local milieu. The trend was exacerbated by colonialism in North Africa and elsewhere. But the activities and ideology of the schools of the Alliance which considered the West to be the superior civilization also constituted a central factor in this development.

The story of the organization in Turkey illustrates the complex relationship that began to evolve between Western Jewry and the Jews in the lands of Islam in the nineteenth century. A vanguard of French Jews, new members of a triumphalist French metropolitan culture, attempted, with all the zeal of neophytes, to reproduce the model of their emancipation and integration into French society in communities which lived under circumstances far removed from their own. Local conditions dictated the success or failure of the various aspects of their program of "regeneration" or led it toward completely unforeseen directions. Nevertheless, by the powerful impetus for change and Westernization that it provided, and by the reactions that it elicited, the action of the Alliance came to occupy the center stage in the life of most of the Jewish communities of Muslim countries, and set the parameters of the encounter between Western and Eastern Jewries in the nineteenth and twentieth centuries.

ABBREVIATIONS

AAIU Archives of the Alliance Israélite Universelle
AI   *Archives Israélites*
AIU   Alliance Israélite Universelle
AZJ   *Allgemeine Zeitung des Judenthums*
BAIU *Bulletin semestriel de l'Alliance Israélite Universelle*
CZA   Central Zionist Archives, Jerusalem
ENIO *Ecole Normale Israélite Orientale*
JC   *Jewish Chronicle*
MAE   Archives of the *Ministère des Affaires Etrangères*, Paris
PRO   Public Records Office, London
UI   *Univers Israélite*

NOTES

Full titles of books are to be found in the Bibliography.

Introduction

1. "Appel à tous les israélites" in AIU, *Alliance Israélite Universelle* (Paris, 1860), 10–11.
2. Ibid., 14.
3. Ludwig Philippson, the editor of the *Allgemeine Zeitung des Judenthums,* coined the term in 1854 in an article on the Jews of Turkey. See AZJ 18 (1854): 152–154.
4. Aron Rodrigue, *De l'instruction à l'émancipation: Les enseignants de l'Alliance israélite universelle et les Juifs d'Orient, 1860–1939* (Paris, 1989), 21.

I. The Emergence of the "Jewish Eastern Question"

1. On the Damascus Affair, see Albert N. Hyamson, "The Damascus Affair of 1840," *Transactions of the Jewish Historical Society of England* 16 (1945–1951): 47–71. The latest study is by Tudor Parfitt, " 'The Year of the Pride of Israel': Montefiore and the Blood Libel of 1840" in Sonia and V. D. Lipman, eds., *The Century of Moses Montefiore* (Oxford, 1985), 131–148.
2. For a study of blood libel accusations in premodern Europe, see R. Po-Chia Hsia, *The Myth of Ritual Murder: Jews and Magic in Reformation Germany* (New Haven, 1988).
3. Reported in AI 1 (1840): 264.
4. AI 1 (1840): 170.
5. UI 20 (1864–65): 371.
6. JC, 3 June 1853.
7. A French translation of this edict is in Moïse Franco, *Essai sur l'histoire des Israélites de l'Empire ottoman* (Paris, 1897), 159–160. It was also publicized in the European Jewish press.
8. AI 1 (1840): 208–209.
9. AI 1 (1840): 259–262.
10. Louis Loewe, ed., *Diaries of Sir Moses and Lady Montefiore,* 2 vols. (London, 1890), 1: 206–207. It is interesting to note that the signatories of this appeal, Isaac Camondo, Salomon Mio Fua, and Samuel N. Treves, were all Italian Jewish notables—*Francos*—residing in Istanbul who had commercial links with Western Europe. On the *Francos,* see chapter 2.
11. For example, the Sephardic community of London had a special fund, that of the *cautivos,* for this purpose. See Richard D. Barnett, "The Correspondence of the Mahamad of the Spanish and Portuguese Congregation of London during the Seventeenth and Eighteenth Centuries," *Transactions of the Jewish Historical Society of England* 20 (1959–1961): 23. See also Ya'akov Blidstein, "Pidyon shevuyim ba-masoret ha-hilkhatit: metaḥim u-mediniyut," in Binyamin Pinkus and Ilan Troen, eds., *Solidariyut yehudit le'umit ba'et ha-ḥadashah* (Beersheba, 1988), 19–27.
12. See Barukh Mevorakh, "'Ikvotehah shel 'alilat Damesek be-hitpathutah shel ha-'itonut ha-yehudit ba-shanim 1840–1860," *Ẕiyon* 23–24 (1958–1959): 46–65; Jonathan Frankel, "Crisis as a Factor in Modern Jewish Politics, 1840 and 1881–82" in Jehuda Reinharz, ed., *Living with Antisemitism: Modern Jewish Responses* (Hanover,

N.H., 1987), 52–54; Michael Graetz, *Les Juifs en France au XIXe siècle: De la Révolution française à l'Alliance israélite universelle* (Paris, 1989), 135.

13. Lucien Wolf, *Sir Moses Montefiore* (New York, 1885), 93–94.

14. Loewe, ed., *Diaries*, 1: 258; Salomon V. Posener, *Adolphe Crémieux* (Philadelphia, 1940), 119, and *Israelitische Annalen*, 24 December 1840.

15. Loewe, ed., *Diaries*, 1: 268–269.

16. For the beginning of the Westernizing reforms in Turkey and the *Tanzimat* see Enver Ziya Karal, *Nizam-ı Cedit ve Tanzimat Devirleri, 1789–1856,* 2nd ed. (Ankara, 1961).

17. Wolf, *Sir Moses,* 96–97.

18. *Israelitische Annalen,* 1 January 1841.

19. Wolf, *Sir Moses,* 97.

20. Loewe, ed., *Diaries,* 1: 270; The *Allgemeine Zeitung des Judenthums* published the declaration in its Hebrew and Judeo-Spanish original in 1841. See AZJ 5 (1841): 16–17. The proclamation began by referring to the benefits of the Imperial Rescript of 1839, moved on to point out the value and honor attached to people who mastered the Turkish language, and ended with asking the Jews to teach their sons Turkish and to have teachers of Turkish in places of learning. Like many similar attempts in the following half century, this remained a dead letter. The fact that the proclamation was issued upon the insistence of Montefiore is not mentioned in Abraham Galanté, *Turcs et Juifs* (Istanbul, 1932). See pages 143–145. It is referred to briefly in Naphtali Nathan, "Notes on the Jews of Turkey," *The Jewish Journal of Sociology* 6 (December 1964): 183.

21. See the text in Simon Schwarzfuchs, *Ha-yehudim ve-ha-shilton ha-ẓarfati be-Alǧiryah, 1830–1855* (Jerusalem, 1981), 35.

22. On the ideology of emancipation among German Jews, the latest study is that of David Sorkin, *The Transformation of German Jewry* (New York, 1987).

23. For a discussion of Dohm, see Jacob Katz, *Out of the Ghetto* (Cambridge, Mass., 1973), 58.

24. See Henri Baptiste (Abbé) Grégoire, *Essai sur la régénération physique, morale et politique des Juifs* (Metz, 1789). The hope of Grégoire was that the Jews would ultimately convert to Christianity. On this see Ruth F. Necheles, "The Abbé Grégoire and the Jews," *Jewish Social Studies* 33 (April-July 1971): 120–140. See also Ruth F. Necheles, *The Abbé Grégoire, 1787–1831: The Odyssey of an Egalitarian* (Westport, Conn., 1971), 3–50. On the wider implications of Grégoire's writings and actions see Pierre Birnbaum, "Sur l'étatisation révolutionnaire: L'abbé Grégoire et le destin de l'identité juive," *Le Débat* 53 (January-February 1989): 157–173. For the Enlightenment discourse on the Jews, the best work is Arthur Hertzberg, *The French Enlightenment and the Jews* (New York, 1968).

25. Phyllis Cohen Albert, *The Modernization of French Jewry* (Hanover, N.H., 1977), 124–125. For Napoleon and the Jews, see the important book by Simon Schwarzfuchs, *Napoleon, the Jews, and the Sanhedrin* (London, 1979).

26. "Regeneration" as an ideology among French Jewry has been studied by Jay R. Berkovitz, "French Jewry and the Ideology of *Régénération* to 1848" (Ph.D. diss., Brandeis University, 1982).

27. Berkovitz, "French Jewry," 190.

28. Ibid.

29. On these Jewish societies created in Paris, see Léon Kahn, *Les professions manuelles et les institutions de patronage* (Paris, 1885).

30. On this aspect, see Lee Shai Weissbach, "The Jewish Elite and the Children of the Poor: Jewish Apprenticeship Programs in Nineteenth-Century France," *Association for Jewish Studies Review* 12 (Spring 1987): 123–142.

31. See Peter Burke, *Popular Culture in Early Modern Europe* (London, 1978).

32. There is a huge literature on the *instituteur*. For the larger process of cultural and social change in which the *instituteur* was a major actor, see Eugen Weber, *Peasants into Frenchmen* (Stanford, Calif., 1976).

33. Graetz, *Les Juifs en France,* 100–101.

34. The report, entitled *Rapport sur l'état moral et politique des Israélites de l'Algérie et des moyens de l'améliorer,* is printed in its entirety in Schwarzfuchs, *Ha-yehudim,* 67–190. The continuity between the 1840s and 1860s in this respect is exemplified in the figure of Altaras himself who was born into a well known family in Aleppo in the Ottoman Empire. He, as a member of the Alliance, was to be especially active in attempts to establish an Alliance school in Izmir. See chapter 3.

35. Ibid., 128–129.

36. Ibid., 150.

37. Ibid., 172.

38. Ibid., 50.

39. Barukh Mevorakh, "'Ikvotehah shel 'alilat Damesek," 47.

40. For the Judeo-Spanish press of Izmir, see Avner Levi, "Ha-'itonut ha-yehudit be-Izmir," *Pe'amim,* no. 12 (1982): 87–104.

41. This image has been studied in Michel Abitbol, "The Encounter between French Jewry and the Jews of North Africa: Analysis of a Discourse (1830–1914)" in Frances Malino and Bernard Wasserstein, eds., *The Jews in Modern France* (Hanover, N.H., 1985), 31–53; Esther Benbassa, "Israël face à lui-même: Judaïsme occidental et judaïsme ottoman (19ᵉ-20ᵉ siècles)," *Pardès,* no. 7 (1988): 105–129.

42. AI 1 (1840): 198–201, 249–251.

43. AZJ 5 (1841): 81–83, 97–102, 129–132.

44. AI 2 (1841): 216–222, 270–274, 480–483.

45. AZJ 5 (1841): 82.

46. Ibid., 129–132. The editor of the *Archives Israélites,* Samuel Cahen, in a note at the end of the French paraphrase of these letters, indicated that he agreed with this recommendation, but also thought that a school in Turkey itself could be very useful. See AI 2 (1841): 482.

47. See Lois C. Dubin, "Trieste and Berlin: The Italian Role in the Cultural Politics of the *Haskalah*" in Jacob Katz, ed., *Toward Modernity* (New Brunswick, N.J., 1987), 206–207.

48. The question of the image and perception of the "Orient" has given rise to a large literature. For some representative works, see Hichem Djait, *L'Europe et l'Islam* (Paris, 1978) and Edward Said, *Orientalism* (New York, 1978).

49. AZJ 5 (1841): 129.

50. On the perception of the *Ostjuden* in Germany, see Steven E. Ascheim, *Brothers and Strangers: The East European Jew in German and German Jewish Consciousness, 1800–1923* (Madison, Wis., 1982); Jack Wertheimer, *Unwelcome Strangers: East European Jews in Imperial Germany* (New York, 1987).

51. AI 1 (1840): 198.

52. AI 4 (1843): 736–741, and AI 5 (1844): 18–22, 180–182.

53. AI 7 (1846): 358–359.

54. UI 8 (1852–1853): 158–164; JC, October 29 and November 19, 1852.

55. On the Reform Edict, see Karal, *Nizam-ı Cedit,* 248–252, and Roderic H. Davison, *Reform in the Ottoman Empire, 1856–1876* (Princeton, N.J., 1963), 52–60.

56. AI 15 (1854): 228–230.

57. AI 15 (1854): 448.

58. JC, 21 April 1854.

59. For a Turkish text of the edict see Karal, *Nizam-ı Cedit,* 258–264.

60. AI 17 (1856): 189–190; UI 11 (1855–56): 340; AZJ 20 (1856): 99–101; JC, 4 April 1856.

61. JC, 21 April 1854.

62. UI 11 (1855–56): 340.

63. AZJ 18 (1854): 152–154.

64. AI 15 (1854): 316–317.

65. JC, 9, 16, and 25 June 1854.

66. AZJ 18 (1854): 295.

67. AI 15 (1854): 445–446. See also Graetz, *Les Juifs en France,* 146–147.

68. Isidore Loeb, *Biographie d'Albert Cohn* (Paris, 1878), 64–85.

69. Yehudah Nehama, *Zikhron tov, o biografia del muy afamado savido y filantropo Avraham Ha-Kohen, ke lo yaman Albert Kohn de Paris* (Salonica, 1877), 104–106.

70. AZJ 18 (1854): 463–464.

71. Graetz, *Les Juifs en France,* 63–111.

72. AI 15 (1854): 370.

73. On this organization see Jacob Barnai, *Yehudei Erez Yisrael ba-meah 18 be-ḥasut "Pekidei Kushta"* (Jerusalem, 1982).

74. Mordecai Eliav, *Erez Yisrael vi-yishuvah ba-meah ha 19, 1777–1917* (Jerusalem, 1978), 110–143. On a partial corrective on this view, see Yisrael Bartal, " 'Old Yishuv' and 'New Yishuv': Image and Reality," *The Jerusalem Cathedra* 1 (1981): 215–231.

75. Jacob Kellner, *Le ma'an Ẓiyon* (Jerusalem, 1976), 13.

76. Eliezer Manneberg, "The Evolution of Jewish Educational Practices in the *Sancak (Eyalet)* of Jerusalem under Ottoman Rule" (Ph.D. diss., University of Connecticut, 1976), 138.

77. AI 15 (1854): 445.

78. On this campaign, see Jonathan Isaac Helfand, "French Jewry during the Second Republic and Second Empire (1848–1870)" (Ph.D. diss., Yeshiva University, 1979), 84–87. See also Graetz, *Les Juifs en France,* 300–306.

79. Phyllis Cohen Albert, "Ethnicity and Jewish Solidarity in Nineteenth-Century France" in Jehuda Reinharz and Daniel Swetschinski, eds., *Mystics, Philosophers, and Politicians: Essays in Jewish Intellectual History in Honor of Alexander Altmann* (Durham, N.C., 1982), 255–260.

80. Quoted in André Kaspi, "La fondation de l'Alliance Israélite Universelle" (Mémoire de maîtrise, Faculté des Lettres, Paris, 1950), 123.

81. AI 15 (1854): 366.

82. Quoted from the Hebrew newspaper *Ben Hanania* by UI 20 (1864-1865): 52–53.

83. Helfand, "French Jewry," 289.

84. The two standard histories of the Alliance devote considerable space to its origins. See Narcisse Leven, *Cinquante ans d'histoire. L'Alliance Israélite Universelle (1860–1910),* 2 vols. (Paris, 1911–20), 1: 63–92; André Chouraqui, *Cent ans d'histoire. L'Alliance Israélite Universelle et la renaissance juive contemporaine (1860–1960)* (Paris, 1965), 15–41.

85. See Graetz, *Les Juifs en France.*

86. J. Tchernof, "Documents pour l'histoire de l'Alliance," undated manuscript in the AIU Library in Paris.

87. Kaspi, "La fondation," 123.

88. Graetz, *Les Juifs en France,* 152–193, 220–363.

89. UI 6 (1850–1851): 255.

90. UI 8 (1852–1853): 394–395.

91. Graetz, *Les Juifs en France,* 390–393.

92. Graetz, *Les Juifs en France,* 370–375.

93. Quoted in Kaspi, "La fondation," 138.

94. AI 19 (1858): 624–625.

95. AI 19 (1858): 697.

96. Quoted in Kaspi, "La fondation," 147.

97. "Manifeste de Juillet 1860," in Chouraqui, *Cent ans,* 408.
98. "Appel à tous les Israélites" in AIU, *Alliance Israélite Universelle* (Paris, 1860), 11–12.
99. Graetz, *Les Juifs en France,* 419–426.
100. AZJ 18 (1854): 201–203. His critical comments on the Alliance are found in AZJ 24 (1860): 557–559.
101. Georges Weill, "The Alliance Israélite Universelle and the Emancipation of the Jewish Communities in the Mediterranean," *Jewish Journal of Sociology* 24 (1982): 119–121.
102. See chapter 7.
103. AIU, *Procès-verbal de l'Assemblée générale de l'Alliance Israélite Universelle tenue le 10 avril 1862* (Paris, 1862), 93.
104. AIU, *Procès-verbal de l'Assemblée générale de l'Alliance Israélite Universelle tenue le 18 juin 1863* (Paris, 1863), 3.
105. AIU, *L'oeuvre des écoles* (Paris, 1865), viii–ix.
106. UI 6 (1850–1851): 255.
107. AIU, *Procès-verbal de l'Assemblée générale de l'Alliance Israélite Universelle tenue le 31 mai 1864* (Paris, 1864), 12.

II. Turkish Jewry in the Age of the *Tanzimat*

1. [Jean Henri] A[bdolomyne] Ubicini, *Letters on Turkey,* tr. Lady Easthope (London, 1859; reprint, New York, 1973), 18–19, 22. This is the only source that reports the results of the census of 1844. See Kemal H. Karpat, *Ottoman Population 1830-1914: Demographic and Social Characteristics* (Madison, Wis., 1985), 116.
2. BAIU 36 (1911): 86–115. For Ottoman censuses, see the discussions in Stanford J. Shaw, "The Ottoman Census System and Population, 1831–1914," *International Journal of Middle East Studies* 9 (1978): 325–338 and Kemal H. Karpat, *Ottoman Population.* For the figures reported in Ottoman censuses in the first decade of the twentieth century, see Justin McCarthy, *The Arab World, Turkey and the Balkans (1878–1914): A Handbook of Historical Statistics* (Boston, 1982), 64, 101, and Kemal H. Karpat, *Ottoman Population,* 161–190.
3. For the most recent summation of this view see Bernard Lewis, *The Jews of Islam* (Princeton, N.J., 1984), 166–170. See also Benjamin Braude and Bernard Lewis, eds., *Christians and Jews in the Ottoman Empire,* 2 vols. (New York, 1982), 1: 24–26. For a view of the decline of Jewish commerce in the Balkans, see Traian Stoianovich, "The Conquering Balkan Orthodox Merchant," *Journal of Economic History* 20 (1960): 234–313. See also William H. McNeill, "Hypotheses Concerning Possible Ethnic Role Changes in the Ottoman Empire in the Seventeenth Century" in Osman Okyar and Halil İnalcık, eds., *Social and Economic History of Turkey* (Ankara, 1980), 128–129.
4. Ali İhsan Bağış, *Osmanlı Ticaretinde Gayri Müslimler* (Ankara, 1983), 129–138.
5. Ibid., 88–89.
6. Ubicini, *Letters on Turkey,* 18–19, 22. Also cited by Karpat, *Ottoman Population,* 116.
7. For the guilds, see Jacob Barnai and Haim Gerber, "Gildot yehudiyot be-Kushta be-shilhei ha-meah ha-18," *Mikhael* 7 (1981): 206–226; Jacob Barnai, "Gildot yehudiyot be-Turkiyah ba-meot ha-16–19" in Gross, *Yehudim,* 133–148.
8. For a study of the Jewish community of Istanbul in the eighteenth century, see Jacob Barnai, "Kavim le-toldot kehilat Kushta ba-meah ha-18" in Jacob Barnai, Yosef Shitrit, Bustanai 'Oded, Aliza Shenhar, and Zvi Yehudah, eds., *Mi-kedem u-mi-yam* (Haifa, 1981), 53–66. For the most recent account of the relationship with the Janissaries, see Lewis, *The Jews of Islam,* 133, 173–174. Also see Robert W. Olson,

"Jews in the Ottoman Empire in Light of New Documents," *Tarih Enstitüsü Dergisi* 7–8 (1976–1977): 119–144; idem, "Jews in the Ottoman Empire in Light of New Documents," *Jewish Social Studies* 41 (Winter 1979): 75–88. Also cited in Lewis, *The Jews of Islam*, 214, n. 33.

9. See Moïse Franco, *Essai sur l'histoire des Israélites de l'Empire ottoman* (Paris, 1897), 132–134; Abraham Galanté, *Histoire des Juifs d'Istanbul*, 2 vols. (Istanbul, 1941–42), 1: 24–29; Salomon A. Rozanes, *Korot ha-yehudim be-Turkiyah u-ve-arẓot ha-kedem*, 2nd ed., 6 vols. (Tel-Aviv, Jerusalem, 1930–1946), 6: 64–67. See also Mosheh David Gaon, *Yehudei ha-mizraḥ be-Ereẓ Yisrael*, 2 vols. (Jerusalem, 1928-1938), 2: 23, 748.

10. AI 38 (1877): 274; 52 (1891): 349; 53 (1892): 133–134, 150-151, 166. See also the references to the works of Franco, Galanté, and Rozanes cited in note 8. Carmona is mentioned in several letters sent by the *Va'ad ha-Pekidim ve-ha-Amerkalim* of Amsterdam. See for example Yosef Yoel and Binyamin Rivlin, eds., *Igrot ha-Pekidim ve-ha-amerkalim be-Amsterdam*, 3 vols. (Jerusalem, 1965–1977), 3: 57. Also see Yisrael Bartal's "Introduction" to the same volume, 16, note 21. I would like to thank Yisrael Bartal for drawing my attention to this source.

11. Ahmed Lütfi, *Tarih-i Lütfi*, 2 vols. (Istanbul, 1290/1873–1328/1910), 1: 245–246. Also cited in Franco, *Essai*, 139–140.

12. Yoel and Rivlin, *Igrot ha-Pekidim*, 1: 162–163; ibid., 2: 228.

13. For example, see David Cazès in the *Bulletin mensuel de l'Alliance Israélite Universelle* (July 1877): 43.

14. Quoted in JC, 19 November 1852.

15. On ethnicity in the Middle East and North Africa, see Lucette Valensi, "La tour de Babel: Groupes et relations ethniques au Moyen Orient et en Afrique du Nord," *Annales, E. S. C.,* no. 4 (July-August 1986): 817–835.

16. For the *dhimma*, see *Encyclopedia of Islam*, "Dhimma," s.v.; Bernard Lewis, *The Jews of Islam* (Princeton, N.J., 1984), 3–66. The work of Bat Ye'or, *Le Dhimmi: Profil de l'opprimé en Orient et en Afrique du Nord depuis la conquête arabe* (Paris, 1980), though polemical, supplies many interesting documents on this theme.

17. There is a large literature on this subject. For the latest work, see Simon Schwarzfuchs, *Kahal: La communauté juive de l'Europe médiévale* (Paris, 1986).

18. See Jacob Barnai and Haim Gerber, *Yehudei Izmir ba-meah ha-19* (Jerusalem, 1985); Joseph Hacker, "Gvuloteyah shel ha-otonomiyah ha-yehudit: Ha-shiput ha-'aẓmi ha-yehudi ba-imperyah ha-'otomanit ba-meot ha-16–ha-18" in Shmuel Almog, Yisrael Bartal, Michael Graetz et al., eds., *Temurot ba-historyah ha-yehudit ha-ḥadashah: Koveẓ ma'amarim, shay li-Shmu'el Etinger* (Jerusalem, 1987), 349–388; Gilles Veinstein, "Une communauté ottomane: les Juifs d'Avlonya (Valona) dans la deuxième moitié du XVIᵉ siècle" in Gaetano Cozzi, ed., *Gli Ebrei e Venezia, secoli XIV-XVIII* (Milan, 1987), 781–828. The very extensive use made by Jews of the Jerusalem Muslim *sicil* courts in the sixteenth century is in full evidence in Amnon Cohen, *Jewish Life under Islam* (Cambridge, Mass., 1984).

19. "Introduction" in Braude and Lewis, eds., *Christians and Jews*, 1: 12–15. See also in the same volume Benjamin Braude, "Foundation Myths of the *Millet* System," 69–88; Mark A. Epstein, "The Leadership of the Ottoman Jews in the Fifteenth and Sixteenth Centuries," 101–115; Joseph Hacker, "Ha-rabanut ha-rashi' ba-imperyah ha-'otomanit ba-meot ha-15 ve ha-16," *Ẓiyon* 49 (1984): 225–263.

20. See Leah Bornstein-Makovetsky, "Mivne ha-rabanut ba-imperyah ha-'otomanit ba-meah ha-16 u-va-meah ha-17," *Mi-Mizraḥ u-mi-ma'arav* 1 (1974): 223–258; idem., "Ha-hanhagah shel ha-kehilah ha-yehudit ba-mizraḥ ha-karov mi-shilhei ha-meah ha-15 ve-'ad sof ha-meah ha-18" (Ph.D. diss., Bar Ilan University, 1978).

21. For the classical period of the Ottoman Empire, see Halil İnalcık, *The Ottoman Empire: The Classical Age, 1300–1600* (London, 1973).

22. For an analysis of the Ottoman state and social formation, see the recent studies by Metin Heper, *The State Tradition in Turkey* (Beverley, North Humberside, 1985), and Çağlar Keyder, *State and Class in Turkey: A Study in Capitalist Development* (London, 1987). For a discussion of state traditions in an Islamic context see Brian S. Turner, *Weber and Islam* (London, 1974), and Bertrand Badie, *Les deux Etats: pouvoir et société en Occident et en terre d'Islam* (Paris, 1986).

23. The major studies of the impact of world capitalism on the Empire have been conveniently collected in Huri İslamoğlu-İnan, ed., *The Ottoman Empire and the World Economy* (Cambridge and Paris, 1987). See also Şevket Pamuk, *Osmanlı Ekonomisi ve Dünya Kapitalizmi (1820–1913)* (Ankara, 1984) and Keyder, *State and Class.*

24. On the "strong" French state, see Bertrand Badie and Pierre Birnbaum, *The Sociology of the State* (Chicago, 1983).

25. For an English translation of the rescript, see Jacob C. Hurewitz, ed., *The Middle East and North Africa in World Politics,* 2 vols. (1975–79), 1: 269–271.

26. The changes in local government have been discussed by İlber Ortaylı, *Tanzimat'tan sonra Mahalli İdareler* (Ankara, 1974).

27. See the discussion in Kemal H. Karpat, "*Millets* and Nationality: The Roots of the Incongruity of Nation and State in the Post-Ottoman Era" in Braude and Lewis, eds., *Christians and Jews,* 162–163.

28. Stanford J. Shaw, "The Nineteenth-Century Ottoman Tax Reforms and Revenue System," *International Journal of Middle East Studies* 6 (1975): 342–431.

29. For an English translation of the relevant clause (no. 12), see Hurewitz, *The Middle East,* 1: 317.

30. Bülent Tahiroğlu, "Tanzimat'tan sonra Kanunlaştırma Hareketleri," *Tanzimat'tan Cumhuriyet'e Türkiye Ansiklopedisi* 3 (1985): 588–596.

31. In the case of the Jews, some commercial litigation still found its way to the Jewish religious courts. But in the light of the clauses of the 1856 decree, the ruling of these courts in this area did not have the force of the law. The erosion in the juridical autonomy of the *millets* has been discussed in passing in several works dealing with the Christian communities under Ottoman rule. For example, see Télémaque Tutundjian, *Du pacte politique entre l'Etat ottoman et les nations non-musulmans de la Turquie* (Lausanne, 1904), 56–58; F. van den Steen de Jehan, *De la situation légale des sujets ottomans non-musulmans* (Brussels, 1906), 95–108; Constantine G. Papadopoulos, *Les privilèges du Patriarcat oecuménique dans l'Empire ottoman* (Paris, 1924), 103–113; Vartan Artinian, "A Study of the Historical Development of the Armenian Constitutional System in the Ottoman Empire" (Ph.D. diss., Brandeis University, 1970), 51. None of these works, however, provide a close study of this problem in the nineteenth century. It is to be hoped that, eventually, Ottoman archives will be more accessible and that scholars will undertake thorough examinations of this question.

32. "asar-ı medeniyet ve malümat-ı müktesibenin icap ettirdiği islahat," from the Turkish text of the decree to be found in Enver Ziya Karal, *Nizam-ı Cedit ve Tanzimat Devirleri, 1789–1856,* 2nd ed. (Ankara, 1961), 259.

33. For the Judeo-Spanish translation of the statutes concerning the Jews, see *La Konstitusion para la nasion israelita de Turkia* (Istanbul, 1865).

34. Bayram Kodaman, *Abdülhamid Devri Eğitim Sistemi* (Istanbul, 1980), 43; İlhan Tekeli, "Tanzimat'tan Cumhuriyet'e Eğitim Sistemindeki Değişmeler," *Tanzimat'tan Cumhuriyet'e Türkiye Ansiklopedisi* 2 (1985): 468.

35. Kodaman, *Abdülhamid Devri,* 100–101.

36. Ayas, *Türkiye Cumhuriyeti,* 689; Cemil Koçak, "Tanzimat'tan sonra Özel ve Yabancı Okullar," *Tanzimat'tan Cumhuriyet'e Türkiye Ansiklopedisi* 2 (1985): 488.

37. See chapter 7.

38. Stanford J. Shaw and Ezel Kural Shaw, *History of the Ottoman Empire and Modern Turkey,* 2 vols. (Cambridge, 1976–1977), 2: 113.

39. For the Russian Empire, the most recent analysis of this policy is in Michael Stanislawski, *Tsar Nicholas I and the Jews* (Philadelphia, 1983), 97–109. For the Hapsburg Empire, see Lois C. Dubin, "Trieste and Berlin: The Italian Role in the Cultural Politics of the *Haskalah*" in Jacob Katz, ed., *Toward Modernity* (New Brunswick, N.J., 1987), 189–224. Also, in the same book, see Hillel J. Kieval, "Caution's Progress: The Modernization of Jewish Life in Prague, 1780–1830," 71–105 and Michael Silber, "The Historical Experience of German Jewry and Its Impact on the *Haskalah* and Reform in Hungary," 107–157.

40. For example, Ludwig August Frankl compared the Reform Decree of 1856 to the *Toleranzpatent* of 1782 in Austria and to the emancipation of the Jews of the Austrian Empire in 1849. See Ludwig August Frankl, *The Jews in the East*, tr. Patrick Beaton, 2 vols. (London, 1859), 1: 170.

41. Alexander Ben Giat, *Suvenires del meldar: Estudio verdadero de loke se pasava en un tiempo* (Izmir, 1920), 8. Slightly different versions of this song are given in Abraham Galanté, *Histoire des Juifs d'Anatolie*, 2 vols. (Istanbul, 1937–39) 2: 342–343, and in David Benvenisti, "Zikhronot le-ne'urim" in Centre de Recherches sur le Judaïsme de Salonique, ed., *Saloniki, 'Ir Va-em be-Yisrael* (Tel-Aviv, 1967), 83.

42. This seems to resemble the custom in Italy. See Simḥah Assaf, *Mekorot le-toldot ha-ḥinukh be-Yisrael*, 4 vols. (Tel-Aviv, 1925–42), 2: v. See also Shlomoh Simonsohn, *History of the Jews in the Duchy of Mantua* (Jerusalem, 1977), 590–596.

43. Benvenisti, "Zikhronot," 83; Ben Giat, *Suvenires*, 5.

44. David Benvenisti, *Yehudei Saloniki be-dorot ha-aḥaronim* (Jerusalem, 1973), 80–85; Benvenisti, "Zikhronot," 85.

45. On the history of the *Talmud Torah* of Salonica, see Avraham Shaul Amarillio, "Ḥevrat talmud-torah ha-gadol be-Saloniki," *Sefunot* 13 (1971–1978): 274–309.

46. Yitsḥak Emanuel, "Toldot yehudei Saloniki" in David A. Recanati, ed., *Zikhron Saloniki*, 2 vols. (Tel-Aviv, 1972-1985), 1: 129.

47. José M. Estrugo, *El Retorno a Sefarad* (Madrid, 1933), 61.

48. Franco, *Histoire*, 262. This was a veritable encyclopedia of rabbinical learning. The commentary on Genesis was published in 1732 by Ya'akov Kuli, the other books of the Bible being treated by various authors through the nineteenth century. Designed for mass consumption, it was the single most important work that shaped the popular Judeo-Spanish religious universe. See Michael Molho, *Le Meam Loez, encyclopédie populaire du sépharadisme levantin* (Salonica, 1945); Pascual Recuero, *Me'am Loez: El gran comentario bíblico sefardí*, 4 vols. (Madrid 1964–74); David N. Barocas, *In Search of Our Sephardic Roots* (New York, 1970). Most of the volumes have now been translated by Aryeh Kaplan under the title of *The Torah Anthology*, 13 vols. (New York, 1977–1987).

49. Emanuel, "Toldot," 129.

50. Ibid., 130.

51. Franco, *Histoire*, 261; Galanté, *Histoire des Juifs d'Istanbul*, 1: 149–150.

52. JC, 10 October 1856, also reproduced in AI 17 (1856): 505.

53. See for example *El Nasional*, 21 March 1873; *El Tiempo*, 6, 20, 24 November 1872, 23 August 1874.

54. Itshak Emanuel, "Los jidios de Salonique" in David A. Recanati, ed., *Zikhron Saloniki*, 1: 19.

55. Galanté, *Histoire des Juifs d'Anatolie*, 2: 108.

56. Frankl, *The Jews*, 1: 101.

57. JC, 29 October 1852, 19 November 1852.

58. AI 19 (1858): 743.

59. William Thomas Gidney, *The History of the London Society for Promoting Christianity amongst the Jews, from 1809 to 1908* (London, 1908), 176.

60. Ibid., 295.

61. Ibid., 364.
62. *Levant Times,* 18 October 1873, as reported in AI 34 (1873): 722–724.
63. Gidney, *History,* 364.
64. Şevket Pamuk, *Osmanlı Ekonomisi ve Dünya Kapitalizmi (1820–1913)* (Ankara, 1984), 18–19; Charles Issawi, ed., *The Economic History of Modern Turkey, 1800–1914* (Chicago, 1980), 74-82.
65. Frankl, *The Jews,* 1: 199.
66. For a general history of the Italian Jews in the Levant, see Attilio Milano, *Storia degli Ebrei Italiani nel Levante* (Firenze, 1949).
67. The "protection" enjoyed by the *Francos* under the capitulations and the relations of the *Francos* of Salonica with the French in the late seventeenth and early eighteenth centuries have been discussed in Simon Schwarzfuchs, "Sulam Saloniki," *Sefunot* 15 (1971–1981): 77–102. The status of the Jews is discussed in Mina Rozen, "Strangers in a Strange Land: The Extraterritorial Status of Jews in Italy and the Ottoman Empire in the Sixteenth to the Eighteenth Centuries" in Aron Rodrigue, ed., *Ottoman and Turkish Jewry: Community and Leadership* (forthcoming).
68. Frankl, *The Jews,* 1: 201.
69. On Camondo, see Aron Rodrigue, "Abraham de Camondo of Istanbul: The Transformation of Jewish Philanthropy" in Frances Malino and David Sorkin, eds., *From East and West: Jews in a Changing Europe, 1750–1870* (forthcoming).
70. On the visit of Albert Cohn and the foundation of the school, see AI 16 (1855): 36–37; UI 10 (1854–1855): 207; Isidore Loeb, *Biographie d'Albert Cohn* (Paris, 1878), 81–85; Yehudah Nehama, *Zikhron tov, o biografia del muy afamado savido y filantropo Avraham ha-Kohen, ke lo yaman Albert Kohn de Paris* (Salonica, 1877), 104–106; N. M. Gelber, "Dr. Albert Cohn u-vikuro bi-Yerushalayim," *Yerushalayim* 2 (1949): 191–195.
71. UI 11 (1855–56): 342.
72. Ibid., 342–344. This is the only report on the circular in existence. The circular has never been discussed in the scholarly literature.
73. UI 14 (1858–59): 247–248, reported from the *Presse d'Orient.*
74. UI 14 (1858–59): 357.
75. UI 14 (1858–59): 247–248, reported from the *Presse d'Orient.* Rabbi Yitshak Akrish, a leading opponent of the school justified the excommunication by arguing that the teaching of European languages would lead to the conversion of the Jews to Christianity. See Yitshak Akrish, *Kiryat arba* (Jerusalem, 1876), folios 185 verso–186 recto. See also Simhah Assaf, *Mekorot le-toldot ha-hinukh be-yisrael,* 4 vols. (Tel-Aviv, 1925-1942), 4: 212–213.
76. AZJ 23 (1859): 159.
77. Galanté, *Histoire des Juifs d'Istanbul,* 1: 183.
78. Franco, *Essai,* 162–164. Also in UI 17 (1861–1862): 497–499.
79. Unfortunately, very few copies of this journal survive, all of them from 1867, long after the conflict of 1862.
80. *Tasvir-i Efkâr,* 4 Recep 1279/26 December 1862, from reprint in İbrahim Şinasi, *Külliyat,* ed. Fevziye A. Tansel (Ankara, 1960), 43–46. Also mentioned by Lewis, *The Jews of Islam,* 221–222, note 29. See also UI 17 (1861–1862): 497–502, reporting from the *Journal de Constantinople.*
81. UI 17 (1861–1862): 468.
82. Galanté, *Histoire des Juifs d'Istanbul,* 1: 76.
83. A French translation of the text of the statutes is to be found in Galanté, *Documents officiels,* 16–27.
84. See Hacker, "Ha-rabanut ha-rashit." See also Mark A. Epstein, "The Leadership of Ottoman Jews."
85. See Galanté, *Histoire des Juifs d'Istanbul,* 1: 107.

86. Ibid., 1: 27.

87. For the significance of Mahmut II's reign, see Bernard Lewis, *The Emergence of Modern Turkey,* 2nd ed. (London, 1968), 74–106 and Niyazi Berkes, *Türkiye'de Çağdaşlaşma* (Istanbul, 1978), 149–186.

88. For the situation in Jerusalem see Jacob Barnai, "Ma'amadah shel 'ha-rabanut ha-kolelet' bi-Yerushalayim ba-tekufah ha-'otomanit," *Katedrah* 13 (1979): 54–56. Moïse Franco, in a letter to the Alliance on the rabbis of Edirne, makes a clear distinction between rabbis who became officially *Hahambaşı* in the 1830s and others. AAIU, Turquie VII. E., Franco, received 10 June 1897.

89. Izmir adopted the *nizamname* in 1896. See Galanté, *Histoire des Juifs d'Anatolie,* 1: 18. This was published in Judeo-Spanish under the title of *Regulamiento de administration de la komunidad israelit de Izmirna* (Izmir, 1896). Jerusalem had not adopted it as late as 1914. See Avraham Hayim, "Ḥakham bashi shel Kushta ve-'milḥemet ha-rabanut' bi-Yerushalayim," *Pe'amim,* no. 12 (1982): 105–113.

90. Isidore Loeb, *Biographie,* 86.

91. AI 18 (1857): 361. On the Chief Rabbi of Izmir in this period, see Simon L. Eckstein, "The Life, Work, and Influence of Rabbi Chayim Palaggi on the Jewish Community Izmir" (Ph.D. diss., Yeshiva University, 1979).

92. According to Milano, there were 377 Italian Jews in Izmir in 1871. Milano, *Storia,* 187.

93. On the negotiations with the Alliance over this school, see chapter 3. See also Galanté, *Histoire des Juifs d'Anatolie,* 1: 109–112. On Sidi and the *Aziziye* school, see AI 18 (1867): 324–325.

94. See *El Tiempo,* 29 April 1925. There is also other evidence pointing in this direction. A. H. Navon mentions that when he arrived to Edirne, he communicated only in Hebrew, implying that he did not know any Judeo-Spanish. See A. H. Navon, "La fondation de l'école de l'Alliance à Andrinople," *Paix et Droit* 3 (April 1923): 13–15. Halevi's letters to the Alliance are in the Ashkenazic Hebrew cursive and not in the Sephardic one. See his letters in AAIU, Turquie I. J. 1. For a discussion of this topic see Shelomoh Haramati, *Sheloshah she-kadmu le-Ben Yehudah* (Jerusalem, 1978), 13, notes 2 and 3.

95. Narcisse Leven, *Cinquante ans d'histoire. L'Alliance Israélite Universelle (1860–1910),* 2 vols. (Paris, 1911–20), 2: 67.

96. Navon, "La fondation," 13–15.

97. Mercado J. Covo, "Contribution à l'histoire des institutions scolaires de la communauté israélite de Salonique jusqu'à la fondation de l'école des garçons de l'Alliance Israélite Universelle," *Almanach Nationale au profit de l'hôpital Hirsch* 8 (1916): 98–100; Joseph Nehama, *Histoire des Israélites de Salonique,* 7 vols. (Salonica, 1935–1978), 6–7: 658–665.

98. James Etmekjian, *The French Influence on the Western Armenian Renaissance, 1843–1915* (New York, 1964), 164.

99. Artinian, "A Study," 59–50.

100. Ibid., 164–167.

101. Koçak, "Tanzimat'tan sonra," 492.

102. Tekeli, "Tanzimat'tan Cumhuriyet'e," 461–462.

103. Ibid., 462.

104. Alexis Alexandris, *The Greek Minority of Istanbul and Greek-Turkish Relations, 1918–1974* (Athens, 1983), 45.

105. Ibid.

106. Shaw and Shaw, *History,* 2: 112.

107. Tekeli, "Tanzimat'tan Cumhuriyet'e," 468. On the foundation of the imperial *lycée* of Galatasaray, see İhsan Sungu, "Galatasaray Lisesi'nin Kuruluşu," *Belleten* 7, no. 26 (1943): 315–347.

III. The Politics of Schooling

1. AAIU, Grèce III. B. 20, Nehama, 14 April 1863.
2. AAIU, Grèce III. B. 20, two letters both dated 18 August 1863.
3. AAIU, France III. A. 17, Abraham Camondo, minutes of the meeting of 31 November 1863.
4. See AIU, *Compte rendu des séances du Comité central tenues pendant le premier trimestre de l'année 1864* (Paris, 1864), 9; AIU, *Procès-verbal de l'Assemblée générale de l'Alliance Israélite Universelle tenue le 31 Mai 1864* (Paris, 1864), 35; AIU, *Extrait des procès-verbaux des séances du Comité central tenues pendant le deuxième et le troisième trimestre 1864* (Paris, 1864), cxxxiii; AIU, *Procès-verbal de l'Assemblée du 25 Mai 1865* (Paris, 1865), 70.
5. See for example *El Nasional,* 25 August 1873 and *El Tiempo,* 14 October 1872, 28 December 1872, 24 November, 1 December 1873, and 10 February 1874.
6. Narcisse Leven, *Cinquante ans d'histoire. L'Alliance Israélite Universelle (1860–1910),* 2 vols. (Paris, 1911–1920), 2: 11–13; Sarah Leibovici, *Chronique des Juifs de Tétouan (1860–1896)* (Paris, 1984), 48–51.
7. Leven, *Cinquante,* 2: 15.
8. AAIU, France III. A. 17, Camondo, 3 March 1864.
9. AIU, *Extrait des procès-verbaux de séances tenues pendant le deuxième et le troisième trimestre 1864* (Paris, 1864), 12–13.
10. AAIU, Grèce VII. B. 31, Fraggi, 13 June 1864.
11. AAIU, Grèce VII. B. 31, Fraggi, 4 October 1864.
12. Most of the letters from Volos in the late 1860s and the early 1870s refer to the financial problems of the school. See AAIU, Grèce XX. E. 247–261. See also Leven, *Cinquante,* 2: 61–65.
13. AAIU, France III. A. 17, Camondo, 3 March 1864.
14. Ibid., 4 April 1864.
15. Ibid.
16. See the letters of Camondo in AAIU, France III. A. 17, dated 21 April 1868, 12 June 1868, and 17 July 1868. See also AAIU, Turquie I. B. 3, de Castro, 17 July 1868, and AAIU, Turquie L. E., Abraham Franco, 2 February 1870.
17. AAIU, France III. A. 17, Camondo, 1 September 1868.
18. AAIU, Turquie I. J. 1, Halevi, 14 Nisan 5625/1865.
19. AAIU, Turquie IV. E., de Toledo, 11 May 1865.
20. A. H. Navon, "Contribution à l'histoire de la fondation des écoles de l'Alliance Israélite Universelle," *Le Judaïsme Sephardi,* no. 1 (July 1932): 8–9.
21. Moïse Franco, who was a teacher at Alliance schools, wrote an extremely interesting and detailed account of the history and customs of the Jews of Edirne which was not included in his *Essai sur l'histoire des Israélites de l'Empire ottoman* (Paris, 1897). For the two rabbinical dynasties of this town, see this account which is to be found in AAIU, Turquie VII. E., received in Paris on 10 January 1897.
22. A. H. Navon, "Contribution," *Le Judaïsme Sephardi,* no. 4 (November 1932): 64–66.
23. AAIU, Turquie IV. E., letter dated 18 June 1867 and signed by Joseph Chouchami, Samuel Sabetai Pisa, Salomon Bohor Eliakim, Yochai Nardea, Elia Navon.
24. A. H. Navon, "Contribution," *Le Judaïsme Sephardi,* no. 4 (November 1932): 64–66.
25. AAIU, Turquie I. J. 1, Halevi, 27 June 1867.
26. A. H. Navon, "La fondation de l'école de l'Alliance à Andrinople," *Paix et Droit* 3 (1923): 15.
27. AAIU, Turquie I. B. 2, Rodrigue, 24 October 1867.

28. Abraham Galanté, *Histoire des Juifs d'Anatolie,* 2 vols. (Istanbul, 1937–39), 1: 58–66.

29. AAIU, Turquie LXXIII. E., Crispin, 30 June 1864, 25 August 1864, 30 August 1864; Altaras, 25 August 1864, 30 August 1864.

30. AAIU, Turquie LXXIII. E., Crispin, 19 September 1867.

31. AAIU, Turquie LXXIII. E., Sidi et al., 17 August 1868, Sidi, 18 August 1868.

32. AAIU, Turquie LXXIII. E., Sidi, 18 August 1868.

33. AAIU, Turquie LXXIII. E., B. Hazan, 17 November 1871.

34. Ibid., 29 November 1872.

35. Ibid.

36. AAIU, Turquie LXXIII. E., Sidi, 29 August 1873.

37. AAIU, Turquie I. C. 1, Cazès, received 26 October 1873, also in BAIU (2ᶜ semestre 1873): 141.

38. See for example *El Nasional,* 20 March 1873, 8 April 1873, 21 April 1873, 18 August 1873.

39. *Jurnal Israelit,* 16 October 1867.

40. See Abraham Galanté, *Histoire des Juifs d'Istanbul,* 2 vols. (Istanbul, 1941–42), 1: 186. Galanté does not make it clear whether this committee was in fact created with the help of the Chief Rabbinate.

41. *El Tiempo,* 15 October 1872, 16 October 1872.

42. Galanté, *Histoire des Juifs d'Istanbul,* 1: 186. See also *El Tiempo,* 20 November 1872.

43. See, for example, *El Tiempo,* 21 October 1872.

44. *El Tiempo,* 5 January 1873.

45. *El Tiempo,* 16 October 1872. A Mme. Arlaud was in charge of the new girls' school in Hasköy. Pierre Baudin taught the Karaites in Hasköy and gave lessons at the new school in Kuzguncuk, and a Mme. Furet was to teach in Ortaköy.

46. *El Tiempo,* 31 October 1872.

47. AAIU, Turquie I. B. 3, de Castro, reporting on the general assembly of the Alliance in Istanbul, 29 April 1869.

48. Galanté, *Histoire des Juifs d'Istanbul,* 2: 59.

49. AAIU, France VIII. A. 63, Veneziani, 7 March 1873.

50. Ibid.

51. AAIU, France VIII. A. 63, Veneziani, minutes of the meeting of the Committee, 16 October 1873 and 23 October 1873.

52. Ibid., minutes, 2 December 1873, 6 February 1874.

53. Ibid., 6 February 1874.

54. BAIU (1ᵉʳ semestre 1874): 3–4.

55. Ibid., 4.

56. Sarah Leibovici, *Si tu fais le bien* (Paris, 1983), 13. For more details on Baron de Hirsch, see Kurt Grunwald, *TürkenHirsch: A Study of Baron Maurice de Hirsch, Entrepreneur and Philanthropist* (Jerusalem, 1966).

57. AAIU, France VIII. A. 63, Veneziani, minutes of the meeting of the Regional Committee, 13 January 1874.

58. Ibid., minutes, 6 February 1874.

59. AAIU, France VIII. A. 63, Bloch, received 19 June 1874.

60. Here, in chronological order, is a list of these schools and the dates of their foundation:

school for boys, Dağhamamı:	January 1875
school for boys, Balat:	July 1875
school for girls, Hasköy:	August 1875
school for boys, Galata:	October 1875

coeducational school, Ashkenazi community, Galata:	1876
school for boys, Hasköy:	January 1877
school for boys, Kuzguncuk:	July 1879
school for girls, Galata:	August 1879
school for girls, Dağhamamı:	August 1880
coeducational school, Ortaköy:	February 1881
school for girls, Balat:	April 1882

See BAIU 7 (2e semestre 1883): 37–38.

61. The *Bulletins* of the Alliance listed the details about the finances of schools in each issue. See BAIU (1873–1913).

62. See the discussion in chapter 4. On the foundation of the *Ecole Normale Israélite Orientale,* see A. H. Navon, *Les 70 ans de l'Ecole Normale Israélite Orientale* (Paris, 1935), 14-18.

63. AAIU, Turquie VI. E., Bloch, 21 October 1869.

64. Ibid., 25 September 1867.

65. Ibid.

66. AAIU, Turquie VI. E., Bloch, 25 September 1867, 23 October 1867.

67. Ibid., 19 March 1868.

68. Ibid., 18 February 1869, 20 May 1869.

69. Ibid., 5 November 1868, 21 October 1869.

70. Ibid., 5 November 1868.

71. Ibid.

72. AAIU, Turquie VI. E., Bloch, 19 March 1868, 21 May 1868.

73. Ibid., 18 February 1869, 22 April 1869.

74. Ibid., 26 May 1870. See the discussion on the Alliance and female education in chapter 4.

75. Ibid., 25 September 1867.

76. Ibid., 21 October 1869.

77. Ibid., 25 September 1867.

78. AAIU, Turquie I. B. 2, de Toledo, 18 July 1875.

79. The most recent study that deals with Mitrani's activities in some detail is to be found in Shelomoh Haramati, *Sheloshah she-kadmu le-Ben Yehudah* (Jerusalem, 1978), 48–81. See also the article entitled "Tnu'at ha haskalah be-Adrianopoli" in *ha-Magid,* 12 Heshvan 5649/1888.

80. Barukh Mitrani, *Diskorso de Perashat Shemot* (Salonica, 1868), 42–43.

81. Ibid., 26–27.

82. Ibid., 1.

83. Ibid., 47.

84. *Jurnal Israelit,* 12 January 1867.

85. Barukh Mitrani, *Sefer ḥinukh Banim* (Jerusalem, 1875).

86. Haramati, *Sheloshah,* 48.

87. Ibid., 55.

88. AAIU, Turquie VI. E., Bloch, 21 September 1871.

89. See for example *Ḥavaẓelet,* 22 Av 5633/1873.

90. AAIU, Turquie IV. E., Mitrani, received 16 August 1875.

91. Ibid., received 24 February 1874.

92. AAIU, Turquie V. E., Bendelac, 26 May 1874.

93. Haramati, *Sheloshah,* 48.

94. See Michael Graetz, *Les Juifs en France au XIXᵉ siècle* (Paris, 1989), 380–383.

95. AAIU, Turquie VI. E., Bloch, 21 May 1868.

96. See for example the letters of Bloch dated 21 May 1868, 10 March 1870 in AAIU, Turquie VI. E.

97. Ibid., 7 September 1871.

98. Ibid., 11 January 1872, 18 January 1872, 8 February 1872, 4 April 1872.
99. Ibid., 6 July 1871.
100. Leibovici, *Chronique,* 88–99.
101. AAIU, Turquie LXXX. E., Cazès, 10 October 1874, 27 December 1874.
102. Ibid., 21 August 1874, 1 October 1874, 19 February 1875.
103. Ibid., 21 August 1874, 1 October 1874, 19 February 1875.
104. Ibid., 30 April 1875.
105. Navon, *Les 70 ans,* 117.
106. AAIU, Turquie LXXXV. E., Pariente, 26 April 1878, 24 May 1878.
107. Ibid., 24 May 1878, 16 August 1878.
108. Ibid., 6 September 1878.
109. Ibid., AIU to Pariente, 25 July 1884.
110. Ibid.
111. Ibid., Pariente, received 16 December 1884.
112. AAIU, Turquie LXXXVI. E., Pariente, 9 January 1885.
113. Ibid., 27 February 1885.
114. Ibid., 18 January 1885.
115. AAIU, Turquie LXXXVI. E., AIU to Pariente, 9 January 1885.
116. Ibid., AIU to Pariente, 13 November 1884.
117. Ibid.
118. AAIU, Turquie XLIII. E., Bloch, 27 May 1884, 3 June 1884.
119. AAIU, Turquie LXXXV. E., AIU to Pariente, 10 October 1884.
120. Ibid., Pariente, 2 December 1884.
121. Ibid, note scribbled on Pariente's letter of 2 December 1884 by Loeb (?), General Secretary of the AIU.
122. AAIU, Turquie LXXXVI. E., AIU to Pariente, 6 February 1885.
123. On the guilds, see Jacob Barnai, "Gildot yehudiyot be-Turkiyah ba-meot ha-16–19" in Nahum Gross, ed., *Yehudim ba-kalkalah* (Jerusalem, 1985), 133–148; On class conflict in Izmir, see Avner Levi, "Social Cleavage, Class War, and Leadership in a Sephardi Community: The Case of Izmir in 1847" in Aron Rodrigue, ed., *Ottoman and Turkish Jewry: Community and Leadership* (forthcoming).
124. AAIU, Turquie I. C. 1, Cazès, received 26 October 1873.
125. AAIU, Turquie LXXXV. E., Pariente, 9 August 1878.
126. Ibid., 14 November 1878, 20 October 1879, 28 October 1879, and 30 October 1879.
127. AAIU, Turquie LXXXVI. E., Pariente, 25 November 1887.
128. Ibid., Pariente, 7 December 1887; AAIU, Turquie LXXXVI. E., AIU to Pariente, 22 December 1887.
129. AAIU, Turquie LXXXVI. E., Pariente, 8 March 1888, 6 April 1888.
130. Ibid., 8 June 1888.
131. Ibid., 1 December 1887, 16 December 1887, received 12 February 1888.
132. Ibid., 27 April 1888.
133. Ibid., AIU to Pariente, 25 March 1888.
134. Ibid., Pariente, 13 April 1888.
135. Ibid., AIU to Pariente, 10 May 1888.
136. Ibid.
137. Ibid., Pariente, received 14 December 1888.
138. AAIU, France VII. A. 45, Loeb to AIU, 16, 19, and 20 November 1888.
139. Ibid., 13 November 1888.
140. Galanté, *Histoire des Juifs d'Anatolie,* 1: 115.
141. AAIU, Turquie LXXX. E., Cazès, 29 September 1875.
142. AAIU, Turquie LXXXV. E., Pariente, 3 June 1879, 14 February 1879, 7 March 1879, 26 March 1879, 2 May 1879, 25 April 1879, and 27 June 1879.

143. For one such report see AAIU, Turquie I. C. 1, Pariente, received 15 May 1884.

144. AAIU, Turquie LXXXVII. E., Pariente, 7 December 1893.

IV. Educating Turkish Jewry

1. See Paul Silberman, "An Investigation of the Schools Operated by the Alliance Israélite Universelle from 1862 to 1940" (Ph.D. diss., New York University, 1973), 73–116. See also Aron Rodrigue, *De l'instruction à l'émancipation: Les enseignants de l'Alliance israélite universelle et les Juifs d'Orient, 1860–1939* (Paris, 1989), 31–39.

2. AAIU, France XI. F. 1, Instructions pour les professeurs, 2.

3. Ibid.

4. Ibid., 4–5.

5. AIU, *Instructions générales pour les professeurs* (Paris, 1903), 63.

6. AIU, *Instructions,* 27. For further details, see Silberman, "An Investigation," 73–86.

7. In Jacques Bigart, *L'Alliance Israélite: son action educatrice* (Paris, 1900), 14. The same themes are expanded in Jacques Bigart, "Le Professeur de l'Alliance doit être un educateur," *Revue des Ecoles de l'Alliance Israélite Universelle* (April-June 1901): 6–17. For the ideology of the Alliance, see also Georges Weill, "Emancipation et humanisme: Le discours idéologique de l'Alliance Israélite Universelle au XIXᵉ siècle," *Les Nouveaux Cahiers,* no. 52 (Spring 1978): 1-20, and Georges Weill, "L'enseignement dans les écoles de l'Alliance au XIXᵉ siècle," *Les Nouveaux Cahiers,* no. 78 (Fall 1984): 51–58.

8. AIU, *Procès-verbal de l'Assemblée générale de l'Alliance Israélite Universelle tenue le 31 Mai 1864* (Paris, 1864), 12.

9. See for example AAIU, Turquie I. E., Rahmané, 7 February 1905; AAIU, Turquie LXIV. E., Ouannou, 18 January 1904.

10. AIU, *Instructions,* 28.

11. AAIU, Turquie XXXVIII. E., Behar, letter received on 16 September 1875. For a study of the activities of Nissim Behar, see Shelomoh Haramati, *Sheloshah she-kadmu le-Ben Yehudah* (Jerusalem, 1978), 84–134.

12. AAIU, France XVII. F. 28, A. H. Navon, annual report, Balat, 1900–1901.

13. AAIU, France XVI. F. 27, Albala, annual report, Bursa, 1898-1899.

14. Ibid., Rahmané, annual report, Aydın, 1901–1902.

15. See Rodrigue, *De l'instruction,* 41.

16. Silberman, "An Investigation," 123–134. The only study of the *Ecole Normale* is A. H. Navon, *Les 70 ans de l'Ecole Normale Israélite Oriental* (Paris, 1935).

17. See Rodrigue, *De l'instruction,* 57–60.

18. Ibid., 59.

19. See, among many other examples, AAIU, France XVII. F. 28, Sémach, annual report, Balat, 1888–1889; France XVII. F. 27, Cardozo, annual report, Aydın, 1894–1895; France XVI. F. 27, Loupo, annual report, Edirne, 1899–1900.

20. See Institut Colonial International, *L'Enseignement aux indigènes* (Brussels, 1931), 316–319.

21. AAIU, France XI. E. 2, Central Committee, circular, 24 February 1925.

22. On this, see Maurice Crubellier, *L'enfance et la jeunesse dans la société française* (Paris, 1979), 92. See also Eugen Weber, *Peasants into Frenchmen* (Stanford, Calif., 1976).

23. See Robert R. Palmer, *The Improvement of Humanity: Education and the French Revolution* (Princeton, N.J., 1985), 3, 52–55; Françoise Mayeur, *De la révolution à l'école républicaine* (Paris, 1981), 30–50; Patrick J. Harrigan, *Mobility, Elites, and Education in French Society of the Second Empire* (Waterloo, Ontario, 1980), 125;

Harvey Chisick, *The Limits of Reform in the Enlightenment: Attitudes toward the Education of the Lower Classes in Eighteenth-Century France* (Princeton, N.J., 1981), 39.

24. Harrigan, *Mobility,* 120.

25. Ferdinand Buisson and Frederic Ernest Farrington, eds., *French Educational Ideals of Today; An Anthology of the Molders of French Educational Thought of the Present* (Yonkers, N.Y., 1919), 5–8.

26. Pierre Giolitto, *Histoire de l'enseignement primaire au XIXᵉ siècle,* 2 vols. (Paris, 1983–1984), 2: 43–44.

27. The report is printed in its entirety in Michel de Certeau, Dominique Julia, and Jacques Revel, *Une Politique de la langue: La Révolution française et les patois* (Paris, 1975), 300–317.

28. Crubellier, *L'enfance,* 242.

29. Buisson and Farrington, *French Educational,* 27–28.

30. AAIU, France VII. A. 45, Loeb, 7 December 1888.

31. AAIU, France XVIII. F. 29, Fresco, annual report, Hasköy, 1895–96.

32. AIU, *Instructions,* 13.

33. Ibid.

34. Ibid.

35. Ibid.

36. AAIU, Turquie L. E., Loeb to Franco, 26 March 1888.

37. Léon Kahn, *Les professions manuelles et les institutions de patronage* (Paris, 1885), 36; Léon Kahn, *Histoires des écoles communales et consistoriales israélites de Paris, 1809–1884* (Paris, 1884), 81. See also Lee Shai Weissbach, "The Jewish Elite and the Children of the Poor: Jewish Apprenticeship Programs in Nineteenth-Century France," *Association for Jewish Studies Review* 12 (Spring 1987): 123–142.

38. Ecole de Travail, *Compte rendu des années 1884–1886* (Paris, 1887), 11.

39. Silberman, "An Investigation," 121.

40. Ibid., 132–133.

41. Harrigan, *Mobility,* 118; Giolitto, *Histoire de l'enseignement,* 2: 9. See also Chisick, *The Limits of Reform.*

42. AAIU, Turquie XLVII. E., Loeb to Dalem, 14 August 1889.

43. See for example AAIU, France XIX. F. 30, Arié, annual report, Izmir, 1895–1896.

44. AAIU, Turquie XXVIII. E., Fernandez, 19 June 1896.

45. AAIU, France III. F. 8, Bénédict, 26 July 1901.

46. AAIU, Turquie L. F., Loeb to Franco, 29 July 1889.

47. See for example, AAIU, France XVIII. F. 29, Nabon, annual report, Hasköy, 1902–1903.

48. Ibid., and AAIU, France XVI. F. 27, Loupo, annual report, Edirne, 1900–1901.

49. AIU, *Procès-verbal de l'Assemblée générale du 25 Mai 1865* (Paris, 1865), 26.

50. BAIU (2ᵉ semestre 1866): 34. The Alliance's "regeneration" of the Eastern Jewish woman is a complex topic that merits a separate study on its own. One article has traced the ideological aspects of this work as seen in the correspondence of the women teachers of the Alliance in Salonica. See Annie Benveniste, "Le rôle des institutrices de l'Alliance Israélite à Salonique," *Combat pour la Diaspora,* no. 8 (1982): 13–26.

51. AAIU, France XVII. F. 28, Navon, annual report, Balat, 1896-97.

52. AAIU, France XVIII. F. 29, Nabon, annual report, Hasköy, 1891–1892.

53. Ibid.

54. AAIU, France XVII. F. 27, Ungar, annual report, Edirne, 1891-92.

55. AIU, *Instructions,* 99. The only study of an Alliance school for girls is that of Esther Benbassa, "L'école de filles de l'Alliance Israélite Universelle à Galata (1879–1912)" (Paper delivered in the Première rencontre internationale d'etudes et de re-

cherches sur l'Empire ottoman et la Turquie contemporaine: Recherches sur la ville ottomane, le cas du quartier de Galata, Paris, 18–22 January 1985).

56. Françoise Mayeur, *L'éducation des filles en France au XIXe siècle* (Paris, 1979), 23.

57. Ibid., 113.

58. Crubellier, *L'enfance,* 268. On the popularization of the notions of the *mère educatrice,* see also Linda L. Clark, *Schooling the Daughters of Marianne* (Albany, N.Y., 1984), 16-29; Mayeur, *De la révolution,* 120–140.

59. AAIU, France XVI. F. 27, Rahmané, annual report, Aydın, 1905–1906.

60. AIU, *Instructions,* 96.

61. Ibid., 49–50.

62. Haramati, *Sheloshah,* 84–125.

63. For example in Balat, AAIU, France XVII. F. 28, Sémach, annual report, Balat, 1892–1893.

64. AIU, *Instructions,* 33–34; AAIU, Turquie XXXVIII. E., Behor, 18 May 1877.

65. AAIU, Turquie LIV. E., 22 June 1908, Fresco.

66. AAIU, France III. F. 8, Bénédict, 1 January 1909; France XVII. F. 28, I. Danon, Galata, annual report, 1894–1895; ibid., Benveniste, annual report, 1908–1909.

67. AAIU, Turquie VIII. E., Loupo, 14 February 1886.

68. On the Alliance attempt to create a new rabbinate in Turkey, see Aron Rodrigue, "The Alliance Israélite Universelle and the Attempt to Reform Rabbinical and Religious Instruction in Turkey" in Simon Schwarzfuchs, ed., *L'"Alliance" dans les communautés du bassin méditerranéen à la fin du XIXe siècle et son influence sur la situation sociale et culturelle* (Jerusalem, 1987), liii–lxx.

69. Ibid.

70. AIU, *Instructions,* 95.

71. Ibid., 95–96.

72. Ibid., 96.

73. See for example AAIU, Turquie XXVIII. E., Fernandez, 23 April 1896.

74. For example in Galata, AAIU, Turquie XLVII. E, Dalem, 8 July 1884; in Edirne, Turquie VIII. E., AIU to Loupo, 26 March 1885.

75. See Michael M. Laskier, *The Alliance Israélite Universelle and the Jewish Communities of Morocco, 1862–1962* (Albany, New York, 1983), 241–242.

76. AAIU, Turquie I. M. 1, Behar, 26 August 1909.

77. BAIU 33 (1908): 35–36.

78. Ibid., 30.

79. Ibid, 34–35. On the 1908 mission, see also Lucien Lazare, "L'Alliance Israélite Universelle en Palestine à l'époque de la révolution des 'Jeunes Turcs' et sa mission en Orient du 29 octobre 1908 au 19 janvier 1909," *Revue des Etudes Juives* 138 (July-December 1979): 307–335.

80. AAIU, France XVIII. F. 29, Fresco, annual report, Hasköy, 1892–93.

81. AAIU, Turquie X. E., Loupo, 5 March 1900.

82. AIU, *Instructions,* 30–32.

83. Quoted in Narcisse Leven, *Cinquante ans d'histoire. L'Alliance Israélite Universelle (1860–1910),* 2 vols. (Paris, 1911–1920), 2: 34.

84. AAIU, France XVII. F. 28, Navon, annual report, Balat, 1897-1898.

85. See de Certeau et al., *Une politique,* 300–317.

86. Henri Baptiste (Abbé) Grégoire, *Essai sur la régénération physique, morale et politique des Juifs* (Metz, 1789), 160.

87. AAIU, Turquie XLII. E., Bloch, 28 December 1879.

88. AAIU, France XVII. F. 28, Navon, annual report, Balat, 1897-1898.

89. AAIU, France XVII. F. 28, Fresco, annual report, Galata, 1907–1908.

90. See introductory essay in Aron Rodrigue, *A Guide to the Ladino Collection in the Harvard College Library* (forthcoming).

91. For an example of the polemics surrounding this issue, see *El Tiempo*, 21 January 1901, 13 June 1901, and 17 June 1901.

92. Mayeur, *De la révolution*, 54–55; Crubellier, *L'enfance*, 242.

93. See for example AAIU, France XVIII. Г. 29, Arić, annual report, Ortaköy, 1881–1882.

94. AAIU, Turquie XXV. E., 7 March 1884, Regional Committee to the Central Committee.

95. AAIU, France XVII. F. 28, Fresco, annual report, Galata, 1907–1908.

96. AAIU, Turquie XXV. E., minutes of the meeting of the Regional Committee, 7 March 1884.

97. See AAIU, Turquie XLII. E., Bloch, 17 March 1876; Turquie XXV. E., Fernandez, 11 October 1876.

98. AAIU, Turquie L. E., Franco, 31 March 1891.

99. AAIU, Turquie XXVI. E., Fernandez, minutes of the meeting of the Regional Committee, 9 August 1884.

100. AAIU, Turquie XLII. E., Bloch, 28 December 1879.

101. AAIU, Turquie XXVI. E., Fernandez, 9 August 1884.

102. See for example AAIU, France XVII. F. 28, Bassous, annual report, Kuzguncuk, 1907–1908; Turquie XLVII. E., Dalmedico, received 18 September 1888.

103. AAIU, Turquie XLIII. E., AIU to Bloch, 22 June 1887.

104. AAIU, Turquie XLVII. E., Dalem, 16 August 1882; also in the same vein in ibid., 13 December 1882; and in AAIU, France XVII. F. 28, Dalem, annual report, Galata, 1882–1883. See also AAIU, Turquie XLII. F., Bloch, 28 December 1879.

105. AAIU, Turquie LI. E., Fresco, 6 May 1891.

106. AAIU, France VII. A. 45, Loeb, received 25 October 1888.

107. AAIU, Turquie XXVI. E., Fernandez, 16 Jan. 1888.

108. AAIU, Turquie LXI. E., Nabon, 10 January 1904.

109. AAIU, Turquie XLVIII. E., I. Danon, 12 September 1894. See also David Kushner, *The Rise of Turkish Nationalism, 1876–1908* (London, 1977), 93.

110. AAIU, France XVI. F. 27, Loupo, annual report, Edirne, 1897-1898.

111. See *El Tiempo,* 17 January 1901. Almost every issue of the newspaper in the years 1900–1901 contains articles on this matter. The same call for the increased teaching of Turkish was also taken up by the Jewish press in the provinces.

112. *El Tiempo,* 3 May 1900, 24 December 1900, 25 December 1900. The same discussions and resolutions took place in Izmir. See *El Meseret,* 9 Haziran, 2, 6, 24 Tişrinevvel 1316.

113. See David Kushner, *The Rise,* 94.

114. AAIU, France XVI. F. 27, Ungar, annual report, Edirne, 1908-1909; France XIX. F. 30, Nabon, annual report, Izmir, 1908–1909; Turquie XXXIV. E., Alchalel, 29 March 1910.

115. AAIU, Turquie XXXIV. E., Alchalel, 24 April 1909.

116. AAIU, France XVI. F. 27, Mitrani, annual report, Edirne, 1909–1910.

117. AAIU, Turquie XIII. E., note attached to Toussié's letter dated 13 April 1904.

118. AAIU, France XVIII. F. 29, Alchalel, annual report, Hasköy, 1909–1910.

119. Leven, *Cinquante,* 2: 10.

120. AIU, *Instructions,* 37–46.

121. The language of instruction in the model *lycée* created by the state in 1869, Galatasaray, was French. On this school, see İhsan Sungu, "Galatasaray Lisesi'nin Kuruluşu," *Belleten* 7, no. 26 (1943): 315–347.

122. On the spread of the usage of French in the Ottoman Empire, see Jacques Thobie, "La France a-t-elle une politique culturelle dans l'Empire ottoman à la veille

de la première guerre mondiale?" *Relations Internationales,* no. 25 (Spring 1981): 21–40.

123. AIU, *Instructions,* 27.

124. AAIU, France XVII. F. 28, Balat, annual report, 2 November 1889.

125. AAIU, Turquie IX. E., AIU to Loupo, 25 September 1899.

126. AAIU, France XVIII. F. 28, Dalem, annual report, Galata, 1889–1890.

127. AAIU, France XVIII. F. 29, Fresco, annual report, Hasköy, 1892–1893; Turquie LII. E., Fresco, 18 November 1898; France XVII. F. 28, Fresco, annual report, Galata, 1898–1899.

128. Ibid.

129. AAIU, France XIX. F. 30, Nabon, annual report, Izmir, 1906–1907.

130. AAIU, France XIX. F. 30, Pariente, annual report, Izmir, 1881–1882. On the polyglot nature of the Istanbul Jewish community, see the excellent survey in Mahir Şaul, "The Mother-Tongue of the Polyglot: Cosmopolitism and Nationalism among the Sepharadim of Istanbul," *Anthropological Linguistics* 25 (Fall 1983): 326–358.

131. For a study of the politics and impact of an Alliance school in a small community, see Aron Rodrigue, "Jewish Society and Schooling in a Thracian Town: The Alliance Israélite Universelle in Demotica, 1897–1924," *Jewish Social Studies* 45 (Summer-Fall 1983): 263–286.

132. The dates in which the smaller communities established Alliance schools are as follows:

Community	Date of foundation of school
Çanakkale (Dardanelles)	1878
Bursa	1886
Manisa (Magnesia)	1892
Aydın	1894
Tire	1897
Turgutlu (Kassaba)	1897
Tekirdağ (Rodosto)	1904
Gelibolu (Gallipoli)	1905
Kırklareli (Kirklisse)	1911
Çorlu	1911

Source: BAIU (1878–1913).

133. Ibid. The Jewish schools of the communities of Vurla, Melas, Akhisar, Nazilli, and Menemen all began to receive subsidies from the Alliance in the first decade of the twentieth century and reformed their institutions under the direction of the Alliance school directors of Izmir. But they were not part of the network, as they were not directed by teachers sent from the Alliance, and though teaching French, their programs did not conform to those adopted in the organization's schools. See BAIU 36 (1911): 86-115. For the history of the small communities in Asia Minor, see Abraham Galanté, *Histoire des Juifs d'Anatolie,* 2 vols. (Istanbul, 1937–39).

134. BAIU (1879–1908).

135. BAIU 18 (1893): 79.

136. See Benbassa, "L'école de filles."

137. BAIU 36 (1911): 86–115. This list excludes those schools, such as those of the smaller communities of Asia Minor, which received subsidies from the Alliance but did not follow its curricula. It also excludes the Alliance kindergartens, the Istanbul Rabbinical Seminary subsidized by the organization as well as the Alliance training farm of *Or Yehudah* in Asia Minor.

138. See the statistics to be found in Kemal H. Karpat, *Ottoman Population 1830–1914: Demographic and Social Characteristics* (Madison, Wis., 1985), 162–190. See

also Justin McCarthy, *The Arab World, Turkey, and the Balkans (1878–1914): A Handbook of Historical Statistics* (Boston, 1982), 64–83. The population statistics cited in these books are from the years 1906–1907 and 1914–1915. Nevertheless, these dates are close enough to 1911 to make comparisons between the figures and those of the Alliance meaningful.

139. Karpat, *Ottoman Population,* 161.

140. AAIU, France XI. 2, circular dated 5 January 1904.

141. AIU, *Instructions générales pour les professeurs* (Paris, 1903), 63.

142. Stanford Shaw, "The Population of Istanbul," *Türk Tarih Dergisi* 32 (1979): 413.

143. See Karpat, *Ottoman Population,* 161.

144. AAIU, Turquie LIV. E., Fresco, received 27 April 1906.

145. MAE, Série D, vol. 27, fol. 28–108.

146. Maurice Pernot, *Rapport sur un voyage d'étude à Constantinople, en Egypte, et en Turquie d'Asie (janvier-août 1912)* (Paris, 1913?), 330–331.

147. This is the case in all the statistics provided in the publications of the education ministry. See for example the list of the *idadis* in the *vilayet* of Edirne, which does not have a breakdown according to each *millet.* See *Salname-i Nezareti Maarif-i Umumiyesi* (Istanbul, 1316/1898), 778–784. The same is true five years later. See *Salname-i Nezareti Maarif-i Umumiyesi* (Istanbul, 1321/1903), 294–296.

148. For example, in the *vilayet* of Edirne, the *Salname* of 1316 does not indicate the existence of the *Talmud Torah* of the city of Edirne with close to 1000 students. There is also no evidence of the Alliance school in Dimetoka (Demotica). See *Salname* (1316/1898), 794–795.

149. Cemil Koçak, "Tanimat'tan sonra Özel ve Yabancı Okullar," *Tanzimat'tan Cumhuriyet'e Türkiye Ansiklopedisi* 2 (1985): 488.

150. Stanford J. Shaw and Ezel Kural Shaw, *History of the Ottoman Empire and Modern Turkey,* 2 vols. (Cambridge, 1976–1977), 2: 113. This figure includes the Galatasaray *lycée.*

151. Ibid.

152. AAIU, Turquie LXXXIII, Nabon, Izmir, received 1 April 1912.

153. The Alliance's reforming of the *Talmudei Torah* has been discussed in Rodrigue, "The Alliance Israélite Universelle and the Attempt to Reform."

154. Ibid.

155. Ibid.

156. Ibid.

157. Ibid.

V. The Alliance Schools and Jewish Society in Turkey

1. See Michael Graetz, *Les Juifs en France au XIXe siècle* (Paris, 1989), 101–105; Phyllis Cohen Albert, *The Modernization of French Jewry* (Hanover, N.H., 1977), 124–128.

2. See Salo W. Baron, *A Social and Religious History of the Jews,* 3 vols. (New York, 1937), 3: 276. On attempts to change Jewish social structure in Europe see Bernard Dov [Sucher Ber] Weinryb, *Der Kampf um die Berufsumschichtung: Ein Ausschnitt aus der Geschichte der Juden in Deutschland* (Berlin, 1936) and idem, *Jewish Vocational Education: History and Appraisal of Training in Europe* (New York, 1948).

3. AAIU, Grèce XX. E. 251, Cazès, 25 September 1872.

4. Ibid., Cazès, 10 October 1872.

5. Ibid., Cazès, 31 October 1872.

6. Narcisse Leven, *Cinquante ans d'histoire. L'Alliance Israélite Universelle (1860–*

1910), 2 vols. (Paris, 1911–1920) 2: 290. For a summary of the origins of the apprenticeship program, see Paul Silberman, "An Investigation of the Schools Operated by the Alliance Israélite Universelle from 1862 to 1940" (Ph.D. diss., New York University, 1973), 152–155.

7. AAIU, Turquie I. C. 1, Cazès, received 26 October 1873, also in BAIU (2ᵉ semestre 1873): 141. Quoted also in Paul Dumont, "Jewish Communities in Turkey during the Last Decades of the Nineteenth Century in Light of the Archives of the Alliance Israélite Universelle" in Benjamin Braude and Bernard Lewis, eds., *Christians and Jews in the Ottoman Empire,* 2 vols. (New York, 1982), 1: 216.

8. AAIU, Turquie VIII. E., Loupo, 1 August 1889.

9. AAIU, Turquie II. C. 8, A. H. Navon, 15 January 1900. See the discussion of this report in Dumont, "Jewish Communities in Turkey," 220.

10. See Léon Kahn, *Les professions manuelles et les institutions de patronage* (Paris, 1885), 36. On these *sociétés de patronage,* see Lee Shai Weissbach, "The Jewish Elite and the Children of the Poor: Jewish Apprenticeship Programs in Nineteenth-Century France," *Association for Jewish Studies Review* 12 (Spring 1987): 123–142.

11. On the history of vocational training in France, see Antoine Léon, *Histoire de l'éducation technique* (Paris, 1968) and André Prévot, *L'enseignement technique chez les frères des Ecoles chrétiennes au 18ᵉ et au 19ᵉ siècles* (Paris, 1964).

12. Albert, *The Modernization of French Jewry,* 124–128. See also Weissbach, "The Jewish Elite."

13. AIU, *Instructions générales pour les professeurs* (Paris, 1903), 82.

14. Ibid.

15. Ibid., 82–84.

16. AAIU, Turquie LXIII. E., Navon, 15 September 1899.

17. *Jurnal Israelit,* 15 December 1867.

18. AAIU, Turquie I. C. 1, Cazès, received 26 October 1873. Also in BAIU (2ᵉ semestre 1873): 144.

19. AAIU, Turquie XXV. E., Bloch, 6 January 1879.

20. AAIU, Turquie LXXXV. E., Pariente, 8 March 1878, 12 July 1878.

21. AAIU, Turquie VI. E., A. Cazès, 20 August 1878.

22. *Boletino de la Sosiedad Dorshei ha-Haskalah* (Edirne, 1889), 6.

23. AAIU, Turquie IX. E., Loupo, 14 July 1897.

24. AAIU, Turquie XLIII. E., Bloch, received 18 December 1879.

25. AAIU, Turquie XXVI. E., Hamouth, minutes of the meeting of the apprenticeship society, 3 November 1886.

26. AAIU, Turquie LVI. E, Hamouth, 1 September 1889.

27. See Esther Benbassa and Aron Rodrigue, "L'artisanat juif en Turquie à la fin du 19ᵉ siècle," *Turcica* 17 (1985): 113-126.

28. AAIU, Turquie X. E., Loupo, 12 January 1900.

29. AAIU, Turquie X. E., Loupo, 12 January 1900.

30. AAIU, Turquie LXXVI. E., Arié, 27 November 1899.

31. Benbassa and Rodrigue, "L'artisanat," 119.

32. AAIU, Turquie LXIII. F., Navon, 15 August 1899. The list is also published in Benbassa and Rodrigue, "L'artisanat," 122.

33. AAIU, Turquie LXXV. E., Arié, 16 June 1897.

34. AAIU, Turquie LXIII. E., Navon, 15 August 1899.

35. On Antébi, see the interesting monograph by Michael M. Laskier, "Avraham Albert Antebi: Perakim be-fo'alo bi-shenot 1897–1914," *Pe'amim,* no. 21 (1984): 50–82.

36. AAIU, Israël IV. E. 11, Antébi, 26 August 1900.

37. AAIU, Turquie LXIII, E., Navon, 15 August 1899.

38. Ibid., 15 September 1899.

39. Ibid., 7 November 1900.
40. AAIU, Israël IV. E. 11, Antébi, 26 August 1900.
41. AIU, *Instructions*, 83.
42. Ibid.
43. AAIU, Turquie XII. E., Mitrani, 12 January 1912.
44. Ibid. The total number of artisans enumerated by Mitrani adds up to 67 and not to 65 as he claims.
45. AAIU, Israël IV. E. 11, Antébi, 21 September 1900.
46. AAIU, Turquie XII. E., Mitrani, 12 January 1912.
47. Ibid.
48. AAIU, Turquie LXXVII. E., Arié, 12 July 1906.
49. Abraham Galanté, *Histoire des Juifs d'Istanbul*, 2 vols. (Istanbul, 1941–1942), 2: 72.
50. Aron Rodrigue, "Jewish Society and Schooling in a Thracian Town: The Alliance Israélite Universelle in Demotica, 1897-1924," *Jewish Social Studies* 45 (Summer-Fall 1983): 275.
51. See Charles Issawi, ed., *The Economic History of Turkey 1800-1914* (Chicago, 1980), 275. For the state of the handicrafts, see Vedat Eldem, *Osmanlı İmparatorluğunun İktisadi Şartları Hakkında Bir Tetkik* (Ankara, 1970), 141-149. A recent overview of the evolution of the Ottoman economy following the 1838 treaty is that of Salgur Kancal, "La conquête du marché interne ottoman par le capitalisme industriel concurrentiel (1838–1881)" in Jean-Louis Bacqué-Grammont and Paul Dumont, eds., *Economie et sociétés dans l'Empire ottoman (Fin du XVIIIe-Début du XXe siècle)* (Paris, 1983), 355–409.
52. Benbassa and Rodrigue, "L'artisanat," 123–124.
53. See "Die wirtschaftliche Lage der Juden in Konstantinopel" in AZJ of 1912, excerpts published in Issawi, *The Economic*, 69–71. The Ashkenazic tailors formed a distinct congregation within the larger Ashkenazic community made up of several congregations. Auswärtiges Amt, Abteilung A, *Akten betreffend die Juden in der Turkei*, 1907–1912, "Die Aschkenasische Kultusgemeinde zu Konstantinopel 1890–1910," K176261. Microfilm in the Central Archives of the Jewish People, Jerusalem.
54. AIU, *Instructions*, 86–89.
55. AIU, *L'Alliance Israélite Universelle, 1860–1895* (Paris, 1895), 24–25. Also quoted in Silberman, "An Investigation," 162.
56. AAIU, Turquie LXVI. E., Salzer, 23 May 1884; see also Esther Benbassa, "L'école de filles de l'Alliance Israélite Universelle à Galata (1879–1912)" (Paper delivered in the Première rencontre internationale d'études et de recherches sur l'Empire ottoman et la Turquie contemporaine: Recherche sur la ville ottomane, le cas du quartier de Galata, Paris, 18–22 January 1985).
57. AAIU, Turquie LXVI. E., Salzer, 19 September 1884. Also discussed in Benbassa, "L'école."
58. AAIU, Turquie IV. E., Abramowitz, 3 November 1887.
59. AAIU, Turquie LXVI. E., AIU to Salzer, 12 June 1889.
60. Ibid., 1 September 1889.
61. AAIU, Turquie LXII. E., L. Nabon, 1 September 1899.
62. AAIU, Turquie XLVI. E., Confino, 13 December 1905, AIU to Confino, 20 December 1905.
63. AAIU, France XIX. F. 30, Nabon, annual report, Izmir, 1908-1909.
64. AAIU, Turquie, XI. E., AIU's response to Mitrani's letter of 18 January 1910.
65. Benbassa, "L'école."
66. Ibid.
67. AAIU, Turquie LXIX. E., Sémach, 6 July 1898. Also noted in Benbassa, "L'école."

68. On the foundation of *Mikveh Yisrael*, see Georges Weill, "Charles Netter ou les oranges de Jaffa," *Les Nouveaux Cahiers,* no. 21 (Summer 1970): 2–36.

69. Leven, *Cinquante*, 2: 314.

70. For an analysis of the work of the Jewish Colonization Association in Palestine, see Simon Schama, *Two Rothschilds and the Land of Israel* (New York, 1978).

71. Leven, *Cinquante*, 2: 321–394. See also Georges Weill, "Les oliviers de Djedeida" (Paper presented during the "Maghreb-Mashrek" congress held in Jerusalem, Spring 1984).

72. AAIU, Turquie LXXXVII. E., Pariente, 7 June 1889, 12 December 1889, 20 December 1889.

73. AAIU, Turquie LXXXVII. E., Pariente, 7 December 1893.

74. Ibid., and AAIU, Turquie LXXXVII. E., AIU to Pariente, April 1890, 13 June 1890, 19 June 1890.

75. AAIU, Turquie LXXIV. E., Arié, 19 October 1894, 16 May 1895.

76. AAIU, Turquie, LXXIV. E., Arié, 29 May 1896, 23 November 1896.

77. AAIU, ICA 4, Alliance to ICA, 5 November 1902; France II. H. 5, ICA to Alliance, 21 November 1900. See also Abraham Galanté, *Histoire des Juifs d'Anatolie,* 2 vols. (Istanbul, 1937–1939), 2: 117–120.

78. AAIU, France V. F. 10, Bénédict, *Or Yehudah,* August 1901; Turquie II. H. 7, Saporta to ICA, 14 November 1900; Turquie LXXVI. E., Arié, 5 July 1901; AAIU, ICA 4, Alliance to ICA, 5 November 1902.

79. AAIU, ICA 4, Alliance to ICA, 5 November 1902.

80. AAIU, ICA 4, Joseph Niégo, 25 September 1908.

81. AAIU, Turquie XLIII. E., Bloch, 7 February 1887.

82. AAIU, France XVII. F. 28, Bassous, annual report, Kuzguncuk, 1895–1896.

83. Ibid., Weismann, annual report, Kuzguncuk, 1895–1896.

84. Ibid. The rate of exchange is determined by the figures applied in AAIU, Turquie XLIX. E., Eskenazi, 13 December 1897.

85. AAIU, Turquie XLIX. E., Eskenazi, 13 December 1897.

86. AAIU, Turquie LXXIV. E., AIU to Arié, 25 January 1895.

87. AAIU, Turquie XLIX. E., Eskenazi, 13 December 1897.

88. For a discussion on the state of Turkish Jewry at the end of the nineteenth century, see Dumont, "Jewish Communities."

89. AAIU, Turquie LXXIV. E., Arié, 6 January 1895. The list is published in full in Benbassa and Rodrigue, "L'artisanat," 115.

90. AAIU, Turquie II. C. 8, Navon, 15 January 1900.

91. AAIU, France XVIII. F. 29, Arié, annual report, Ortaköy, 1883–1884, list of students who left the school.

92. AAIU, France XVII. F. 28, Dalem, annual report, Galata, 1883-1884, list of students who left the school.

93. AAIU, France XIX. F. 30, Pariente, annual report, Izmir, 1880–1881, list of students who left school.

94. Ibid., Arié, annual report, Izmir, 1895–96, list of students who left school.

95. AAIU, France XVI. F. 27, Loupo, annual report, Edirne, 1888-1889, list of students who left the school.

96. These statistics have been compiled from the information about the destinations of students leaving at the end of each year supplied to Paris by the teachers. AAIU, France XVI. F. 27, Loupo, annual reports, Edirne, 1895–1903, lists of students leaving the school; AAIU, France XVI. F. 27, Mitrani, annual reports, Edirne, 1903–1905, lists of students leaving the school.

97. AAIU, France XVI. F. 27, Loupo, annual report, Edirne, 1899-1900.

98. Ibid.

99. See for example AAIU, France XVIII. F. 29, Fresco, annual report, Hasköy, 1891–1892; AAIU, France XVI. F. 27, Sémach, annual report, Bursa, 1911–1912.

100. See the report about Galata in AAIU, Turquie XLVII. E., Dalem, 9 July 1879; about Balat in AAIU, Turquie XXXVIII. E., Behar, 21 September 1879.

101. Compiled from the statistics in AAIU, France XIX. F. 30, Arié, annual reports 1896–1897, 1898–1899, and 1900–1901.

102. AAIU, Turquie XLIII. E., Bloch, 7 February 1887.

103. AAIU, Turquie XLIII. E., Bloch, no date, compiled in 1890 before his departure.

104. *Hamenora*, no. 7 (September 1925): 216.

105. AAIU, France XVII. F. 28, Israel Danon, annual report, Galata, 1885–1886.

106. AAIU, France XIX. F. 30, Arié, annual report, Izmir, 1894–1895; AAIU, Turquie LXXIV. E., Arié, 19 July 1895.

107. AAIU, France XIX. F. 30, Arié, annual report, Izmir, 1901–1902; AAIU, France XVII. F. 28, Fresco, annual reports, Galata, 1900–1901, 1903–1904; AAIU, France XVII. F. 28, Bassous, annual report, Kuzguncuk, 1907–1908.

108. This was spelled out very succinctly in a report published in *L'Aurore*, the major Zionist newspaper of Istanbul. See *L'Aurore*, 30 July 1909. A similar situation existed in Salonica. See AAIU, France X. F. 18, Benghiat, 11 December 1910.

109. All the school directors repeatedly reported this fact. See for example AAIU, Turquie LXXXIII. E., Nabon, Izmir, letter received on 1 April 1912.

110. For the specifically French economic penetration, see the magisterial study of Jacques Thobie, *Intérêts et impérialisme français dans l'Empire ottoman, 1895–1914* (Paris, 1977). See also Jacques Thobie, *La France impériale, 1880–1914* (Paris, 1982), 17–54.

111. There is a vast literature on this subject. Bourdieu's work is arguably the best and the most representative. See Pierre Bourdieu and Jean-Claude Passeron, *La Reproduction, éléments pour une théorie du système d'enseignement* (Paris, 1970).

112. See the discussion in Henry A. Giroux, *Ideology, Culture and the Process of Schooling* (Philadelphia, 1981), 15, 103. See also the preface to the same book by Stanley Aronowitz, 2–3, and M. D. Shipman, *Education and Modernisation* (London, 1971), 34, 43, 49-50.

113. AAIU, Turquie L. E., Franco, 27 June 1889.

114. Ibid., also noted by Mitrani in AAIU, Turquie XI. E., received 10 January 1894.

115. AAIU, Turquie XLIII. E., Bloch, 7 February 1887.

116. Noted by Fresco in AAIU, France XVII. F. 28, annual report, Galata, 1902–1903. Indeed, this is very much in evidence in the Judeo-Spanish press beginning with the 1870s when more and more French words were hispanicized and incorporated into the Judeo-Spanish vocabulary. The meaning of the new word was given in brackets. Very often, the French import replaced a word of Turkish origin in Judeo-Spanish. For good examples of this phenomenon, see *El Tiempo* of the 1870s.

117. Robert L. Bee, *Patterns and Processes: An Introduction to Anthropological Strategies for the Study of Socio-Cultural Change* (New York, 1974), 105–108.

118. For "diglossia" see Joshua A. Fishman, *Advances in the Sociology of Language,* 2 vols. (The Hague, 1971–1972).

119. See the studies of Karen Gerson on the Turkish Jewish community of today. Karen Gerson, "Language Change as Influenced by Cultural Contact: A Case, Ladino" (MA thesis, Boğaziçi University, 1983) and idem, "The Relation of Language, Ethnicity, and Ethnic Group Identity. A Case: Judeo-Spanish" (MA thesis, University of Reading, 1986). I would like to thank Karen Gerson for having sent me the manuscripts of her work.

VI. The Alliance and the Emergence of Zionism in Turkey

1. AAIU, Turquie IX. E., Loupo, 5 January 1891.
2. Ibid. In 1891 it produced a play of Molière in Judeo-Spanish.
3. AAIU, Turquie IX. F., Loupo, 10 November 1898.
4. AAIU, Turquie LXXVII. E., Arié, received 23 December 1897, November 1898.
5. AAIU, Turquie LXXVII. E., Bigart, 26 March 1903.
6. AAIU, Turquie IX. E., Loupo, 6 January 1899, 30 January 1899, AAIU, Turquie X. E., Loupo, 29 January 1901, 22 January 1902, 7 February 1903, 5 June 1903.
7. AAIU, Turquie LXXV. E., Arié, 16 June 1897.
8. On associations and societies among the Jews of Turkey in this period, see Esther Benbassa, "Associational Strategies in Ottoman Jewish Society in the Nineteenth and Twentieth Centuries" in Avigdor Levy, ed., *The Jews in the Ottoman Empire* (forthcoming).
9. AAIU, France XIX. F. 30, Arié, annual report, Izmir, 1898-1899.
10. See Michael Graetz, *Les Juifs en France au XIXᵉ siècle* (Paris, 1989).
11. AAIU, Turquie VII. E., Loupo, 8 September 1893.
12. AAIU, Turquie II. B. 5, Abraham Palacci, letter received in July 1895.
13. AAIU, France XIX. F. 30, Nabon, annual report, Izmir, 1912-1913.
14. See his articles in *La Vara*, 28 July 1905, 11 May 1906, 25 May 1906, 22 June 1906, 20 July 1906, 18 January 1907, and 10 May 1907.
15. AAIU, Turquie XXX. E., Nahum, 4 January 1892, 28 December 1897, 19 January 1898. On the career of Haim Nahum, see the important work by Esther Benbassa, "Haim Nahum Effendi, dernier Grand Rabbin de l'Empire ottoman (1908–1920): Son rôle politique et diplomatique" (Thèse de doctorat d'état ès lettres, Université de Paris III, 1987).
16. AAIU, Turquie XXX. E., Nahum, 18 January 1899, Bigart to Nahum, 27 January 1899. See also Benbassa, "Haim Nahum," 56.
17. AAIU, Turquie XXX. E., Nahum, 6 September 1908; AI 69 (1908): 299; AI 70 (1909): 28. *El Tiempo*, 12 August 1908. For further details on the events surrounding his election, see Benbassa, "Haim Nahum," 78–82.
18. *El Tiempo*, 1 January 1909, 4 January 1909, and 8 January 1909; AI 70 (1909): 28; AAIU, Turquie XXX. E., Nahum, 23 December 1908. On the background of these letters, see Benbassa, "Haim Nahum," 101–102.
19. *El Tiempo*, 25 January 1909; AI 70 (1909): 35. Benbassa, "Haim Nahum," 115.
20. See Esther Benbassa, "L'Alliance Israélite Universelle et l'éléction de Haim Nahum au Grand Rabbinat de l'Empire ottoman (1908–1909)" in World Union of Jewish Studies, *Proceedings of the Ninth World Congress of Jewish Studies* 3: 84.
21. AAIU, Turquie XXX. E., Bigart to Nahum, 15 September 1908.
22. Ibid., Nahum, 23 September 1908.
23. AAIU, Registre, Secrétariat 219, Bigart to Nahum, 25 January 1909.
24. AAIU, Turquie XXX. E., Nahum, 22 November 1901.
25. AAIU, Turquie II. C. 8, Fresco, 28 July 1908; AAIU, LXXXIII. E., Nabon, 2 August 1908; *El Tiempo*, 27, 28, 31 July 1909.
26. For the reaction of the Jews to the Young Turk Revolution, see Feroz Ahmad, "Unionist Relations with the Greek, Armenian, and Jewish Communities of the Ottoman Empire" in Benjamin Braude and Bernard Lewis, eds., *Christians and Jews in the Ottoman Empire*, 2 vols. (New York, 1982), 1: 401. The situation in Salonica is examined in David Farhi, "Yehudei Saloniki be-mahapekhat ha-'turkim ha-ẓe'irim,' " *Sefunot* 15 (1971–1981): 135–152. For a detailed study of the reaction in one Judeo-Spanish newspaper in Istanbul, see Esther Benbassa, "La 'nation' juive au lendemain

de la revolution Jeune-Turque (1908) à travers *El Tiempo,* journal judéo-espagnol d'Istanbul" (Paper read at the conference "Istanbul dans la Presse. La Presse à Istanbul," Istanbul, May 1985). The myth of the Young Turk Revolution as the result of a conspiracy by Jews and Freemasons has been analyzed by Elie Kedourie, "Young Turks, Freemasons and Jews," *Middle East Studies* 7 (January 1971): 89–104.

27. See for example AAIU, Turquie I. G. 1, Alchalel, 8 January 1911, AAIU, France XIX. F. 30, Nabon, annual report, Izmir, 1908-1909.

28. BAIU 33 (1908): 73–74.

29. AAIU, Registre, Secrétariat 219, Bigart to Nahum, 25 January 1909.

30. BAIU 33 (1908): 40.

31. Hilmi Yücebaş, *Filozof Rıza Tevfik: Hayatı, Hatıraları, Şiirleri* (Istanbul, 1978), 8. His Judeo-Spanish was perfect and after the revolution he gave lectures in Judeo-Spanish to Jewish audiences. See pages 78 and 144.

32. Sina Akşin. *Jön Türkler ve İttihat ve Terakki* (Istanbul, 1980), 298.

33. Galanté dealt with Zionism in some detail only in the context of Herzl's encounter with the Sultan. See Abraham Galanté, *Abdul Hamid II et le Sionisme* (Istanbul, 1933). The subject of the Zionist movement in Turkey was treated only very tangentially in his voluminous writings. For an example, see the brief references to the "pseudo-Zionists" in his account of the Chief Rabbinate of Nahum in Abraham Galanté, *Histoire des Juifs d'Istanbul,* 2 vols. (Istanbul, 1941–42) 1: 140–143. He does not mention Nessim Rousso's important role in Turkish Zionism when he gives an account of his public activities. See Abraham Galanté, *Turcs et Juifs* (Istanbul, 1932), 89–90. Other studies, including Zionist ones, have ignored the ramifications of Zionism in the Sephardic world. Feroz Ahmad, basing his study on these accounts, asserts that "[w]hile the Zionist movement had an office in Istanbul, it found virtually no support amongst local Jews." See Feroz Ahmad, "Unionist Relations" in Braude and Lewis, eds., *Christians and Jews,* 1: 426.

34. *El Tiempo,* 13 June 1898, 25 July 1898, 26 July 1898, 6 June 1901, and 13 June 1901.

35. Neville Mandel, *The Arabs and Zionism before World War I* (Berkeley, 1976), 60.

36. On this aspect, see David Farhi, "Documents on the Attitude of the Ottoman Government towards the Jewish Settlement in Palestine after the Revolution of the Young Turks, 1908–1909" in Moshe Maoz, ed., *Studies on Palestine in the Ottoman Period* (Jerusalem, 1975), 190–210; Mandel, *The Arabs;* Isaiah Friedman, *Germany, Turkey and Zionism, 1897–1918* (Oxford, 1977); and most recently in Turkish by Mim Kemal Öke, *Siyonizm ve Filistin Sorunu (1880–1914)* (Istanbul, 1982).

37. See Benbassa, "Haim Nahum," passim. See also Esther Benbassa, "Le Sionisme dans l'Empire ottoman à l'aube du 20e siècle," *Vingtième Siècle,* no. 24 (October-December 1989): 69–80 and idem, "Le Sionisme et la politique des alliances dans les communautés juives ottomanes" in Aron Rodrigue, ed., *Ottoman and Turkish Jewry: Community and Leadership* (forthcoming).

38. CZA, L5/1, Jacobson to Cologne, 8 July 1911; Friedman, *Germany,* 149. On the Zionist utilization of the local press, see Esther Benbassa, "Presse d'Istanbul et de Salonique au service du sionisme," *Revue Historique* 276 (October-December 1986): 337–365.

39. Benbassa, "Le Sionisme et la politique" (forthcoming).

40. CZA, L5/1, Jacobson to Cologne, 8 July 1911. A short historical account of Zionism among Turkish Jews, where the role of the *Makabi* is stressed, is to be found in PRO, FO 371/801, 68021, report prepared by A. H. Orenstein, lieutenant in intelligence, and sent by Admiral Calthorpe on 16 April 1919 to the Foreign Office, London.

41. *L'Aurore,* 4 March 1910.

42. Central Archives of the History of the Jewish People, P112/109, Minute Book of

the Alliance Regional Committee, Constantinople, 1903–1917, meetings of 24 June 1906, 8 November 1908, and 3 April 1914.

43. *L'Aurore*, 20 January 1911.

44. AAIU, Turquie I. G. 1, Nathan, 16 November 1910, 4 February 1912, and 21 March 1912; ibid., Alchalelel, 8 January 1911; AAIU, Turquie XXIX. E., Fernandez, 3 March 1911.

45. AAIU, Turquie I. G. 1, reference in the letter of Bigart to Fernandez, 5 May 1911.

46. *El Tiempo*, 28 October 1910; *L'Aurore*, 4 November 1910, 29 November 1910.

47. Benbassa, "Haim Nahum," 386; AAIU, Turquie XL. E., Benveniste, 19 May 1911, 7 February 1912, 12 February 1912, 27 February 1912, and 28 March 1912.

48. AAIU, Turquie XLI. E., Benveniste, 3 May 1913; AAIU, Turquie I. G. 1, 26 February 1914. See also Benbassa, "Haim Nahum," 414.

49. Herzl accused the Alliance of being neither a universal alliance nor Jewish. Quoted in Michel Abitbol, *Les deux terres promises: Les Juifs de France et le sionisme, 1897–1945* (Paris, 1989), 33–34. For examples of attacks against the Alliance in the official Zionist press, see *Die Welt*, 14 February 1902, 28 March 1902, 6 June 1902, 20 June 1902, 15 August 1902, 24 April 1903, 1 July 1904, and 12 April 1911.

50. On this affair, see CZA Z2/31, Friedman to Cologne, 9, 12, and 28 April 1911; CZA Z2/31, circular, Cologne, 8 May 1911; ibid., circular, Berlin, 12 May 1911; CZA, L5/24, Friedman to Jacobson, 11 May 1911; *L'Aurore*, 31 December 1910, 23 May 1911, 3 June 1911, 13 June 1911, 20 June 1911, 23 June 1911, 7 July 1911, and 17 October 1911; AAIU, Turquie XL. E., Benveniste, 26 May 1911; BAIU 36 (1911): 38–51. The 1911 affair has been referred to only in passing by the historians of the Alliance. The history of the relationship between the German membership of the Alliance and the Central Committee, from the foundation of the organization to 1914, is a topic that has not been treated at all in the scholarly literature. A good study is of interest not only for the history of the Alliance, but also for the understanding of the relationship between German and French Jewries in the second half of the nineteenth and the early twentieth centuries.

51. AAIU, France XVIII. F. 28, Sémach, annual report, Galata, 1909–1910.

52. *Hamenora*, no. 7–8 (July-August 1924): 214.

53. AAIU, Turquie I. G. 1, Nathan, 4 February 1912; AAIU, Turquie XL. E., Benveniste, 8 May 1910.

54. AAIU, Turquie XXXIV. E., Alchalel, 11 December 1910.

55. Benbassa, "Haim Nahum," 283–285.

56. *Bulletin de l'Amicale* (1910): 12.

57. See the statutes in André Chouraqui, *Cent ans d'histoire. L'Alliance Israélite Universelle et la renaissance juive contemporaine (1860–1960)* (Paris, 1965), 412.

58. *Bulletin de l'Amicale* (1910): 31.

59. Ibid.

60. See for example *Die Welt*, 24 April 1903, 7 January 1910, and 27 October 1911. For a classic Zionist interpretation of the early years of the Alliance and its leaders reflecting this line of thought, see Nahum Sokolow, *History of Zionism, 1600–1918*, 2 vols. (London, 1919), 1: 180–183.

61. *L'Aurore*, 22 April 1910, 29 April 1910, 6 May 1910, and 1 July 1910.

62. *L'Aurore*, 25 February 1910.

63. Ibid., 13 May 1910.

64. Ibid., 4 November 1910.

65. Ibid., 27 June 1911. On the relationship between the Alliance and other Jewish organizations, see Zosa Szajkowski, "Conflicts in the AIU and the Founding of the Anglo-Jewish Association, the Vienna Allianz and the Hilfsverein," *Jewish Social Studies* 19 (January-April 1957): 29–50. Unfortunately, there is no study on the

Hilfsverein that treats all of its activities. Its relations with Zionists is studied in Friedman, *Germany, Turkey*, passim. Its work in Palestine is the subject of Mosheh Rinot, *Ḥevrat ha-'ezrah le-yehudei Germanyah bi-yeẓirah u-ve-ma'avak: perek betoldot ha-ḥinukh ha-'ivri be-Ereẓ-Yisrael u-ve-toldot yehudei Germanyah* (Jerusalem, 1971).

66. CZA, Z2/10, Jacobson to Wolffsohn, 30 December 1910; CZA, Z2/11, Jacobson to Wolffsohn, 28 March 1911.

67. David Fresco, *Le Sionisme* (Istanbul, 1909).

68. Ibid., 71–72.

69. The latter had already expressed such fears with the emergence of the official Zionist movement. AAIU, Turquie I. G. 1, Arié, 10 June 1898; ibid., Fernandez, 6 September 1897.

70. Nahum Sokolow, *Trajikomedia o yorar y riir: Estudio psikolojiko sovre el estado de alma del sinior David Fresko, direktor del "Tiempo"* (Istanbul, 1910).

71. *El Tiempo*, 23 September 1910; *L'Aurore*, 8 November 1910; Benbassa, "Haim Nahum," 312.

72. AAIU, Turquie XXX. E., Nahum, 15 November 1910. This was the interpretation of the Zionist leadership. See CZA Z2/10, Jacobson, 30 December 1910.

73. CZA, Z2/31, Wolffsohn to Leven, 21 February 1911; ibid., Leven and Bigart to Wolffsohn, 3 March 1911. The letters are reproduced in English in CZA, Z2/32. Also cited in Benbassa, "Haim Nahum," 318–319.

74. See PRO, FO 371/62 12910, 10 January 1919. Benbassa, "Haim Nahum," 595.

75. See Benbassa, "Le Sionisme," 77.

76. Ibid.

77. *La Nation*, 23 July 1920. Also quoted in Paul Dumont, "Une communauté en quête d'avenir: Le sionisme à Istanbul au lendemain de la première guerre mondiale" in Université de Nice–Centre de la Méditerranée moderne et contemporaine, ed., *Les Juifs dans la Méditerranée médiévale et moderne*, 101–102; Benbassa, "Haim Nahum," 658. For a list of the local organizations affiliated to this *Fédération*, see PRO, FO 371/ 801 165700, 22 December 1919.

78. AAIU, Turquie XII. E., Mitrani, 20 May 1921, 17 July 1921.

79. See, for example *La Nation*, 13 February 1920, 20 February 1920, 9 June 1922.

80. AAIU, Turquie I. G. 1, Nathan, 4 February 1912.

81. *L'Aurore*, 4 March 1910.

82. Ibid., 2 January 1910.

83. Ibid., 2 September 1910.

84. On these two, see Aron Rodrigue, *De l'instruction à l'émancipation: Les enseignants de l'Alliance israélite universelle et les Juifs d'Orient, 1860–1939* (Paris, 1989), 61, 187.

85. Benbassa, "Le Sionisme," 74.

86. See Henry A. Giroux, *Ideology, Culture and the Process of Schooling* (Philadelphia, 1981), 2–3, 15, 103.

87. See the report in AAIU, Turquie L. E., Franco, 31 March 1891. See also UI 49 (1893–1894): 201–203; *El Tiempo*, 17 January 1901.

88. AAIU, Turquie I. B. 2, Jacques Danon to Bigart, 7 September 1903.

89. Ibid.

90. AAIU, Turquie LXXXI. E., Galanté, 17 June 1904. The articles by Galanté are in AI 62 (1901): 198, 211–212; AI 63 (1902): 190–191, 270, 342–343, 396. See also Albert E. Kalderon, *Abraham Galante: A Biography* (New York, 1983), 18–19, 26.

91. *L'Aurore*, 3 March 1911.

92. *L'Aurore*, 27 June 1911.

93. *L'Aurore*, 23 May 1911.

94. On the foundation of the *B'nai B'rith* order and its work in the United States,

see Deborah Dash Moore, *B'nai B'rith and the Challenge of Ethnic Leadership* (Albany, N.Y., 1981). The *Bulletin de la Grande Loge de District XI et de la Loge de Constantinople* and *Hamenora* are the two publications of the Lodges in Turkey and in the Middle East which provide important information about their activities.

95. On the philanthropic activities of the lodges, see the *Bulletin de la Grande Loge* (1911–1921).

96. Benbassa, "Haim Nahum," 298.

97. On this, see chapter 7.

98. *El Tiempo*, 21 April 1915. On the foundations of this *lycée*, see AAIU, Turquie XLII. E., Benveniste, 5 February 1928; Turquie II. C. 8, Nathan, 19 November 1937.

99. On his career, see Joseph Niégo, *Cinquante années de travail dans les oeuvres juives* (Istanbul, 1933).

100. CZA, Z2/10, Jacobson to Wolffsohn, 30 December 1910. See also Benbassa, "Haim Nahum," 297.

101. *Bulletin de la Grande Loge* (1911–1913): 14.

102. *El Tiempo*, 25 November 1921, 22 February 1922, and 7 March 1922.

103. *El Tiempo*, 16 October 1923.

104. *L'Aurore*, 27 June 1911.

105. For a study of the Turkish nationalist Moïse Kohen, see Jacob M. Landau, *Tekinalp, Turkish Patriot, 1883–1961* (Leiden, 1984). Galanté has been studied by Kalderon, *Galante*.

106. MAE, Archives des Postes, Turquie, Ambassade, Carton 5/711, Wiet (Bagdad) to Bompard (Istanbul), 27 May 1911.

107. *L'Aurore*, 18 February 1910.

108. The most recent study on Bulgarian Jewry does not analyze in depth the factors that led to the rise of Zionism. See Vicki Tamir, *Bulgaria and Her Jews* (New York, 1979), 136–158. For an earlier account of the clash with the Alliance, see Saul Mézan, *Les Juifs espagnols en Bulgarie* (Sofia, 1925), 54–65.

109. AAIU, Bulgarie I. G. 17, Tatar-Bazardjik, Sémach, 17 March 1895.

110. Ibid., 26 December 1895.

111. Ibid., 26 December 1895, received 19 March 1896 and 24 May 1897.

112. AAIU, Bulgarie I. G. 17, Tatar Bazardjik, Bigart to Sémach, 31 May 1897.

113. AAIU, Bulgarie I. G. 14, Philippopoli, Bigart to Cohen, May 1897.

114. See for example AAIU, Bulgarie I. G. 14, Philippopoli, Cohen, 20 June 1899.

115. AAIU, Bulgarie I. G. 7, Sofia, S. Danon, 14 May 1911.

116. AAIU, Bulgarie I. G. 14, Philippopoli, Cohen, 8 August 1898.

117. AAIU, Bulgarie I. G. 15, Astruc, 31 January 1899.

118. AAIU, Bulgarie I. G. 14, Bulgarian Zionist Central Committee to the Alliance Central Committee, received 6 August 1903.

119. Ibid.

120. AAIU, Bulgarie I. D. 3, Arié, 29 May 1913; BAIU 38 (1913): 123.

121. AAIU, Bulgarie VII. B. 163 bis, AIU to the French consul in Varna, 12 March 1908.

122. AAIU, Turquie XXV. E., Fernandez, 25 November 1881.

123. AAIU, Turquie XXVIII. E., Fernandez, 20 October 1896, 28 November 1898. On Ottoman policy, see Mandel, *The Arabs*, 1–31, and Öke, *Siyonizm*, 51–100.

124. AAIU, Turquie XXVIII. E., Fernandez, 20 October 1896.

125. AAIU, Turquie I. G. 1, Fernandez, 6 September 1897; AAIU, Turquie I. G. 1, Benveniste, 3 March 1911; AAIU, Turquie XL. E., Benveniste, 3 May 1911.

126. See for example BAIU (2ᵉ semestre 1866): 9.

127. *Bulletin mensuel de l'Alliance Israélite Universelle* (April 1892): 18.

128. AAIU, Turquie I. C. 7, Bigart to Nabon, 25 May 1893.

129. AAIU, Turquie II. B. 6, Bigart, 22 April 1912.

130. Bayram Kodaman, *Abdülhamid Devri Eğitim Sistemi* (Istanbul, 1980), 49–50; Osman Ergin, *Türkiye Maarif Tarihi*, 5 vols. (Istanbul, 1939–1943, reprint ed., Istanbul 1977) 1–2: 769–809.

131. For the capitulations, see Nasim Susa, *The Capitulatory Regime of Turkey* (Baltimore, 1933); Necdet Kurdakul, *Osmanlı Devletinde Ticaret Andlaşmaları ve Kapitulasyonlar* (Istanbul, 1981).

132. Mandel, *The Arabs*, 4–7, and Friedman, *Germany*, 32–49.

133. AAIU, Turquie XLIII. E., Bloch, 10 March 1885.

134. AAIU, Turquie XXVIII. E., Fernandez, 1 July 1898.

135. AAIU, Turquie LIII. E., Fresco, 3 January 1901.

136. AAIU, Turquie XXX. E., Nahum, 1 August 1907.

137. AAIU, Turquie I. G. 1, Fernandez, 6 September 1897.

138. Ibid., 29 October 1897.

139. AAIU, Turquie I. G. 1, Nathan, 21 March 1912.

140. AAIU, Turquie XXIX. E., Fernandez, 3 March 1911, Bigart to Fernandez, 3 July 1913; AAIU, Turquie XLI. E., Benveniste, 3 May 1913.

141. AAIU, Grèce I. G. 3, Bigart to Benghiat, 7 December 1909.

142. BAIU 34 (1909): 50–51.

143. Ibid., 51.

144. See AI 70 (1909): 226–227; JC, 13 August 1909.

145. See for example *L'Aurore*, 9 April 1911; Richard J. H. Gottheil, *Zionism* (Philadelphia, 1914), 159. See also CZA, Z2/11, Jacobson to Wolffsohn, 28 March 1911.

146. AAIU, Turquie XXX. E., Bigart to Nahum, 26 November 1909.

147. Ibid., Bigart to Nahum, 22 November 1910. On this question, see also Benbassa, "Haim Nahum," 268–269.

148. See Mandel, *The Arabs*, 93–116; Benbassa, "Haim Nahum," 270.

149. AAIU, Turquie I. G. 1, Bigart to Nathan, 22 November 1910.

150. Ibid., Bigart to Fernandez, 5 May 1911.

151. On this, see Abitbol, *Les deux terres,* 78–79.

152. *La Nation*, 2 January 1920.

VII. Between French Imperialism and Turkish Nationalism

1. On this see the magisterial dissertation of Albert Salon, "L'Action culturelle de la France dans le monde" (Thèse pour le doctorat d'état ès lettres, Université de Paris I, Sorbonne, 1980).

2. *Bulletin de la Mission laïque* 9 (1909): 72.

3. *Bulletin de l'Alliance française* 2 (1885): 86. For a recent discussion of the cultural component of French imperialism, see Christopher M. Andrew and A. S. Kanya-Forstner, *France Overseas* (London, 1981), 26–28.

4. *Bulletin de l'Alliance française* 8 (1891): 53.

5. *Bulletin de l'Oeuvre des Ecoles en Orient*, no. 248 (1902): 607.

6. For the French protection of the Catholics in the Ottoman Empire, see Francis Rey, *De la protection diplomatique et consulaire dans les échelles du Levant et de Barbarie* (Paris, 1899). For an attack against this protectorate from the anti-clericalist standpoint, see J. L. De Lanessan, *Les Missions et leur Protectorat* (Paris, 1907), especially 208–228.

7. Salon, "L'Action culturelle," 94–116. See also Matthew Burrows, " 'Mission civilisatrice': French Cultural Policy in the Middle East, 1860–1914," *The Historical Journal* 29 (1986): 109–135.

8. Jacques Thobie, "La France a-t-elle une politique culturelle dans l'Empire otto-

man à la veille de la première guerre mondiale?" *Relations Internationales*, no. 25 (1981): 33.

9. Other Catholic powers such as Austria and Italy had done their best to erode the French "protection." In 1902, France was obliged to relinquish its claim to protect non-French Catholics in the Ottoman Empire. See William I. Shorrock, *French Imperialism in the Middle East* (Madison, Wis., 1976), 33. See also Joseph N. Hajjar, *Le Vatican, la France et le Catholicisme Oriental (1878–1914)* (Paris, 1979), 265–278.

10. See for example the attack on missionary schools by A. Aulard reported in MAE, Série D, Administrative, vol. 19, February 1908, fol. 11–12. See also De Lanessan, *Les Missions*, 208–228.

11. Apart from foreign policy considerations, the French diplomatic service was very much the preserve of the French Right in this period, which predisposed it to be sympathetic to the Catholic cause. The missionary schools were also supported in the influential *Revue des deux mondes*. See for example Louis Bertrand, "Les Ecoles d'Orient," *Revue des deux mondes* 52 (July-August 1909): 755–794.

12. Thobie, "La France," 34.

13. MAE, Série D, Administrative, vol. 1, report compiled on 6 October 1910, fol. 44–77.

14. Maurice Pernot, *Rapport sur un voyage d'étude à Constantinople, en Egypte et en Turquie d'Asie (janvier-août 1912)* (Paris, 1913?).

15. Jacques Thobie, "Relations internationales et zones d'influence: Les intérêts français en Palestine à la veille de la première guerre mondiale" in Saul Friedlaender, Harish Kapur, André Reszler, eds., *L'Historien et les relations internationales: Receuil d'études en hommage à Jacques Freymond* (Geneva, 1981), 437.

16. Thobie, "La France," 24. These statistics have to be modified, as Pernot included the figures of only two of the Alliance schools in Istanbul. With this rectification, the Jewish share goes to over 30 percent of the total.

17. Ibid.

18. Ibid.

19. These figures are arrived at using the data in the Pernot account, which is thorough for the large centers, and the statistics in the *Bulletins* of the Alliance. See Pernot, *Rapport sur un voyage*, 310–333; BAIU 36 (1911): 80–85. Pernot conducted his visit in the first half of 1912 and, as shown by the figures he cites for the Alliance schools, seems to have used the statistics supplied to him for 1911.

20. The figures for Salonica and Edirne can be taken as definitive, as they are based upon statistics compiled by the *Quai d'Orsay* about the ethnic-religious composition of the students in all the French language institutions of these two towns and upon the information to be found in the Bulletin of the Alliance for 1909. See MAE, Série D, Administrative, vol. 28, 1909, fol. 4–12; BAIU 34 (1909): 104. One has to allow for a statistically insignificant margin of error, as there were a few non-Jews in the Alliance schools. The percentages for the Asian side of the Ottoman Empire are much more imprecise, as they are based partially upon the Pernot statistics, which provide information about the religious and ethnic composition of only 55 percent of the total student body surveyed.

21. Netter to Leven, letter dated 9 May 1862, quoted in Georges Weill, "Charles Netter ou les oranges de Jaffa," *Les Nouveaux Cahiers*, no. 21 (Summer 1970): 31.

22. Quoted in MAE, NS, Turquie, vol. 137, Boppe (Jerusalem) to Paris, 17 November 1903. Also mentioned in Catherine Nicault-Lévigne, "La France et le sionisme, 1896–1914" (Thèse de doctorat de IIIᵉ cycle, Université de Paris I, Sorbonne, 1986), 589. I would like to thank Mme. Nicault-Lévigne for allowing me to read the manuscript of her dissertation before it had been submitted.

23. The entire text of the Waddington memorandum is to be found in AAIU,

Turquie I. C. 6, note from the French Embassy in Istanbul, 28 April 1874. See also AAIU, Turquie LXXXVI. E., Pariente, appendix to letter dated 11 November 1887.
24. Ibid. This note is also quoted in MAE, NS, Turquie, vol. 137, Boppe (Jerusalem) to Paris, 17 November 1903.
25. AAIU, Turquie LXXXVII. E., Bigart to Pariente, 24 March 1892.
26. AAIU, Turquie IV. E., Courtois to Crémieux, 14 August 1869.
27. Ibid., Courtois to Bloch, 15 May 1873.
28. See for example MAE, Correspondance politique des Consuls, Andrinople, vol. 4, Peyraud to Paris, 16 August 1887.
29. MAE, Correspondance politique des Consuls, Andrinople, vol. 4, Laffon to Paris, 17 January 1882.
30. MAE, Correspondance politique des Consuls, Smyrne, vols. 6–11 (1869–1895).
31. For example in AAIU, Turquie LXXXVI. E., Pariente, 11 November 1887; AAIU, Turquie LXXXVII. E., Pariente, 17 April 1892.
32. See for example AAIU, Turquie LXXX. E., Cazès, 26 November 1875; Turquie XLII. E., Bloch, December (?), 1878; AAIU, Turquie XLIII. E., Bloch, 31 December 1886.
33. Ibid., AAIU, Turquie I. B. 1, Adès, 3 June 1898; AAIU, Turquie LXXVI. E., Arié, 14 March 1900; AAIU, Turquie LXXVII. E., Arié, 8 June 1904.
34. The most thorough study of the relationship between France and the Alliance in North Africa is that of Joan Gardner Roland, "The Alliance Israélite Universelle and French Policy in North Africa, 1860–1918" (Ph.D. diss., Columbia University, 1969). See also Michael M. Laskier, *The Alliance Israélite Universelle and the Jewish Communities of Morocco, 1862–1962* (Albany, N.Y., 1983), 66–68, 152–171; Aron Rodrigue, *De l'instruction*, 18–19, 167–182.
35. AAIU, Turquie XXVII. E., Fernandez, 6 May 1892.
36. On this affair, see Shorrock, *French Imperialism*, 25.
37. AAIU, Turquie XXVIII. E., Bigart to Fernandez, 24 November 1901.
38. AAIU, Turquie XXIX. E., Bigart to Fernandez, 19 May 1908.
39. Central Archives for the History of the Jewish People, Jerusalem, Dossiers de correspondance reçues par les directeurs d'écoles (AIU): 1er série, lettres reçues de Paris par Nissim Behar, D1, Loeb to Behar, 6 August 1886.
40. AAIU, Turquie LIII. E., Loeb to Bloch, 12 January 1887.
41. Most notably in MAE, NS, Turquie, vols. 137–138. On the attitude of the French to Zionism, see Catherine Lévigne, "Le 'Quai', et les débuts du sionisme," *Les Nouveaux Cahiers*, no. 50 (Fall 1977): 50–55; Catherine Lévigne, "Le mouvement sioniste en France et la politique française au Levant," *Relations Internationales*, no. 12 (1977): 307–325.
42. See Andrew and Kanya-Forstner, *France Overseas*, 40–54.
43. MAE, Archives des Postes, Ambassade Turquie, Carton 175/712, Jerusalem to embassy in Istanbul, 5 March 1900.
44. MAE, NS, Turquie, vol. 137, Ministre d'Affaires Etrangères to Ministre de l'Intérieur et des Cultes, 6 July 1904. Also quoted in Nicault-Lévigne, "La France et le sionisme," 683.
45. MAE, NS, Turquie, vol. 137, Boppe (Jerusalem) to Paris and Istanbul, 17 November 1903.
46. Ibid., 66–73.
47. MAE, NS, Turquie, vol. 137, note of direction politique, 5 February 1904. MAE, NS, Turquie, vol. 137, copy of note verbale, 6 February 1905.
48. MAE, NS, Turquie, vol. 137, Copy of note verbale, 6 February 1905.
49. For this affair, see MAE, NS, Turquie, vol. 137, Boppe (Jerusalem) to Paris, 17 November 1903; ibid., Bercy (Beirut) to Paris, 13 January 1904; ibid., Bapst, Chargé

d'affaires of France in Istanbul to Paris, 25 February 1904; ibid., Ottoman Foreign Ministry to French embassy, 11 September 1904; ibid., Paris to Constans, French Ambassador in Istanbul, 27 December 1904; ibid., Constans (Istanbul) to Paris, 9 February 1905; MAE, Archives des Postes, Ambassade, Turquie, Carton 175/711, Fernandez to Constans, 24 April 1908. See also Nicault-Lévigne, "La France et le sionisme," 587–591.

50. Nicault-Lévigne, "La France et le sionisme," 655–665; Lévigne, "Le 'Quai'," 53.

51. MAE, Archives des Postes, Ambassade, Turquie, Carton 175/711, Boppe to Paris, 26 November 1907. The same letter is also to be found in MAE, Série C, Administrative, vol. 142, fol. 321.

52. Ibid.

53. MAE, Archives des Postes, Ambassade, Turquie, Carton 175/711, embassy circular to consuls, 8 January 1908.

54. MAE, Série D, Administrative, Istanbul to Paris, vol. 21, 21 June 1908.

55. AAIU, Turquie LXXXIV. E., Bigart to Nabon, 18 February 1910.

56. MAE, NS, Turquie, vol. 137, Leven to Foreign Ministry, 18 February 1904.

57. MAE, NS, Turquie 138, copy of a letter from the Alliance to the Foreign Ministry, 30 December 1912.

58. For this question of Salonica, see AAIU, Grèce I. C. 51, Nehama, 3 January 1913; MAE, NS, Turquie vol. 138, French Ambassador in Athens to Paris, 20 February 1913; ibid., French Ambassador in Istanbul, to Paris, 17 March 1913; ibid., French Ambassador in London to Paris, 3 April 1913.

59. See CZA, Z2/648, letters between Wolffsohn and Nathan, 1906-1908.

60. AAIU, Israël I. G. 2, Antébi, 17 August 1908, 2 September 1908.

61. AAIU, Turquie XXX. E., Bigart to Nahum, 10 December 1908.

62. Lévigne, "Le mouvement sioniste," 291; Nicault-Lévigne, "La France et le sionisme," 670. See also David Farhi, "Yehudei Saloniki be-mahapekhat ha-'Turkim ha-Ze'irim,' " *Sefunot* 15 (1971–1981): 150–151; MAE, Série D, Administrative vol. 21, several letters of Choublier of 1911, fol. 184–197.

63. Central Archives of the Jewish People, P112/109, Minute Book of the Alliance Regional Committee, Istanbul, 1903–1917, minutes of the meeting of 10 December 1914.

64. On the work of philanthropic organizations during the war, see Esther Benbassa, "Haim Nahum Effendi, dernier Grand Rabbin de l'Empire ottoman (1908–1920): son rôle politique et diplomatique" (Thèse de doctorat d'état ès lettres, Université de Paris III, 1987), 522–542. The fact that the Alliance schools received money from the charity commissions set up by the united effort of the various philanthropic organizations in Istanbul during the war is mentioned in AAIU, Turquie XLI. E., Benveniste, 11 February 1921.

65. AAIU, Turquie XXIX. E., Central Committee to Fernandez, 14 December 1914, 25 March 1915; AAIU, Turquie XLI. E., Benveniste, 18 March 1919.

66. MAE, Guerre 1914–1918, vol. 960, Foreign Ministry to the Ministry of War, 7 October 1915.

67. Ibid., vol. 960, Foreign Ministry to the Ministry of Public Instruction, 9 March 1916, 38 verso.

68. MAE, Guerre 1914–1918, vol. 965, Ministry of Interior, 14 November 1914.

69. See Michel Abitbol, *Les deux terres promises: Les Juifs de France et le sionisme, 1897–1945* (Paris, 1989), 70.

70. Ibid., 78–79.

71. Salon, "L'action culturelle," 193.

72. AAIU, Turquie XLI. E., Benveniste, 24 July 1919, 17 October 1919, 13 February 1920, 21 February 1921, 17 August 1921, 13 October 1922.

73. MAE, Levant 1918–1940, Turquie, vol. 112, 31 July 1919, Defrance to Paris; AAIU, Turquie XLI. E., Benveniste, 24 July 1919.

74. *La Nation*, 2 January 1920.

75. 16,000 francs were given for the schools in Istanbul in 1920. See AAIU, Turquie XLI. E., Benveniste, 12 February 1920. This was increased to 25,000 in 1922. See AAIU, Turquie XLI. E., Benveniste, 13 October 1922, 27 October 1922.

76. AAIU, Turquie XLVII. E., Dalem, 24 August 1882.

77. Bayram Kodaman, *Abdülhamid Devri Eğitim Sistemi* (Istanbul, 1980), 66–67; Faik Reşit Unat, *Türkiye Eğitim Sisteminin Gelişmesine Tarihi Bir Bakış* (Ankara, 1964), 25, 28, This was duly noted by the Alliance. See AAIU, Turquie XXVI. E., Fernandez, 3 August 1886.

78. The best book on this subject is Kodaman, *Abdülhamid Devri*.

79. See for example AAIU, Turquie XLIII. E., Bloch, 15 June 1886.

80. See for example AAIU, Turquie XLVIII. E., Israel Danon, 18 September 1894; AAIU, Turquie XXX. E., Nahum, 27 February 1900.

81. AAIU, Turquie II. C. 8, Fresco, 26 June 1902.

82. See Aron Rodrigue, "Jewish Society and Schooling in a Thracian Town: The Alliance Israélite Universelle in Demotica, 1897–1924," *Jewish Social Studies* 45 (Summer-Fall 1983): 278, and AAIU, Turquie I. B. 7, Franco, 4 November 1906.

83. AAIU, Turquie XXIX. E., Fernandez, 4 December 1906.

84. Nevzad Ayas, *Türkiye Cumhuriyeti Milli Eğitimi* (Ankara, 1948), 690; Cemil Koçak, "Tanzimat'tan sonra Özel ve Yabancı Okullar," *Tanzimat'tan Cumhuriyet'e Türkiye Ansiklopedisi* 2 (1985): 488.

85. Ayas, *Türkiye Cumhuriyeti*, 690; Koçak, "Tanzimat'tan Sonra," 488.

86. AAIU, Turquie XXXIV. E., Alchalel, 21 May 1909; AAIU, Turquie II. B. 6, (Tire) Politi, 2 May 1911.

87. AAIU, Turquie XXX. E., Nahum, 9 July 1914, 22 July 1914.

88. AAIU, Turquie XXVII. E., Fernandez, 28 November 1889.

89. Ibid.

90. Yahya Akyüz, *Türk Eğitim Tarihi* (Ankara, 1982), 118.

91. AAIU, Turquie XXVII. E., Fernandez, 28 November 1889.

92. Ibid., Fernandez, 8 October 1889.

93. See for example AAIU, Turquie XXVIII. E., Fernandez, 2 June 1899.

94. See AAIU, Turquie LXIV. E., Ouannou, 16 November 1902; AAIU, Turquie XXX. E., Nahum, 1 July 1902; AAIU, Turquie LXVII. E., Danon, 7 October 1902.

95. AAIU, Turquie XXX. E., Nahum, 12 October 1900. See also Benbassa, "Haim Nahum," 51–52.

96. AAIU, Turquie XXX. E., Nahum, 29 September 1909.

97. Ibid., Nahum, 12 September 1910.

98. Ibid., Nahum, 12 December 1911.

99. David Kushner, *The Rise of Turkish Nationalism 1876–1908* (London, 1977), 93; AAIU, Turquie XLVIII. E., I. Danon, 12 September 1894.

100. Ayas, *Türkiye Cumhuriyeti*, 691.

101. *El Tiempo*, 20 November 1914. See also AAIU, Turquie XXX. E., Nahum, 27 April 1919.

102. AAIU, Turquie XLI. E., Benveniste, 9 April 1918; AAIU, Turquie XII. E., Mitrani, letter received 16 February 1919.

103. AAIU, Turquie XLI. E., Benveniste, 9 April 1918; AAIU, Turquie XII. E., Mitrani, 1 January 1920.

104. Ayas, *Türkiye Cumhuriyeti*, 691; Akyüz, *Türk Eğitim*, 179; Koçak, "Tanzimat'tan sonra," 489.

105. There is only one mention of this regulation in the Alliance archives. The Izmir school director reported on the law, but did not mention whether it was ever implemented. See AAIU, Turquie LXXXIII. E., Nabon, 20 August 1915.

106. See especially the letter by Nabon from Izmir in 1920. AAIU, Turquie LXXXIII. E., 17 March 1920.

107. On this phenomenon, see Jacob Barnai, " 'Blood Libels' in the Ottoman Empire of the Fifteenth to the Nineteenth Centuries" in Shmuel Almog, ed., *Antisemitism through the Ages* (Oxford, 1988), 189–194.

108. See Aron Rodrigue, *De l'instruction à l'émancipation: Les enseignants de l'Alliance israélite universelle et les Juifs d'Orient, 1860–1939* (Paris, 1989), 175-178.

109. AAIU, Turquie LXXXIII. E., Nabon, 4 April 1921.

110. *Paix et Droit* 3 (December 1923): 12.

111. The best work on the rise of the Republic is still that of Bernard Lewis, *The Emergence of Modern Turkey*, 2nd ed. (London, 1968).

112. See the texts of the Lausanne treaty, clauses 38 to 44 in Jacob C. Hurewitz, *The Middle East and North Africa in World Politics*, 2 vols. (New Haven, 1975–79) 2: 330–331. Clause 40 concerns the schools. The latest work on the Lausanne treaty is by Mim Kemal Öke, *İngiliz Belgelerinde Barış Konferansı*, 2 vols. (Istanbul, 1983–1984).

113. National Archives, US Department of State, Records relating to Turkey, 1910–29 (roll 32), 867.4016/967, Bristol, 1 December 1923; 867.4016/984, Bristol, 30 July 1923; PRO, FO 371/10207, Lindsay to Chamberlain, 18 November 1924. See also the long report summing up all the notes and protests sent by the allies to Turkey over this problem between 1923–1925 in PRO, FO 371/10866, Lindsay to Chamberlain, 3 February 1925; for other accounts, see *El Telegrafo*, 24 September 1923; *El Tiempo*, 23 October 1923, 7 November 1923, 16 November 1923; *Jewish Chronicle*, 23 November 1923; *Stamboul*, 25 February 1924; *Paix et Droit* 3 (October 1923): 11.

114. *İkdam*, 3 November 1923, and *Akşam*, 22 November 1923, cited in MAE, *Bulletin périodique de la presse turque*, no. 33 (23–24 February 1924).

115. *El Telegrafo*, 24 September 1923; *El Tiempo*, 23 October, 7 November, 16 November 1923.

116. *El Tiempo*, 23 October 1923.

117. The original text of this decree was later sent by the director of the Galata school to the Central Committee in Paris. See AAIU, Turquie II. C. 8, Nathan, 14 May 1935. See also the *Jewish Chronicle*, 13 July 1923; *İkdam*, 2 August 1923, cited in MAE, *Bulletin*, no. 31 (18–19 November 1923); *El Tiempo*, 14 September 1923; Alexis Alexandris, *The Greek Minority of Istanbul and Greek-Turkish Relations, 1918–1974* (Athens, 1983), 133.

118. "*Öz Türk*," in the words of the then–inspector of foreign schools, İsmail Hakkı [Uzunçarşılı], who would later have a distinguished career as a historian of the Ottoman Empire. See *Akşam*, 12 February 1926, cited in Mustafa Ergün, *Atatürk Devri Türk Eğitimi* (Ankara, 1982), 59. The fact that no non-Muslims were to be appointed to these positions was also reported in the Jewish press. See *El Tiempo*, 23 October 1923.

119. *El Tiempo*, 14 September 1923.

120. *El Tiempo*, 19, 28 September 1923.

121. Ibid., 5 October 1923.

122. İlhan Başgöz and Howard E. Wilson, *Educational Problems in Turkey, 1920–1940* (Bloomington, Ind., 1968), 77, Akyüz, *Türk Eğitim*, 230; Hasan Cicioğlu, *Türkiye Cumhuriyetinde İlk ve Orta Öğretim* (Ankara, 1982), 33.

123. AAIU, Turquie XXXI. E., Nathan, 2 October 1936.

124. See for example the case of Edirne in AAIU, Turquie XII. E., Mitrani, 9 January 1924.

125. The original text of the note sent to the Alliance school in Galata was later sent by the director to Paris and is to be found in AAIU, Turquie II. C. 8, Nathan, 14 May 1935.

126. Robert Mantran, "L'enseignement français en Turquie entre 1925 et 1930" in Paul Dumont and Jean-Louis Bacqué-Grammont, eds., *La Turquie et la France à l'époque d'Atatürk* (Paris, 1981), 180.

127. Ibid., 181–182.

128. The original text of the note is to be found in AAIU, Turquie II. C. 8, Nathan, 14 May 1935. See also *El Tiempo*, 20 June 1924; *Stamboul*, 24 June 1924, and *Akşam*, 22 June 1924, *Cumhuriyet*, 29 June and 7 July 1924, cited by Ergün, *Atatürk Devri*, 58.

129. AAIU, Turquie XLI. E., Benveniste, 16 July 1924; *Stamboul*, 2, 11, and 27 July 1924.

130. *Stamboul*, 15 April 1925; AAIU, Turquie XLII. E., Benveniste, 12 August 1926, 5 February 1928; AAIU, Turquie XII. E., Mitrani, 23 February 1927.

131. AAIU, France XVI. F. 27, Mitrani, Edirne, 1927–1928 annual report.

132. Ayas, *Türkiye Cumhuriyeti*, 695.

133. See *El Telegrafo*, 16 September 1925; *Stamboul*, 15, 20 October 1925; *El Tiempo*, 14 October 1925; *Jewish Chronicle*, 23 October 1925; Alexandris, *The Greek Minority*, 135. The exact circumstances in which these clauses were renounced need further research. For a beginning, see AAIU, Turquie II. C. 8, Fresco, 4 March 1926, 24 March 1926; National Archives, US Department of State, Records relating to Turkey, 1910–1929, 867.4016/988, 31 March 1926. See also PRO, FO 371/10866, Lindsay to Chamberlain, 8 December 1925.

Conclusion

1. BAIU 38 (1913): 108.

2. See for example AAIU, France XIX. F. 30, Pariente, annual report, Izmir, 1882–1883.

3. AAIU, Turquie XLIII. E., Bloch, 7 February 1887.

4. AAIU, Turquie I. B. 1, Bigart to Adès, 8 March 1899.

5. AAIU, Turquie LXXXV. E., Pariente, 6 August 1884.

6. AAIU, Turquie LXXIV. E., Arié, 17 November 1893.

7. Ibid.

8. Ibid.

BIBLIOGRAPHY

Archival Documentation

Archives of the Alliance Israélite Universelle (Paris)

The documentation in the archives has been divided by country. Each file comprises the letters and reports received by the Alliance Central Committee, as well as the drafts of the letters sent from Paris. The following files have been consulted:

France (each entry represents one file)

III. A. 16, Albert Cohn, 1860/1876.
III. A. 17, De Camondo.
V. A. 34, Baron de Hirsch.
VI. A. 43bis, Israël Lévi.
VII. A. 45, Isidore Loeb, rapport d'inspection en Turquie, 1888.
VIII. A. 63, Emmanuel Veneziani, 1871/1889.
IX. A. 70, Séances annuels du Comité central, 1911/1913.
XI. A. 73, Rapport sur les Ecoles (Comité central).
XI. A. 76, Mission Nahoum aux USA.
XI. A. 79, Mission Halevy aux Falashas.
XI. A. 80, Mission Nahoum aux Falashas.
XII. A. 1, Procès-verbaux des séances du Comité central, 1898/1904.
XXXVII. B. 326, 1877/1914, Souscription en faveur des Juifs de Turquie.
I. D. 1, Questions générales, situation des Juifs en Orient, 1867. Protection des Juifs en Orient, 1876. Statistiques 1903/4.
II. D. 8, Question Sioniste.
IV. D. 16, Rapport avec le Ministère des Affaires Etrangères. Correspondance concernant les écoles du Levant, 1895/1909, 1909/1916. Interventions auprès des représentants français, 1903/1913.
VII. D. 33, Situation des Juifs par pays, Grèce 1897/1935.
VIII. D. 48, Situation des Juifs par pays, Turquie 1864/1904, 1913/1914.
I. E. 1a, Ecole Normale Israélite Orientale.
I. E. 1b, Ecole Normale Israélite Orientale.
VIII. E. 18, Projets divers, écoles d'agriculture, 1900/1936.
IX. E. 1, Instructions—écoles.
IX. E. 2, Instructions—écoles.
IX. E. 23, Ecoles de l'AIU, suggestions etc., Grèce 1872/1923.
IX. E. 31, Ecoles de l'AIU, suggestions etc., Turquie 1873/1916.
XI. E. 1, Instructions pour les professeurs.
III. F. 8, Rapport d'inspection de S. Bénédict, Alep- Jaffa (1897/1905).
V. F. 10–11, Rapport d'inspection de S. Bénédict, Le Caire-Yamboli (1896/1908).
X. F. 18, Rapports annuels des écoles, Grèce.
XVI. F. 27, Rapports annuels des écoles, Turquie.
XVII. F. 28, Rapports annuels des écoles, Turquie.
XVIII. F. 29, Rapports annuels des écoles, Turquie.

XIX. F. 30, Rapports annuels des écoles, Turquie (each of the last five entries contain files for each school).
I. G. 1–6, Sionisme et l'AIU (several files).
I. H. 1, AIU et Hilfsverein (several files).
II. H. 2–7, AIU et ICA (several files).
ICA 4, Turquie 1902/3.

Turquie (each entry represents one box with several files)

General Subjects
I. B. 1–3, Comités locaux et communautés.
I. B. 4–7, Comités locaux et communautés.
I. C. 1–3, Situation générale intérieure des Juifs.
I. C. 4–7, Situation générale intérieure des Juifs.
I. C. 8–9, Situation générale intérieure des Juifs.
I. C. 10–14, Situation générale intérieure des Juifs.
I. G. 1, Sionisme et Alliance.
I. H. 1, Sociétés en relations avec l'AIU.
I. J. 1, Lettres de Joseph Halevy d'Andrinople.
I. L. 1, Aide sociale, legs divers.
I. M. 1, Activités intellectuelles.

Schools and communities (alphabetical according to place and correspondent)
Aydın:
I. E., Adès—Guéron.
II. E., Halegua—Rahmané.
III. E., Rahmané—Valadji.

Andrinople (Edirne):
IV. E., Abramowitz—Bassan.
V. E., Behar—Benveniste.
VI. E., Bezareth—Confino.
VII. E., Daffa—Guéron.
VIII. E., Habib—Loupo.
IX. E., Loupo.
X. E., Loupo—Toledo.
XI. E., Mitrani.
XII. E., Mitrani.
XIII. E., Mizrahi—Ungar.
XIV. E., Ungar—Zecharia.

Brousse (Bursa):
XV. E., Abravanel—Azouz.
XVI. E., Barouch—Ibensaal.
XVII. E., Kowo—Matalon.
XVIII. E., Matalon—Schaki.
XIX. E., Sémach—Zechariah.

Constantinople (Istanbul):
XXIV. E., Divers.
XXV. E., Comité régional, Fernandez.
XXVI. E., Comité régional, Fernandez.
XXVII. E., Comité régional, Fernandez.
XXVIII. E., Comité régional, Fernandez.
XXIX. E., Comité régional, Fernandez.
XXX. E., Généraux, Haim Nahoum, Grand Rabbin.

XXXI. E., Généraux, Nathan.
XXXII. E., Abeles—Adès.
XXXIII. E., Adès—Albala.
XXXIV. E., Alboher—Alchalel.
XXXV. E., Alchalel (Mme.)—Altabev.
XXXVI. E., Amon—Azouz.
XXXVII. E., Babani—Bassous.
XXXVIII. E., Bassous—Bechar, Nissim.
XXXIX. E., Bechar, Rachel—Behor.
XL. E., Belilos—Benveniste.
XLI. E., Benveniste.
XLII. E., Benveniste—Bloch.
XLIII. E., Bloch.
XLIV. E., Bornstein—Cheni.
XLV. E., Cheni—Cohen.
XLVI. E., Confino—Conorté.
XLVII. E., Daffa—Danon.
XLVIII. E., Danon—Dufour.
XLIX. E., Eblagon—Eskenazi.
L. E., Faraggi—Franco.
LI. E., Frances—Fresco, Moïse.
LII. E., Fresco.
LIII. E., Fresco.
LIV. E., Fresco—Fried.
LV. E., Gaby—Grossman.
LVI. E., Grun—Hamouth.
LVII. E., Hasson—Korvo.
LVIII. E., Kralowitz—Levy, Samson.
LIX. E., Levy (Mme. Sarah)—Loria, Jacques.
LX. E., Loria, Jacques—Misrahi.
LXI. E., Mitrani—Nabon.
LXII. E., Nabon (Mme.).
LXIII. E., Nahmias—Navon.
LXIV. E., Navon (Mme.)—Paves.
LXV. E., Peilmann—Saltiel.
LXVI. E., Salzer, Hélène—Salzer, Rachel.
LXVII. E., Saporta—Schuck.
LXVIII. E., Sémach, Haim.
LXIX. E., Sémach, Haim—Sémach (Mme.).
LXX. E., Sémach (Mme.)—Somekh.
LXXI. E., Soriano—Victorias.
LXXII. E., Weismann—Zonana.

Smyrne (Izmir):
LXXIII. E., Affaires locales—Auerbach.
LXXIV. E., Arié.
LXXV. E., Arié.
LXXVI. E., Arié.
LXXVII. E., Arié.
LXXX. E., Caleb—Dufour.
LXXXI. E., Farhi—Jerusalmi.
LXXXII. E., Jousselin (Mme.).
LXXXIII. E., Lahana—Nabon.
LXXXIV. E., Nabon.

LXXXV. E., Nabon (Mme.)—Pariente.
LXXXVI. F., Pariente.
LXXXVII. E., Pariente.
LXXXVIII. E., Polako—Schahevitch.

Or Yehudah:
XCV. E.

Grèce (each entry represents one box with several files)

General subjects
III. B. 20, Comités et communautés (Salonique).
IV. B. 21–22, Comités et communautés (Salonique).
V. B. 23–24, Comités et communautés (Salonique).
VI. B. 25–26, Comités et communautés (Salonique).
VII. B. 27, Comités et communautés (Salonique).
I. C. 1–10, Situation générale intérieure des Juifs.
I. C. 41–52, Situation générale intérieure des Juifs.
I. D. 1–3, Politique extérieure, consuls, etc.
I. G. 1–3, Sionisme et l'Alliance.

Schools and communities
I. E. 11–17, Demotica.
II. E. 18–29, Demotica.
VIII. E. 103–114, Salonique (no. 108, Allatini file).
XX. E. 253–258, Volo.

Bulgarie (each entry represents one box with several files)

VII. B. 163bis, Consulat de France, Varna (one file only).
I. D. 1–8, Politique extérieure, Consuls.
I. G. 1–12, Sionisme.
I. G. 13–18, Sionisme.

Israël

I. G. 1–3, Sionisme.
IV. E. 11–12, Antébi (1900).

Registre

Secrétariat, 219.

Archives of the Ministère des Affaires Etrangères (Paris)

Correspondance politique des consuls
Andrinople 1869–1891, Vols. II-V.
Smyrne 1869–1891, Vols. VI-XI.
Salonique 1841–1895, Vols. I-X.

Série C, Administrative (1890–1907)
Vol. 116: Correspondance générale, 1900–1907.
Vol. 117: Affaires diverses.
Vol. 141: Alliance française, Turquie.
Vol. 142: Alliance Israélite Universelle, 1905–1907.
Vols. 143–165: Secours réligieux, allocations.

Série D, Administrative (1907–1914), Sous diréction du Levant
Vol. 1: Dossier général et notes, 1908–1911.
Vol. 4: Turquie, dossier général, 1906–1910.

Vol. 7: Smyrne, 1908–1911.
Vol. 18: Alliance française, 1908–1911.
Vol. 19: Mission laique, 1908–1911.
Vol. 20: Etablissements de Salonique, 1908–1911.
Vol. 21: Alliance Israélite Universelle, 1908–1911.
Vols. 25–33: Allocations, 1908–1911.

Correspondance politique et commerciale
Nouvelle Série
Turquie, vols. 135–138: Palestine, Sionisme.

Archives des postes
Turquie, Ambassade, Carton 175/711–712: Alliance Israélite Universelle.

Guerre 1914–1918
Vol. 960: Alliance Israélite Universelle.
Vols. 961–964: Français en Turquie, Ecoles.
Vols. 965–971: Ottomans en France.
Vols. 1197–1201: Sionisme.

Série E, Levant 1918–1929
Vols. 10–17: Palestine, Sionisme.
Vol. 112: Turquie, Religion israélite.
Vols. 255–256: Turquie.
Vols. 520–523: Turquie, Instruction publique.

Central Archives for the History of the Jewish People (Jerusalem)

P112/109: Minute Book of the Alliance Regional Committee, Istanbul, 1903–1917.
Dossiers de correspondance reçue par les directeurs d'écoles (AIU): ler série, lettres
    reçues de Paris par Nissim Behar, D1-D3: 1884–1896.
(microfilm) Auswärtiges Amt: Akten betreffend die Juden in der Turkei, 1897–1912,
    K692/175834–176145.

Central Zionist Archives (Jerusalem)

Z2/ 6–12: Files on the correspondence of Zionist representatives in Istanbul and the
    Central Zionist Office, Cologne, 1905–1911.
Z2/ 31–32: Files on relations with the Alliance Israélite Universelle.
Z2/ 516: File on the Alliance Israélite Universelle and Zionism in Turkey.
Z2/ 541: File on the Jews of Turkey.
Z2/ 648: File on relations with the Hilfsverein der Deutschen Juden.
L5: Files on the correspondence of the Zionist Agency at Constantinople, 1909–1917.

Public Records Office (London)

Correspondence of the British High Commissioner and later the British Ambassador
    in Turkey with London concerning the Jews and other minorities, 1919–1927:
FO 195/2452
FO 371/521
FO 371/62
FO 371/801
FO 371/10207
FO 371/10865
FO 371/10866

FO 371/11522
FO 371/11541
FO 371/12318
FO 371/13080

National Archives, US Department of State (Washington) (microfilm)

Records relating to Turkey, 1910–1929
(roll 32) 867.4016: Peoples of Turkey, Protection of Minorities, Race Problems.

Primary Printed Sources

Brochures, Books, and Periodicals published by the Alliance Israélite
Universelle, 1860–1939 (by date of publication)

Alliance Israélite Universelle. Paris, 1860.
Compte rendu de l'Assemblée générale annuelle du 30 mai 1861. Paris, 1861.
Compte rendu sommaire des séances du Comité depuis l'Assemblée générale du 30 mai 1861. Paris, 1861.
Procès-verbal de l'Assemblée générale de l'Alliance Israélite Universelle tenue le 10 avril 1862. Paris, 1862.
Procès-verbal de l'Assemblée générale tenue le 18 juin 1863. Paris, 1863.
Extrait des procès-verbaux des séances du Comité central tenues pendant le dernier trimestre de l'année 1863. Paris, 1864.
Compte rendu des séances du Comité central tenues pendant le premier trimestre de l'année 1864. Paris, 1864.
Procès-verbal de l'Assemblée générale de l'Alliance Israélite Universelle tenue le 31 mai 1864. Paris, 1864.
Extrait des procès-verbaux des séances du Comité central tenues pendant le deuxième et le troisième trimestre de 1864. Paris, 1864.
Extrait des procès-verbaux des séances du Comité central tenues pendant le dernier trimestre de 1864. Paris, 1865.
L'oeuvre des Ecoles. Paris, 1865.
Procès-verbal de l'Assemblée générale du 25 mai 1865. Paris, 1865.
Bulletins semestriels de l'Alliance Israélite Universelle (1860/1865–1913).
Bulletins mensuels de l'Alliance Israélite Universelle (1873–1913).
Brochure publiée à l'occasion du 25ᵉ anniversaire de la fondation de l'oeuvre. Paris, 1885.
L'Alliance Israélite Universelle, 1860–1895. Paris, 1895.
Bigart, Jacques. *L'Alliance Israélite: son action éducatrice.* Paris, 1900.
Instructions générales pour les professeurs. Paris, 1903.
Revue des Ecoles de l'Alliance Israélite (1901–1904).
Bulletin des Ecoles de l'Alliance Israélite (1910–1914).
Association des Anciens Eleves de l'AIU, *Bulletin de l'Amicale* (1910–1913). Constantinople.
Bigart, Jacques. *L'action de l'Alliance Israélite en Turquie.* Paris, 1913.
Paix et Droit (1920–1939).

Documents, Books, Memoirs, Official Publications

Akrish, Yitshak. *Kiryat arba.* Jerusalem, 1876.
Assaf, Simhah. *Mekorot le-toldot ha-hinukh be-yisrael* [Sources for the History of Education among the Jews]. 4 vols. Tel-Aviv, 1925–42.
Ben Giat, Alexander. *Suvenires del meldar: Estudio verdadero de lo ke se pasava en un tiempo* [Memories of the *Meldar*: A Real Account of What Used to Happen Once upon a Time]. Izmir, 1920.

Cevdet Paşa, Ahmet. *Tezâkir* [Memoirs], edited by Cavid Baysun. 4 vols. Ankara, 1953–67.

Danon, Abraham. *Yosif da'at o El Progreso* [The Growth of Wisdom or Progress]. Edirne, 1888.

———. *Boletino de la Sosiedad Dorshei ha-Haskalah* [Bulletin of the Society of the Seekers of Enlightenment]. Edirne, 1889.

Ecole de Travail. *Compte rendu des années 1884–1886.* Paris, 1887.

Frankl, Ludwig August. *The Jews in the East*, Patrick Beaton tr. 2 vols. London, 1859.

Fresco, David. *Le Sionisme.* Istanbul, 1909.

Grégoire, Baptiste Henri (Abbé). *Essai sur la régénération physique, morale et politique des Juifs.* Metz, 1789.

La konstitusion para la nasion israelita de Turkia [The Constitution of the Jewish *Millet* in Turkey]. Istanbul, 1865.

Lütfi, Ahmed. *Tarih-i Lütfi* [The Chronicle of Lütfi]. 2 vols. Istanbul, 1290/1873–1328/1910.

Mitrani, Barukh. *Diskorso de Perashat Shemot* [Discourse on a Portion of Exodus]. Salonica, 1868.

———. *Sefer ḥinukh Banim* [The Book of Education of Barukh (N) Mitrani]. Jerusalem, 1875.

Nehama, Yehudah. *Zikhron tov, o biografia del muy afamado savido y filantropo avraham ha-kohen, ke lo yaman albert kohn de paris* [Good Memory, or Biography of the Very Famous Scholar and Philanthropist Avraham ha-Kohen who is called Albert Kohn of Paris]. Salonica, 1877.

———. *Mikhtevei dodim mi-yayin* [Letters to Friends from Yehudah Nehama]. Salonica, 1890.

Niégo, Joseph. *Cinquante années de travail dans les oeuvres juives.* Istanbul, 1933.

Pernot, Maurice. *Rapport sur un voyage d'étude à Constantinople, en Egypte et en Turquie d'Asie (janvier-août 1912).* Paris, 1913 (?)

Regulamiento de administration de la komunidad israelit de izmirna. Izmir, 1896.

Salname-i Nezareti Maarif-i Umumiyesi [The Yearbook of the General Education Ministry]. Istanbul, 1316/1898, 1321/1903.

Şinasi, İbrahim. *Külliyat* [Complete Works], edited by Fevziye A. Tansel. Vol. 4: *Makaleler* [Articles]. Ankara, 1960.

Sokolow, Nahum. *Trajikomedia o yorar y riir: Estudio psikolojiko sovre el estado de alma del sinior David Fresko, direktor del "Tiempo"* [Tragi-comedy or to Cry and to Laugh: A Psychological Study on the State of Soul of Mr. David Fresco, the Editor of "El Tiempo"]. Istanbul, 1910.

Ubicini, [Jean Henri] A[bdolomyne]. *Letters on Turkey*, translated by Lady Easthope. 2 vols. London, 1856, reprinted, New York, 1973.

Yoel, Yosef, and Rivlin, Binyamin, eds. *Igrot ha-Pekidim ve-ha-Amerkalim be-Amsterdam* [Letters of the Committee of Officials of Amsterdam]. 3 vols. Jerusalem, 1965–78.

Newspapers and Periodicals

Allgemeine Zeitung des Judenthums
Archives Israélites
L'Aurore
Bulletin de l'Alliance française
Bulletin de la Grande Loge de District XI et de la Loge de Constantinople [B'nai B'rith, Istanbul]
Bulletin périodique de la press turque (MAE)
Hamenora [B'nai B'rith, Istanbul]
Israelitische Annalen
Jewish Chronicle

Jurnal Israelit
El Meseret
Stamboul
El Telegrafo
El Tiempo
Univers Israélite
Die Welt

Secondary Sources

Abitbol, Michel. "The Encounter between French Jewry and the Jews of North Africa: Analysis of a Discourse (1830–1914)." In *The Jews in Modern France,* edited by Frances Malino and Bernard Wasserstein, 31–53. Hanover, New Hampshire, 1985.

————. *Les deux terres promises: Les Juifs de France et le sionisme, 1897–1945.* Paris, 1989.

Ahmad, Feroz. *The Young Turks: The Committee of Union and Progress in Turkish Politics, 1908–1914.* Oxford, 1969.

————. "Unionist Relations with the Greek, Armenian and Jewish Communities of the Ottoman Empire, 1908–1914." In *Christians and Jews in the Ottoman Empire,* edited by Benjamin Braude and Bernard Lewis, vol. 1, 401–434. New York, 1982.

Akşin, Sina. *Jön Türkler ve İttihat ve Terakki* [The Young Turks and (the Committee of) Union and Progress]. Istanbul, 1980.

Akyüz, Yahya. *Türk Eğitim Tarihi* [History of Turkish Education]. Ankara, 1982.

Albert, Phyllis Cohen. *The Modernization of French Jewry: Consistory and Community in the Nineteenth Century.* Hanover, New Hampshire, 1977.

————. "Ethnicity and Jewish Solidarity in Nineteenth-Century France." In *Mystics, Philosophers, and Politicians: Essays in Jewish Intellectual History in Honor of Alexander Altmann,* edited by Jehuda Reinharz and Daniel Swetschinski, 249–274. Durham, North Carolina, 1982.

Alexandris, Alexis. *The Greek Minority of Istanbul and Greek-Turkish Relations, 1918–1974.* Athens, 1983.

Amarillio, Avraham Shaul. "Ḥevrat talmud torah ha-gadol be-Saloniki" [The Great Talmud Torah Society in Salonica]. *Sefunot* 13 (1971–1978): 274–309.

————. "Ḥevrot ẓedakah ve-ḥesed" [Societies of Charity and Philanthropy]." *Sefunot* 15 (1971–1981): 103–134.

Anderson, R. D. *Education in France, 1848–1870.* Oxford, 1975.

Andrew, Christopher M., and Kanya-Forster, A. S. *France Overseas: The Great War and the Climax of French Imperial Expansion.* London, 1981.

Angel, Marc D. *The Jews of Rhodes: The History of a Sephardic Community.* 2nd ed. New York, 1980.

Artinian, Vartan. "A Study of the Historical Development of the Armenian Constitutional System in the Ottoman Empire, 1838–1863." Ph.D. diss., Brandeis University, 1969.

Ascheim, Steven E. *Brothers and Strangers: The East European Jew in German and German Jewish Consciousness, 1800–1923.* Madison, Wisconsin, 1982.

Assaf, Simḥah. *Mekorot le-toldot ha-ḥinukh be-yisrael* [Sources for the History of Education among the Jews]. 4 vols. Tel-Aviv, 1925–1942.

Ayas, Nevzad. *Türkiye Cumhuriyeti Milli Eğitimi* [National Education in the Turkish Republic]. Ankara, 1948.

Badie, Bertrand. *Les deux Etats: Pouvoir et société en Occident et en terre d'Islam.* Paris, 1986.

Badie, Bertrand, and Birnbaum, Pierre. *The Sociology of the State.* Chicago, 1983.

Bağış, Ali İhsan. *Osmanlı Ticaretinde Gayri Müslimler* [Non-Muslims in Ottoman Commerce]. Ankara, 1983.

Barnai, Jacob. "Ma'amadah shel 'ha-rabanut ha-kolelet' bi-Yerushalayim ba-tekufah ha-'otomanit" [The Status of the 'General Rabbinate' in Jerusalem in the Ottoman Period]. *Katedrah* 13 (1979): 47–69.

———. "Kavim le-toldot kehilat Kushta ba-meah ha-18" [Aspects of the History of the Constantinople Community in the Eighteenth Century]. In *Mi-kedem u-mi-yam* [From the Orient and the Occident], edited by Jacob Barnai, Yosef Shitrit, Bustanai 'Oded, Aliza Shenhar, and Zvi Yehudah, 53–66. Haifa, 1981.

———. "Ha-yehudim ba-imperyah ha-'otomanit" [The Jews in the Ottoman Empire]. In *Toldot ha-yehudim be-arẓot ha-islam: ha-'et ha-ḥadashah* [History of the Jews in Islamic Countries: Modern Times], edited by Shmuel Ettinger, vol. 1, 73–118, Jerusalem, 1981.

———. *Yehudei Ereẓ Yisrael ba-meah ha-18 be-ḥasut "Pekidei Kushta"* [The Jews of Erets Israel in the Eighteenth Century under the Patronage of the Constantinople Committee Officials of Erets Israel]. Jerusalem, 1982.

———. "Kavim le-toldot ha-ḥevrah ha-yehudit be-Izmir be-shilhei ha-meah ha-18 u-ve-reshit ha-meah ha-19" [Aspects of Jewish Society in Izmir at the End of the Eighteenth and the Beginning of the Nineteenth Centuries]. *Ẓiyon* 47 (1982): 56–76.

———. "Gildot yehudiyot be-Turkiyah ba-meot ha-16–19" [Jewish Guilds in Turkey from the Sixteenth to the Nineteenth Centuries]. In *Yehudim ba-kalkalah* [Jews in the Economy], edited by Nahum Gross, 133–148. Jerusalem, 1985.

———. "Ha-yehudim ba-imperyah ha-'otomanit" [The Jews in the Ottoman Empire]. In *Toldot ha-yehudim be-arẓot ha-islam: ha-'et ha-ḥadashah* [History of the Jews in Islamic Countries: Modern Times], edited by Shmuel Ettinger, vol. 2, 183–297. Jerusalem, 1986.

———. " 'Blood Libels' in the Ottoman Empire of the Fifteenth to the Nineteenth Centuries." In *Antisemitism through the Ages,* edited by Shmuel Almog, 189–194. Oxford, 1988.

Barnai, Jacob, and Gerber, Haim. "Gildot yehudiyot be-Kushta be-shilhei ha-meah ha-18" [Jewish Guilds in Constantinople at the End of the Eighteenth Century]. *Mikhael* 7 (1981): 206–226.

———. *Yehudei Izmir ba-meah ha-19* [The Jews of Izmir in the Nineteenth Century]. Jerusalem, 1985.

Barnett, Richard D. "The Correspondence of the Mahamad of the Spanish and Portuguese Congregation of London during the Seventeenth and Eighteenth Centuries." *Transactions of the Jewish Historical Society of England* 20 (1959–1961): 1–50.

Barocas, David N. *In Search of Our Sephardic Roots,* translated by Paula O. de Benardete. New York, 1970.

Baron, Salo W. *A Social and Religious History of the Jews.* 3 vols. New York, 1937.

———. *The Jewish Community: Its History and Structure to the American Revolution.* 3 vols. Philadelphia, 1942.

———. *A Social and Religious History of the Jews.* 2nd ed., vol. 18. *The Ottoman Empire, Persia, Ethiopia, India and China.* New York and Philadelphia, 1983.

Bartal, Yisrael. " 'Tokhniot ha-hityashvut' mi-yemei masa'o ha-sheni shel Montefiore le-Ereẓ Yisrael (1839)" [Settlement Proposals during Montefiore's Second Visit to Erets Israel, 1839]. *Shalem* 2 (1976): 231–296.

———. " 'Old Yishuv' and 'New Yishuv': Image and Reality." *The Jerusalem Cathedra* 1 (1981): 215–231.

———. "A Nationalist before His Time or Belated *Shtadlan?* Guidelines for the

Activities of Moses Montefiore." Paper delivered at the conference on "Britain and the Holy Land, 1800–1914," University College, London, 8 February 1989.

Bashan, Eliezer. "Pe'ilutam ha-kalkalit shel yehudei Izmir ba-meot ha-17 ve ha-18 lefi ha-arkhionim shel ḥevrat ha-levant ha-britit" [The Economic Activity of the Jews of Izmir in the Seventeenth and Eighteenth Centuries in the Archives of the British Levant Company]. In *Yehudim ba-kalkalah* [Jews in the Economy], edited by Nahum Gross, 149–68. Jerusalem, 1985.

Başgöz, İlhan, and Wilson, Howard E. *Educational Problems in Turkey, 1920–1940.* Bloomington, Indiana, 1968.

Bat Ye'or. *Le Dhimmi: Profil de l'opprimé en Orient et en Afrique du Nord depuis la conquête arabe.* Paris, 1980.

Bee, Robert L. *Patterns and Processes: An Introduction to Anthropological Strategies for the Study of Socio-Cultural Change.* New York, 1974.

Benbassa, Esther. "L'école de filles de l'Alliance Israélite Universelle à Galata (1879–1912)." Paper delivered at the Première rencontre internationale d'études et de recherches sur l'Empire ottoman et la Turquie contemporaine: Recherches sur la ville ottomane, le cas du quartier de Galata, Paris, 18–22 January 1985.

———. "La 'nation' juive au lendemain de la Révolution jeune-turque (1908) à travers *El Tiempo,* journal judéo-espagnol d'Istanbul." Paper read at the conference Istanbul dans la Presse. La Presse à Istanbul, Istanbul, 23–24 May 1985.

———. "L'Alliance Israélite Universelle et l'élection de Haim Nahum au Grand Rabbinat de l'Empire ottoman (1908–1909)." In *Proceedings of the Ninth World Congress of Jewish Studies* (Division B), edited by the World Union of Jewish Studies, vol. 3, 83–90. Jerusalem, 1986.

———. "Presse d'Istanbul et de Salonique au service du sionisme (1908–1914). Les motifs d'une allégeance." *Revue Historique* 276 (October-December 1986): 337–65.

———. "Haim Nahum Effendi, dernier Grand Rabbin de l'Empire ottoman (1908–1920): son rôle politique et diplomatique." Thèse de doctorat d'état ès lettres, Université de Paris III, 1987.

———. "Israël face à lui-même: Judaïsme occidental et judaïsme ottoman (19e-20e siècles)." *Pardès* 7 (1988): 105–129.

———. "Le Sionisme dans l'Empire ottoman à l'aube du 20e siècle." *Vingtième Siècle,* no. 24 (October-December 1989): 69–80.

———. "Le Sionisme et la politique des alliances dans les communautés juives ottomanes." In *Ottoman and Turkish Jewry: Community and Leadership,* edited by Aron Rodrigue. Forthcoming.

———. "Associational Strategies in Ottoman Jewish Society in the Nineteenth and Twentieth Centuries." In *The Jews in the Ottoman Empire,* edited by Avigdor Levy. Forthcoming.

Benbassa, Esther, and Rodrigue, Aron. "L'artisanat juif en Turquie à la fin du XIXe siècle: l'Alliance Israélite Universelle et ses oeuvres d'apprentissage." *Turcica* 17 (1985): 113–126.

Benveniste, Annie. "Le rôle des institutrices de l'Alliance Israélite à Salonique." *Combat pour la Diaspora,* no. 8 (1982): 13–26.

Benvenisti, David. "Zikhronot le-ne'urim" [Memories of Youth]. In *Saloniki, 'ir va-em be-yisrael* [Salonica, the Mother City of the People of Israel], edited by the Centre de Recherches sur le Judaïsme de Salonique, 82–98. Tel-Aviv, 1967.

———. *Yehudei Saloniki be-dorot ha-aḥaronim* [The Jews of Salonica in the Last Generations]. Jerusalem, 1973.

Berkes, Niyazi. *The Development of Secularism in Turkey.* Montreal, 1964.

———. *Türkiye'de Çağdaşlaşma* [Modernization in Turkey]. Istanbul, 1978.

Berkovitz, Jay R. "French Jewry and the Ideology of *Régénération* to 1848." Ph.D diss., Brandeis University, 1982.

Bertrand, Louis. "Les écoles d'Orient: Ecoles chrétiennes et israélites." *Revue des deux mondes* 52 (July-August 1909): 755–794.

Besso, Henry V. *Ladino Books in the Library of Congress: A Bibliography.* Washington, 1963.

Birnbaum, Pierre. "Sur l'étatisation révolutionnaire: L'abbé Grégoire et le destin de l'identité juive." *Le Débat,* 53 (January-February 1989): 157–173.

Blidstein, Ya'akov. "Pidyon shevuyim ba-masoret ha-hilkhatit: metaḥim u-mediniyut" [The Ransoming of Captives in the Halakhic Tradition: Tensions and Politics]. In *Solidariyut yehudit le'umit ba-'et ha-ḥadashah* [Jewish National Solidarity in the Modern Period], edited by Binyamin Pinkus and Ilan Troen, 19–27. Beer-sheba, 1988.

Bornstein-Makovetsky, Leah. "Mivne ha-rabanut ba-imperyah ha-'otomanit ba-meah ha-16 u-va-meah ha-17" [The Structure of the Rabbinate in the Ottoman Empire in the Sixteenth and Seventeenth Centuries]. *Mi-mizraḥ u-mi-ma'arav* [From the East and the West] 1 (1974): 223–258.

――――. "Ha-hanhagah shel ha-kehilah ha-yehudit ba-mizraḥ ha-karov me-shilhei ha-meah ha-15 ve-'ad sof ha-meah ha-18" [The Jewish Communal Leadership in the Near East from the End of the Fifteenth Century through the Eighteenth Century]. Ph.D. diss., Bar-Ilan University, 1978.

――――. "Yehudim portugezim be-ḥaẓer ha-malkhut be-Kushta ba-me'ah ha-16: Don Yosef Nasi" [Portuguese Jews in the Royal Court in Constantinople in the Sixteenth Century: Don Joseph Nasi]. In *Mi-Lisbon le-Saloniki ve-Kushta* [From Lisbon to Salonica and Constantinople], edited by Zvi Ankori, 69–94. Tel-Aviv, 1988.

Bourdieu, Pierre, and Passeron, Jean-Claude. *La Reproduction, éléments pour une théorie du système d'enseignement.* Paris, 1970.

Braude, Benjamin. "Foundation Myths of the *Millet* System." In *Christians and Jews in the Ottoman Empire,* edited by Benjamin Braude and Bernard Lewis, vol. 1, 69–88. New York, 1982.

Braude, Benjamin, and Lewis, Bernard, eds. *Christians and Jews in the Ottoman Empire.* 2 vols. New York, 1982.

Buisson, Ferdinand, and Farrington, Frederic Ernest, eds. *French Educational Ideals Today: An Anthology of the Molders of French Educational Thought of the Present.* Yonkers, New York, 1919.

Burke, Peter. *Popular Culture in Early Modern Europe.* London, 1978.

Burrows, Matthew. " 'Mission civilisatrice': French Cultural Policy in the Middle East, 1860–1914." *The Historical Journal* 29 (1986): 109–135.

Certeau, Michel de, Julia, Dominique, and Revel, Jacques. *Une Politique de la langue: La Révolution française et les patois.* Paris, 1975.

Chisick, Harvey. *The Limits of Reform in the Enlightenment: Attitudes toward the Education of the Lower Classes in Eighteenth-Century France.* Princeton, New Jersey, 1981.

Chouraqui, André. *Cent ans d'histoire: L'Alliance Israélite Universelle et la renaissance juive contemporaine (1860–1960).* Paris, 1965.

Cicioğlu, Hasan. *Türkiye Cumhuriyetinde İlk ve Orta Öğretim* [Elementary and Secondary Education in the Turkish Republic]. Ankara, 1982.

Clark, Linda L. *Schooling the Daughters of Marianne: Textbooks and the Socialization of Girls in Modern French Primary Schools.* Albany, New York, 1984.

Cohen, Amnon. *Jewish Life under Islam: Jerusalem in the Sixteenth Century.* Cambridge, Massachusetts, 1984.

Cohen, Eliahou. "L'influence intellectuelle et sociale des écoles de l'Alliance Israélite

Universelle sur les Israélites du Proche-Orient." Thèse de Doctorat, Université de Paris, 1962.

Covo, Mercado J. "Contribution à l'histoire des institutions scolaires de la communauté israélite de Salonique jusqu'à la fondation de l'école des garçons de l'Alliance Israélite Universelle." *Almanach nationale au profit de l'hôpital de Hirsch* 8 (1916): 97–103.

Crubellier, Maurice. *L'enfance et la jeunesse dans la société française, 1800–1950.* Paris, 1979.

Davison, Roderic H. "Turkish Attitudes concerning Christian- Muslim Equality in the Nineteenth Century." *American Historical Review* 59 (1954): 844–864.

———. *Reform in the Ottoman Empire, 1856–1876.* Princeton, New Jersey, 1963.

Devereux, Robert. *The First Ottoman Constitutional Period: A Study of the Midhat Constitution and Parliament.* Baltimore, 1963.

De Lanessan, J. L. *Les Missions et leur Protectorat.* Paris, 1907.

Djait, Hichem. *L'Europe et l'Islam.* Paris, 1978.

Dubin, Lois C. "Trieste and Berlin: The Italian Role in the Cultural Politics of the Haskalah." In *Toward Modernity: The European Jewish Model,* edited by Jacob Katz, 189–224. New Brunswick, New Jersey, 1987.

Dumont, Paul. "Une source pour l'étude des communautés juives en Turquie: Les Archives de l'Alliance Israélite Universelle." *Journal Asiatique* 267 (1979): 101–135.

———. "La condition juive en Turquie à la fin du XIXᵉ siècle." *Les Nouveaux Cahiers,* no. 57 (Summer 1979): 25–38.

———. "La structure sociale de la communauté juive de Salonique à la fin du dix-neuvième siècle." *Revue Historique* 263 (April-June 1980): 351–393.

———. "Jewish Communities in Turkey during the Last Decades of the Nineteenth Century in the Light of the Archives of the Alliance Israélite Universelle." In *Christians and Jews in the Ottoman Empire,* edited by Benjamin Braude and Bernard Lewis, vol. 1, 209–242. New York, 1982.

———. "La Turquie dans les archives du Grand Orient de France: Les loges maçonniques d'obédience française à Istanbul du milieu du XIXᵉ siècle à la veille de la première guerre mondiale." In *Economie et sociétés dans l'Empire ottoman (Fin du XVIIIᵉ-Début du XXᵉ siècle),* edited by Jean-Louis Bacqué-Grammont and Paul Dumont, 171–201. Paris, 1983.

———. "Une communauté en quête d'avenir—Le sionisme à Istanbul au lendemain de la première guerre mondiale." In *Les Juifs dans la Méditerranée médiévale et moderne,* edited by Université de Nice-Centre de la Méditerranée moderne et contemporaine—Centre d'études médiévales, 97–124. Nice, 1987.

Eckstein, Simon L. "The Life, Work, and Influence of Rabbi Chayim Palaggi on the Jewish Community in Izmir." Ph.D. diss., Yeshiva University, 1970.

Eldem, Vedat. *Osmanlı İmparatorluğunun İktisadi Şartları Hakkında Bir Tetkik* [A Study on the Economic Circumstances of the Ottoman Empire]. Ankara, 1970.

Eliav, Mordecai. *Ereẓ Yisrael vi-yishuvah ba-meah ha-19, 1777–1917* [Erets Israel and Its (Jewish) Settlement in the Nineteenth Century, 1777–1917]. Jerusalem, 1978.

Emanuel, Yitshak. "Toldot yehudei Saloniki" [History of the Jews of Salonica]. In *Zikhron Saloniki* [Memory of Salonica], edited by David A. Recanati, vol. 1, 1–275. Tel-Aviv, 1972.

———. "Los jidios de Salonique" [The Jews of Salonica]. In *Zikhron Saloniki* [Memory of Salonica], edited by David A. Recanati, vol. 1, 13–37. Tel-Aviv, 1972.

Encyclopaedia Judaica, s. v. "Camondo."

Epstein, Mark A. *The Ottoman Jewish Communities and Their Role in the Fifteenth and Sixteenth Centuries.* Freiburg, 1980.

Ergin, Osman. *Türkiye Maarif Tarihi* [History of Education in Turkey]. 5 vols. Istanbul, 1939–43. Reprinted, Istanbul, 1977.

Ergün, Mustafa, *Atatürk Devri Türk Eğitimi* [Turkish Education in the Time of Atatürk]. Ankara, 1982.

Estrugo, José M. *El Retorno a Sefarad: Un Siglo despues de la Inquisicion.* Madrid, 1933.

Etmekjian, James. *The French Influence on the Western Armenian Renaissance, 1843–1915.* New York, 1964.

Farhi, David. "Yehudei Saloniki be-mahapekhat 'ha-turkim ha-ẓe'irim' " [The Jews of Salonica in the Young Turk Revolution]. *Sefunot* 15 (1971–1981): 135–152.

———. "Documents on the Attitude of the Ottoman Government towards the Jewish Settlement in Palestine after the Revolution of the Young Turks, 1908–1909." In *Studies on Palestine during the Ottoman Period,* edited by Moshe Maoz, 190–210. Jerusalem, 1975.

Fattal, Antoine. *Le statut légal des non-musulmans en pays d'Islam.* Beirut, 1958.

Findley, Carter V. *Bureaucratic Reform in the Ottoman Empire: The Sublime Porte, 1789–1922.* Princeton, New Jersey, 1980.

Fishman, Joshua A. *Advances in the Sociology of Language.* 2 vols. The Hague, 1971–72.

Franco, Moïse. *Essai sur l'histoire des Israélites de l'Empire ottoman depuis les origines jusqu'à nos jours.* Paris, 1897.

Frankel, Jonathan. "Crisis as a Factor in Modern Jewish Politics, 1840 and 1881–82." In *Living with Antisemitism: Modern Jewish Responses,* edited by Jehuda Reinharz, 42–58. Hanover, New Hampshire, 1987.

Friedman, Isaiah. *Germany, Turkey and Zionism, 1897–1918.* Oxford, 1977.

Galanté, Abraham. *Documents officiels turcs concernant les Juifs de Turquie.* Istanbul, 1931.

———. *Turcs et Juifs.* Istanbul, 1932.

———. *Abdul Hamid II et le Sionisme.* Istanbul, 1933.

———. *Histoire des Juifs d'Anatolie.* 2 vols. Istanbul, 1937–1939.

———. *Histoire des Juifs d'Istanbul.* 2 vols. Istanbul, 1941–1942.

———. *Türkler ve Yahudiler* [Turks and Jews]. 2nd ed. Istanbul, 1947.

———. *Receuil de nouveaux documents inédits concernants l'historie des Juifs de Turquie.* Istanbul, 1949.

———. *Türk Harsı ve Türk Yahudisi* [Turkish Culture and the Turkish Jew]. Istanbul, 1953.

Gaon, Mosheh David. *Yehudei ha-mizraḥ be-Ereẓ Yisrael* [The Jews of the East in Erets Israel]. 2 vols. Jerusalem, 1928–1938.

———. *Ha-'itonut be-Ladino: Bibliografyah* [The Ladino Press: A Bibliography]. Jerusalem, 1965.

Gat, B. Z. *Ha-yishuv ha-yehudi be-Ereẓ Yisrael bi-shenot 5600–5641* [The Jews of Erets Israel in the Years 5600–5641]. Jerusalem, 1963.

Gelber, N. M. "Dr. Albert Cohn u-vikuro bi-Yerushalayim" [Dr. Albert Cohn and His Visit to Jerusalem]. *Yerushalayim* 2 (1949): 175–195.

Gerber, Haim. "Yehudim be-ḥayei ha-kalkalah shel ha-'ir ha-anatolit Bursa ba-meah ha-17" [Jews in the Economic Life of the Anatolian Town of Bursa in the Seventeenth Century]. *Sefunot* 16 (1980): 235–272.

———. *Yehudei ha-imperyah ha-otomanit ba-meot 16–17: kalkalah ve-ḥevrah* [The Jews of the Ottoman Empire in the Sixteenth and Seventeenth Centuries: Economy and Society]. Jerusalem, 1982.

Gerber, Jane S. "The Damascus Blood Libel—Jewish Perceptions and Responses." In *Proceedings of the Eighth World Congress of Jewish Studies* (Division B), 105–110. Jerusalem, 1982.

Gerson, Karen. "Language Change as Influenced by Cultural Contact: A Case, Ladino." MA thesis, Boğaziçi University, 1983.

———. "The Relation of Language, Ethnicity, and Ethnic Group Identity. A Case: Judeo-Spanish." MA thesis, University of Reading, 1986.

Gibb, H. A. R., and Bowen, Harold. *Islamic Society and the West.* 1 vol., 2 parts. London, 1950–1957.

Gidney, William Thomas. *The History of the London Society for Promoting Christianity amongst the Jews, from 1809 to 1908.* London, 1908.

Giolitto, Pierre. *Histoire de l'enseignement primaire au XIXe siècle: L'organisation pédagogique.* 2 vols. Paris, 1983–84.

Girard, Patrick. *Les Juifs de France de 1789 à 1860: De l'émancipation à l'égalité.* Paris, 1976.

Giroux, Henry A. *Ideology, Culture and the Process of Schooling.* Philadelphia, 1981.

Gottheil, Richard J. H. *Zionism.* Philadelphia, 1914.

Graetz, Michael. *Les Juifs en France au XIXe siècle: De la Révolution française à l'Alliance israélite universelle,* translated by Salomon Malka. Paris, 1989.

Grunwald, Kurt. *Türkenhirsch: A Study of Baron Maurice de Hirsch, Entrepreneur and Philanthropist.* Jerusalem, 1966.

Hacker, Joseph. "Istanbul Jewry 1750–1850." In *A Tale of Two Cities: Jewish Life in Frankfurt and Istanbul, 1750–1850,* edited by Vivian B. Mann, 38–49. New York, 1982.

———. "Ottoman Policy towards the Jews and Jewish Attitudes towards the Ottomans during the Fifteenth Century." In *Christians and Jews in the Ottoman Empire,* edited by Benjamin Braude and Bernard Lewis, vol. 1, 117–126. New York, 1982.

———. " 'Ha-rabanut ha-rashit' ba-imperyah ha-'otomanit ba-meot ha-15 ve-ha-16" [The "Chief Rabbinate" in the Ottoman Empire in the Fifteenth and Sixteenth Centuries]," *Ẓiyon* 49 (1984): 225–263.

———. "Gvuloteyah shel ha-otonomiyah ha-yehudit: ha-shiput ha-'aẓmi ha-yehudi ba-imperyah ha-'otomanit ba-meot ha-16—ha-18" [Jewish Autonomy in the Ottoman Empire: Its Scope and Limits]. In *Temurot ba-historyah ha-yehudit ha-ḥadashah: Koveẓ ma'amarim, shay li-Shmuel Etinger* [Transition and Change in Modern Jewish History. Essays in Honor of Shmuel Ettinger], edited by Shmuel Almog, Yisrael Bartal, Michael Graetz, et al., 349–388. Jerusalem, 1987.

Hajjar, Joseph. *Le Vatican, la France et le Catholicisme oriental (1878–1914): Diplomatie et histoire de l'Eglise.* Paris, 1979.

Haramati, Shelomoh. *Sheloshah she-kadmu le-Ben Yehudah* [Three Who Preceded Ben-Yehudah]. Jerusalem, 1978.

Harrigan, Patrick J. *Mobility, Elites, and Education in French Society of the Second Empire.* Waterloo, Ontario, 1980.

Hayim, Avraham. "Ha-ḥakham bashi shel Kushta ve-'milḥemet ha-rabanut' bi-Yerushalayim" [The Chief Rabbi of Constantinople and the 'War of the Rabbinate' in Jerusalem]. *Pe'amim,* no. 12 (1982): 105–113.

Helfand, Jonathan Isaac. "French Jewry during the Second Republic and Second Empire (1848–1870)." Ph.D. diss., Yeshiva University, 1979.

Henriques, Ursula R. "Who Killed Father Thomas?" In *Sir Moses Montefiore: A Symposium,* edited by V. D. Lipman, 50–75. Oxford, 1982.

Heper, Metin. "Center and Periphery in the Ottoman Empire, with Special Reference to the Nineteenth Century." *International Political Science Review* 1 (1980): 81–105.

———. *The State Tradition in Turkey.* Beverley, North Humberside, 1985.

Hertzberg, Arthur. *The French Enlightenment and the Jews.* New York, 1968.

Hertzberg, Arthur, ed. *The Zionist Idea: A Historical Analysis and Reader.* New York, 1966.

Heyd, Uriel. "The Jewish Communities of Istanbul in the Seventeenth Century." *Oriens* 6 (1953): 299–314.

Hirschberg, Hirsch Z. "The Oriental Jewish Communities." In *Religion in the Middle East,* edited by A. J. Arberry, vol. 1, 119–225. London, 1969.

Hsia, R. Po-Chia. *The Myth of Ritual Murder: Jews and Magic in Reformation Germany.* New Haven, 1988.

Hurewitz, Jacob C., ed. *The Middle East and North Africa in World Politics: A Documentary Record.* 2 vols. 2nd ed. New Haven, 1975–1979.

Hyamson, Albert M. "The Damascus Affair of 1840." *Transactions of the Jewish Historical Society of England* 16 (1945–1951): 47–71.

Hyman, Paula. *From Dreyfus to Vichy: The Remaking of French Jewry.* New York, 1979.

Israël, Gérard. *L'Alliance Israélite Universelle, 1860-1960. Cent ans d'efforts pour la libération et la promotion de l'homme par l'homme.* Paris, 1960.

İnalcık, Halil. *The Ottoman Empire: The Classical Age, 1300–1600,* translated by Norman Itzkowitz and Colin Imber. London, 1973.

Institut Colonial International. *L'enseignement aux indigènes.* Brussels, 1931.

İslamoğlu-İnan, Huri, ed. *The Ottoman Empire and the World Economy.* Cambridge and Paris, 1987.

Issawi, Charles, ed. *The Economic History of Turkey, 1800–1914.* Chicago, 1980.

Kahn, Léon. *Histoire des écoles communales et consistoriales israélites de Paris, 1809–1884.* Paris, 1884.

———. *Les professions manuelles et les institutions de patronage.* Paris, 1885.

———. *Le Comité de Bienfaisance.* Paris, 1886.

Kalderon, Albert E. *Abraham Galante: A Biography.* New York, 1983.

Kancal, Salgur. "La conquête du marché interne ottoman par le capitalisme industriel concurrentiel (1838–1881)." In *Economie et sociétés dans l'Empire ottoman (Fin du XVIIIᵉ-Début du XXᵉ siècle),* edited by Jean-Louis Bacqué-Grammont and Paul Dumont, 355–409. Paris, 1983.

Karal, Enver Ziya. *Nizam-ı Cedit ve Tanzimat Devirleri, 1789–1856* [The Ages of the New Order and Reform]. 2nd ed. Ankara, 1961.

Karpat, Kemal H. *An Inquiry into the Social Foundations of Nationalism in the Ottoman State: From Social Estates to Classes, from Millets to Nations.* Princeton, New Jersey, 1973.

———. "Ottoman Population Records and the Census of 1881/82–1893." *International Journal of Middle East Studies* 9 (1978): 237–274.

———. "*Millets* and Nationality: The Roots of the Incongruity of Nation and State in the Post-Ottoman Era." In *Christians and Jews of the Ottoman Empire,* edited by Benjamin Braude and Bernard Lewis, vol 1, 141–169. New York, 1982.

———. *Ottoman Population, 1830–1914: Demographic and Social Characterisitics.* Madison, Wisconsin, 1985.

Kaspi, André. "La fondation de l'Alliance Israélite Universelle." Mémoire de maîtrise, Faculté des Lettres, Paris, 1950.

Katz, Jacob. *Tradition and Crisis: Jewish Society at the End of the Middle Ages.* New York, 1961.

———. *Out of the Ghetto: The Social Background of Jewish Emancipation, 1770–1870.* Cambridge, Massachusetts, 1973.

Katz, Jacob, ed. *Toward Modernity: The European Jewish Model.* New Brunswick, New Jersey, 1987.

Kazamias, Andreas M. *Education and the Quest for Modernity in Turkey.* London, 1966.

Kazancıgil, Ali. "The Ottoman Turkish State and Kemalism." In *Atatürk, Founder of a Modern State,* edited by Ali Kazancıgil and Ergun Özbudun, 37–56. Hamden, Connecticut, 1981.

Kedourie, Elie. "The Alliance Israélite Universelle, 1860–1960." *The Jewish Journal of Sociology* 9 (June 1967): 92–99.

———. "Young Turks, Freemasons and Jews." *Middle Eastern Studies* 7 (January 1971): 89–104.

Kellner, Jacob. *Le-ma'an Ẓiyon* [For Zion's Sake]. Jerusalem, 1976.

Keyder, Çağlar. *State and Class in Turkey: A Study in Capitalist Development.* London, 1987.

Kieval, Hillel J. "Caution's Progress: The Modernization of Jewish Life in Prague, 1780–1830." In *Toward Modernity: The European Jewish Model,* edited by Jacob Katz, 71–105. New Brunswick, New Jersey, 1987.

Koçak, Cemil. "Tanzimat'tan sonra Özel ve Yabancı Okullar" [Private and Foreign Schools after the Tanzimat]. *Tanzimat'tan Cumhuriyet'e Türkiye Ansiklopedisi* 2 (1985): 485–494.

Kodaman, Bayram. *Abdülhamid Devri Eğitim Sistemi* [The Educational System in the Age of Abdülhamid]. Istanbul, 1980.

Kuran, Ercümend. "Repércussions sociales de la réforme de l'éducation dans l'Empire ottoman." In *Economie et sociétés dans l'Empire ottoman (Fin du XVIIIᵉ– Début du XXᵉ siècle),* edited by Jean-Louis Bacqué-Grammont and Paul Dumont, 145–148. Paris, 1983.

Kurdakul, Necdet. *Osmanlı Devletinde Ticaret Andlaşmaları ve Kapitülasyonlar* [Commercial Treaties and Capitulations in the Ottoman State]. Istanbul, 1981.

Kushner, David. *The Rise of Turkish Nationalism, 1876–1908.* London, 1977.

Landau, Jacob M. *Jews in Nineteenth-Century Egypt.* New York, 1969.

———. *Tekinalp, Turkish Patriot, 1883–1961.* Leiden, 1984.

Laqueur, Walter. *A History of Zionism.* New York, 1972.

Laskier, Michael M. *The Alliance Israélite Universelle and the Jewish Communities of Morocco, 1862–1962.* Albany, New York, 1983.

———. "Aspects of the Activities of the Alliance Israélite Universelle in the Jewish Communities of the Middle East and North Africa: 1860–1918." *Modern Judaism* 3 (May 1983): 147–172.

———. "Avraham Albert Antebi: Perakim be-fo'alo bi-shenot 1897–1914" [Avraham Albert Antébi: Aspects of His Activities in the Years 1897–1924]. *Pe'amim,* no. 21 (1984): 50–82.

Lazare, Lucien. "L'Alliance Israélite Universelle en Palestine à l'époque de la révolution des 'Jeunes Turcs' et sa mission en Orient du 29 octobre 1908 au 19 janvier 1909." *Revue des Etudes Juives* 138 (July-December): 307–335.

Leibovici, Sarah. *Si tu fais le bien.* Paris, 1983.

———. *Chronique des Juifs de Tétouan (1860–1896).* Paris, 1984.

Léon, Antoine. *Histoire de l'éducation technique.* Paris, 1968.

Leven, Narcisse. *Cinquante ans d'histoire. L'Alliance Israélite Universelle (1860–1910).* 2 vols. Paris, 1911–1920.

Levi, Avner. "Ha-'itonut ha-yehudit be-Izmir" [The Jewish Press in Izmir]. *Pe'amim,* no. 12 (1982): 87–104.

———. "Social Cleavage, Class War, and Leadership in a Sephardi Community: The Case of Izmir in 1847." In *Ottoman and Turkish Jewry: Community and Leadership,* edited by Aron Rodrigue. Forthcoming.

Lévigne, Catherine. "Le 'Quai' et les débuts du sionisme," *Les Nouveaux Cahiers,* no. 50 (Fall 1977): 50–55.

———. "Le mouvement sioniste en France et la politique française au Levant." *Relations Internationales,* no. 12 (1977): 307–325.

Levy, Sam. "Les grandes familles Sephardi: Les Allatini." *Le Judaisme Sephardi,* no. 51 (1937): 58–59.

Lewis, Bernard. *The Emergence of Modern Turkey.* 2nd ed. London, 1968.

———. *The Jews of Islam.* Princeton, New Jersey, 1984.

Loeb, Isidore. *Biographie d'Albert Cohn.* Paris, 1878.

Loewe, Louis, ed. *Diaries of Sir Moses and Lady Montefiore.* 2 vols. London, 1890.

Löwy, A. *The Jews of Constantinople: A Study of Their Communal and Educational Status.* London, 1890.

Lutski, Alexander. "Ha-'Frankos' be-Haleb ve-hashpa'at ha-kapitulaziot 'al toshaveha ha-yehudim" [The *Francos* of Aleppo and the Influence of the Capitulations on the Inhabitants of the City]. *Ziyon* 6 (1941): 46–79.

Maarif Vekâleti, ed. *Tanzimat.* Istanbul, 1940.

Mandel, Neville J. *The Arabs and Zionism before World War I.* Berkeley and Los Angeles, 1976.

Manneberg, Eliezer. "The Evolution of Jewish Educational Practices in the *Sancak (Eyalet)* of Jerusalem under Ottoman rule." Ph.D. diss., University of Connecticut, 1976.

Mantran, Robert. "L'enseignement français en Turquie entre 1925 et 1930." In *La Turquie et la France à l'époque d'Atatürk,* edited by Paul Dumont and Jean-Louis Bacqué-Grammont, 179–189. Paris, 1981.

Mardin, Şerif. *The Genesis of Young Ottoman Thought: A Study in the Modernization of Turkish Political Ideas.* Princeton, New Jersey, 1962.

———. "Power, Civil Society and Culture in the Ottoman Empire." *Comparative Studies in Society and History* 11 (1969): 258–281.

Marrus, Michael R. *The Politics of Assimilation: A Study of the French Jewish Community at the time of the Dreyfus Affair.* Oxford, 1971.

Mayeur, Françoise. *L'éducation des filles en France au XIXᵉ siècle.* Paris 1979.

———. *De la révolution à l'école républicaine.* Paris, 1981.

McCarthy, Justin. *The Arab World, Turkey, and the Balkans (1878–1914): A Handbook of Historical Statistics.* Boston, 1982.

———. *Muslims and Minorities: The Population of Ottoman Anatolia and the End of the Empire.* New York, 1983.

McNeill, William H. "Hypotheses Concerning Possible Ethnic Role Changes in the Ottoman Empire in the Seventeenth Century." In *Social and Economic History of Turkey,* edited by Osman Okyar and Halil İnalcık, 128–129. Ankara, 1980.

Mevorakh, Barukh. "'Ikvotehah shel 'alilat Damesek be-hitpathutah shel ha-'itonut ha-yehudit ba-shanim 1840–1860" [The Influence of the Damascus Blood Libel on the Development of the Jewish Press in the Years 1840–1860]. *Ziyon* 23–24 (1958–1959): 46–65.

Mézan, Saul. *Les Juifs espagnols en Bulgarie.* Sofia, 1925.

Milano, Attilio. *Storia degli Ebrei italiani nel Levante.* Firenze, 1949.

Modiano, Léon. *Le Judaïsme et l'Alliance Israélite Universelle.* Salonica, 1909.

Molho, Michael. *Le Meam Loez, encyclopédie populaire du sépharadisme levantin.* Salonica, 1945.

Moody, Joseph N. *French Education since Napoleon.* Syracuse, New York, 1978.

Moore, Deborah Dash. *B'nai B'rith and the Challenge of Ethnic Leadership.* Albany, New York, 1981.

Nathan, Naphtali. "Notes on the Jews of Turkey." *The Jewish Journal of Sociology* 6 (December 1964): 172–189.

Navon, A. H. "La fondation de l'école de l'Alliance à Andrinople." *Paix et Droit* 3 (April 1923): 13–15.

———. "Contribution à l'histoire de la fondation des écoles de l'Alliance Israélite Universelle." *Le Judaïsme Sephardi,* no. 1 (July 1932): 8–9.

————. "Contribution à l'histoire de la fondation des écoles de l'Alliance Israélite Universelle." *Le Judaïsme Sephardi*, no. 4 (November 1932): 64–66.

————. *Les 70 ans de l'Ecole Normale Israélite Orientale*. Paris, 1935.

Necheles, Ruth F. *The Abbé Grégoire, 1787–1831: The Odyssey of an Egalitarian*. Westport, Connecticut, 1971.

————. "The Abbé Grégoire and the Jews." *Jewish Social Studies* 33 (April-July 1971): 120–140.

Nehama, Joseph. *Histoire des Israélites de Salonique*. Vols. 6–7. Thessaloniki, 1935–1978.

Nicault-Lévigne, Catherine. "La France et le sionisme, 1896–1914." Thèse de doctorat de IIIᵉ cycle, Université de Paris I, Sorbonne, 1986.

Niégo, Joseph. "Abraham Danon." *Hamenora* 3 (February 1925): 127–130.

Öke, Mim Kemal. *Siyonizm ve Filistin Sorunu (1880–1914)* [Zionism and the Question of Palestine]. Istanbul, 1982.

————. *İngliz Belgelerinde Barış Konferansı* [The Lausanne Peace Treaty according to English Documents]. 2 vols. Istanbul, 1983–1984.

Olson, Robert W. "Jews in the Ottoman Empire in Light of New Documents." *Tarih Enstitüsü Dergisi* 7–8 (1976–1977): 119–144.

————. "Jews in the Ottoman Empire in Light of New Documents." *Jewish Social Studies* 41 (Winter 1979): 75–88.

Ortaylı, İlber. *Tanzimat'tan sonra Mahalli İdareler* [Local Government after the *Tanzimat*]. Ankara, 1974.

Palmer, Robert R. *The Improvement of Humanity: Education and the French Revolution*. Princeton, New Jersey, 1985.

Pamuk, Şevket. *Osmanlı Ekonomisi ve Dünya Kapitalizmi (1820–1913)* [The Ottoman Economy and World Capitalism (1820–1913)]. Ankara, 1984.

Papadopoulos, Constantine G. *Les privilèges du Patriarcat oecuménique dans l'Empire ottoman*. Paris, 1924.

Parfitt, Tudor. " 'The Year of the Pride of Israel': Montefiore and the Blood Libel of 1840." In *The Century of Moses Montefiore*, edited by Sonia and V. D. Lipman, 131–148. Oxford, 1985.

Polk, William R., and Chambers, Richard L., eds. *Beginnings of Modernization in the Middle East: The Nineteenth Century*. Chicago, 1968.

Posener, Salomon V. *Adolphe Crémieux: A Biography,* translated by Eugene Golob. Philadelphia, 1940.

Prévot, André. *L'enseignement technique chez les frères des Ecoles chrétiennes au 18ᵉ et au 19ᵉ siècles*. Paris, 1964.

Prost, Antoine. *Histoire de l'enseignement en France 1800–1967*. Paris, 1968.

Ramsaur, E. E. *The Young Turks: Prelude to the Revolution of 1908*. Princeton, New Jersey, 1957.

Recuero, Pascual. *Me'am Loez: El gran comentario bíblico sefardí*. 4 vols. Madrid, 1964–74.

Rey, Francis. *De la protection diplomatique et consulaire dans les échelles du Levant et de Barbarie*. Paris, 1899.

Rinot, Mosheh. *Ḥevrat ha-'ezrah le-yehudei Germanyah bi-yeẓirah u-ve-ma'avak: perek be-toldot ha-ḥinukh ha-'ivri be-ereẓ-yisrael u-ve-toldot yehudei germanyah* [The Hilfsverein der Deutschen Juden during the Years of Foundation and Struggle: A Chapter in the History of Hebrew Education in Erets Israel and in the History of German Jewry]. Jerusalem, 1971.

Rodrigue, Aron. "Jewish Society and Schooling in a Thracian Town: The Alliance Israélite Universelle in Demotica, 1897–1924." *Jewish Social Studies* 45 (Summer-Fall 1983): 263–286.

————. "The Alliance Israélite Universelle and the Attempt to Reform Rabbinical and Religious Instruction in Turkey." In *L'"Alliance" dans les communautés du bassin méditerranéen à la fin du XIXe siècle et son influence sur la situation sociale et culturelle,* edited by Simon Schwarzfuchs, liii-lxx. Jerusalem, 1987.

————. *De l'instruction à l'émancipation: Les enseignants de l'Alliance israélite universelle et les Juifs d'Orient, 1860–1939.* Paris, 1989.

————. "Abraham de Camondo of Istanbul: The Transformation of Jewish Philanthropy." In *From East and West: Jews in a Changing Europe, 1750–1870,* edited by Frances Malino and David Sorkin. Forthcoming.

————. *A Guide to the Ladino Collection in the Harvard College Library.* Cambridge, Massachusetts. Forthcoming.

Roland, Joan Gardner. "The Alliance Israélite Universelle and French Policy in North Africa, 1860–1918." Ph.D. diss., Columbia University, New York, 1969.

Rozanes, Salomon A. *Korot ha-yehudim be-Turkiyah u-ve-arzot ha-kedem* [History of the Jews in Turkey and in the Middle East]. Vol. 6: *Ha-dorot ha-aharonim* [The Last Generations]. Jerusalem, 1945.

Rozen, Mina. "Arkhion lishkat mishar be-Marseille; makor le-toldot kehilot yisrael ba-Levant u-vi-Zfon Afrika" [The Archives of the Chamber of Commerce of Marseilles; a Source for the History of the Jewish Communities of the Levant and North Africa]. *Pe'amim,* no. 9 (1981): 112–124.

————. "Strangers in a Strange Land: The Extraterritorial Status of Jews in Italy and the Ottoman Empire in the Sixteenth to the Eighteenth Centuries." In *Ottoman and Turkish Jewry: Community and Leadership,* edited by Aron Rodrigue. Forthcoming.

Said, Edward. *Orientalism.* New York, 1978.

Salon, Albert. "L'action culturelle de la France dans le monde." Thèse pour le doctorat d'état ès lettres, Université de Paris I, Sorbonne, 1980.

Schama, Simon. *Two Rothschilds and the Land of Israel.* New York, 1978.

Schwarzfuchs, Simon. *Les Juifs de France.* Paris, 1975.

————. *Napoleon, the Jews, and the Sanhedrin.* London, 1979.

————. "Sulam Saloniki" [The Salonica Scale]. *Sefunot* 15 (1971–1981): 77–102.

————. *Ha-yehudim ve-ha-shilton ha-Zarfati be-Algiryah, 1830–1855* [Les Juifs d'Algérie et la France (1830–1855)]. Jerusalem, 1981.

————. *Kahal: La communauté juive de l'Europe médiévale.* Paris, 1986.

Shaw, Stanford J. "The Nineteenth-Century Ottoman Tax Reforms and Revenue System." *International Journal of Middle East Studies* 6 (1975): 421–459.

————. "The Ottoman Census System and Population, 1831–1914." *International Journal of Middle East Studies* 9 (1978): 325–338.

————. "The Population of Istanbul in the Nineteenth Century." *Türk Tarih Dergisi* 32 (1979): 403–414.

Shaw, Stanford J., and Shaw, Ezel Kural. *History of the Ottoman Empire and Modern Turkey.* 2 vols. Cambridge, 1976–1977.

Shipman, M. D. *Education and Modernisation.* London, 1971.

Shmuelevitz, Aryeh. *The Jews of the Ottoman Empire in the Late Fifteenth and Sixteenth Centuries: Administrative, Economic, Legal, and Social Relations as Reflected in the Responsa.* Leiden, 1984.

Shorrock, William I. *French Imperialism in the Middle East: The Failure of Policy in Syria and Lebanon, 1900–1914.* Madison, Wisconsin, 1976.

Silber, Michael. "The Historical Experience of German Jewry and Its Impact on the *Haskalah* and Reform in Hungary." In *Toward Modernity: The European Jewish Model,* edited by Jacob Katz, 107–157. New Brunswick, New Jersey, 1987.

Silberman, Paul. "An Investigation of the Schools operated by the Alliance Israélite Universelle from 1862 to 1940." Ph.D. diss., New York University, 1973.

Simonsohn, Shlomoh. *History of the Jews in the Duchy of Mantua.* Jerusalem, 1977.

Soboul, Albert, and Blumenkranz, Bernhard, eds. *Les Juifs et la révolution française: Problèmes et aspirations.* Toulouse, 1976.

Sokolow, Nahum. *History of Zionism, 1600–1918.* 2 vols. London, 1919.

Sorkin, David. *The Transformation of German Jewry.* New York, 1987.

Stanislawski, Michael. *Tsar Nicholas I and the Jews: The Transformation of Jewish Society in Russia, 1825–1855.* Philadelphia, 1983.

Stillman, Norman, ed. *The Jews of Arab Lands: A History and Source Book.* Philadelphia, 1979.

Stoianovich, Traian. "The Conquering Balkan Orthodox Merchant." *Journal of Economic History* 20 (1960): 234–313.

Sungu, İhsan. "Galatasaray Lisesi'nin Kuruluşu" [The Foundation of the Galatasaray *Lycée*]. *Belleten* 7, no. 26 (1943): 315–347.

Susa, Nasim. *The Capitulatory Regime of Turkey.* London, 1933.

Szajkowski, Zosa. "Conflicts in the AIU and the Founding of the Anglo-Jewish Association, the Vienna Allianz and the Hilfsverein." *Jewish Social Studies* 19 (January-April 1957): 29–50.

———. "Jewish Diplomacy: Notes on the Occasion of the Centenary of the Alliance Israélite Universelle." *Jewish Social Studies* 22 (July 1960): 131–158.

———. "The Schools of the Alliance Israélite Universelle." *Historia Judaica* 22 (1960): 3–22.

———. *Jews and the French Revolutions of 1789, 1830 and 1848.* New York, 1970.

Şaul, Mahir, "The Mother Tongue of the Polyglot: Cosmopolitism and Nationalism among the Sepharadim of Istanbul." *Anthropological Linguistics* 25 (Fall 1983): 326–358.

Tahiroğlu, Bülent. "Tanzimat'tan sonra Kanunlaştırma Hareketleri" [Legislation (and Legal Codes) after the *Tanzimat*]. *Tanzimat'tan Cumhuriyet'e Türkiye Ansiklopedisi* 3 (1985): 588–601.

Tamir, Vicki. *Bulgaria and Her Jews: The History of a Dubious Symbiosis.* New York, 1979.

Tchernof, J. "Documents pour l'histoire de l'Alliance." Undated manuscript in the AIU Library in Paris.

Tekeli, İlhan. "Tanzimat'tan Cumhuriyet'e Eğitim Sistemindeki Değişmeler" [Changes in the Educational System from the *Tanzimat* to the Republic]. *Tanzimat'tan Cumhuriyet'e Türkiye Ansiklopedisi* 2 (1985): 456–475.

Thobie, Jacques. *Intérêts et impérialisme français dans l'Empire ottoman, 1895–1914.* Paris, 1977.

———. "La France a-t-elle une politique culturelle dans l'Empire ottoman à la veille de la première guerre mondiale?" *Relations Internationales,* no. 25 (Spring 1981): 21–40.

———. "Relations internationales et zones d'influence: Les intérêts français en Palestine à la veille de la première guerre mondiale." In *L'Historien et les relations internationales: Receuil d'études en hommage à Jacques Freymond,* edited by Saul Friedlaender, Harish Kapur, and André Reszler, 427–446. Geneva, 1981.

———. *La France impériale, 1880–1914.* Paris, 1982.

Tritton, A. S. *The Caliphs and their Non-Muslim Subjects: A Critical Study of the Covenant of Umar.* London, 1930.

Turner, Brian S. *Weber and Islam.* London, 1974.

Tutundjian, Télémaque. *Du pacte politique entre l'Etat ottoman et les nations non-musulmans de la Turquie.* Lausanne, 1904.

Unat, Faik Reşit. *Türkiye Eğitim Sisteminin Gelişmesine Tarihi Bir Bakış* [A Historical Look at the Evolution of the Educational System of Turkey]. Ankara, 1964.

Valensi, Lucette. "La tour de Babel: Groupes et relations ethniques au Moyen-Orient et en Afrique du Nord." *Annales, E. S. C.,* no. 4 (July-August 1986): 817–838.

van den Steen de Jehan, F. *De la situation légale des sujets ottomans non-musulmans.* Brussels, 1906.

Veinstein, Gilles. "Une communauté ottomane: les Juifs d'Avlonya (Valona) dans la deuxième moitié du XVIe siècle." In *Gli Ebrei e Venezia, secoli XIV-XVIII,* edited by Gaetano Cozzi, 781–828. Milan, 1987.

Vital, David. *The Origins of Zionism.* Oxford, 1975.

———. *Zionism: The Formative Years.* Oxford, 1982.

———. *Zionism: The Crucial Phase.* Oxford, 1987.

Weber, Eugen. *Peasants into Frenchmen: The Modernization of Rural France, 1870–1914.* Stanford, California, 1976.

Weill, Georges. "Charles Netter ou les oranges de Jaffa." *Les Nouveaux Cahiers,* no. 21 (Summer 1970): 2–36.

———. "Emancipation et humanisme: Le discours idéologique de l'Alliance Israélite Universelle au XIXe siècle." *Les Nouveaux Cahiers,* no. 52 (Spring 1978): 1–20.

———. "The Alliance Israélite Universelle and the Emancipation of the Jewish Communities in the Mediterranean." *The Jewish Journal of Sociology* 24 (1982): 117–134.

———. "Les oliviers de Djedeida." Paper delivered at the "Maghreb-Mashrek" congress, Jerusalem, Spring, 1984.

———. "L'enseignement dans les écoles de l'Alliance au XIXe siècle." *Les Nouveaux Cahiers,* no. 78 (Fall 1984): 51–58.

———. "L'Alliance Israélite Universelle et la condition sociale des communautés méditérranéennes à la fin du XIXe siècle (1860–1914)." In *L'"Alliance" dans les communautés du bassin méditerranéen à la fin du XIXe siècle et son influence sur la situation sociale et culturelle,* edited by Simon Schwarzfuchs, vii-lii. Jerusalem, 1987.

Weinryb, Bernard Dov [Sucher Ber]. *Der Kampf um die Berufsumschichtung: Ein Ausschnitt aus der Geschichte der Juden in Deutschland.* Berlin, 1936.

———. *Jewish Vocational Education: History and Appraisal of Training in Europe.* New York, 1948.

Weissbach, Lee Shai. "The Jewish Elite and the Children of the Poor: Jewish Apprenticeship Programs in Nineteenth-Century France." *Association for Jewish Studies Review* 12 (Spring 1987): 123–142.

Wertheimer, Jack. *Unwelcome Strangers: East European Jews in Imperial Germany.* New York, 1987.

Wolf, Lucien. *Sir Moses Montefiore: A Centennial Biography with Extracts from Letters and Journals.* New York, 1885.

Yaari, Abraham. *Reshimat sifrei ladino ha-nimẓaim be-veit ha-sefarim ha-le'umi ve-ha-universita'i bi-Yerushalayim* [Catalogue of Judeo-Spanish Books in the Jewish National and University Library, Jerusalem]. Jerusalem, 1934.

———. *Ha-defus ha-'ivri be-Kushta* [Hebrew Printing in Constantinople]. Jerusalem, 1967.

Yücebaş, Hilmi. *Filozof Rıza Tevfik: Hayatı, Hatıraları, Şiirleri* [The Philosopher Rıza Tevfik: His Life, Memories, and Poems]. Istanbul, 1978.

INDEX

Agricultural Training, 9, 16–17, 56, 110–111. See also *Mikveh Yisrael*; *Or Yehudah*; Vocational Education

Algerian Jewry, 4, 18; "regeneration" of, 7–9

Alkalai, Yehudah, 59, 61

Allatini, Moïse, 39, 45

Allgemeine Zeitung des Judenthums, 9, 10, 11; on the Reform Edict of 1856, 14; on Turkish Jewry, 13, 14, 15

Alliance française, 145, 151

Altaras, Jacques Isaac, 48, 53; report on Algerian Jewry, 7–9

Amicale, 127–129, 142

Antébi, Albert, 104–105, 152, 155

Archives Israélites, 9, 10, 11, 133; and the Jewish Eastern Question, 15; on Jewish solidarity, 17–19, 20, 21

Arié, Gabriel, 167–170

Armenians, 26, 47; and Turkish Jewry, 25, 27–28

Ashkenazim, 16; schools of, 91; Western view of, 13, 152; and Zionism, 127

Astruc, Elie-Aristide, 22

Atatürk, 162

L'Aurore, 128, 131; and Zionism, 127, 142

Avigdor, Jacob, 42

Balat, schools of, 37, 54, 57

Barbier, Adolph, 47

Baruch, Marco, 139

Behar, Nissim, and the *Alliance française,* 151; on Hebrew, 80, 81, 82; view of Jews of Balat, 72

Bénédict, Sylvain, 78

Benveniste, Abraham, 156

Berr, Berr Isaac, 6

Bigart, Jacques, 127, 133, 150, 156; and Haim Nahum, 123, 124, 143; on "regeneration," 169; and the Young Turk revolution, 125; and Zionism, 134, 139, 143–144, 155

Bloch, Félix, 113; and the AIU, 62; in Edirne, 52, 57–62; and the Hasköy school, 50, 65; in Istanbul, 65; and Barukh Mitrani, 60–61; and Shemtob Pariente, 65–66; on Yiddish, 85

Bloch, Simon, 21

B'nai B'rith, 117, 171; and the AIU, 134, 135

Bnei Yisrael, 128

Board of Deputies of British Jews, 14, 23; and the Damascus affair, 2, 3

Boppe, on France and the AIU, 153–154; on the Jews, 152

Buisson, Ferdinand, 76

Bulgaria, and the AIU-Zionist conflict, 137–140; compared to Turkey, 167–170

Cahen, Isidore, 18, 21, 22

Cahen, Samuel, 17–19, 20

Camondo, Abraham de, 40, 41; and the AIU, 44, 47; on education as "regeneration," 48; and educational reform, 42, 47–50, 55

Carmona, Behor Isaac, 27

Carmona, Moshe, 27

Carré, I., 76

Carvallo, Jules, 22; on emancipation, 24; on Jewish unity, 20, 21

Castro, Eliezer de, 102

Castro, Jacques de, 47, 50

Cazès, David, 62, 63; report on Turkish Jewry, 53–54, 66, 101; and vocational education, 100–101

Central Committee of the AIU, xiv; and alumni associations, 121; on education, 71–72, 77–79; and the need for local support in Turkey, 47–49; relationship with affiliates, 57–58, 64–66, 67, 77, 132–134; and the Alliance teachers, 74–77; and Zionism, 127–130, 140–143

Central Consistory of French Jews, and Algerian Jewry, 4, 8; and the AIU, 22–23; and the Damascus affair, 2; on education, 6–7; and the Jewish Eastern Question, 15; and Palestine, 17; and the Reform Edict of 1856, 14; and "regeneration," 16; role of, 16, 19

Cercle Israélite, 121

Chief Rabbinate, in Turkey, 87; and the AIU, 122–123; revival of, 43; role of, 29

Cohen, Joseph, 7–9

Cohn, Albert, 167; and the Damascus affair, 2; in the Middle East in 1854, 15; and schools in Turkey, 38, 40, 44, 46

Comité de bienfaisance, 7, 15, 16

Crémieux, Adolphe, 15, 129, 167; and the AIU, 22, 47; and the Damascus affair, 1–2, 3, 4; on education, 3; on the "regeneration" of women, 77–79

Crispin, Nissim, 53

Dalem, Jules, 86, 157

Damascus Affair, 1–3

Danon, Abraham, 45, 81; and Haim Nahum, 123–124; and vocational education, 102

Danon, Bekhor, 45

231

ARON RODRIGUE is Associate Professor of History and Jewish Studies at Indiana University, Bloomington, and author of *De l'instruction à l'émancipation: Les enseignants de l'Alliance israélite universelle et les Juifs d'Orient, 1860–1939*.